D0938654

WOBBLY WAR

THE CENTRALIA STORY

WOBBLY WAR

THE CENTRALIA STORY

John McClelland, Jr.

FOREWORD BY
Richard Maxwell Brown

WASHINGTON STATE HISTORICAL SOCIETY

Washington State Historical Society
315 N. Stadium Way
Tacoma, Washington 98403

© 1987 by the Washington State Historical Society. All rights reserved.

First Edition

Library of Congress Catalog Card Number: 87-51095
ISBN 0-917048-62-8

To Burdette

CONTENTS

FOREWORD

In the course of one day in 1919 a small city in southwest Washington went from obscurity to national notoriety. Like many American communities on November 11 of that year, Centralia, Washington, was the scene of a parade in celebration of the first anniversary of the end of World War I. Taking no part in the parade were the Centralia members of the Industrial Workers of the World, a radical labor organization commonly known as the Wobblies. As the large American Legion contingent of Centralia's Armistice Day parade paused near the local IWW hall, gunfire erupted. Within an hour four Legionnaires were dead or dying, and three were wounded. Soon an angry mob converged on the jail where Wobblies accused of the deaths were held in custody. That night one of the Wobblies — Wesley Everest — was taken out of the jail and lynched by anti-IWW vigilantes. Months later a controversial trial resulted in prison terms for eight Wobblies convicted of murder in the second degree.

During the 1920s and 1930s Centralians were still bitter over the violence of 1919. Beyond Centralia, the episode became a cause célèbre as a growing number of Americans came to believe that the Wobblies had been unjustly convicted in the trial of 1920. One died in prison, but a long campaign in behalf of the others led to the parole of six in 1930-33. Finally, the eighth and last prisoner (who had refused parole) became a free man in 1939 when the governor commuted his sentence to the time served.

Long of interest to scholars, the Centralia tragedy of 1919 is also engraved in the minds of the many Americans who have read novelist John Dos Passos's arresting sketch of the episode in *1919*, the second volume of his classic fictional trilogy, *U.S.A.*[1] Yet, the violent event and its long aftermath are only now given full and adequate treatment in *Wobbly War: The Centralia Story* by John M. McClelland, Jr.[2] As a distinguished newspaper editor and publisher of southwest Washington who grew up not far from Centralia and as a perceptive Pacific Northwest regionalist, McClelland brought ideal credentials to the preparation of this striking study of an American community in conflict. Many years of research and thought have gone into the making of *Wobbly War,* and the result is a compelling study of a searing chapter in the history of the Pacific Northwest. Above all we have here a very human story. The incidents and emotions of 1919 and afterward come to life in the pages of this book. We owe a debt of gratitude to John McClelland for ending the long neglect of this significant event in Pacific Northwest history.

In McClelland's authoritative account of the Centralia episode we have much more than a chronicle of events. Readers will find here an objective, analytical treatment of the issues raised by the conflict in Centralia and its violent climax. In the course of exhaustive research in oral as well as archival sources, John McClelland uncovered much new material. All readers will be absorbed in the story told here, and scholars will find especially useful the richness of detail and explanation. McClelland deals judiciously with the numerous questions that have arisen about the outbreak of 1919. Who initiated the violence on that fateful November 11? Was Wesley Everest mutilated before he was lynched? These and other key questions are thoroughly explored in the pages of *Wobbly War,* whose author also provides an extended, careful treatment of the background to the violence of November 11, 1919.

The context of the Centralia conflict was the timber industry of the Pacific Northwest,[3] whose loggers and mill workers had been the objects of aggressive organizing efforts by the IWW in the early part of the century. Founded in Chicago in 1905, the IWW was a far-left labor union dedicated to the ultimate revolutionary goal of abolishing capitalism, but also oriented to the immediate objective of on-the-job improvement for workers.[4] Headed by the charismatic William D. (Big Bill) Haywood,[5] the Wobblies' rhetoric of revolution spearheaded a radical agitation that usually stopped short of violence.[6] To many, the prototypical Wobbly was a class-conscious, untrammelled individualist who resisted the constraints of modern industrial organization. Thus, the folklore of the IWW focusing on the roving Wobbly with his "Little Red Song Book" and bundle of belongings became an important part of the mystique of the movement[7] — a type exemplified by Ray Becker in *Wobbly War*. More typical of the Wobblies who figure in the Centralia story are those who were longtime residents of Centralia and its vicinity.

Melvyn Dubofsky and other scholars have made us aware of the impact of the IWW on the workers of the East, but the image of the IWW as a typically Western organization persists and is grounded in the reality of its impressive strength in the West. Certainly, the Wobblies were well entrenched in the timber industry of the Pacific Northwest and were prominent players in the industry's tumultuous history in the 1910s.[8] The Wobblies gained fame in the Pacific Northwest for a series of free-speech campaigns that began in Spokane in 1909 and came to a violent climax in the "Everett Massacre" of 1916.[9] Beset by low wages, long hours, job insecurity, and oppressive and dangerous working conditions,[10] Pacific Northwest loggers and sawmill workers turned increasingly to the IWW in a time of labor unrest and prowar extremism during World War I. Upon American entry into World War I in 1917, the patriotism of prowar activists clashed with the radicalism of IWW militants, many of whom opposed the war. A long strike of IWW and American Federation of Labor (AFL) timbermen in the summer of 1917 curtailed the wartime production effort. The federal government responded with a policy that established the eight-hour day in the woods and mills of the Northwest. This concession to workers was, however, balanced by the creation of a new labor union — the federally sponsored Loyal Legion of Loggers and Lumbermen — to counteract the radical influence of the IWW.[11]

Yet, a radical labor tradition in the Pacific Northwest antedated both the IWW and the First World War.[12] Worker militance hit an early peak in the 1892 uprising of silver miners in the Coeur d'Alene country of northern Idaho.[13] The outbreak of World War I exacerbated the already turbulent labor relations in the Pacific Northwest. In Butte, Montana, Frank Little, an IWW official and antiwar activist, was lynched by vigilantes in 1917.[14] Similar in spirit to the lynching of Frank Little, although occurring in the Southwest, was a notable event which took place in the copper-mining town of Bisbee, Arizona, on July 12, 1917. Early on that day an extralegal combination of 2,000 law officers and antilabor vigilantes forcibly loaded 1,186 striking AFL and IWW copper miners and their supporters onto a special train and deported them into the desert in New Mexico.[15]

The IWW had been a main target of the Bisbee vigilantes, and 426 Wobblies had been among the deportees, but the IWW did not play a leading role in a traumatic event of labor insurgency in the Pacific Northwest in early 1919: the Seattle general strike of February 6-11.[16] Although the IWW eagerly supported the general strike, the more conservative AFL leaders who were in control of the work stoppage kept the Wobblies on the fringe of the effort. The Seattle general strike was nonviolent and quickly collapsed, but it bred a mood of antilabor, antiradical hysteria that was still very much alive both regionally and nationally on Armistice Day, 1919. The crushing of the Seattle general strike was just one notable event in a 1917-1920 national campaign of antiradical/antilabor suppression that was fed by prowar hysteria and escalated by fears resulting from the Communist triumph in the Russian Revolution of 1917.[17] A highlight in the oppressive trend was a federal trial of IWW leaders for sedition that produced the conviction of Big Bill Haywood and ninety-one others. By 1920, a nationwide "Red Scare" — inspired in part by the Centralia violence of 1919 — had spawned a massive violation of the civil liberties of those accused of radicalism or disloyalty.[18] Contributing importantly to the antiradical drive was the American Legion, a mass-membership organization of World War I veterans founded early in 1919. The American Legion stressed a strongly antiradical, ultrapatriotic version of Americanism that was enthusiastically endorsed by the new Legion post in Centralia.[19]

Aside from the inherent interest of the story it

tells, *Wobbly War* thus significantly increases our understanding of a number of important aspects of early-twentieth-century American history and the history of the Pacific Northwest: the timber industry, labor history, the IWW, and the antiradical vendetta of the era of World War I. Several new approaches to American history and the history of our region are also reflected in *Wobbly War*. Before 1960, professional historians largely neglected local history, but since then an emphasis on the local community has been one of the most successful strategies for deepening our knowledge of American history.[20] This is an approach that has also been used with great profit by labor historians. A landmark in the combination of community history and labor history is *Mill Town*, Norman H. Clark's study of the "Everett Massacre" and its background.[21] Like Clark's book on Everett, *Wobbly War* is a salient example of the union of community history with labor history, for it is a treatment in depth of a community in crisis. The community-history method is also a major approach for the study of American violence. Thus, vigilantism and lynch law, as in the case of *Wobbly War*, have been deeply probed at the local level. Centralia in 1919 represented a common pattern in which the established leaders of a local community — often supported by officers of the law — sponsored vigilante violence.[22]

Not to be overlooked, however, is that Centralia in 1919, although well into the modern age of the automobile, was still quite close to the frontier. John McClelland emphasizes that anti-IWW forces in Centralia and the Pacific Northwest were inspired by the tradition of frontier vigilantism. In broader terms, Carlos A. Schwantes has offered the concept of the "wageworkers' frontier" for interpreting labor history in the West.[23] By this concept, Schwantes means that labor relations in the West of the late nineteenth and early twentieth centuries combined modern industrial conditions with the ambience and psychology of the frontier. It is just such a linkage that we find in Centralia's "Wobbly War." McClelland tellingly reveals the coexistence of the modern development of Centralia in the 1910s with the raw spirit of a community whose ethos and ideals were still strongly shaped by the frontier. Surrounded by high, dark forests of Douglas fir dotted with crude logging camps owned by hardbitten timber kings but often dominated by two-fisted Wobblies, Centralia in 1919 was an example of the explosive mixture of modern industry with the combative frontier spirit.

In conjunction with his study of violent conflict, John McClelland has given us a nuanced and sensitive community history. One of his many virtues as a historian is that he is not content to end the story with the conclusion of the trial of the Wobblies in 1920 or with the release of the last of the IWW prisoners in 1939, but brings us right up to the present. Memories are long in Centralia, and, as McClelland shows, those of 1919 are still alive. Many a reader of this engrossing achievement in Pacific Northwest regionalism will wish to swing off Interstate 5 and into today's Centralia — an attractive little city where, thanks to *Wobbly War,* those attuned to the regional traditions and identity may sense the ghosts of 1919 around the town square, along the northern stretch of Tower Avenue, and above the flowing waters of the Skookumchuck and the Chehalis.

Eugene, Oregon
April 7, 1987

RICHARD MAXWELL BROWN
*Beekman Professor of Northwest
and Pacific History
University of Oregon*

PREFACE

I grew up in the 1920s in the newly established city of Longview on the Columbia River. It was a sawmill town in the beginning. Most of the men worked for the Long-Bell Lumber Company. The company called it a model city, not a sawmill town, and actually it was a model in many respects. The founder of both the company and the city, Robert A. Long, had presided over the building of smaller sawmill towns in the South. Longville, Louisiana, was one, Ludington another. A standard pattern was followed there. Near the sawmill were a company store and a dormitory for single workers, and rows of small houses for families. A big house was provided for the superintendent. And there was a church — always a church.

The loggers who cut timber for the mills lived in crude camps in the woods. Places to sleep, called bunkhouses, and places to eat, cookhouses, were provided. Nothing more was considered necessary. Logging was done mostly by transient workers. When a tree was felled, the saws, the axes, the wedges, and the bottles of oil to keep the saws from sticking in the pitch were moved to the next tree. When the tree line receded a half-mile or so, the camp was moved. When the mill pond at the sawmill was glutted, the camp might be shut down and the men laid off. The camps — the early ones — didn't provide bedding or blankets. The loggers had to carry their own, rolled in backpacks, when they quit or were laid off and moved to another camp.

R. A. Long, seventy-three years old and a veteran in the lumber industry when his Western venture at Longview was conceived in 1923, knew that labor unrest was common in West Coast lumbering.

His chief engineer, Wesley Vandercook, who came to the Northwest in 1918 to scout for a sawmill site, wrote a lengthy report that included warnings about labor trouble. They were militant, these North-west loggers and mill workers, he reported. Most belonged to the Industrial Workers of the World —the notorious "one big union" advocates whose leaders were in prison for opposing the war effort. IWW, many said, stood for "I Won't Work." They would work, but usually only on their own terms: eight hours a day, bedding provided in the camps, no payment to a job shark to get on a payroll, no blacklisting by employers to identify and starve out union members.

There weren't many strikes, Vandercook reported, unless walking off the job at the end of eight hours was a strike, or unless slowdowns and maybe some sabotage to cause machine breakdowns could be called striking. Stories about such tactics are what led to the derisive sobriquet, "I Won't Work."

Long and his lieutenants never had dealt with a union — not since the company was founded in 1875 — and since everything they heard about them was bad, they decided that the operation to be set up at Longview would minimize chances for labor trouble. Working conditions would be made better than any the men in the area were used to.

This precaution accounted for one of the wonders of the new enterprise, a satellite town for the loggers — Ryderwood — twenty miles up the Cowlitz River near Winlock, so the men could live in company houses and come home from the woods to their families every night on railroad cars rather than huddle in dismal bunkhouses far up in the hills. And those without families could come back to a clean dormitory and in the evening play pool or go to the picture show.

Growing up in the '20s I heard discussions about Ryderwood and the St. Helens inns — a row of five large boardinghouses for single men built by the company to house the single workers in Longview. And I heard about the going wage — $3.60 a day — that a lot of men didn't think was enough, even though the workday during the war had been reduced from ten to eight hours. Three-sixty a day came to $21.60 for a six-day week. A family could get by on that. It had to.

And I heard talk among the adults about the strange menace from up north around Centralia, thirty miles away. Something terrible had happened in Centralia a few years before. It was a massacre, everybody said. Men were shot. One was hanged. The people were terrorized. But it was all very vague. No one seemed to know just what happened, or if they did, wouldn't elaborate.

Our minister — Longview's first — came from Tacoma. He told about being advised to get an ax handle and keep it handy, like the rest of the men in town, just in case there was trouble. What kind of trouble were they expecting? What was this menace? The IWW? They must be monsters. Everybody was afraid of them. I had better be afraid too.

The years went by and the menace did not materialize. Something must have calmed down the labor scene in western Oregon and Washington. What was it? Was it those mysterious happenings in Centralia back in 1919?

The answers to these questions seemed to be at hand when I opened a history of Centralia produced as a class project in Centralia High School in 1954. To my disappointment, and surprise, all it contained about the notorious "massacre" was one paragraph.

The Armistice Day case — the massacre, the tragedy, whatever it might be called — obviously was not a subject Centralia cared to talk about or to have others discuss, much less write about, thirty-five years after the event.

Why not? I wondered. What shame was being concealed? What scandal was being glossed over? What really happened up there in Centralia that day in November 1919, when the first anniversary of the Armistice was observed?

My curiosity aroused, I began to look into the card indexes of libraries to see what had been published. Quite a lot, it turned out, including magazine and newspaper articles by the score, and many pamphlets, produced in a slowly accelerating stream beginning in 1920, during and after a nationally publicized trial, and on through the whole decade of the 1920s and into the 1930s. But what was published, with almost no exceptions, was chiefly exhortation, strongly biased for or against one faction or the other in what came to be

identified by many writers as a labor-capitalist confrontation — an episode in a continuing "class war" conflict, a union-management battle, or a struggle between American Legion patriots and IWW traitors.

The full story obviously wasn't there. I set out to find it. It has taken a long time, the effort interrupted, sometimes for years, by lack of enough time away from newspapering to devote to the kind of painstaking research required in the production of any kind of history. Fortunately the search was started early enough to enable me to get much information directly from some who were participants — one juror, the judge, three defendants, the leading prosecutor, some who were shot at or wounded, many who saw the shooting, and a number of those who lived through the stormy aftermath.

I learned at last what was being whispered about darkly when I was a boy in early Longview and why Centralians, even a half-century after 1919, were reluctant to talk about the case or even refused to. I found the 3,750-page transcript of the lengthy trial at Montesano, stored and forgotten in the Legion offices in Seattle. I located the son of DeWitte Wyckoff, who was sent out from New York by three church groups — Catholic, Protestant, and Jew — to find out, once and for all, whether justice was served in the Centralia case. He could provide much of the material used by his father in writing the report, published in 1930, that came closer than any other to a true account of the events and a fair evaluation of what ensued.

And I found in the corner of a cemetery outside Centralia the grave of the lynch victim, Wesley Everest, long unmarked but now with a modest granite monument, bearing the emblem of the IWW, and beside it a vase of artificial flowers.

In the park in the center of Centralia is a soldier monument and on its base are the faces in bas-relief bronze of Warren O. Grimm, Arthur McElfresh, Ben Casagranda, and Dale Hubbard, the four Legionnaires who survived battles in France only to come back and be slain on the street in their hometown. The inscription on the monument doesn't attempt to explain what happened on November 11, 1919, or why. A few words cannot do that. Hence this account.

1

The Early Warfare

In the gray early morning of February 5, 1915, the community of Centralia, Washington, midway between Seattle and Portland, discovered that overnight a serious crisis had developed. Forty-seven unwanted, undesirable, and possibly dangerous men had come down the main-line tracks from the north and were hanging around the streets, up to something.

The unpleasant news spread quickly. The men were mostly Wobblies,[1] out on the road, moving to a new place. They had to be gotten rid of and quickly. It was not that the visitors were causing any trouble. They sat on their bedrolls, leaned against buildings, or stood on street corners, looking around to see who was watching them. All wore dark hats, brims drooping from repeated drenchings, heavy work shoes, and coats that on many extended down to their knees. They were on the move, as Wobblies often were and expected to be, looking for what they needed — work, food, a roof to get under. Many were young loggers. Many were unskilled. All were unemployed.

Centralia, population 7,300, like any other place of this size, was not prepared to do much for hungry transients, whether they were ordinary tramps, traveling along, or men carrying the red membership card of the Industrial Workers of the World, out of a job and hoping to find one no matter how low the pay. Only the large cities had breadline facilities or soup kitchens.

Town ordinances commonly identified persons without means of support or sustenance as vagrants. Vagrancy was a misdemeanor punishable by a fine which could seldom be collected, by a jail sentence with the consequent cost of meals provided at public expense, or by work performed with a pick, shovel, or ax on some public undertaking. The most common disposition of a vagrancy case was none of these alternatives, however, but an edict, issued by a police officer or, if necessary, a local court, for the unwanted visitor to get out of town by sundown.

Four dozen Wobblies were too many vagrants for a town such as Centralia to jail, feed, or put to work. They had to be moved on. News stories of the episode do not say to what extent the men were argued with on the point of moving voluntarily, but they did not. Wobblies by 1915 had a reputation for being generally contemptuous of law enforcement and examples of their defiance were numerous, especially in Spokane where the police, in an attempt to stop IWW recruiting speeches on street corners, started jailing the speakers. Those jailed were replaced on their soap boxes so rapidly that the jails soon were jammed and the city forced to negotiate a compromise on a subject of vital consequence to the IWW — free speech.

The Wobblies on that February day in Centralia would not move on at the mere insistence of the police, and since the lawmen were in such a small minority, a decision was made to resort to tactics commonly used and widely accepted in Western towns since frontier times and well remembered by older and still able-bodied residents. Citizens were called upon to take a hand in dealing with the problem. This was the twentieth century, however, and vigilantism had been refined and subjected to discipline. Those eager to help run the Wobblies out of town were sworn in as "special policemen" and by early afternoon nearly a hundred men were gathered around the police station and given their assignment — round up the Wobblies and march them, using no force unless necessary, to a point well beyond the southern city limits. The visitors, outnumbered, moved without resistance.

Midway between Centralia and Chehalis, the county seat four miles south, are the Southwest Washington Fairgrounds, with empty open livestock buildings offering shelter. The Wobblies decided to camp there for the night. Many carried the characteristic

1

luggage of the itinerant logger — two or three blankets with a few personal possessions rolled into them, the whole tied with a piece of rope and slung over a shoulder. A "bindle" it was called, and those seen trudging along, a little bent over, lugging a bindle, were identified by a term that had just a slight ring of sympathy — "bindle stiff."

The men were hungry when they were driven out of town and there was nothing to eat at the fairgrounds. The next morning, after a conference, a delegation of eight was sent to the Centralia police station where Capt. Fred Ingalls was on duty. They didn't want any trouble, the Wobblies explained. But the men were really hungry. They had to have food and they were coming into town to get some, one way or another.

That sounded like an ominous ultimatum to Captain Ingalls, who was in charge since Chief Robert Schneider had left with Mayor W. H. Thompson for a sheriffs' convention in Olympia. He phoned an urgent message to the next town north, Tenino: When the mayor and the chief pull into town, tell them to hurry home. Emergency.

Meanwhile all of the hungry Wobblies trudged back into Centralia. They had developed a plan of action. Some went into the Hub Bakery, asked for free bread and, being refused, helped themselves to a few loaves and walked out. Others went into the Gingrich Grocery and took some apples. These token demonstrations of serious intent were enough to arouse the small police force and its numerous helpers to action again. The "undesirables," as the *Centralia Chronicle* termed them, "were marched to the police station and thrown in the bull pen." They were searched for weapons, but none were found. Asked again to leave, they said they wouldn't budge until they were fed.

Mayor Pro Tem Albert Sears and others asked, Why not? Feed them and then they would be gone. "But wiser heads," reported the *Chronicle,* "pointed out that if this were done, the city would have to run a municipal boardinghouse for days to come."

When the mayor and the chief arrived, irritated at having their trip interrupted, they were in no mood for anything conciliatory, especially for a jail full of what to a local reporter looked like "the toughest-looking bunch of men ever seen in this city."

The tough-looking visitors, waiting to be deported again, "sang songs and shouted. They offered no resistance." Local unionists — members of the Tim-

ber Workers and the Trades and Labor Council — "stoutly asserted" that they were not responsible for the presence of the Industrial Workers in Centralia, despite rumors that Wobblies were to be called into town to help win a strike against local sawmills.

Police and posse then repeated what they had done the day before, only this time they marched the men down the railroad tracks all the way to Chehalis, where they were met by the police, who had been forewarned. They were then escorted, without a pause, straight through town to the south side and told to keep going.

The *Chronicle's* sense of objectivity in its reporting caused it to conclude its front-page story of the day's events with this comment: "The way the bunch arrested this morning were hustled out of the city is an excellent indication of how the public looks upon their presence and it is up to every public-spirited citizen to do his part in keeping the city clear of this class of citizens which is famous for its determination to get their living without work."

Where the wanderers went next is not recorded. Probably they boarded southbound trains and went on to Portland, where free meals were to be had. If rails stretched out toward a Wobbly's destination, he didn't need to walk. Freight trains ran frequently and trainmen, out of either sympathy for those who called themselves "fellow workers" or respect for their ability to resist forcible removal from boxcars, usually allowed men to ride once they were aboard. The red card of IWW membership came to be a pass.

Centralia, the scene of these troubles, lies a hundred miles south of Seattle and a like distance north of Portland on a generally wet expanse of river bottom and beside the main-line railroad tracks, laid originally by the company that put steel on one of the overland wagon trails, the Northern Pacific. Just over the tracks to the east, the Cascade foothills begin, heavily forested and pouring forth snowmelt and rainfall from the mountain range where the dominant peaks are quiet, cold Mt. Rainier, off to the north, and Mt. St. Helens, the more active volcano, on the horizon to the south.

One of the streams pouring out of these hills is the turbulent Skookumchuck, and where it flows into the more placid Chehalis is Centralia, located there because of two happenstances. A man of considerable ambition and enterprise was the first settler in the valley. Then, in time, the Northern Pacific laid its tracks across his property, encouraging a development that was central to so much that its founders called it what other central places in numerous other states had been called — Centerville, later changed to the more euphonious Centralia.

George Washington was that first settler. He was not all white, a circumstance that led him and others who carried that handicap in the nineteenth century to move permanently away from the turmoil over slavery and migrate to the far West. It was not any absence of racial prejudice in the West that drew him. Treatment of the Indians was plain enough evidence that racial tolerance was not a frontier virtue. But they knew the West was generally free and there was so much land to be claimed that even a black man had a chance. That was not the case, however, in Oregon Territory, south of the Columbia.

Oregon aspired to statehood, and if it were to become identified, as all states were in the 1850s, as "slave" or "free," its chance of admission would likely vanish in the bitter struggle of both factions to gain numerical supremacy in Congress. With no blacks at all, slavery could be a moot question in Oregon, so the pioneer Oregonians simply excluded them.

George Washington, George Bush, and a few others with some dark in their skins settled out of necessity north of the Columbia, claiming land by right of settlement as the law of the time allowed. But Washington ran into trouble among his neighbors. He had come up from slavery, hadn't he? He wasn't really a citizen, was he? So he shouldn't be allowed to claim free land, should he, especially good farmland right where two rivers came together? After all, he was not a white man. His claim was not recognized.

Washington understood. Racism didn't end at the Continental Divide. So he devised an ingenious scheme to get around the problem.

Washington's mother was white, and two of her white friends, Mr. and Mrs. James C. Cochran, took the boy as a foster son when his father was sold to a distant owner. The Cochrans moved west to Ohio, and then to northern Missouri. The law prescribed illiteracy for blacks. But young George taught himself to read and write. The Cochrans were able to get a bill through the Missouri legislature declaring that George, because his mother was white, was born free, and so could enjoy all freedoms except holding office.

By 1850 Washington was thirty-three and contracted what was commonly called "Oregon fever." He decided to go west and persuaded the Cochrans to go with him, promising that he would never leave them.

He built a log house for the Cochrans near Cowlitz Landing before taking up a claim on the Skookumchuck, and when his claim was challenged, he simply had his foster parents come north and make the claim in his stead. Once it had been proved, he bought the 640 acres from them for $3,200. Because the land was on the line of travel between the Columbia River and Puget Sound, Washington's farm soon became a stopping place for travelers, like Monticello, Jackson's, Olequa, and Cowlitz Landing — all on the Cowlitz — and John Jackson's home, where court sessions were held, halfway up from the Cowlitz, and Claquato, where the original county seat was located.

The centrality of Washington's claim suggested that it might in time become a town, and he undertook to facilitate that possibility by laying out lot lines, streets, and even alleys. He sold 76-by-150-foot lots and became rich.

The Northern Pacific railroad was the making of George Washington's town. It became a division point where the train crews changed.

At the turn of the century Centralia, claiming a population of 1,600, was well established with a mayor-council form of government, a paid city marshal, and a voluntary fire brigade. There wasn't much money — not after the dismal '90s. Municipal bills were often paid with warrants, interest-bearing promises to pay when cash showed up in the treasury.

Then conditions improved. Lumber mills created new employment. Land values rose again. Some of the businessmen who had left when a previous boom ended heeded the renewed call of opportunity and returned. Municipal improvements had to be made, all meeting with the usual opposition encountered when public money is spent locally. Tower Avenue, named for Philadelphia millionaire Charlemagne Tower, was paved with brick. Residential streets were graded and a power plant made streetlights and a streetcar line possible. A sewer system and concrete sidewalks in place of wooden ones were installed. Thus Centralia went from frontier village to large town in the first decade of the century, and when the census was taken in 1910 the figure of nearly eight thousand brought it the distinction of being called the fastest-growing place in the state of Washington.

Centralians were pleased. They had much to be proud of. Their city was rapidly fulfilling the aspirations of all American cities — a solid economic base, good schools, many churches, and handsome red brick buildings on Main Street replacing worn frame structures. The N.P. displayed its confidence by building the biggest and most elegant brick passenger and freight depot anywhere between Portland and Tacoma. The sound of railroading was something Centralians endured without complaint, day and night, as hissing steam locomotives rumbled into town from the north and south, dozens of times a day, alerting everyone to their arrival with penetrating whistle blasts and a clanging of bells that sounded like a cathedral town at high noon when two or more engines were in the yard at once, which was often.

The early years in Centralia were good years, the older residents remembered. On New Year's Day families would hold open houses and couples would go calling, some of the lumber executives dressing up in long-tailed coats and wearing top hats. "Some of the mill owners came from the East," one elder citizen recalled. "They brought with them Eastern social customs. The mills were the things that kept the town going. I miss it yet when at midnight on New Year's Eve all the mill whistles used to blow."[2]

George Dysart, a local attorney with a realtor's sense of boosterism, wrote in 1909: "Opportunity knocks but once in the East, but . . . here she keeps up a constant clatter. She is fairly screaming to attract the attention of the capitalist and the homeseeker. . . . There are more opportunities to the square inch in Lewis County than in any other place in the world. . . . Here is a domain containing 2,600 square miles of undeveloped wealth."[3]

Dysart noted that the timber valued at $10 million was supplying fifty saw and shingle mills. "Here the laboring man finds employment at good wages and living expenses are low. And here the capitalist finds numerous opportunities for profitable returns on his investments."

Some differences of opinion existed among laboring men on the matter of wages being "good," yet labor unrest in the decade between 1910 and 1920 was less over pay scales than over hours and unsatisfactory conditions of work.

In the woods and mills prior to World War I the ten-hour, six-day week was standard. Wages were computed not by the hour, but by the day. A three-dollar-a-day wage was about average.

The loggers were particularly dissatisfied with their living conditions. They felled and bucked old-growth trees seldom less than six feet in diameter, then dragged them out of the woods. It was hard work and dangerous. Injuries were frequent. First aid was not provided, much less medical assistance. But the men didn't complain as often about hazards or even wages as about hours and camp conditions.

Logging crews were housed in movable company shacks close to the timber. In a typical shack three tiers of plank bunks extended along the walls and a sizable wood stove stood in the center. No bedding of any kind was provided. There was no running water, of course, and an outhouse wasn't built if it seemed likely a camp wouldn't be left in one place for long. Men didn't have outhouses while on the job in the woods, the logging bosses reasoned. They were hardly a necessity in camp, conveniently surrounded as camps usually were by tall stumps.

Meals in the camps were usually fair to good. Loggers ate prodigious amounts of food three times a day and logging outfits came to be known more for the quality of what their cookhouses produced than for any other characteristic.

The bosses had tradition on their side in resisting betterment of working conditions. Woods work had always been done by hardy men who didn't expect to be pampered. Many were foreign-born, often illiterate. Furthermore they were for the most part itinerant drifters. What was the point of providing camp comforts for men who didn't stay around very long?

The long ten-hour days — from sunup till sundown in the winter months — were often wet and, up in the hill country, cold. But loggers were mostly young and invariably hardy. They took pride in what they could do with axes and saws that sometimes were as long as sixteen feet. But it was too much to spend ten hours swinging a four- or five-pound double-bitted ax or pulling and shoving what came to be called a "misery whip" through the tough butts of several-centuries-old Douglas firs. They wanted to work only eight hours.

The logging operators and mill owners were outraged at the demands of both the AFL and the IWW on the matter of hours. Their margins of profit were seldom anything but thin even though stumpage was abundant and cheap. Prices were kept low by that abundance plus the chronic oversupply of lumber resulting from too many enterprising entrepreneurs deciding that sawmilling was the best business to embark on in a country where most of the land was covered with forest, and mill sites on deep water or on the new railroads were easy to find.

The only way to make a go of logging or sawmilling under such circumstances was to cut every corner possible and keep expenses to the barest minimum. If the work week were shortened, production would be curtailed, the bosses reasoned. Costs would go up. So it just couldn't be allowed.

The economic problems of employers were of no concern whatever to the mostly young, largely uned-ucated loggers and mill hands who were willing to accept the IWW contention that workers and employers had nothing in common. To their way of thinking wages were low, hours were long, and camp life uncomfortable, not because employers were struggling to keep costs down and survive, but because they were greedy, and because a system that required men to work for wages was fundamentally wrong and should be abolished.

There is no record of any employer successfully establishing an amicable working relationship with a group of Wobblies. The IWW didn't want agreements. They wanted change. So employers couldn't even try to deal with them. They could only fight them. So they did. And the war was unrelenting.

2

The Militant Mobs

While the 1915 expulsion was the first recorded instance of vigilante action against the IWW in Centralia, officially sanctioned or otherwise, it was by no means the first in the region. After the Wobblies emerged as a menace to the status quo in 1912 by joining an already-called lumber strike in Portland, enmity toward them mounted.

Workers in the Northwest always had been unorganized, dissatisfied, frequently unemployed, and, many thought, oppressed, as they moved about among the mines, mills, orchards, and logging camps on both sides of the Cascade range. The ideological base of the IWW did not have as much appeal to the young and uneducated sons of immigrants and farmers as did the promise of higher wages, a shorter working day, and more comfortable living conditions in the logging camps. They dreamed of a time when the "employing class," as the IWW literature termed it, could be bent to the determined will of a labor force so strong that none could resist it. They listened to the zealous recruiters and speakers and read the literature, supplied at the IWW halls in the cities and spread around the camps, giving details of the utopia that would emerge when all workers could band together, force abolition of private ownership, and end the necessity for anyone to pay or earn wages. It all may have been beyond full understanding, but it sounded noble, provided great goals to aspire to, and proclaimed unrelenting war on employers who were depriving workers of their due.

There was more even than that to the Wobbly appeal. Single men with no permanent jobs, moving about frequently, had no homes. When they joined the Industrial Workers of the World, they became part of a growing alliance that provided a sense of destiny and, perhaps more important, a place to go and a feeling of belonging in any town or city where the IWW had a hall.

Such halls had some of the characteristics of a lodge or club. There were racks of reading material, usually comfortable chairs, tables for playing cards, and, most important, the companionship of those who were living, striving, and hoping in a common way. Their camaraderie was often expressed in song. The tunes of the songs they sang were always borrowed — the melodies were from familiar songs the men already knew. But the words were original. Usually they were biting, cynical, or satirical words that expressed contempt even for such respected institutions as the Salvation Army, which competed with IWW speakers for worker attention on city street corners with pious promises of what the IWW's Little Red Song Book described as "pie in the sky when you die." The Wobblies were concerned with the more down-to-earth matter of regular meals now.

Hungry men would have been wandering on the road in 1915 if there had been no IWW. More men than were needed to fill the work force had been coming West for decades, lured by the legendary abundance of opportunity on the frontier. Unemployment was so widespread, and turnover in the logging camps so common as a result of the miserable conditions in them, that job buying became a prevalent practice. Agents who agreed to supply men for logging camps and other employers opened shops along the city skid roads where, for a fee, a man could get a job when the "job shark" had one to offer. The standard fee for ordinary jobs such as choker setter, whistle punk, or fireman was two dollars. Hook tenders, high climbers, camp cooks, and fallers and buckers paid more because their wages were higher.

"Burnside Street in Portland was lined with job sharks," one worker who sought jobs in that era recalled. "Seattle had them too. Stories of abuse, plots, and plans to keep the men coming and going to and from the camps so the sharks could collect the job fees often were common gossip. There also was the 'clearinghouse' set up by employers to check and keep a record of possible troublemakers. After buying a job, you still had to get an OK from the clearinghouse before you could go to work."[1]

For men caught in a system they considered unjust, the IWW organization provided a means of expressing their grievances. And they were expressed, often and vehemently.

Such expressions were widely reported throughout the West, and people in Centralia and elsewhere heard often of "disturbances" attributed to the radical labor group. When a thousand or more unemployed men staged a demonstration in the Los Angeles Plaza, shouting about "starvation amid plenty," the "disturbance" was blamed on the IWW. In a city as large as Los Angeles the police could handle such outbreaks. With clubs and drawn revolvers they broke up the demonstration. One man was killed. Seventy-five were arrested. A city councilman demanded an investigation. It exonerated the police because "the Industrial Workers of the World who were involved in the trouble stirred up the unemployed to violence," although news stories reported that the gathering in the plaza was peaceful and orderly until the police arrived.[2]

Centralians and others who watched the alarming spread of Wobbly-caused troubles were reminded of the famous Chicago Haymarket case of 1886 when another clash with the police occurred in San Francisco only weeks after the one in Los Angeles. Lucy Parsons, considered one of the founders of the IWW, was the widow of the ill-fated Albert R. Parsons, who was convicted and executed for what the state contended in the Haymarket case was his part in a bomb throwing in which one policeman was killed and seventy wounded. She had lost none of her militancy as late as 1913 and was arrested, along with unemployed IWW agitators, for making a public demand for three dollars for an eight-hour work day and legislation that would require the state to provide jobs for all who couldn't find private employment.

The trouble involving the IWW in the Northwest dates from 1912, when agitation began in earnest for specific reforms in the lumber industry. The mills in that industry were owned for the most part by small companies, all fiercely independent and uncompromising in their determination to resist interference of any kind with their efforts to make a profit in a business climate that often defied profit-making.

With the advent of unionism — the American Federation of Labor craft unions and then the IWW with its "one big union" concept (forerunner of modern industrial unionism) — employers recognized the need to defend themselves against a new threat. The independent entrepreneurs of the woods and mills could not agree among themselves on such matters as marketing practices or lumber standards, but they could willingly stand as one in unremitting resistance to all attempts to organize their workers, to reduce the work day from ten to eight hours, to cause money to be spend needlessly in pampering loggers with amenities such as showers and bed sheets in the camps, and to denounce the IWW in particular as an enemy of all that "good Americans" believed in.

These operators formed the Pacific Lumber Manufacturers Association, electing as its first president E. C. Griggs of Tacoma, an uncompromising mill boss determined to keep unions out of his St. Paul and Tacoma Lumber Company operations. He served for ten years. In 1911 the West Coast Lumbermen's Association was formed, but its antilabor activities were confined to the retention of a detective agency to infiltrate the IWW and keep lumbermen informed of its plots and strategies.

The first alarms were sounded in Grays Harbor towns, the lumber center of southwest Washington, fifty miles west of Centralia. Several thousand men were employed there in the numerous Aberdeen and Hoquiam waterfront mills and logging camps that fed the mills with daily trainloads of logs as thick as a man is tall. The IWW and the AFL recruited successfully among these workers, and by 1912 the union leaders decided the time had come for a showdown on their frequently rejected demands.

When the customary requests for an eight-hour day and higher wages were rejected, the IWW struck. This was a shock to the whole region. Strikes were relatively new in the West. Workers were not conceded to have any "right" to strike. They were expected to assume that they had an obligation to work, to obey their employers and to consider themselves fortunate to have a regular job. Mills — with their screaming head rigs where logs were sawed into lumber, and their towering steel burners where unused parts of sawn logs, as much as a quarter of a whole log, were consumed — stood as symbols of prosperity. Strike? Refuse to work? This was radicalism destructive of the very fabric of society, the employers would have everyone believe. And if any citizens did not agree, at least they did not say so, especially mayors, police chiefs, prosecutors, and other public officials who knew that labor trouble, like any other kind of public disturbance, had to be suppressed. Employers, the real community leaders, had enough to say about who was elected not to be ignored when they demanded protection against sullen hordes forcing mill production lines to shut down.

All the blame for the Grays Harbor strike fell on the Wobblies when the Aberdeen Trades Council, made up of the AFL craft unions, refused to endorse the work stoppage. Then came a tactic often used in the early West when public indignation aroused in the male citizenry a desire to take a personal part in ridding the community of an unquestioned evil. First a "citizens' committee" was formed to find a way to settle the strike. The IWW had a hall in Aberdeen. The strike leaders held forth there. The first move, the citizens' committee decided, should be to raid the hall, tear it apart and then run the Wobblies out of town. They would be loaded into boxcars and sent away — no matter where, just away from Grays Harbor.

All went well at first. The hall was raided, and about 150 Wobblies were forced into boxcars. But the railroad crews, fellow workers of sorts themselves, refused to go along with the vigilantes. They wouldn't move the cars. So the undesirables were sent on their way afoot twenty-four miles toward the next town, Raymond, where 460 of that town's citizens, hastily sworn in as deputies, were waiting when the straggling strikers arrived. Raymond was already deporting its own undesirables and had no trouble dealing with the overflow from Aberdeen.

The systematic expulsions of the IWW continued until only the AFL union leaders were left to speak for the workers. They agreed to a settlement that brought the pay scale to $2.25 a day (22-1/4 cents an hour), gave preference in hiring to American citizens (excluding the numerous Greeks and Finns in the area), and denied employment to any Wobbly.

The Wobblies thus lost their first strike and the mill owners were greatly relieved.

The IWW concentrated its organizing efforts in places where working conditions were considered particularly bad. One of these was the region around Coos Bay, Oregon, where a Wobbly hall was maintained between 1911 and 1913 in the town of Marshfield. Railroad workers there struck, claiming that $1.00 of their $2.50 daily wage was being withheld to pay for food that wasn't up to logging-camp standards, and that when bills at the company store were not paid promptly, personal belongings were confiscated. The dissatisfied railroad workers asked two IWW leaders, F. E. McKay and W. J. Edgeworth, to represent them.

An active organizer for the IWW at that time in Coos County was a young logger from Portland, Wesley Everest, who would carry memories of his treatment in Oregon then to a later year in Centralia, where he encountered Wobbly warfare more intense than that in Marshfield.

In late June 1914, tolerance for the two leading local IWW firebrands, Edgeworth and Everest, ended and they were arrested and jailed. But the business community wasn't satisfied to let the law handle the matter. As the *Coos Bay Harbor* reported, "A committee of citizens went into the jail and took the men from their cells, leading them down the street between escorts to the boat landing at the foot of Market Avenue, where they were placed on board the launch *Bonita*, accompanied by about 300 Marshfield businessmen."[3] The launch took the Wobblies across the bay to Jarvis Landing, where they were told to get out and start walking.

One did not need to be a Wobbly to suffer ill treatment at the hands of vigilantes of that day. A month after Everest and Edgeworth were deported, Dr. Bailey Kay Leach, a chiropractor and editor of a Socialist newspaper in Bandon, was seized. His offense was daring to print criticism of the Wobbly deportation. The Bandon Commercial Club, made up of businessmen, called Dr. Leach to account. No, he said, he was not a member of the IWW nor had he insulted the flag, as was charged. The verdict of the Commercial Club nevertheless was that he had to go. He was taken by boat to Coquille and by car to Marshfield, where he was put on another boat that put him off at Jarvis Landing. He too was instructed to start walking and never come back.

Stores in Bandon closed and employees of the Moore Lumber Company stood by to "back up the businessmen to a man" if Leach and his few supporters dared to resist.[4]

These actions were sufficiently high-handed to attract widespread attention and caused Governor Oswald West to express regrets to the men who were deported. He promised them the protection of the law in the future and directed the attorney general to investigate the widely publicized deportations. The attorney general found no one to criticize, much less to accuse of criminal activity. His report concluded, "The loggers and millmen are a contented class in Coos County and apparently dislike the invasion of agitators and disturbers."[5]

The buildup of public sentiment against the IWW was a satisfying development to employers, who undertook to pour more fuel on the fires of hatred and fear. They were in full flame by 1916.

The newly organized Employers Association of Washington hired as its manager a facile writer and speaker with venom in his oratory, Leigh H. Irvin. He turned out a series of pamphlets, based on his speeches, with such titles as "Conspiracy Against Liberty," "Un-American Ambitions," and "Government by Labor Unions." Not content merely to denounce the IWW and organized labor in general, Irvin proclaimed the noble intentions of employers. The association, he wrote, was engaged in forwarding a great educational campaign. Its task was to convince the country that opposition to labor organizations was not based on selfish motives but because "we know that coercion and violence never promote the general welfare."[6] Irvin referred frequently to the "Labor Trust," which he accused of dynamitings and destruction of property.

The Wobblies were not intimidated by all this. Despite intense opposition, they stepped up their organizing efforts and started their own newspaper in Seattle, the *Industrial Worker,* which every week headlined the clashes and struggles of the war on Wobblies and exhorted the workers to fight on.

Sometimes it seemed as if the Wobblies went out deliberately looking for trouble, as in 1916 when Everett, the big mill town on Puget Sound, provided an attractive opportunity to make an organizing drive among AFL shingle weavers who were on strike and not making any progress. The IWW opened a hall and began recruiting on the streets, an activity that brought the inevitable reaction from those elected with industry support. The sheriff and the police warned the Wobblies to desist from street speaking and go back to Seattle. The AFL strike leaders wanted them out, too. "We don't want them damn anarchists here any more than you do," one of their spokesmen told the police.[7] The Commissioner of Public Safety undertook what others tried with invariably poor results — reasoning with the Wobblies. The shingle weavers' strike was a local thing, he said to a clump of grim-faced IWW organizers. He insisted the strikers wanted to settle it in their own way without interference. The Wobblies were unimpressed. They didn't leave and so were arrested, charged with vagrancy and jailed. But instead of being taken to court the next morning they were transported to the docks and shoved aboard a Seattle-bound steamer. Thus challenged, the Wobblies plotted a next move. One by one they went back to Everett, held street meetings, quoted Patrick Henry and recited from the U.S. Constitution, and they won some sympathizers.

Here was something law enforcement obviously couldn't handle alone. It was time for strong men to step in. The Everett Commercial Club, akin to a chamber of commerce and organized to promote the best interests of the city, determined that one of those best interests was getting rid of the Wobblies. David Clough, the lumber executive usually looked to for leadership, warned that Everett was threatened with an invasion of destructive troublemakers and bums bent on ruining the city. Sheriff Donald McRae, elected with the support of the business community, was given command of the defense endeavors and told to get busy. He began by deputizing two hundred volunteers and drilling them and his regular deputies in strong-arm tactics. The city council made it easier to bring charges against the invaders by passing an ordinance prohibiting meetings on the streets.

The vigilantes went to work and the Wobblies retreated. The tactics were rough — too much so for some Everett citizens, who could see that McRae's brand of law enforcement was making the Wobblies seem like oppressed underdogs. It was no longer entirely a matter of radical outsiders interfering in a local labor dispute. The local leaders, including Ernest P. Marsh, Trades Council president and labor paper editor, were offended when some of their own speakers were suppressed. Marsh called a mass meeting for September 22 in one of the parks and dared provoke the Commercial Club by inviting Seattle Socialists and Wobblies to take part. To make sure the visitors were not molested, local workers provided an escort, including a brass band, from the dock to the park. A huge crowd turned out — fifteen thousand, by estimate. The Wobblies felt encouraged.

But in the days following McRae did not let up. Everyone entering town had to be checked. Anyone who couldn't prove he was not a Wobbly was turned away. Incoming trains, steamers, and interurbans were met. The roads were patrolled.

In an attempt to get around the blockade, a group of Wobblies went by train to Mukilteo, seven miles south of Everett, and hired a launch to take them to a dock in Everett which they presumed would not be guarded. But the Everett spies were alert. Before the launch reached Everett, Sheriff McRae and several deputies aboard a tugboat intercepted it. Shots were fired as a warning to stop. The Wobblies and their pilot were hauled aboard the tug and taken to Everett, where they were held in the county jail for nine days before being released.

Tension in Everett mounted. "An intolerable situation exists in this city," the *Everett Labor Journal* protested. "The beating up of men and boys by citizens clothed with temporary authority and armed with clubs, which is almost a nightly occurrence, reflects but little credit on those who stand for law and order. The *Labor Journal* holds no brief for the IWW. IWW tactics and philosophies have never appealed very strongly to the trade union movement. But if ever there was an asinine policy pursued in the world, it is the policy of going over the heads of the city authorities and policing the city with a mob — mob is the right word — of highly respected citizens."[8]

Undiscouraged, a band of more than forty Wobblies on October 30 boarded a steamer for Everett, expecting to be able to force their way past any deputies who might meet them on the dock. But word of their coming preceded them and the vigilantes were ready — a hundred or more, wearing handkerchiefs tied around their necks for identification.

The forty men were pushed into cars and trucks and transported to Beverly Park on the city's edge. According to later testimony in court, the vigilantes formed a double line along the suburban railroad track where it crossed a road and, with guns drawn, forced the men to run the gauntlet. As they ran they were beaten with clubs, pick handles, and gun butts. Some were made to lower their pants and submit to lashings with devil's club, a stiff stalk with needle-like spines. Some men fell under the blows, and were dragged to their feet and beaten again. Some were sent sprawling on a cattle guard with sharp teeth. The few who made a desperate attempt to escape were caught, brought back and made to run the line.

It was not a silent scene. The men screamed and moaned in pain and the vigilantes cursed and shouted. A man living a quarter-mile away heard the uproar and came running.

"What in God's name is going on here?" he asked breathlessly.

"We're beating the hell out of a bunch of Wobblies," he was told. "That's the only kind of language they understand."[9]

The victims of this violence stumbled down the track toward Seattle, and after a while they were able to board an interurban car. The passengers on the car were shocked by the condition of the bloody, suffering men and were useful witnesses for the IWW when the story of Beverly Park beatings was related later in court hearings.

This brutality stirred some sympathy for the Wobblies. Already, a few Everett merchants were displaying signs in their windows announcing that they did not belong to the Commercial Club. Clergymen organized a public meeting to appeal to the sheriff, but the sheriff was in no mood to let up. Two of his hunting dogs were found poisoned. "Cat's Claw"[10] cards were left at his door. He received threatening letters. Mysterious fires broke out on his property.

The Wobblies who ran the gauntlet in Beverly Park limped back into Seattle and told their story. Enraged, the IWW organization determined to strike back. It felt that sufficient public opinion had been aroused against the use of violence to make it safe to advertise their next move. Handbills by the thousands were strewn about Everett proclaiming:

CITIZENS OF EVERETT

Attention!

A meeting will be held at the corner of Hewitt and Westmore Ave., on Sunday, Nov. 5, at 2 p.m. Come and help maintain yours and our constitutional rights.

— Committee

Meanwhile, the IWW recruited volunteers to join in a mass invasion of Everett. Transportation was a problem. The interurban could not handle large numbers. Trucks were too expensive. So it was decided to charter one of the many passenger steamers that made regular runs on the Sound. One of these was the *Verona*. On the evening of November 4 a Wobbly leader, who was seen to be carrying a large roll of currency, asked the captain of the *Verona,* C. E. Wiman, if his boat could be chartered for the next day. Wiman said no, the *Verona* had its regular run to make, so the Wobbly asked how many the steamer could carry. It held 260, he was told. Taking out his roll, the Wobbly peeled off three ten-dollar bills and gave them to Wiman as passage money for a full load.

Next morning more men than the *Verona* could carry showed up and the surplus embarked on another steamer, the *Calista.* One of the men on the *Verona,* as she set sail for a violent rendezvous with Wobbly intolerance, was a native of Ireland, James McInerney, a thirty-one-year-old native of County Clare, who had drifted west after immigrating in 1910, earning his way as a construction worker, then learning the logging trade. Even an Irish immigrant like McInerney, used to hardship, did not find life in the wet logging camps tolerable. He embraced the IWW philosophy in 1916, joining those vowing to succeed with reforms despite the hostility they encountered everywhere.

McInerney and many others who boarded the *Verona* could sense something of the exhilaration of soldiers going forth to battle after reading the *Industrial Worker* that week. "The entire history of the IWW," it proclaimed, "will be decided at Everett. Workers should go to Everett, not with any thought of starting a fight to get revenge, but to make a stand and go to jail if necessary."

"Workers of America," admonished the Wobbly editor, "if the boss-ruled gang of Everett is allowed to crush free speech and organization, then the Iron Hand will descend upon us all over the country. Will you allow this? It is for you to choose! Every workman should help in every way to put an end to this infamous reign of terror. ACT NOW!"

The IWW had imaginative writers in its ranks, one being Walker C. Smith. "Laughter and jest were on the lips of the men who crowded the *Verona,*" he wrote, "and songs of One Big Union rang out over the sparkling waters of Puget Sound. Loyal soldiers were these in the great class war, enlightened workers who were willing to give their all in the battle for bread, happiness and liberty. . . ."[11]

"One can believe the laughter, the jest and the song," wrote historian Norman Clark much later.

These men were from the logging camps and the hobo jungles, from the dreary monotony of grubby street corners and drafty rooming houses on Skid Road. They carried a kind of tribal memory of Spokane — memories of how others had remembered it — and they talked of brotherhood, wage slavery, social revolution and their obligations to their fellow workers in Everett. Some were cocky with confidence. It would be a great day, part picnic, part holy war. Probably only a few knew where Everett was, and even fewer knew what it looked like or what was really taking place there. To Wobblies less impressed by theory, the free speech fight was at least a sort of ritual in the fraternal order of wage slaves, at best a rousing hell-of-a-good-time — the substance of song and cherished memory. It was what should happen to Everett after the blood of Beverly Park had fixed the city forever in the cartography of class war.[12]

The *Verona*'s trip up the Sound was uneventful and spirits were high as the vessel approached the dock in Everett. Many passengers crowded together on the forward deck to sing one of their defiant songs as the vessel's engines were cut and it drifted slowly toward the dock:

> We meet today in freedom's cause,
> And raise our voices high!
> We'll join our hands in union strong
> To battle or to die.

One enthusiastic young man, Hugo Gerlot, climbed the vessel's foremast and waved to a crowd of spectators gathered on the hillside behind the dock to watch another IWW confrontation. The dock itself was deserted except for three men — Sheriff McRae, Deputy Sheriff Jefferson Beard, and Lt. Charles C. Curtis of the National Guard.

Some of the men on the *Verona,* still seething over the last dockside reception, had brought guns with them. They had these in readiness as the steamer slowly slid alongside the wooden dock and its crew put out a mooring line.

Sheriff McRae stepped forward and shouted, "Who's your leader?"

"We're all leaders," came back the reply in a confused chorus.

"Well, you can't land here," the sheriff warned.

"Why not?" came a reply from the *Verona*. "It's a free country, ain't it?"

Hugo Gerlot started waving something — a red flag, some witnesses said, but only his cap, others claimed. And then a shot was fired. Whether it came from the dock or the *Verona* was never finally determined, although testimony at a subsequent Bureau of Marine Inspection that came to light in 1979 revealed that three armed Wobblies were huddled behind the smokestack, and were seen to fire numerous shots from handguns. The first shot could as well have been fired by one of these as by one of the three officers on the dock who, though armed, were not expecting armed resistance from the Wobblies. A squadron of uniformed men had been stationed inside the warehouse on the dock, ready to be called out if the "invaders" tried to defy the sheriff and leave the ship.[13]

The first shot was followed immediately by a volley of shots in both directions. Gerlot fell to the deck, dead. Deputies on the dock threw open the doors of the warehouse and joined the fray. Several were hit. Sheriff McRae was struck twice, in the leg and foot, but kept on firing.

In a panic, the *Verona*'s passengers rushed to the offshore side of the ship, causing it to list sharply. Some of the wounded and dead rolled across the deck, through the railing and into the water. Other deputies who had been stationed on the tugoat *Edison* fired into the crowds jammed along the *Verona*'s railing and at the wounded struggling in the water. The ship's passageways were blocked by those scrambling to get below decks.

The *Verona*'s captain, who ducked for cover when the firing started, finally got a grasp of the situation and ordered the engines into reverse full power. The line to the dock either broke or was cut and soon the ship was out of gun range. The *Edison* did not pursue the *Verona* as it hastened back to Seattle, warning the *Calista* on the way to turn back.

The dead and wounded on shore were put into automobiles that headed in a stream for the hospital. It was a strange caravan, almost halted when the crowds of onlookers, outraged by what they had seen, went down from the railroad tracks to shout curses and threats at those who — far from being consid-

ered martyrs wounded in a battle to protect Everett from an invading menace — were being jeered for resorting to even more brutal tactics than those used at Beverly Park, especially the vicious firing at men floundering in the water.

Sheriff McRae, wounded, panicky, worried lest the Wobblies send another wave of invaders, and shocked by the hostility toward him expressed by the crowds of onlookers at the dock, called for help from the local naval militia and hurriedly sent a telegram to the governor: "Terrible riot in Everett. At least 25 citizens shot. Some dead and others mortally wounded. Send militia at once without fail and plenty of them." He was not alone in his panic. David Clough and John McChesney, another local industrial leader, signed the telegram also.

Governor Lister was alarmed, too, and ordered two companies of the National Guard sent to Everett at once to preserve order. One was Company M from Centralia. Commercial Club leaders wanted the troops stationed in the streets immediately, but the guard commander, after conferring with McRae, did not see the need and the men were kept out of sight, but ready for action, in the armory.

Despite the extent of the gunfire, only seven persons were known to have been killed — five on the ship and two on the dock. There may have been more. But only five bodies were recovered. Those killed on shore were Deputy Sheriff Beard and Lieutenant Curtis. Nineteen members of the sheriff's squad and thirty-one Wobblies were seriously wounded.

News of what was immediately termed a "massacre" reached Seattle before the bullet-ridden *Verona* arrived at its home dock on Alaskan Way. The police were waiting. Seventy-four Wobblies were arrested and soon taken back to Everett to be jammed into the Snohomish County jail, four in a cell, ten cells to a tank. There they remained for two months while a prosecution strategy was being devised. It was not an easy task. The handling of large groups by vigilantes was seldom difficult. All those rounded up could be considered guilty and dealt with accordingly, as at Beverly Park. But here was a murder situation. The killers had to be prosecuted and legalities had to be observed. Specific charges had to be made and then proven. Frontier justice could not be allowed to carry over to the courtroom.

The men in jail waiting to be charged with a crime

were fed so much foul mush they went on a hunger strike. When their requests for blankets and mattresses were refused, they resorted to the tactic known as "building a battleship." This meant beating on the walls, bars, and metal floors with anything made of metal, shouting in unison and raising a din that could be heard blocks away. The ruckus succeeded and blankets and mattresses were provided.

The IWW retained Fred H. Moore of Los Angeles and George F. Vanderveer of Seattle as defense attorneys. Vanderveer was a forty-one-year-old former prosecuting attorney in King County, educated at Columbia and Stanford, who took more seriously than most one part of the oath all Washington lawyers were required to swear when admitted to the bar. It read, "I solemnly promise and swear that I will never reject from any consideration, personal to myself, the cause of the defenseless or oppressed. . . . "[14]

This was the first time Vanderveer had accepted the IWW as a client, and his wife and friends didn't like it. The case served as his introduction to IWW philosophy and tactics, which puzzled him. The seventy-four men in jail did not seem nearly as interested in winning acquittal as in using the trial as a platform to expound IWW doctrine. IWW headquarters mailed a large bundle of the union's literature to the prosecutor, hoping he would introduce it as evidence to show what kind of organization was on trial. If that were done, they reasoned, the nobility of all that the IWW stood for could be talked about in open court and would be reported in the press, and thousands would be given a chance to see the rightness of the workers' cause as well as their innocence.

This bothered Vanderveer, who angrily admonished his clients that his assignment was to win a murder trial, not preach Wobbly doctrine in court.

The men were kept waiting for trial so long that some public sympathy was aroused. Women's groups brought an occasional dinner to the jail. Others provided reading materials. Then, at last, the prosecution was ready. It filed informations charging four crimes against each man being held. But since seventy-four men were far too many to try simultaneously a beginning was made by trying just one. He was Thomas C. Tracy, identified in the information as the one who fired the shot from a pilothouse window on the *Verona* that killed Deputy Sheriff Beard.

The murder trial went on for nine tedious weeks.

Hundreds of witnesses produced testimony totaling two and a half million words. It was no ordinary murder case, as everyone knew and as the lawyers trying the case conceded. The IWW itself was on trial. The right of a city to defend itself against the onslaughts of radicals was being decided. In his instructions to the jury, Judge J. T. Ronald said, "It is plain that we are making history."

The Wobbly lawyers, as they made history, were given a freedom denied in the Centralia case trial three years later. They were allowed to introduce the whole story of labor oppression in Everett — the denial of free speech on the streets, the forcible expulsions, and the brutal beatings in Beverly Park.

On a Wednesday in April the judge and jury were loaded in cars and taken first to the park, where Judge Ronald pointed to the cattle guard and the place where the men were forced to run the gauntlet. They went then to the dock. The *Verona* was sailed up from Seattle again and positioned with one line to the dock and the stern out, just as it had been when the firing began on November 5. The defense put a man in the pilothouse where Tracy was supposed to have fired the fatal shot, and members of the jury stood at places on the dock where witnesses said they were standing when they saw Tracy shoot. The jurors could not even see the man in the pilothouse.

Members of the jury — one of the first under a new Washington law allowing women to serve — boarded the *Verona* and saw that it was riddled with bullet holes. They reflected on the fact that five and possibly more of the companions of those on trial were killed in the shoot-out.

When the testimony ended, the jury deliberated for twenty-two hours. Numerous ballots were taken before the verdict: not guilty.

The verdict, while not a complete surprise, was a disappointment to many who felt that the Wobblies were being allowed to get away with murder. After all, they were the bad men of the day and Everett was terrorized by them. They were capable of descending on the city and doing great harm. The sheriff and his deputies were fighting a defense action in what amounted to a war. An invasion was being repelled. The defense succeeded and the invaders were forced to flee. In the battle two defenders were killed, which was unfortunate, but the battle was won and besides, more Wobblies were killed than defenders.

George Vanderveer, in his first time out in defense of the IWW, had won. He discovered that being a Wobbly in court did not mean certain conviction.

The acquittal was not generally well received, however, and it stirred vicious impulses in the more rabid Wobbly haters, among them the editor of the *Douglas County Hammer* in Wenatchee, quoted in the *Industrial Worker* as recommending that the citizens of Everett "take a lesson from frontier history when a well executed lynch law made short work of an outlaw class. That this class (the Wobblies) are outlaws goes without saying. . . . The frontier method is worth trying now when the law fails to be effective."

3

Mobilizing to Meet the Menaces

The rough way Wobblies were handled in Centralia, Everett, and elsewhere set no precedents. This was the Far West in the first decades of the twentieth century, only a few years removed from times when a man was expected to volunteer on short notice to serve the local good by fighting off some threatening evil or provide protection against a sudden menace, whether it be marauding Indians, gangs of bandits, laid-off Chinese railroad construction workers willing to work for a dollar a day or, as now, disruptive radicals such as the Industrial Workers of the World.

Frontier self-sufficiency was such that if a sheriff or marshal required assistance, it could always be found among the men of the community, who either carried guns or had them handy and welcomed a little excitement. The resulting armed body was known as a posse. If there was time, members of a posse were "sworn in" as deputies in order to give official sanction to what they were about to do. When such men set out to right wrongs on their own, either spontaneously or on call from a leader who wore no star and held no office, the name applied was vigilantes. A less respectable name, sometimes used, was "mob."

Posses were of an ad hoc nature. They had one assignment, performed it, and dispersed. Vigilantes, however, often considered their attentions to matters of law and order and public safety to be needed over a period of time, either because those charged with duties in these areas were inadequate in number or because they lacked the qualities needed to deal effectively with situations requiring courage and force of numbers. Vigilantes sometimes kept themselves mobilized for indefinite periods, imposing their own version of law enforcement and judicial determination

over that of constituted authority.

The settlers and those who came soon after believed that the ends of justice were best served, promptly and with certainty in many instances, if the aroused citizens in a community bestirred themselves to action in critical times and did what they knew to be right even if it was not exactly legal.

Vigilantes and the law were sometimes at odds. Self-respecting sheriffs and other public officers were not always willing to stand aside and let a band of angry and often irrational citizens take over their duties. The mob instinct was easily aroused, as in Tacoma and Seattle during the uprising against the Chinese in 1886. Law enforcement tried to shield the helpless Chinese against violence, although agreeing with the majority of citizens that the "celestials" had to go. Public officials could not cope with the emotionalism engendered by intense racial feelings.

Washington did not have a legal hanging of a white man until 1877, when a John Thompson killed Solomon Baxter of Renton on a Sunday, claiming self-defense. He was indicted for murder on Tuesday, tried on Thursday, convicted on Friday, sentenced on Saturday, and would have been hanged the following Monday had his attorney not appealed to Governor Ferry for executive clemency, thereby starting a period of legal delays that extended from February to September when the hanging did take place.

Many hangings occurred prior to 1877, of course, as did many afterward, which could not be classified as legal. Quite often these involved Indians, half-breeds, or Chinese, whose offenses, committed with or without an understanding of the white man's laws, could be considered so obviously evil that courtroom delays and expenses in administering punishment should be avoided. Vigilantism was no more nor less commonly resorted to in Washington, however, than elsewhere in the West on occasions when law enforcement officers were too few or too timid, or the courts too slow, to enable the offenders to be dealt with promptly.

Vigilantes were particularly active during the 1860s in the town of Steilacoom. A young man, Stephen Judson, elected sheriff, was bothered by this and was so determined to thwart further interferences with legal processes that he reinforced the five-inch-thick wood door of his brick jail with boiler iron. This precaution was soon tested. A respected citizen was shot in a dispute over a stolen cow and the slayer promptly locked up in what the sheriff considered an impregnable jail. As had happened before in Steilacoom, an enraged group of citizens soon assembled, marched to the jail, seized the sheriff, and put him under guard in a nearby store while an assault was made on the jail in order to bring the culprit to immediate justice.

The reinforced door withstood battering with a thirty-foot log, but the aroused citizens were not to be thwarted. They pounded away at the bricks around the door until the jamb collapsed, providing access to the terrified prisoner. He was seized and taken to a nearby barn, where the log used as a ram was hoisted to the loft with one end protruding to serve as a hanging place for the prisoner, still trussed up in irons.[1]

After this episode, followed, as usual, by no indictments or charges against the lynchers, Sheriff Judson realized that the jail had to be made even stronger, not to prevent escapes, but to protect inmates against the fury of those willing to deny trial to the accused. So he lined the inner walls with six layers of heavy two-by-twelve-inch planks, spiked and cross-spiked in such a way that a saw could not cut through them. As an additional precaution he planked the floor with more two-by-twelve timbers.

Perhaps the most spectacular recorded lynching in Washington occurred in Seattle in 1882, a time when crime flourished there, especially in its "Lava Bed" or slum district, later to be adorned with a no less enigmatic name, Skid Road. After a series of crimes, the respectable pioneer Seattleites became so much concerned that it took only one more fatal shooting —the killing by robbers of a prominent citizen — to arouse them to action. The fire bell was rung and soon two

hundred men assembled in the engine house. A search for the killers was begun. Two armed men found hiding behind some hay on a wharf were seized and taken to jail. The searchers assembled again and soon made their decision: Hang them both now. The sheriff, his son, and the chief of police took a stand behind the locked door of the jail and said no. So the vigilantes broke down the door only to find Sheriff L. V. Syckoff standing with drawn pistol, swearing he would defend the prisoners with his life. This was enough to prevent a lynching that night. Next morning, however, the accused pair were taken to court and evidence against them was presented. The judge ordered them held for the grand jury and with that the action began. A dozen men surged to the front of the courtroom. Amid angry shouts about delays, they seized the two prisoners and hustled them out a back door. The judge and the sheriff were prevented from interfering. Roger Sherman Greene, chief justice of the Supreme Court, had come to the hearing and the vigilantes, knowing he would be there, brought a sheet which they threw over him to keep him from seeing who was administering out-of-court justice. Ropes were quickly looped around the necks of the two men, who stood convicted without a trial beneath a hastily improvised scaffold in Occidental Square. It consisted of a scantling laid in the crotches of adjacent maple trees in front of Henry Yesler's residence. Justice Greene, escaping from the sheet, ran to the scene of the hanging, arriving just as the two were hoisted clear of the ground. There, amid shouts of "Hang him too" and "Shoot him," he began hacking frantically at the hanging ropes with his pocketknife. Again he was grabbed and pulled away.

While the two victims of lynch-mob violence were still swinging, someone remembered that the jail contained another man accused of murder. The lust to lynch was upon them so it was quickly agreed to get him too. The mob rushed to the jail, smashed through the fence surrounding it, battered in the door, seized the prisoner, and dragged him, screaming his protests of innocence, to Occidental Square where he was hanged beside the other two victims.

Justice Greene was incensed by all this but understood the temper of the times well enough not to bring charges against any of those he could himself identify as lynchers. Later he wrote, "That lynching set a bad example to other communities and to posterity, yet it no doubt has operated as a local and powerful

*A typical IWW hall in 1912, with the familiar slogans
prominently displayed: "Boost for the 8 Hour Day,"
"One Union, one label, one enemy."*

deterrent of crime. Its force, however, as a scarecrow to criminals was soon spent; while the pernicious example of Seattle's citizens still remains and will continue to remain, a widely approved fallacious precedent, to invite and sophistically justify or excuse, here and elsewhere, future similar disorder."[2]

Compilers of a history of violence in America commissioned by President Nixon in 1968, a time when the government was bewildered by the changing extent and nature of violence, did enough research to be able to list some of the places where known vigilante actions had taken place in the states. Under Washington State are listed New Dungeness, Tacoma, Pullman, Colfax, Seattle, Walla Walla, Union Gap, Centralia, Aberdeen, and Everett — all places where clubs, guns, and rope were used against Wobblies.

The researchers made this reasonable observation: "Fundamentally, the pioneers took the law into their own hands for the purpose of establishing order and stability in newly settled areas. . . . The hurtful presence of outlaws and marginal types in a context of weak and ineffectual law enforcement created the spectre and, often, the fact of social chaos. The solution hit upon was vigilantism. A vigilante roundup of ne'er-do-wells and outlaws followed by the flogging, expulsion, or killing of them not only solved the problem of disorder but had crucial symbolic value as well. . . . Vigilantism was a violent sanctification of the deeply cherished values of life and property."[3]

Posses and vigilantes could handle most local emergencies, but as early as 1855 Washington's first residents learned that armed bodies of men functioning under military discipline were needed to deal with major troubles. In the mid-1850s several Indian tribes, finally understanding the terms of treaties negotiated with their chiefs by Gov. Isaac Stevens, rose up in a wrath they considered righteous enough to justify attacking whites wherever they might be likely to get away with it. The settlers hastily erected log blockhouses and stockades where families could take refuge. One of these blockhouses, Fort Borst, was left standing long after the Indians were subdued and survives as an historic relic in Borst Park near the Skookumchuck River in Centralia.

The Indian wars necessitated the recruitment of volunteer troops who helped the regular army put down the uprisings. They continued to serve as volunteer militia during the rest of the territorial period.

When statehood was finally achieved in 1889, framers of the new state constitution had little difficulty agreeing that a militia should be made a permanent arm of state government. The militia was to be divided into two parts, one to be maintained on active duty as the National Guard of Washington, and the other to consist of reserves subject to military duty on call.

Uses to which the state's new military contingent could be put were demonstrated as early as 1894 when coal miners struck in Roslyn. Northern Pacific train crews refused to move trains through the strike area. The resourceful general manager of the mining company, George Dickerson, climbed into a locomotive and piloted a short train to St. Paul, Minnesota, covering the distance in five days. There he recruited six hundred blacks with promises of good pay in the mines, loaded them on his train, and headed west. At Helena the recruits were given guns, which they were told might be needed to hold off Indians who were on the warpath again. Meanwhile, the governor had been persuaded to call for federal troops from Vancouver to reinforce the sixty deputy marshals who were holding off strikers trying to block rail traffic in and out of the mines. Strikers and the St. Paul strikebreakers turned the mining towns into armed camps, leading Governor Ferry to send in National Guardsmen to disarm everyone. Peace finally was restored with the mining companies claiming total victory over the union.

Strikes were considered public disorders. No laws sanctified them and no laws recognized those who might call a strike. All men were expected to work and to accept what an employer was willing or able to pay, under conditions he felt he could afford and be successful. The time of labor rights — to collective bargaining, to union recognition, and to strike — was still far away. The use of the militia, men carrying arms to defend against those threatening to disturb the public tranquility, was generally accepted as proper to prevent strikers from interfering with production.

In 1910 the IWW, organized in the East five years before, was getting a foothold in the West, and that year Company M, 161st Infantry, National Guard, was organized to serve Southwest Washington with Centralia as its base.

Those recruited to serve under E. F. Kirklin, a Spanish-American War veteran selected as the first captain of the unit, were nearly all from Centralia, Chehalis, and other parts of Lewis County. Dr. David

Special Collections Division, University of Washington Libraries, neg. #UW6635

Livingstone was appointed first lieutenant and William Scales second lieutenant.

"When the move was made to organize a militia," a local historian wrote in later years, "all agreed that it was a fine idea, and one which reflected a great deal of credit on the city. Probably most of us were thinking of the grandeur which would be ours on future Fourth of Julys and Memorial Days."[4]

Kirklin soon resigned and Dr. Livingstone, commissioned captain, took command of the unit. Livingstone, a thin, intense-looking man, was a native of Canada with a medical degree from Trinity University in Toronto. He was a grandnephew of David Livingstone, the noted African explorer.

Scales, who helped organize the company, had served through the war with Spain and was listened to with respect by the younger recruits when he and Captain Kirklin told about the exploits of Col. Teddy Roosevelt, and other inspiring aspects of that short war's triumphs in Cuba and the Philippines.

The Guard unit met regularly to drill, review tactics, keep the equipment maintained, and experi-

Wobblies often went to jail rather than relinquish their right to speak on the street to recruit members and preach their brand of reform. A loud-voiced speaker always drew a crowd.

ence the pleasures of fraternal association. Nearly all members of Company M were young, serving a common purpose, and elated by the respect accorded around town by those they were charged with protecting. Company M developed such a high degree of camaraderie that it was kept alive as the Company M Association, though not as a military unit, until 1978 when a final annual reunion was held.

In June 1916, Company M received orders to travel to the Mexican border on what was called a "punitive expedition." The unit assembled in uniform in Centralia and marched to the depot. It being July 4, feelings of pride and patriotism ran high. "As they marched to the station," wrote the local chronicler of the unit's history, "a wave of pride thrilled through us, for there is something about the thud of marching feet and the beat of drums that brings a 'cheer to the throat and a blur in the eye.' These were not boys!

Photo by D. D. Kinsey; Special Collections Division, University of Washington Libraries

These were men — fighting men! And suddenly we began to realize that in just such boys as these lay the nation's security."

While they were gone, the IWW fanned the flames of discontent, as they liked to put it, in its new weekly, the *Industrial Worker.* In its fourth issue the *Worker* took note of a bill in Congress federalizing the militia, saying the capitalists "would crow about this. . . Plu-

A typical crowded logging-camp bunkhouse scene in the days before the Wobblies achieved objectives such as company-provided bedding, showers, and bunks with mattresses.

tocracy wants a slave driving army on the federal payroll to be sure of their legions in time of strike. . ." Therefore, the workers should "use every effort, legal and illegal, to so discredit the militia that none but the very lowest type of working men would join its ranks, for this type can be depended upon to preach the necessity of social revolution in stronger terms than all the rebel agitators on earth. . . . "[6]

A year later the *Industrial Worker* had not softened its attitude. "The National Guard," it complained, "is the strong-arm of capitalism in the prostitution of the women of the working class, and the degeneracy of manhood. Unthinking and incapable of thinking, they are the dregs at the bottom of society that administer to the scum on top."[7]

Such comments, clipped from the papers and passed around, did nothing to create a tolerance for Wobblies among men of the National Guard.

Company M remained near Calexico on border patrol until September 1916, when it was sent home.

4

Conservative Town, Conservative People

Pioneering calls for self-reliance of a high order. Those who come first to settle a place have no others to help them. They build from their own beginnings, take pride in what they accomplish, and are reluctant to accept changes in what they decided was right in the first place. As a consequence Centralia, like all other towns in Washington in the first quarter of this century, developed as hard-rock conservative. What was orthodox and customary was respected. Anything otherwise was viewed with suspicion, especially in political affairs.

The Republican Party, stronghold of conservatives, controlled all state and most county and local offices, year after year, with a few exceptions, as in the recession year of 1896 when a fusion of Democrats, Populists, and Silver Republicans swept the state, and again in 1912 and 1916 when the Democrats won the governor's office. During this whole period there was only one dissident movement of significant size and, while not actually political, it was as offensive to the conventionally minded as a gathering of athiests in a churchyard. It would cause Centralia to become unwillingly the object of world attention. It was, of course, the Industrial Workers of the World.

The IWW moved into Centralia after it became a sizable lumber and logging town as well as a railroad center. When the mills were built logging trains shuttled daily between the woods and the ponds where logs were sorted and stored for sawmills. The mills often kept their head rigs rattling back and forth on double shifts to produce "green" lumber that was stacked in the yards to be air-dried, a slow process in the drizzle season, which was long. Some companies could afford drying kilns, heated by steam from boilers fired with an ever-abundant supply of bark, slabs, and sawdust, good for nothing but burning in a time when there were no pulp mills.

Men who didn't work with wood had jobs calling for more skills in the railroad shops, on the trains, and in the stores along Tower Avenue that made Centralia the shopping center of Lewis County.

Mill operators knew some of their employees belonged to unions but they felt no obligation to accord union recognition, and none was given. Union strength in Centralia lay with the small, conservative craft unions, each with its rigid set of apprentice rules to prevent worker oversupply, and jealously guarded limits of jurisdiction. Such unions viewed with disdain the contention of the Wobblies that all workers should belong to one big union. Radicals were no more welcome in the central labor temple than in the Chamber of Commerce or the Elks lodge. Samuel Gompers was the revered leader of labor, not "Big Bill" Haywood, the leader of the IWW.

The Wobblies, with few friends and no allies in organized labor, went their own way, publishing their own newspaper and establishing their own places to meet — halls, they were called, none pretentious enough to deserve so dignified a name as "temple."

In Centralia and other mill towns owners and managers enjoyed prominent places in local affairs, providing, as they did, the paychecks for half or more of the local workers. They were, of course, staunchly Republican, and were strongly resistant to changes threatening to industrial profitability, and especially the kinds of changes advocated by the IWW. Their views were listened to and usually heeded, even at election time, although once there was an exception.

Mrs. Archie Black, widow of a Saltzer Valley saw-mill worker, came to the Northwest from the South, where Republicans were as scarce as Democrats were in the West. She was struggling to support her five children by sewing and taking in washing when, in 1915, in order to fill out an election ticket, the handful of other Democrats in the county persuaded her to file for county clerk. The unprecedented happened. The poor widow — the Democrat — won.

The Blacks were close friends of the pioneer Samuel Edwin Grimm family, which included five children, Warren, Huber, Francis, Mary, and William. Mary Grimm served as Mrs. Black's chief deputy after her election, and later succeeded her in office.

Warren Ort Grimm, destined to be at the fatal storm center of the 1919 Centralia explosion when he was only thirty-two, had a short but unusually eventful life. He was four when his family moved from the East to the village of Centralia in 1891. He developed into a tall, heavy youth, strong and athletic. His face was handsome, his forehead high, and there was a set to his jaw that gave him a look of determination. Football was his favorite sport, played in high school and at the University of Washington where he enrolled in 1908. In the hazing practices of that time, the freshmen and sophomore men were allowed to engage in a free-for-all skirmish, the winner being the one that subdued and tied up the largest number from the other side. Grimm, because of his size, was chosen captain of the freshman group. He surprised the opponents by grouping his team of fifty in the form of a wedge that scattered the sophomores so effectively that his nick-name thereafter was "Wedge." "Wedge" Grimm was awarded the Flaherty medal in 1912, indicating his selection as the most inspirational player on the foot-ball team. He was elected to several honor societies, including Phi Delta Phi, the national law honorary fraternity. In the summers he was able to get employ-ment in the Lewis County Courthouse in Chehalis.

After graduation Grimm returned to his home-town where he was appointed deputy prosecuting attorney. Later he entered a law partnership with his older brother, Huber.

Another young law school graduate, Elmer Stuart Smith, settled in Lewis County at about the same time Warren Grimm started his career. His father, James Smith, living in Minnesota, was aware that some of the free land that lured settlers to the Northwest after the

University Archives, University of Washington Libraries

Warren Grimm played football under the legendary coach Gil Dobie whose teams at the University of Washington never lost a game.

C. D. Cunningham, as he looked when serving as prosecutor.

lawyer. He attended the St. Paul College of Law, an outpost of legal learning that was able to recruit a faculty only by inducing practicing attorneys to teach classes, which were all held in the evenings. In 1913 Elmer, after graduation, qualified automatically, as did all Minnesota law school graduates of that time, for admission to the bar.

Minnesota was not dominated by the conservatism that prevailed in newer states on the Pacific coast, and Macalester College, most of whose graduates went into the ministry, could expose its students to liberal leanings strong enough to bring about the selection of a black educator, Booker T. Washington, president of Tuskegee Institute, to be the commencement speaker the year Smith graduated. "Red" Smith, as he was called, and his classmates, who included DeWitt Wallace, the founder of *Reader's Digest,* heard the venerable Washington admonish them "to go out from this institution (and) carry with you a resolve in your heart ... of giving to all men whatever their race or color, the highest and truest freedom because without the freedom of the lower individual in the community there cannot exist the highest degree of happiness in any part of the nation."[1]

The Macalester students, required to take Bible courses and to attend chapel daily, were well conditioned for a final lecture on brotherhood from one who had suffered the injustices of racial intolerance.

James Smith was easily persuaded to heed his father's call to join him and his mother in a homesteading venture in Washington, and Elmer finally agreed also. The claims were filed and legal residences established by constructing cabins on land near Hanaford, east of Centralia. When word of this reached Centralia, the lumber establishment was upset. The lumbermen knew the government land was out there, within an hour's log train trip from their mills, and it was valuable. Now here were complete strangers, out from Minnesota, claiming it right under their noses. And besides the timber on the land there was coal.

Still another law school graduate who found Lewis County a place of opportunity was Clifford Dorwin Cunningham, who graduated from Washburn College in Topeka, Kansas, and then earned a law degree at the University of Washington in 1909. A college friend who worked on a newspaper in Centralia convinced him that it would be a good place to begin a law practice. Cunningham, a tall, handsome man,

British flag was finally hauled down in 1846 was still available as late as 1914. The elder Smith went to King County to pursue an occupation he had long followed, coal mining. He studied maps and found some heavily timbered public land near coalfields fifteen miles east of Centralia. An individual could file a claim for 160 acres on such land and become the owner after living on the premises and developing the property for two years. Smith couldn't do this himself because he had already availed himself of that privilege in the Midwest. But he had two sons, Elmer and James, who could qualify for a latter-day adventure in pioneering.

Elmer, a tall, athletic redhead, was not entirely pleased with the opportunity his father offered. He was the only one of the six children in the Smith family who went to college. He was graduated in 1910 from Macalester College, a small Presbyterian institution in St. Paul, and after a year of teaching decided to become a found residence where single males usually did — in a boardinghouse — and there he met a schoolteacher, Mame Joack. They married. Their children — one of whom became a nationally famous dancer and choreographer, Mercier Cunningham — attended the Catholic school and suffered the taunts and occasional stone throwings of their public school peers, who were advancing religious prejudice into still another generation. The mother was the Catholic in this marriage partnership, not Cunningham. He was a Republican, of course, and took an opportunity to make a name for himself as a lawyer by running for county prosecutor. He was able to get the support of those most concerned with local politics, the mill operators, and won. He succeeded a second time, then relinquished the position to begin a private law practice, including among his clients the largest industry of the area, Francis Hubbard's Eastern Railway and Lumber Company.

Hubbard was like other first-generation timber entrepreneurs of the Northwest such as Henry Hewitt, Jr., and Chauncey Griggs of Tacoma, David Clough of Everett, and Alex Polson, Charles Clemons and the Schafer brothers of Grays Harbor. He came west and was awed by the thick, towering stands of timber he found. The urge to cut, produce lumber, and make money was irresistible.

Hubbard was born in 1847 and grew up to become fascinated with wires being strung on poles from one town to the next. The whole country would soon be linked by telegraph, he concluded, and so he became a telegraph operator, first with the Michigan Central Railroad and then Western Union and the Northern Pacific Railroad. By 1900, when he was fifty-three, Hubbard was well acquainted with leaders in the telegraph field and knew that they bought vast quantities of wooden cross arms. Every pole had to have at least one cross arm. Some had a dozen. So he built the mill in Centralia, after acquiring a sizable tract of timber, and began producing cross arms and shipping them east. D. F. Davis was vice-president of his company and George Dysart, the pioneer lawyer of the valley, was the corporate secretary.

Hubbard enjoyed being classified in the puff books of that time as a "captain of industry." His mill was the largest in the county. It could cut 150,000 board feet a day. He paid $25,000 a month in wages to 225 employees, an average of $111 apiece or 42 cents an hour for a 6-day, 60-hour week.

Elmer Smith, about the time he began to practice law in Centralia.

Courtesy of D.A. Waddell

"Mr. Hubbard has never regarded his workmen as part of a great machine," his complimentary biographer wrote, "but as individuals with human interests, ambitions, needs and possibilities. It is said that he regards his men with almost a paternalistic solicitude and recognizes no class distinction. He has himself worked his way up from the ranks and his success should be an inspiration and source of encouragement to others." [2] Hubbard built the largest house in town, at 717 North Washington Avenue, and had not only one of the town's first automobiles but also quarters for a chauffeur over the garage.

H. H. Martin & Sons were lumber-mill operators in Centralia also, with a logging railroad extending ten miles into the timbered hills. One of the sons, Frank Martin, married F. W. Hubbard's one adopted daughter, Mellie, in 1906, and the union of the two families so pleased her father that he built the couple a handsome house as a wedding gift.

Hubbard and Martin, operating the two largest industries and related by marriage, were dominant figures in the affairs of Centralia. They were among the founders and early leaders of the regional employer and lumber associations organized, among other reasons, to ward off unionism, a menace that persisted and grew from the turn of the century to a climactic point of change during World War I, when one IWW goal, shared by every woods and mill worker — the eight-hour day — came to a point of decision.

Earnest Dale Hubbard, who was to fall to gunfire by the Skookumchuck on November 11, 1919, was a nephew of F. W. Hubbard. He also was a large, well-proportioned youth who played football in high school and at the university. Described as a quiet type of person, he left college to enlist in the army three months after war was declared and served with the Tenth Army Engineers doing construction work in France until his discharge in January 1919. On October 15, 1919, a month before his death, he was married to Jean Rogers of Montevideo, Minnesota, in San Diego.

Warren Grimm, Elmer Smith, Dale Hubbard, and the other young men of Centralia, especially those in the National Guard, followed carefully the news of the European war that began in Europe in 1914. An entire continent and an ocean lay between the quiet valley of the Chehalis and the Marne, the Rhine, the Dardanelles, and other strange places where battles were fought for causes not easily understood. But understood or not, the war was a reality and daily news accounts of it plainly identified the adversaries. It was the Germans — the Kaiser, the Huns — against Great Britain, the mother country; France, whence came Lafayette in time of need; and Belgium, where towns were burned and babies killed, or so the newspapers reported. The brutality of the Kaiser's army and navy was accepted as truth in Lewis County, so surprise was not great when the U-boats began sinking American ships, and President Wilson, abandoning his stance of neutrality, on April 6, 1917, asked Congress to take the nation into the conflict.

The men of Company M were already on duty by then. Seasoned from service on the Mexican border and disciplined in Everett, where they had been sent to protect the city from the IWW menace in 1916, the Lewis County soldiers were among the first guard units called up by President Wilson on March 26 to protect industries from domestic disorders "in the event of open hostilities with Germany."

When the call to duty came, Captain Livingstone was instructed to increase his company's strength to 150, an assignment that proved impossible, despite the war fever which brought most of Centralia to a hastily organized patriotic rally in the city park the night the mobilization order was received. The Reverend H. W. Thompson, the Civil War veteran always ready with a flow of patriotic oratory, made a speech, after which the crowd, estimated at five thousand, trooped up Tower Avenue on the usual line of parade march to First Street, then countermarched and returned to the park.

By March 31 only nineteen more men had volunteered to join the company, bringing the total to just over one hundred. Then, with the Elks band leading the way, the soldiers marched from the armory to the depot where, amid cheers and much embracing by relatives, they boarded a train for an encampment at Camp Lewis on American Lake near Tacoma. Two days earlier at a "mass meeting" of women, a Centralia Red Cross society had been organized.

Either because the men of Company M understood the situation in Everett or by coincidence, Company M's first assignment was to go back there and do industrial guard duty. Lt. Frank Van Gilder, home on furlough a few weeks later, reported that the men of Company M were encountering "much insolence" from the Wobblies in Everett. "Several threats," the Centralia Chronicle quoted Van Gilder as saying, "had been made to the effect that the IWWs would later on keep the guards busy. One who refused to halt at the mouth of a railroad tunnel when commanded to do so was knocked senseless by a Company M guard who used the butt of his rifle."

By this time the Wobblies' reputation for engaging in industrial sabotage was well known, however much or little deserved. Wobblies denied vigorously all accusations that they were responsible for spikes in logs that sprayed teeth of whirling band-saw blades like bullets, or emery dust found in machine bearings, or copper nails driven into fruit trees to make orchards die. But in the same IWW publications that protested the accusations there frequently were articles praising sabotage and urging the use of it. Accusers could always point to a resolution passed without debate at the ninth convention of the IWW in 1914 which called

The IWW hall on the southeast corner of First and B streets in Centralia after it was raided and wrecked during the April 15, 1918, Red Cross parade. Some of the broken windows have been boarded up.

for "all speakers to be instructed to recommend to the workers the necessity of curtailing production by a means of 'slowing down' and sabotage. All rush work should be done in a wrong manner."

Louis Adamic, a laborer before he was an author, encountered Wobblies who told him about sabotage and why it was used: "Sabotage and 'striking on the job' are forms of revenge that the working class of America — blindly, unconsciously, desperately — exacts for the employers' relentless, brutal opposition to its strivings in the past. . . ."[3]

The indifference of the IWW toward what it termed "the capitalistic war" in Europe soon generated widespread belief that the Wobblies, since they did not want to help win the war, must be sympathetic to Germany. Evidence to support such a belief has not been found. When the war began in 1914 the IWW declared that "we, as members of the Industrial army, will refuse to fight for any purpose except the realization of industrial freedom." The IWW did not take the side of the enemy. Its stance was essentially one of neutrality and was based on an unwillingness to post-

pone its ideological struggle while the nation put aside all else to fight a war.

Reports of sabotage, strikes impeding war production, and the defiant militancy of the IWW press all combined to blacken the image of the organization, which proceeded as if it had no concern at all for public opinion. It persisted in the delusion that its cause was so just — so right — that in time it would prevail and the public would understand.

So black had its image become by 1918 that Zane Grey, the West's preeminent novelist, chose the IWW as the villain for his story of struggle in the Eastern Washington farm belt — *Desert of Wheat.* In this book patriotic wheat ranchers, alarmed at the wartime conduct of the Wobblies, seized a Wobbly leader and hanged him from a railroad trestle. The body was left there, swinging and twisting, for several days. It was a righteous and necessary act, the way Grey related it, and was accepted as such, when the novel was published in January 1919, by the growing corps of loyal Zane Grey readers — including those in Centralia, where the fictional account of vigilante violence turned out to be prophetic, if not suggestive.

Anti-Wobbly sentiment was whipped up by newspapers of the nation. Northwest newspapers in particular were critical of anyone or anything that suggested a lack of patriotism. The papers in Centralia frequently roared angry denunciations of the IWW from their editorial pages.

The Wobblies came to be called "Emperor Wilhelm's Warriors." "The outrageous eruption of the IWW in the far West," thundered the *Chicago Tribune*, ". . . is nothing less than rebellion." As the storm of denunciation and opposition grew more intense, the IWW became ever more plainly identified as an enemy — one to be feared and fought.

5

Suzzallo, Parker, Disque, and the Eight-hour Day

The war on Wobblies might be said to have opened with a speech made in 1912 by Everett C. Griggs, president of the National Lumber Manufacturers Association, and a founder of the St. Paul and Tacoma Lumber Company.

"The anarchistic doctrines (of the IWW) now running riot are against law and order and stand for revolution," he declared. "Given free rein, their leaders openly advocate a Labor Trust, and preach sedition, disrespect to the flag and the abolishment of the wage system. . . Our forefathers sacrificed too much blood in establishing the great American republic to allow sedition, riot and revolution to be preached throughout the land. Must it ever take some frightful holocaust, some explosion like the (Los Angeles) *Times,* some Titanic disaster to turn the American people from paths that lead but to loss of life and principles?"[1]

The kind of employer opposition resulting from such warnings was staunch enough to withstand every weapon used by the determined Wobbly assailants. Slowdowns, sabotage, and strikes, intermingled with public demonstrations and general hell-raising, far from wearing down the bosses, made them more furious and unyielding. Then in 1917 the war broke out. It provided the IWW with unexpected new leverage. Lumber was much needed by the military. The lumber operators, the Wobblies thought, wouldn't dare let the war effort be impeded. They would have to yield to the union's demands in order to keep the mills working.

Their demands were clearly stated a month before the United States entered the European war. Large IWW posters, listing nine demands, were posted in public places as well as at mills and logging camps.

These were:

1. An eight-hour day and no Sunday or holiday work.
2. A minimum wage of $60 per month with free board.
3. Wholesome food served on porcelain dishes with no overcrowding at dining tables. Cook houses to be supplied with sufficient help to keep them sanitary.
4. Sanitary sleeping quarters with not more than 12 men in each bunkhouse. Single spring beds and bedding furnished without charge. Houses to be well lighted and furnished with reading tables. Laundry room with shower baths to be installed.
5. Free hospital services.
6. Five dollars per day minimum for river drivers.
7. Two pay days a month with pay by bank check.
8. All hiring to be done on the job or from the union hall, with transportation furnished to the job.
9. No discrimination against members of the IWW.

Most of these aspirations were those of the AFL as well as the IWW and the strikes that followed involved both unions. But when there was labor trouble, it was easy for the public to believe that Wobblies were the real cause of it.

Demands such as these could not be discussed at a bargaining table. There was no such thing. Unions were not recognized by employers. There was no bargaining with something that was not even accorded the right to exist. But the menace of the unions was real enough, and the employers organized to meet it. The Lumbermen's Protective Association was formed in Seattle on July 9, 1917. The members agreed to raise a strike fund of $500,000 and to impose a fine of $500 a day on any member who dared yield anything on the

THE WHITE HOUSE
WASHINGTON

10 January, 1917

My dear Gregory:

I would be very much obliged if
you would look over the enclosed papers.
If true, they state a very grave situation
and it is thoroughly worth our while to
consider what, if anything, should and can
be done about the influences proceeding from
Seattle. Perhaps you will be kind enough to
speak to me about the matter when we see each
other again.

Cordially and faithfully yours,

Woodrow Wilson

encs.

Hon. T. W. Gregory,
The Attorney General.

Attorney General papers, National Archives

*Letter from President Wilson to the attorney general asking
for information about labor troubles in Seattle in early 1917.*

chief issue — the eight-hour day. Every work shift was to be ten hours, as usual. The operators contended, with some logic, that they could not compete successfully with sawmills in the Southern states, all on the ten-hour day, if they submitted to the eight-hour demand. Furthermore, the maximum production required by wartime demands couldn't be achieved on a shortened shift schedule.

The wartime strike spread through the industry. By midsummer an estimated ten thousand men were out. The IWW printed stickers, known as "silent agitators," and pasted them by the thousands on walls, trees, and fences. One read, "The hours are long and the pay is small. Take your time and buck them all." Another urged, "Slow up, Bill, and live longer. When you speed up, the job will end quicker."

Employers countered with half-page newspaper ads headed, "A friendly statement from the Lumber industry to its employees and the people of the Pacific Northwest." These ads appealed for increased production to help the war effort.

The mill owners could not contend that the strikes were actually impeding the war effort yet, since most of them had excessive inventories of lumber on hand at the start of the war — more than enough to fill military orders. But "to a certain extent," the ad went on to say cautiously, needed production was prevented "by a strike seemingly controlled by an organization which preaches sedition, the slowing down of industry and disorganization." Then came an appeal for the men to go back to work on a ten-hour day until government contracts were filled and then "let the men on the job decide for themselves whether they will work eight or ten hours."

The Wobblies didn't wait to decide. They adopted a new tactic. They would go back to work but at the end of eight hours walk off the job. Whole crews would be fired promptly for doing this and a new crew hired. Then the process would be repeated, infuriating and frustrating mill and logging camp bosses. A few gave in. One of the first was the Snow Lumber and Shingle Company at Littell, near Chehalis.

The assistant attorney general assigned to the Seattle office at this time was Clarence Reames, a lawyer who developed an intense animosity toward the IWW and reported to Washington, D.C., on what he perceived to be the union's evil behavior in the Northwest so often and in such vitriolic language that his

The wooden shoes on the worker have significance. The French word sabotage, preached by the Wobblies, is supposed to have originated when French workers threw their wooden shoes (sabots) into factory machinery.

IWW messages were printed on posters and stickers that were posted where workers were likely to see them.

A scissorbill, in Wobbly parlance, was one who wouldn't join the union and instead preferred to keep on the good side of an employer.

superiors finally told him to calm down.

Reames was not the only one the administration heard from. The strikes and the IWW's lack of patriotism brought from aroused citizens a stream of letters and telegrams demanding federal action. Other states passed antisyndicalism laws, enabling local law enforcement officers to arrest radicals just for being radicals.[2] The Washington legislature passed such a law early in 1917 but it was vetoed by Gov. Ernest Lister. According to one source, he did so because of intimidation. Anonymous "black hand" letters warned him that the executive mansion would be blown up if he signed the bill. Alarmed, he hired bodyguards and moved his family out of the governor's mansion, adjacent to the capitol, to an apartment.[3]

Governor Lister was sympathetic toward some of the demands of the strikers, including the eight-hour day, but his feelings about the IWW itself were no less hostile than those of Clough, Griggs, Hartley, Hubbard, and other employers.

In the early months of the wartime strikes, Governor Lister instigated a statewide organization of vigilantes called the Patriotic League. He approved the eager actions of these patriots and sheriffs who, with citizen-deputy helpers, began rounding up radicals in such numbers that stockades to hold them had to be built in several cities, among them Yakima, Ellensburg, Pasco, Cle Elum, and Wenatchee. Governors from adjoining states met with Lister to compare strategies for suppressing the troublemakers, who remained defiant, even when locked up. In Spokane James Rowan, one of the IWW's most active orators, published an ultimatum, demanding release of all class-war prisoners and calling for a general strike to force such action. The city, thoroughly alarmed, declared martial law, raided and closed the local IWW hall, and accelerated the rounding up of Wobblies.

In other Western cities the aroused citizenry, like their fathers in frontier days, concluded that undesirables could not be dealt with effectively under the law and intervened. In Jerome, Arizona, hundreds of miners and other citizens, armed with pick handles and rifles, started out at sunrise on a July day to rid the town of the IWW mine-worker agitators who the day before had called a strike. Warned of what might happen, most of the strikers fled during the night. Sixty who remained were seized and forced into the boxcars of a departing freight train.

Two days later equally enraged citizens in Bisbee, Arizona, as the press put it, "took the law into their own hands." Business in the town was suspended while the Citizens Protective League, numbering some fifteen hundred members, grabbed all known or suspected Wobblies and corralled them in the fenced baseball park where they were searched for weapons and incriminating red membership cards. Later they were loaded on railroad cattle cars and deported without food or water into the Arizona desert.

The Bisbee deportation was so brutal it attracted national attention. Newspapers commented that such wholesale sending of Wobblies into the countryside or out of cities and into smaller communities was really not the proper way to handle the problem. But they could not suggest better ways. How to deal effectively with the IWWs, editorial writers admitted, was one of the paramount issues of the day.

President Wilson was sufficiently disturbed by reports from the strike scenes of the West to appoint a Mediation Commission to investigate, find the causes of the trouble, and, if possible, clear them up. W. B. Wilson, secretary of labor, was named chairman and Felix Frankfurter, a young lawyer, secretary.

After making a study of the copper-mine troubles in Arizona, the commission went to Seattle and began immediate hearings, day and night. Although most of the witnesses were employers, the commission also heard from Seattle AFL labor council spokesmen — but no Wobblies. The IWW was too loosely put together to have spokesmen or elected officers. The commission would not have known whom to call if it had wanted to dignify the radicals by giving them a chance to be heard. The real voices of the IWW were its writers, the ones who produced voluminous literature and periodicals, such as the *Industrial Worker* in Seattle, and it was by their writings, consistently inflammatory and contemptuous of established ways in industry and society generally, that the IWW was judged. The commission knew that such judgments were uniformly negative. The Wobblies were pariahs.

The Wilson Commission soon concluded that the eight-hour day was the chief issue and set out to convince the operators that, if they would give in on that, they would undermine IWW propaganda, the men would stop walking off the job, and the needed war work would get done.

The commission's report was written by the sec-

The Wobblies were adept at propagandizing. This poster appealed for the support of those who deplored child labor.

retary, Felix Frankfurter. The workers' grievances were real, he wrote. "The uncompromising attitude on the part of the employers has reaped for them an organization of destructive rather than constructive radicalism. The IWW is filling the vacuum created by the operators. . . . The hold of the IWW is riveted instead of weakened by the unimaginative opposition on the part of employers to the correction of real grievances. . . . The greatest difficulty in the industry is the tenacity of the habits of individualism."[4]

The report focused on the chief obstacle — opposition to the eight-hour day — reminding the timbermen that theirs was almost the only industry on the coast still clinging to the long work day. "In truth," Frankfurter wrote, "we cannot escape the conviction that with too many employers opposition (to unions) has become a matter of pride instead of judgment, a reluctance to yield after having defeated the strike."[5] Frankfurter, the liberal lawyer of 1918, became the liberal Supreme Court Justice twenty-one years later.

The war created an urgent need for a particular specie of wood — Sitka spruce, straight grained, light and strong enough to be used for the frames and struts of the new fighter planes. Another need was for ship timbers. Keels for ships built of Douglas fir were laid in large numbers when war caught the nation short of vessels and German subs began taking a serious toll.

Disorganized and disrupted, the private operators could not be counted on to fill the needs. Furthermore, spruce grew mostly in remote areas of the coastal range where no logging railroads existed. The army sent Col. Bryce P. Disque to get something done.

In Seattle, Colonel Disque was briefed by Dr. Henry Suzzallo, president of the University of Washington, and Dr. Carleton Parker, head of the Graduate School of Business. Some young university faculty members, working under Parker's direction, had undertaken to find out for themselves about working conditions in the woods. They verified the loggers' complaints. Parker studied the IWW on the West Coast and gained attention as one of the leading writers about progressive and liberal causes of the time.

Disque made a rapid tour of logging camps and mills, met industry leaders, and let it be known he had come to the Northwest to take action. He induced George W. Long, manager of the Weyerhaeuser Timber Company, to call a meeting of the seven largest companies on October 25 in Portland to discuss ways of increasing spruce production. Parker and Suzzallo were invited.

Disque proved to be a persuasive speaker as well as a strategist. He planted sympathetic individuals in the audience to ask questions that he and Parker had worked out together.

As a result of this meeting the major lumber operators, who together employed some twelve thousand workers, agreed to join in forming an organization whose members would swear loyalty to the United States and try to increase the output of lumber for the military. That organization was to be called the Loyal Legion. This was not Disque's idea. It was Parker's.

Disque then went east and conferred at length with Samuel Gompers, president of the AFL and a solid ally of the Wilson administration, whose approval was needed if the army was going to work with labor in the Northwest. He did not talk to Gompers about the Loyal Legion idea, fearing it might sound like a rival to the AFL. Instead he outlined plans for a new army unit, to be called the Spruce Production Division, which would not engage in any kind of economic activity, including advocacy of the eight-hour day. For when that great battle was won, Disque knew from his talks with Parker, the AFL would want the credit. The Loyal Legion, if ever it were formed, would be strictly a civilian organization, Disque concluded, and he did not want to be involved in it. His job was to get the lumber out, not to achieve the worker objectives Parker had lectured to him about.

Gompers finally agreed to a plan calling for the use of army troops as loggers and lumber workers provided they received regular civilian wages, less their army pay. The Spruce Division was then approved and Disque given command of it.

While he was gone, the lumbermen in the Northwest grew more enthusiastic about the Loyal Legion idea. They met in Centralia on November 10 and, after listening to Suzzallo and Parker, voted to sponsor Loyal Legion units in all their operations, expecting Disque and the army to be pleased with their show of patriotism. They resolved "to keep an active organization of all logging interests" alive and to ask Disque to "meet with all the loggers at his earliest convenience to go over the labor situation thoroughly." The operators were sure that with the army on their side, and their workers sworn to produce as a matter of patriotic necessity, the IWW would at last be put down.

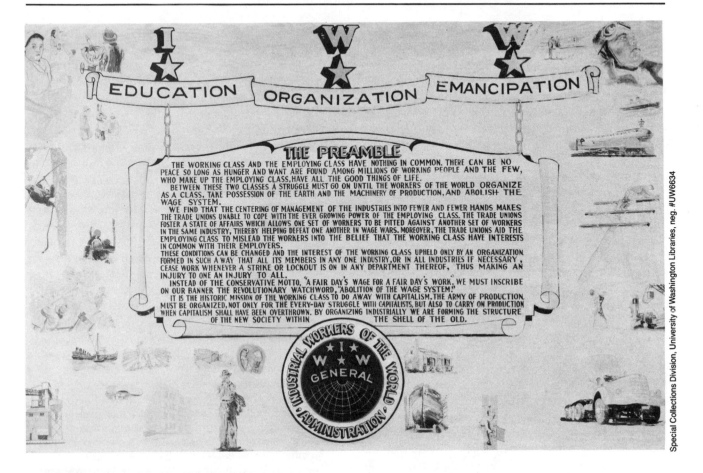

Special Collections Division, University of Washington Libraries, neg. #UW6634

On this banner is the famous IWW "Preamble" often used as proof of the basic radicalism of the organization.

Back in Portland, Disque issued a confidential circular explaining the Spruce Production Division and asking that all instances of labor shortages and sabotage be reported directly to him. He said nothing about the legion.

But Parker had been busy while Disque was in the East. Seeing in the legion a chance to improve the working conditions he knew were at the heart of the labor troubles, he collaborated on a set of instructions for the legion units and procedures for organizing what became the Loyal Legion of Loggers and Lumbermen — the famed 4-L.

Disque had trouble getting troops assigned to his Spruce Division. It was something new. The generals were too busy with the American Expeditionary Force to be much concerned with the lumber supply in the Northwest. So to get action Disque warned again about the IWW menace. He didn't say they were being pro-German when they refused to work a full shift or to work at all. But he implied it. They had an urge, as he

put it, "to destroy industry for the sake of destruction." It was a commonly held belief and it attracted sufficient attention in the War Department to get the troops Disque needed to begin his strange wartime enterprise, logging and lumbering with soldiers.

It was the relentless pursuit of the eight-hour day — the Holy Grail of labor's crusades — that concerned the Wobblies most in 1917, not the ultimate fate of industry. They used their wartime leverage relentlessly, realizing that the legion would concentrate on spruce production while chaos still prevailed in the fir operations. A scattered few employers gave in, but the major operators — the members of the Lumbermen's Protective Association — were sworn not only never to yield but to penalize any members who weakened and worked men less than ten hours a day.

But the pressure for more production persisted

and another meeting was called for February 27, 1918, in Portland. There the operators, still adamantly opposed to the shorter day, agreed to a compromise. They would let Colonel Disque make the decision. After all, he represented the army and ought to be able to decide what was best for the war effort. If there had to be an eight-hour day, let it be the army's decision. Disque decided quickly. It was better to have everyone working on an eight-hour basis than to have constant interruptions on a ten-hour schedule.

Given authority on the hours issue, Disque decided to go further. He issued a whole set of labor regulations for the industry. They included, besides the eight-hour day, time and a half for overtime, a charge of no more than $7.35 a week for board in logging camps, and a charge of $1.00 a week for bedding with a weekly change of sheets and pillow slips, all to be furnished "at the earliest practicable date." Some operators were slow to comply but, sooner or later, most did.

The Disque edict was a memorable turning point in Northwest labor relations. The ten-hour-day barrier at last was broken. In later times there were arguments about who should get credit for achieving this great objective. The eight-hour day was granted, some contended, only to get the men to stop striking and get back to work, in which case the strikers were responsible. They raised the issue. The issue was resolved in their favor. But it would not have been so resolved, at least then, had it not been for Disque. He won the confidence of the employers despite their suspicions about Parker, Suzzallo, and others who kept telling him there would be no lasting peace in the woods and the mills unless the old grievances were resolved. Those

two academicians therefore could be rightly identified as the eight-hour-day achievers.

Suzzallo, though prolabor, was not pro-Wobbly and hoped the Loyal Legion would give itinerant workers the organization and camaraderie they wanted without the radical philosophy. He hoped patriotic fervor would replace revolutionary leanings. Suzzallo's part in the eight-hour-day affair was not forgotten by Roland Hartley, one of the lumber operators in Everett, when he became governor and set out to have Suzzallo ousted as president of the university.

The Department of Justice office in Seattle had been in the forefront of the anti-IWW crusade and had voluminous files on what the radicals did or were suspected of doing. Suzzallo arranged for the Loyal Legion officers to have access to these files so they could learn what they were up against. What they were confronted with, they found, was something that had as firm a hold on the minds of many men as a religion or a cult. Their newspaper, *The Industrial Worker,* expressed it on May Day, in that first year of the war:

> The songs we sing are not the songs of race or creed. They sound the might of a class. We are confined to no country, no flag. Our songs herald your overthrow. This is our day. We are the forgers of revolution — the destroyers of the old and the outgrown. We are the nemesis of idlers — the doom of masters — the emancipators of slaves. We are revolt. We are progress. We are revolution.

Wobblies might join the Loyal Legion to get and keep a job, and many did, but that did not mean they stopped being Wobblies.

6

Wobbly War in Wartime

Centralia's Company M became bored with guard duty in Everett. There was no trouble. Whether because of previous difficulties there or otherwise, the Wobblies concentrated their activities elsewhere. The guardsmen were glad to be ordered back to Camp Lewis on American Lake, this time to prepare for service overseas.

The day before they left Everett they read news reports from Butte, Montana, where six masked men, acting just before dawn, had seized Frank Little, one of the most outspoken and defiant IWW leaders in the Rocky Mountain area. He was taken from his hotel room at night, tied with a rope to the back of a car, and dragged over rutted streets for several blocks to a railroad trestle, where his battered body was trussed up and hanged. It was a bad thing, many said, but understandable.

William Scales saw that the company he helped organize would soon be going overseas and decided he was not going to be left behind, even though at the age of forty-four he was considered too old to serve as an officer. He resigned his reserve commission, closed his store in Centralia, and, when the train carrying Company M pulled out of Camp Murray headed east, he climbed aboard, took an oath as a private en route, and made it to France with a supply company. The members of Company M did not stay together in France but were scattered among other units.

When Washington men put on their uniforms and went off to war, feelings intensified against those who would not so much as wave a flag at home. Just to be a member of the IWW was not yet illegal in Washington and Oregon, but the Department of Justice sent instructions for the U.S. District Attorneys on the West Coast to begin charging Wobblies with treason and sedition under a wartime espionage act. The department announced that it was "prepared to deal swiftly and severely with IWW activities in the Northwest where they relate to the stoppage or curtailment of production in industries whose continuation is essential to the war."[1]

Antisyndicalism bills were introduced in the legislatures of Washington and Oregon, inspiring the *Industrial Worker* to offer its version of a definition:

> The word syndicalism is derived from the French word "syndicat" and means something terrible: It means a union. . . . There are those who think that all that is necessary when slavery leads to discontent is to pass a law making discontent a crime. Most of the tyrants of history thought the same until they were engulfed in the wrath of those they had betrayed. If there is anything clearly written in the history of human progress, from revolution to revolution, it is that laws made to crush discontent have been the augury of gigantic social upheavals which have dealt in no gentle manner with lawmakers and legislators.[2]

The eagerness of citizens to move on their own to suppress radicalism during the war years was not confined to cities. Local patriots in the town of Winlock, eighteen miles south of Centralia, discovered two organizers for Labor's Non-Partisan League in their midst. A. Knutson, the state manager for the league, and R. W. Edwards took lodging in a local hotel.

Several apprehensive citizens stationed themselves with ears to the thin wall in an adjacent room where conversations on the other side could be plainly heard. What was heard, according to an extensive account in the *Chehalis Bee-Nugget*,[3] was sufficiently alarming to call for action. The worst of what had been rumored about the Non-Partisan League was confirmed. The members were radicals. Back in North Dakota the league had been able to elect enough members to the legislature to pass laws authorizing

Special Collections Division, University of Washington Libraries, neg. #UW6633

such unheard-of ventures into the unknown as the use of public funds to make farm loans. The league's platform called for government seizure and operation of all factories having labor disputes that did not yield to mediation, bond issues to raise funds for public projects, and a system of state-owned grain mills, elevators, packing houses, and cold-storage plants. It also favored state-controlled world credit banks, short-term government loans to farmers secured by crops, and other strange social experiments.

The *Oregonian* of Portland, commenting on the Non-Partisan League, pronounced the ultimate condemnation: The league was on a par with the IWW.

The hotel eavesdroppers, who summarized what they heard in a signed affadavit, were R. W. Rees, W. W. Webb, Lacey P. Arnold, and Charlotte Arnold. They swore they had heard the two visitors criticize democracy and approve oligarchial rules with control in the hands of a few (like big business). The reporters of this heresy issued a judgment:

A typical wartime Sunday afternoon rally to raise funds for IWW members imprisoned under the syndicalism law or other laws passed to suppress radicals. The banner announces, "Liberty bonds, war savings stamps and cash from $5 and up accepted here as loan for bail of Class War Prisoners." Eventually enough funds were raised to bring about the release of IWW national leaders while their case was appealed. They lost the appeal and went back to prison.

"These men, aside from being disloyalists, are rascals — just mercenary rascals. They are organizing a system of Bolsheviki under the guise of a farmers' league. What their ultimate object is can be spelled in the word 'revolution.' Is this not pro-German propaganda, the same as disrupted Russia and relieved the Hun hordes that they might attack in force on the western front?"[4]

Knutson had done most of the talking, so when the irate Winlock citizens banged on the hotel room door and revealed that their plotting had been discovered, he was selected to receive a coat of hot tar decorated with wads of cotton, an unaccountable adornment inasmuch as Winlock proclaimed itself the egg capital of Lewis County and feathers were plentiful.

Edwards, who was escorted out of town with his blackened companion, was not molested after he promised to abandon any remaining enthusiasm he might have for Labor's Non-Partisan League. Toledo, ten miles away to the east, where the pair went to recover from their painful eviction from Winlock, did not regard Edwards' intransigence so lightly. Several days later eight auto loads of Toledo citizens took him into the countryside, smeared him with tar, showered him with feathers, and elicited a promise that he would return to his home in California.

Edwards, however, was not completely intimidated by his reception in southern Lewis County. The next month, while engaged in organizing efforts north of Centralia, he and H. S. Stoddard were arrested and placed in protective custody in the Lewis County jail when Sheriff John Berry heard that they were being threatened by farmers who had read about them in the *Bee-Nugget.* The pair were held long enough to become convinced that this time, when they were told to move on, they should.

The prosecutor, Herman Allen, while not the least tolerant of radicals, as subsequent events proved, was disturbed enough by vigilante violence in his county to issue a strong statement:

"I wish to state that mob violence will not be tolerated under any circumstances.... If such things as have been enacted at Winlock and Toledo are not stopped at once, it will result in the death of someone and this office will get the blame.... I will state here and now that mob violence in this county, as far as I am able to prevent it, will cease."[5]

As American involvement in the war deepened, patriotic fervor at home intensified. Intolerance of any utterance or action that even suggested less than full support for the great fight extended to others besides radical Wobblies.

Inducements to give to the Red Cross and buy Liberty Bonds in Centralia and Chehalis sometimes extended to the publication on the front pages of newspapers of names of donors and the amounts they gave or invested. Minutemen organizations were formed "to investigate all rumors of disloyalty and to do this without publicity." After a patriotic Chehalis parade in April 1918, a speaker declared, "There are

The top poster spells out what the worker might expect to get if he joined the One Big Union. The lower message, issued in 1917, was a takeoff on the Army recruiting poster showing Uncle Sam pointing and saying, "I want you."

This placard, widely used after World War I began, did much to identify the IWW as unpatriotic.

only two kinds of people in America today — Americans or traitors, and we should not allow the traitors and others who do not assist the government to live in this country."

The wartime zeal extended even to the advocacy of compulsion in getting proper support for the war's needs. C. A. Studebaker, vice-chairman of the Chehalis Liberty Loan Drive, publicly proposed a federal law making it possible to confiscate the assets of person who would not purchase war bonds voluntarily. He was able to get 250 signatures on a petition supporting this view. It was not enough for a person to assert his patriotism; he was expected also to demonstrate it. Those fighting the war not only had to be supported at home with money and work; they had to be cheered on, sung about, prayed for, marched for, and openly admired. When Centralia teachers were called in to sign contracts for the next school year, they were asked to "show their loyalty and patriotism by signing an oath of allegiance" which included the following:

> To the best of my ability I will assist and encourage every movement that is made in the interests of the American Red Cross Association. I will encourage the sale of Liberty bonds. I will purchase thrift and savings stamps, subscribe to the YMCA war fund, teach and practice conservation of food, do all in my power to encourage the cultivation of home gardens by the

pupils. . . . I will by thought, word and deed do everything that lies within my power to inculcate in the minds of the pupils the spirit of loyalty to the government and teach them that it is their imperative duty to support every national prosecution of the war.[7]

If teachers had reservations about signing such a document, they hardly dared express them. One who did, however, was Elmer Smith. His high school teaching career came to an end at this point. It was time, he decided, to begin full-time practice of the law. He rented a small space, heated by a wood stove, on North Tower Avenue, sharing it with another beginning lawyer, Lucien J. Birdseye.[8] There he began serving persons not welcome in other law offices, including those who had grievances against employers.

Not far from Smith's office was the rectangular city park that George Washington had donated. Any outdoor speaking in Centralia was done there. One afternoon Elmer Smith saw a small crowd around a speaker who was expressing thoughts that sounded sufficiently like IWW philosophy to stir angry murmurs and then vocal protests among the audience. The speaker was jostled when he decided to go away and Smith, the tall young redhead, offered to walk with him to the depot, if he was headed that way, to see that he came to no harm. The offer was accepted. Smith explained the situation in Centralia, which by then he fully understood.

This friendly act toward a radical was noticed, of course, and widely talked about. Shortly afterward a businessman approached Smith, not with a reprimand but to make what was intended to be a helpful offer and suggestion. If Smith would "come in with them," meaning the established conservative business interests who effectively controlled the city, he could expect to develop a lucrative practice. He would get his share of the law business. He could prosper. But that would mean abandoning any radical leanings he may have acquired and certainly not accepting the kind of clients he had started with. Smith related this incident to his family and others without quoting his precise reply. He may have thanked the man who approached him, but the answer was that he felt compelled to follow his conscience. His unconventional convictions were widely known even before he decided not to continue teaching in the high school. Ora Black Kennedy remembers that her father "hated" Elmer Smith

This was the IWW pennant, with yellow letters on a red background and the globe in blue.

and did not want her to enroll in his classes.

Any scrap of news about local servicemen made front-page news during the war. A troop train carrying 164 men of the Twentieth Engineers stopped in Centralia. The *Chronicle* reported with a note of pride that Dale Hubbard was on the train and that the ladies of the Red Cross canteen served the men homemade pie, coffee, and doughnuts. Lt. Lloyd Dysart wrote home in May that he had been in the thick of the fighting in the frontline trenches. Wendell Baxter and Cecil Keys were in his company.

Newspapers seemed to vie with one another in their patriotic exhortations. The Wobblies' journalistic voice, the *Industrial Worker,* would not join that chorus but it did remain silent on the subject of the European war, concentrating instead on the war on Wobblies at home.

The flag was waved almost daily in the newspapers. "If the people of the earth are not to become toiling minions for the Prussian Junkers," the *Centralia Hub* declared, "if they are not to be terror ridden slaves at the mercy of a German Kaiser's will, Prussianism must be driven back within its own borders and kept there. We are fighting for the safety and liberty of our children, our homes, our country. No price is too great to pay for victory. . . . Invest in Liberty bonds. . . ."[9]

The IWW attitude could not be defended in a wartime atmosphere so charged with excited clamor for sacrifice, hard work, and a sustained high level of enthusiasm for all war-related activities. Any who did not share the excitement felt constrained to conceal that deficiency.

Patriotic zealots were easily moved to action. The publisher of the *Oakville Cruiser,* W. H. Moore, appeared reluctant to publish a notice of one more patriotic rally in that eastern Grays Harbor County town. He was reprimanded by being forced publicly to kiss and then salute an American flag.[10]

The Wobblies could not be hypocritical. Their original judgment about the war remained unchanged, and since their ideological objections did not carry the same weight as those made by others on religious grounds, many Wobblies were drafted and did serve.

If the IWW ever had any real legal rights they all but vanished after the commission appointed by President Wilson came West during the 1917 strike. The AFL supported Woodrow Wilson, and his secretary of labor, W. B. Wilson, who headed the commission, did not want to substantiate reports that the labor troubles in the Northwest might be due to failures of leadership in the AFL. The commission, meeting in Seattle and Portland, could not dignify the IWW by conferring with its members or by seeking an understanding of its methods and motives. Wilson acted as if the IWW was not worthy of attention by a government commission. It was not to be taken seriously. This high-level attitude did not go unnoticed.

If the federal government would accord no recognition to this organization, it could be considered, in effect, outlawed, deserving of being suppressed. The

war on Wobblies could be waged with impunity.

Raids and roundups became more common. A major suppression took place on May 3, 1917, when Mayor Ole Hansen ordered the Seattle police to close a hall that the *Post-Intelligencer* described as "a hotbed of sedition and a place of rendezvous for slackers and loafers and undesirables generally" at 208-1/2 Washington Street. Fifty uniformed police conducted the raid, seizing a "large quantity of seditious literature" and arresting 213 men who either had no draft card or carried an IWW card. A cheering but "otherwise undemonstrative crowd numbering fully 15,000 witnessed the undoing of the unpatriotic horde. Many cheered as wagon load after wagon load of prisoners were hauled away to jail." Doors of the hall were locked by the police.

"Minutemen" (vigilante) organizations were active. W. A. Blackwood, secretary of the Seattle Minutemen, reported to Senator Wesley Jones that "we have been particularly active in running down the most rabid leaders and agitators among the IWW and have been instrumental in making several hundred investigations and having caused many arrests during the past few months."[11] So numerous were the arrests, Blackwood said, that a detention station or prison, large enough to accomodate 2,500 to 3,000 prisoners, was urgently needed in the Puget Sound area. Some cities, including Yakima, built stockades where large numbers of the radicals could be held.

The Wobblies could not resist, but they did protest, though in vain. IWW defense committees were formed. The few lawyers, such as Vanderveer, who would take Wobbly cases were kept busy. E. I. Chamberlin, secretary of the Seattle District Defense Committee, complained bitterly in a message to the attorney general about the rough treatment. Is it justice, he asked, when persons are arrested, thrown into jail, and held incommunicado merely for selling or distributing defense literature? He said bank presidents who loot banks, thieves, and even murderers were not treated as badly as Wobblies "who are denied every constitutional and legal right. . . ."[12] The attorney general, reflecting on such complaints, told his deputy in Seat-

Wobbly tactics called for slowdowns on the job and outright sabotage of industrial equipment. Despite such open advocacy of this, they steadfastly refused to accept responsibility for acts of sabotage such as spikes driven into logs.

RELEASE ALL CLASS WAR PRISONERS

Many hundreds of members of the Industrial Workers of the World and other workers are still held in penitentiaries and jails throughout the United States. Some of these have been convicted and are serving long. terms of imprisonment, others are wasting away their lives waiting for trial. These men are depending upon you for their freedom.

Make all checks and money orders payable to
General Defense Committee
1001 W. Madison St.. Chicago, Ill.

NOTE Enclose this list with your remittance. It will be returned to you properly receipted.

Secretary Gen. Defense Committee

 CONTRIBUTIONS FOR THE DEFENSE FUND

tle that he thought anti-Wobbly activity might be getting too extreme.

William D. Haywood, one of the founders and titular head of the IWW, wrote the following in an impassioned pamphlet entitled *RAIDS! RAIDS! RAIDS!*

The IWW needed to raise funds to defend members in trouble with the law almost from the beginning of the union. Those jailed for union activities were invariably called "class-war prisoners." This is an early appeal for defense funds signed by the union's president, William D. Haywood.

Telegrams are coming in from all parts of the country, telling of raids, of halls and offices having been closed, of furniture, office fixtures and typewriters having been destroyed. Many tons of literature have been confiscated or burned in bonfires; members have been badly beaten and hundreds of them thrown into prison. They have met with the same savage cruelty as perpetrated under the old Russian regime of pogrom when Cossacks committed the foulest and most vicious crimes against the Jews. Here in the United States it matters not what an individual's religion may be, his color, his nationality or the industry in which he is employed. If he is an IWW, he has no rights that profiteers or politicians are compelled to respect.

The threat of enemies from within, IWW or otherwise, was sufficiently real for Governor Lister to organize what he called a Secret Service, headed by C. B. Reed of the Washington Detective Bureau of New York. Reed employed ten operatives beginning in August 1917. Each was assigned a number and ordered to send reports of what they observed, nosing about the state, directly to Lister, the attorney general, and the U.S.

attorney in Seattle, Clay Allen.[13]

All did not go well with Lister's Secret Service. Reed paid his operatives six dollars a day and charged the state ten dollars. Mayor Ole Hansen of Seattle found out about this, accused Reed of grafting, and had the city council revoke his detective license. Hansen and Lister were political enemies.

Others besides the Secret Service undertook to keep the governor informed. Articulate Wobblies did not remain silent as the relentless war against them intensified. Thomas Elliott of Prosser wrote to Lister describing in vivid detail how Frank Meyers, secretary of the Yakima local of IWW, was taken from his hotel room at night, tarred and feathered, then turned loose with a warning that he would be killed if he ever returned to Yakima. "Tell the others," he was told, "that any IWW secretary who comes to Yakima to work, or to spread unpatriotic propaganda, will not be tarred and feathered but will receive the same treatment given Little in Montana."[14] In another letter Elliott described what happened when troops were sent into the Yakima Valley to provide protection against the

IWW menace. "They raided the IWW hall, seized its contents and began indiscriminately arresting every man they found wearing overalls."[15] Elliott himself was thrown into jail, he reported, but sawed through the bars and escaped to carry his tale of woe to an unsympathetic governor.

The ranks of the IWW increased rapidly in the early weeks of the war, Governor Lister noted, and he became particularly alarmed when he and three other Northwest governors received telegrams from a Wobbly leader threatening a general strike among harvest workers if all members of the IWW then held in jail were not released promptly.

The Defense Councils in all the agricultural counties were alerted and the strike, though called, did not succeed. "The strike was a failure," Lister later reported. "Its instigator was arrested, taken to Chicago, tried with about one hundred members of the IWW and convicted and sentenced to twenty years in a Federal penitentiary."[16]

Members of Congress joined the anti-Wobbly chorus. The subversives had to be suppressed, they said. Senator William E. Borah of Idaho, a state where the IWW had been particularly active, tried to convince his colleagues that this could not be done. "You cannot destroy the organization," he said. "It is an intangible proposition. It is something you cannot get at. You cannot reach it. You do not know where it is. It is not in writing. It is not in anything else. It is simply an understanding between men, and they act upon it without any evidence of existence whatever."[17] Borah added that he did not want the people of his state resorting to mob violence even against the IWW.

Senator Porter J. McCumber of North Dakota said he understood that working conditions had gotten so bad in Oregon and Washington that "men are afraid to go into the timber to work. It was all a man's life was worth to leave his home and go into the lumber camps. . . . It seems to me that . . . we are justified in doing exactly what the frontiersmen have had to do in many instances, organize their defense forces and destroy the criminals."[18]

Clarence Reames, on the scene in Seattle, estimated that Wobblies in Washington numbered 140,000 and that at least 5,000 were aliens who should be deported. He expressed disappointment when the Bureau of Labor issued a statement saying alien Wobblies would not be arrested and held for deportation in the absence of any offense other than membership in the union. Reames reported that it was difficult to keep well-meaning citizens from taking the law into their own hands. "A few halls," he wrote, "have been burned and some of the property of the organization destroyed, but on the whole the conduct of the majority of the citizens has been very commendable."[19]

Reames' judgment reflected that of people in the Northwest generally. It was all right to raid halls and destroy what little property was in them, it was believed, especially when the law didn't seem to be taking care of the situation.

7

Postwar Crackdown

November 11 in later years was no occasion for celebration in Centralia but in 1918 it was a day of real joy. The armistice was signed. At last the war was over. The men of Company M, gone more than a year, would come home.

The city exulted, like all others, proud of the part its men, its Red Cross, its Liberty Bond money, and the lumber from its mills played in defeating the hated Huns. Now there would be peace and normal times.

Lewis County's losses in the war were not disproportionately high. More than sixteen hundred went into service. Records compiled in the aftermath listed forty-three who did not return. There may have been more whose fate was known only to their families.

The labor situation at war's end was relatively calm. The Loyal Legion of Loggers and Lumbermen, promoted and encouraged by employers because its members were sworn to stay on the job and produce, had a firm quota of adherents in most camps and mills. The IWW was not idle or discouraged, just quiet. Many of its members and leaders were in jail, convicted under the sedition law, but the organization itself was intact and had not retreated an inch from its original opinion about the war — that it was an unnecessary capitalistic conflict.

The Wobblies in the West suffered one great disappointment at the beginning of 1919. Seattle shipyards, caught at war's end producing ships no longer needed, announced a pay cut. A strike ensued and there was devised a plan that was widely attributed to the scheming Wobblies, many of whom were "two-card men," maintaining membership in both an AFL union and the IWW. The plan called for every worker — literally every one — to go on strike simultaneously. This would produce a powerful show of force that would demonstrate at last the real power of the workers. Such a general strike would spread. It could be the giant leap that would put workers in control.

What came to be known as the Seattle general strike, planned rather carefully, began on February 16. It lasted five days. Most of the conservative local AFL union leaders had gone East before the plans were made and knew nothing about them. They were aghast when they heard what was happening. The international unions threatened revocation of local charters if the men didn't get back to work promptly. This official AFL displeasure — plus a realization that, while the shipyard workers stood to get something if the strike were won, others were only losing wages while off the job — brought to an ignominious termination what came to be listed as the only general strike the United States ever had.

The Wobblies were stunned. They had been exuberantly hopeful, if not confident, that finally, with enough workers using the strike weapon in one massive effort, their great goal could be achieved. They expected the strikers somehow to become so carried away with the excitement of a great display of power that they would become more militant and determined as the days and weeks wore on and the capitalists did not yield. They expected the fire of unrest that burned continually in their own inner yearnings to blaze up like a forest conflagration in a windstorm, spreading from city to city, destroying the oppressive capitalists and leaving the workers triumphant.

When it didn't happen the Wobblies were downcast but not discouraged. The strike failure didn't mean the objective was wrong or even unattainable. It meant only that not enough workers had been reached and persuaded. Organizing had to be intensified.

For labor's foes the collapse of the general strike was a triumphant turning point. It was the biggest confrontation with the radicals yet — a major battle — and it was won. Surely the Wobbly war itself

U. S. OFFICERS TO DISCUSS STRIKE —SEE PAGE 2

The Seattle Star

FINAL EDITION
TWO CENTS IN SEATTLE

FULL Leased Wire of the United Press Association.

COMPLETE Service of the Newspaper Enterprise Association.

THE GREATEST DAILY CIRCULATION OF ANY PAPER IN THE PACIFIC NORTHWEST

SEATTLE, WASH., TUESDAY, FEBRUARY 4, 1919.

Weather Forecast:

VOLUME 21. NO. 230.

STOP BEFORE IT'S TOO LATE

This is plain talk to the common-sense union men of Seattle. You are being rushed pell-mell into a general strike. You are being urged to use a dangerous weapon—the general strike, which you have never used before—which, in fact, has never been used anywhere in the United States.

It isn't too late to avert the tragic results that are sure to come from its use. You men know better than any one else that public sentiment in Seattle— that is, the sentiment of the ninety-per cent of the people who are not directly involved in the wage dispute of the shipworkers—*is against a general strike.* You know that the general public doesn't think the situation demands the use of that drastic, disaster-breeding move. *You know, too, that you cannot club public sentiment into line, and you know, too, that no strike has ever been won without the moral support of the public.*

The people know that there is a decent solution of the issue at stake. And the issue at stake is merely a better wage to the average unskilled worker in the shipyards. To a large extent public opinion is with these unskilled workers now, but public opinion will turn against them if their wage issue brings chaos and disaster upon the whole community unnecessarily. Seattle today is awake to the fact that she is on the brink of a disaster, *and Seattle is getting fighting mad.* The people are beginning to visualize the horrors that a general tie-up will bring. They see the suffering that is bound to come and *they don't propose to be silent sufferers.*

Today Seattle resents this whole miserable mess. Seattle resents the insolent attitude of the shipyard owners; Seattle resents the verbosity of Director General Piez, whose explanation does not explain, and just as emphatically resents the high-handed "rule or ruin" tactics of the labor leaders who propose to lay the whole city prostrate in a vain attempt to show their power. Let us not mince words. A general strike cannot win unless one of two things happens. Either the ship owners and Piez must yield or else the workers must be able to control the situation *by force.* The latter method no doubt would be welcomed by the agitators and the babblers of Bolshevikism. But the latter method is bound to be squelched without much ado, and you decent union men of Seattle will be the sufferers then. *A revolt—and some of your leaders are talking of a revolution—to be successful must have a country-wide application.* There isn't a chance to spread it east of the mountains. There isn't a chance to spread it south of Tacoma *and today fifty per cent of the unions of Tacoma have turned down the proposition for a general strike.*

Confined to Seattle or even confined to the whole Pacific coast, the use of force by Bolsheviks would be, and should be, quickly dealt with by the army of the United States. These false Bolshevik leaders haven't a chance on earth to win anything for you in this country, *because this country is America—not Russia.*

could be won soon, and then there would be real peace.

Mayor Ole Hansen of Seattle was flattered to be assigned the role of hero — the one most responsible for breaking the strike. He was so pleased that he went on the road lecturing about his achievement and in due course wrote a book about it. Employers set out to crack down harder on labor agitators and to request law enforcement to join them. Laws had to be stretched to do this. Employers may have thought vigilante action was all right in individual cases, but day-by-day pressure should be lawful.

At this point the wartime antisedition law was made more useful by a case that originated in Pacific County, adjoining Lewis County to the west. Two IWW organizers, Fred Lowery and Charles Brown, were picked for prosecution. They were charged with "willfully, wrongfully, feloniously and anarchistically" advocating the overthrow of the government by "the unlawful means of an organization known as the Industrial Workers of the World. . . ."[1]

In the trial Lowery's attorney tried to introduce as evidence the report of the Wilson Commission, sent West early in the war to investigate labor troubles. The report, the attorney contended, declared that the IWW was not in fact an anarchical organization. Therefore Lowery was wrongfully charged. The court disallowed this piece of evidence on curious grounds. The Wilson report, it concluded, "was not official and in no way a public record. . . ." Therefore any testimony based on it would be hearsay, which is always inadmissible.

Lowery was convicted and because, if the verdict stood, any Wobbly could be put away for merely being a Wobbly, the case was appealed to the State Supreme Court. There it was upheld.

Other states passed laws to provide better ways to get at Wobblies. These were usually criminal syndicalism laws, aimed at suppressing spoken and written words considered seditious. Washington's legislature had passed such a bill in 1918, but because of intimidation or otherwise, Governor Hart had vetoed it. Early in 1919 the legislature passed the bill again. It provided "penalties for the dissemination of doctrines inimical

Front page of the Seattle Star *on the eve of the general strike in February 1919. The appeal went unheeded and the strike occurred but did not last long, much to the chagrin of the Wobblies, who hoped it would spread and result in the achievement of one of their objectives—the overthrow of capitalism.*

to public tranquility and orderly government." This time the governor signed it. This law made it a felony to advocate, teach, print, publish, or display anything that advocated, advised, taught, or justified crime, sedition, violence, intimidation, or injury as a means of effecting industrial, economic, social, or political change, or even to be a member of or voluntarily assemble with any group formed to advocate what was forbidden.[2] A clause aimed straight at Wobbly halls made it a misdemeanor for any property owner to allow his premises to be used by those engaged in what the law prohibited.

In the same session the legislators were persuaded to define sabotage and make it illegal. The act provided that "whoever, with intent that his act shall, or with reason to believe that it may, injure, interfere with, or obstruct any (commercial) . . . enterprise wherein persons are employed for wages, shall willfully injure or destroy . . . any property whatsoever . . . or derange or attempt to derange any mechanism or appliance, shall be guilty of a felony."[3] The law also made it illegal to teach, advocate, or publish anything about sabotage or to be a member or associate with any group of persons who promoted these now prohibited ideas and procedures.

Thus law enforcement officers in Washington, after March 1919, had two plainly worded laws to use against Wobblies. IWW halls henceforth were to be illegal, but halls would hardly be needed since mere membership in an organization that was on record in countless publications as advocating what was now contrary to law should be enough to get Wobblies out of halls and into jails.

What's more, these laws had the effect of sanctifying all previous acts of suppression. What vigilantes had taken upon themselves to do in the past — raid halls and punish subversives — now could be done with impunity. If someone dared rent space to Wobblies, he could be arrested. The raiding of the hall in Centralia in 1918 didn't have the sanction of law at the time, although that made no difference, but now, in retrospect, it could be regarded as something done to promote the general welfare.

The virtual outlawing of the IWW did not, however, result in its easy suppression in Washington. Those who remained loyal to the radical creed through all the turmoil and angry oppression were too numerous to be arrested, tried, and jailed one at a time. No one knew how many men carried the red cards of membership on both sides of the Cascades, but there were thousands. The dimensions of the uproar they created and the often hysterical nature of what was written and said about them was for some Wobblies a source of wonderment. Here they were, struggling to improve the lot of the common man, rid society of selfish elements who exploited workers, and make life better for everyone, and yet they were hounded and harassed and legislated against at every turn. Why? Though they couldn't answer that precisely, they did coin a phrase to describe it — "the Wobbly horrors." It was used around the logging camps. When a boss became nervous and began firing men suspected of IWW affiliations, it was said that he had a bad case of the "Wobbly horrors."

No records were kept of the number of Wobblies sent to jail under the syndicalism laws, but there were not enough to identify the laws as the ultimate weapon of IWW suppression. Vanderveer was frequently called to defend an accused Wobbly and sometimes he succeeded. The general public, from whose ranks juries were chosen, was not as much afflicted with "the Wobbly horrors" as were employers and public officials. Furthermore, jail expenses were high when they were crowded. Convicted Wobblies entered the jails with almost an attitude of triumph as they joined the ranks of those who gave up their freedom for a cause and became "class-war prisoners."

The *Industrial Worker* printed the text of the Washington syndicalism law on its front page, paralleling it on one side with sections of the "Imperial Russian Penal code prohibiting sedition utterances," and on the other side with similar excerpts from the "Imperial German Criminal code of 1870 signed by Bismarck and William I." Both contained sections remarkably similar to the Washington law.[4]

Criminal laws are written to allow officials to deal at any one time with single offenders or, at most, small groups. Wobblies operated in packs. So they still sometimes had to be dealt with in old, often spectacular ways, such as on July 21 when a squad of twenty-four Seattle police was sent to break up a large crowd assembled at Fourth and Virginia to hear Wobbly speakers denounce American intervention in Russia. The police moved in, swinging billy clubs and inflicting enough bloody head cuts and bruises to succeed in their mission. The crowd was dispersed.

Such actions to suppress radical utterances gave the IWW newspapers reason to scream typographically in protest and to demand that the workers strike back. "Slow down — strike on the job," the *Industrial Worker* demanded. It did not recommend work stoppages. In a strike, it explained, the worker loses wages. Better to stay on the job, but don't do as much.

The number of workers being jailed kept the Wobblies stirred up. Their mutterings and outcries, widely reported, repeated, and often exaggerated, led to the circulation of rumors which, however bizarre, were widely believed. Local and federal officials were sent a telegram by the Justice Department on July 4, 1919, warning them to be on guard against a "gigantic IWW plot to burn down all logging camps where the 4-L was recognized."[5] Spokane was so alarmed by rumors of an IWW invasion that it appealed for troops — state or federal. When these were refused, the Commissioner of Public Safety swore in more ex-soldiers as special policemen and the mayor declared martial law.

This kind of hysteria was cause for real concern among the Spokane Wobblies. They were not that bad, they wanted everyone to know, and took to wearing white buttons with the American flag on them and the words "League for Democracy at Home." The white-button wearers, when they attended a syndicalism trial, identified themselves as Wobblies and so were arrested. The cumulative effect clogged the courts.

Skirmishes in the Wobbly war were not confined to the Northwest. In Superior, Wisconsin, a decision was made that did not go unnoticed among Wobblies elsewhere. Those in charge of an IWW hall, hearing they were to be next in a series of raids in that part of the country, brought in an arsenal of guns and let it be known that if a mob showed up, the raiders would be shot. There was no raid.[6]

The critical year of 1919 moved along. There was much of public concern besides labor troubles and Wobblies. It was the year when the long campaign against the evils of the saloon finally succeeded and the eighteenth amendment, prohibition, was voted in. The right for women to vote was close at hand.

Wobblies, it surprised many to learn, did not often frequent saloons. They did not object to prohibition because their unwritten creed included strong disapproval of anything smacking of "dehorn." Asked to define this unusual term, a Wobbly could explain that when a horned animal, such as a bull, is dehorned, it loses its ability to fight. It is rendered incapable of defending itself or protecting others who need defending. Wobblies were supposed to have unwavering loyalty to their cause and to be fit and ready at all times to fight for that cause, on a street-corner soap box, in a stove-side discussion, or in a confrontation with the police. Alcohol could interfere with union militancy. It would dehorn a man and make him overlook or forget his class-war obligations. Prostitution was similarly frowned on in time of crisis. During a strike in Grays Harbor the whorehouses — and they were numerous — were persuaded by the IWW leaders to close.

The first Fourth of July after the war's end called for more fervent than usual hurrahs for the Red, White and Blue, especially since so many men were safely home and could put on their uniforms and march behind the flag, with bands playing and crowds along the sidewalks shouting their admiration.

In Centralia Lt. Warren O. Grimm, back from an unusual war's-end year of duty with American forces fighting Bolsheviks in Siberia, was the senior officer among the home boys. He shared honors in the parade with Lt. A. F. Cormier, who was the marshal. Capt. David Livingstone rode in an open automobile with city officials. The Red Cross, the Elks, and Boy Scouts provided vehicles converted to floats adorned with colorful crepe paper and flowers. Servicemen marched under a new banner. While still in France American servicemen, knowing their war experience would provide a lasting common bond among them, formed the American Legion. This organization's reason for being, besides comradeship, was to hold high the flag, encourage patriotism, keep America strong, and not yield anything to the enemy at home or abroad. The enemy, it was decided very early in the Legion's history, included Communists and other radicals such as the Industrial Workers of the World.

The first national meeting of the Legion on home soil was held in May 1918, in St. Louis. Sgt. Sherman Curtin of Seattle walked into the meeting carrying reports of renewed Wobbly activities in the Northwest. He described the IWW as the "International," bearing close ties to the Russian revolutionaries.

All over the nation servicemen organized Legion posts. In Centralia the old soldier William Scales took the lead. He had reopened his grocery store and urged all servicemen in the area to come in and register as charter members of a new post. A month later the post was organized with Scales as commander. Trustees included Warren Grimm, Dr. F. J. Bickford, and A. F. Cormier. One Centralia family, waiting for word that their soldier son had returned, was informed on December 6 that he had been killed on September 27 in the battle of the Argonne Forest. All Centralia mourned, the newspapers said, and the Legionnaires named their new post for him — Grant Hodge.

On the same day that the Legion post was organized another meeting was held, in the Centralia Chamber of Commerce. It was called at the request of George F. Russell of Seattle, the full-time secretary of the Employers Association of Washington, to discuss the "labor situation." That meant Wobbly intransigence. Russell was a forceful speaker and urged the Centralia group to form a local organization for the purpose of combating, however best it could, the insidious efforts of the radicals to destroy American business. The local employers listened, none more attentively than mill owner Francis Hubbard. At Rus-

SLOW DOWN

The hours are long, the pay is small So take your time And buck them all.

sell's urging a temporary organization was formed immediately. Hubbard was made chairman and empowered to perfect the organization. Russell said a similar meeting would be held on July 7 in Chehalis.[7]

Russell then went on his way, carrying out his mission — to alert industrialists and businessmen to the continuing menace of the IWW and urging them to recognize the need to do something about it.

8

Entry into Centralia

The ragtag troop of hungry Wobblies who invaded Centralia in February 1915 were not the first in that midway railroad town. Months earlier Wobblies were seen in the north part of town in an old saloon that had been converted to a meeting place by a group of local socialists. C. D. Cunningham recalled that one of his university classmates, Ludwig Katterfeld, running for governor on the Socialist ticket, came to town and spoke in the hall. Katterfeld remained Cunningham's one radical friend even after he went on to become a leading Communist activist and served a term in prison, like many Wobblies, after being convicted under laws that made it illegal to voice views defined as subversive.[1]

This hall fell into disuse by the IWW in the prewar years, when unemployment in the lumber industry became so severe that few workers could afford the fifty cents a month in dues the IWW assessed. War brought back full employment and IWW recruiting resumed with vigor. Halls were needed. Wobblies were mostly itinerant, moving from job to job or running from one place of oppression to another. There had to be places where they could keep in touch, engage in recruiting, pay dues, pick up the latest labor papers from Chicago, Seattle, or San Francisco, cash paychecks when they had them, try to borrow a few dollars when they didn't, and even bed down for a night or two if they had no money for a room. Centralia was the crossroads of southwest Washington and was a logical place for a hall. A decision was made to establish one, and in March 1917, space was rented in the Central Building, 530 North Tower Avenue, close to downtown. The *Chronicle* took note of this unwelcome development and reported that benches were being constructed, making it obvious that the place was going to be used for meetings. "The organization is not taking a chance of meeting opposition by holding meetings in the street," the newspaper observed. It went on to note that "IWWs have been here in numbers during the past few weeks but committed no acts necessary for the authorities to interfere."[2]

Others, however, did interfere, though peaceably. The agent for the Central Building, S. H. Bloomer, was asked if he was aware that he had rented to the IWW. He was not, he said. The renters told him they were simply an organization of lumber workers. Now that he knew, he promptly evicted them and was commended in a *Chronicle* editorial which said that "much credit is due Mr. Bloomer and other prominent citizens for the diplomatic manner in which they handled" the eviction.

"The IWW has given up headquarters in this city," editor Harry L. Bras took satisfaction in announcing, "and it is earnestly hoped they will never attempt such a movement again."[3]

The earnest hopes were unfounded. The Wobblies looked elsewhere for space to rent and were rejected like blacks trying to move into a white neighborhood, until they found an empty former saloon on the corner of First and B streets. The saloon was owned by an estate in Chehalis whose administrator was more concerned with getting the place rented than with the character of the tenants. The *Chronicle* then reported that the IWW had established a base in Centralia after all, "painted signs on the windows, fitted up the interior with tables and benches and apparently is settling for an extended stay."

This was considered intolerable. In April 1917, fifty businessmen met at the Commercial Club to discuss what next should be done to rid the city of the "IWW horde that has opened a hall here." Members of the city commission were of no help. They told the businessmen that they couldn't take action unless the Wobblies did something illegal. Why not prosecute them as vagrants? someone asked. The meeting, as reported by the *Chronicle*, ended by electing A. C. Gesler chairman. He said the IWW were known to be thieves and liars and the sooner the city got rid of them the better. "As a result of the commission expressing itself as powerless to act," the *Chronicle* concluded, "it is considered possible that the businessmen will take matters into their own hands as Everett citizens were forced to do when the authorities there refused assistance. The better element in Centralia has said that the IWW must go; and the next move on their part is awaited with interest."

Centralia had to wait for that move until the spring of 1918 when the city held one of its periodic drives to raise funds for the Red Cross. The occasion called for a bazaar and the customary symbol of patriotism in action, a parade. Centralia's "better element" decided then that it was time again for the city to show it was up with the times by running Wobblies out of town. Furthermore, the governor would be riding in the parade. He would be impressed.

Marching in the parade on May 18 were members of the Home Guard and the Elks. The parade moved north on Tower Avenue to Second, turned around and headed back toward the center of town. When the rear of the parade reached First on the return march, a loud yell was heard and a number of the marchers left the parade and ran down the block to the hall bearing the hated IWW sign. They rushed in, grabbed a few startled men, and herded them into the street. Then the destruction began. Furniture from the hall was stacked in the street and burned. Thrown on this pile was a typewriter, some books, Wobbly literature, and records. What to do with a desk and a phonograph was decided when someone suggested an auction. James Churchill, local glove factory owner, bid high on the Victrola. Francis Hubbard, recently elected president of the Employers Association of Washington, bought the desk for the Chamber of Commerce.

As for the Wobblies, they were "lifted by their ears into a truck," according to a later account, and taken to an open space between Centralia and Chehalis where they were forced to run the gauntlet between two lines of middle-aged vigilantes (the young men being off to war) and endure a flogging with sticks and ax handles as they ran. They were ordered then to march away from town and keep going.[4]

After the hall's destruction, the only IWW pres-ence left in Centralia was a small newsstand operated by a partially blind IWW sympathizer named Tom Lassiter, where the *Industrial Worker*, the *Seattle Union Record,* and Tacoma's labor paper, *Solidarity,* were sold. These papers were widely circulated and seen by foes of the IWW as well as its members. The IWW papers in particular were regarded as viciously subversive, especially on the subject of the Russian revolution. Lassiter ignored abusive remarks about what he was selling and his obstinancy was too much for three local foes of radicalism, who went to Lassiter's stand, seized all the union papers there, and warned the news dealer not to put any more issues on sale. Lassiter disregarded the warning and on June 30, six weeks after the hall was raided, two men drove up to Lassiter's stand, forced him into their car, and drove north to the Thurston County line where they pushed their victim out and into a ditch, warning him never to return to Centralia. A passing motorist soon picked him up and took him on to Olympia.

In a week Lassiter was back, still unafraid and again selling the labor papers. This time the prosecutor was persuaded to have him arrested, but he wasn't charged. Lassiter then sought the help of the one local lawyer who would dare represent a person with radical leanings, Elmer Smith. Smith had recently incurred the wrath of employers by convincing a court that a young woman client was justified in protesting her pay, which was lower than the minimum legal wage for women. In another case, a child of a laid-off worker died and the death was attributed to malnutrition. Smith filed suit on behalf of the worker against his lumber company employer, charging that the child starved because the father had no wages to buy food. This infuriated the Centralia business community.

Smith was accused of being the "real intellectual power of the IWW" in Lewis County. He was considered a member. His friends, who were numerous, admitted he was "very class conscious," and he was at that time the local president of the Triple Alliance, a liberal political organization made up of farmers, railwaymen, and unionists.

Smith carefully assembled the facts in the Lassiter case, knowing his client had violated no law. The prosecutor, knowing that also, declined to file formal charges. Thus deprived of a chance to vindicate a victim of local oppression in court, Smith submitted sworn statements of Lassiter's mistreatment to Governor Hart. They were ignored.

Raids during this period often had official sanction. Search warrants were obtained and the materials to be seized in them were listed.[5] One sanctioned raid was used to suppress *Solidarity* in Tacoma. On December 19, 1917, the U.S. District Court issued a warrant authorizing the seizure of the contents of the IWW newspaper plant at 1314 Commerce Street. The raid was successfully carried out.

The Bolshevik uprising in Russia was a setback for the Allies since German troops who had been fighting Russia were freed to reinforce those arrayed against the Allies on the western front. The IWW's open admiration for this triumph of the proletariat provided one more reason to wage war on Wobblies. On September 5, 1917, agents of the Department of Justice undertook to close, simultaneously, every IWW hall still open in the nation. These mass raids were followed on September 28 by indictments against 166 national IWW leaders, including William Haywood and everyone else on the general headquarters staff in Chicago. George Vanderveer's reputation was such by then that he was sent an urgent appeal to go East and direct the defense of those charged in this major effort at the national level to smash the IWW. The Seattle attorney, not sure he was ready for such a task, was reluctant to go, but he was the best the IWW could find, so he took the assignment, which proved unsuccessful. The Wobbly leaders went to prison.

A Russian ship, the *Shilka,* an auxiliary steamer in the service of the new government, sailed into Seattle on December 21 and tied up at Pier 5. A rumor spread quickly that it had brought $100,000 in gold for use in defending the IWW "class war" prisoners awaiting trial in Chicago. Guards were placed on the pier to inspect any packages brought ashore and the ship itself was searched. No gold was found.

The Seattle Wobblies were greatly excited by the appearance among them of actual participants in a revolution that seemed to be succeeding. They persuaded members of the *Shilka*'s crew to speak at a meeting in their hall. Several thousand handbills were distributed, announcing the event. The hall was thronged when Denil Teraninoff, quartermaster of the *Shilka,* made a dramatic entrance wearing a Russian naval uniform. "Cheer after cheer greeted the representative of real freedom," reported the *Industrial Worker,* "and these increased in volume as the speaker's remarks were translated by a woman member of the Russian colony."

Seattle's officialdom was less enthusiastic. Teraninoff was arrested, booked at the city jail, then returned to his ship and advised to stay on board. Tacoma Wobbies sent gifts to the Russians. A *Shilka* sailor responded with a letter of thanks and the Tacomans sent back a letter saying:

> You no doubt realize that we come as the revolutionists of America, being still in the minority, are unable as yet to follow your example in freeing ourselves from the terrible slave system in which we are enthralled, but confidently look forward to the time when we can reach across the Pacific Ocean and grasp the hands of our progressive fellow workers in Russia and say 'we are with you!' The persecution of the Industrial Workers of the World becomes more severe each day and our organization grows accordingly. We have nothing but great hopes for the future freedom of all mankind. Long live the Russian revolution!
> — A. R. Tucker, W. J. Harrington, K. McClellennon, committee[6]

As the IWW took on a Red tinge, the lines of antagonism tightened still more. This enemy had to be defeated. But how? The laws were proving to be ineffectual. The jails were not large enough. Reflecting in frustration, the editor of the *Centralia Chronicle* decided the time had come to propose a return to the tactics used on the frontier when a menace could not be handled adequately under the law. From 1849 to 1851, he wrote, there was no criminal or civil law in California, so "after three years of terror a small but brave body of men organized what was known as a Vigilante Committee that meted out justice.... It was so in the South during the reconstruction period.... The people of this country will not stand for their property and the sacredness of their homes to be long in jeopardy. In the absence of law enforcement, they will take matters into their own hands and woe be to the transgressors. We believe, in this state, a menace exists that will need to be dealt with in the absence of specific laws by the organized citizenship working in the interest of justice and the perpetuity of the home and Christian government. The IWWs belong to a class that must change...."[7]

The people of Centralia read this thinly veiled call to arms and pondered it. They did not, however, take issue with it.

9

1919, Year of Trouble

The first six months of 1919 were not good ones in the Northwest lumber industry, employing nearly 150,000 men. Mills reported an average loss of fifty-five cents per thousand board feet. Then in July the market improved and operators looked forward to recouping their first-half losses in the final two quarters. At this point the IWW made another move. Its Lumberworkers International Union called strikes. The operators were furious.

They had given in on the eight-hour day, fixed up the camps, and raised wages. Now the radicals were at it again with new demands in addition to old ones.

The Wobblies had always disdained political action, but they changed after the Russian revolution, and when their top leaders went to prison under sedition convictions they began using the strike as a weapon to back demands that the U.S. immediately withdraw its troops from Russia and release those who had come to be called "class-war prisoners." While pursuing these objectives the Wobblies did not overlook their own wants, which now included a minimum wage of five dollars a day; a maximum charge of one dollar a day for board; free blankets, sheets, and pillows; bathhouse wash and dry rooms; right of free speech, press, and assembly; and hiring to be done on the job rather than through job sharks.

"The lumber industry is prosperous just at present," the *Chronicle* commented in November, "and more men are employed at higher wages than ever before. If the radicals . . . cause a disturbance among the lumber workers, they will greatly damage many lines of industry in the West and thousands of people will be out of work."[1]

Oregon loggers, drifting home after being lured north by higher wage scales in Washington, reported that nearly every logging camp in the state was working under IWW conditions. They said, "One never knows whether he will work an hour or half a day or all day when he commences in the morning for the Wobblies are constantly stirring up trouble and walkouts are common. . . . Even the foremen of the camps are obliged to join the IWW." At several places where these Oregon men were employed while in Washington they saw IWW members tear emblems from the clothing of 4-L members and "throw them in the dust." They said nobody dares resist such usage "for the Wobblies are in the ascendency."[2]

L. H. May, an official of the McKenna Lumber Company near Olympia, verified this conclusion. He said a majority of the men working in the logging camps of Washington were members of the IWW.[3]

Such reports of increased Wobbly activity alarmed not only employers but those concerned with patriotism, notably the American Legion and the Benevolent and Protective Order of Elks.

The Elks lodge maintained a spacious hall on the top floor of the largest building in downtown Centralia. In the basement was the *Chronicle* plant. On the second and third floors were offices, including those of C. D. Cunningham. The Elks hall was the convenient meeting place downtown for the lodge's membership, which included most of those who were part of the business establishment. To be an Elk in a city the size of Centralia was to be accepted. It was the largest organization in town and provided a kind of male bastion where men who were friends could gather from noon on, with the bar open and the pool and card tables always available, and, on meeting nights, assemble in a big hall with massive elk heads staring down from the walls to go through a ritual in which patriotism was a dominant theme. A stone fireplace in the entry hall at the top of the stairs provided a welcoming fire on winter nights.

The Centralia lodge sometimes initiated as many

as fifty-four at a time, as it did on July 12, 1919. The occasion was important enough to bring Governor Louis Hart down from Olympia to take part in the ceremonies. He too was an Elk.

"There is no more patriotic order than the BPOE," proclaimed the *Chronicle* on November 7, quoting from a resolution passed by the Grand Lodge at its recent convention. "Whereas the Benevolent and Protective Order of Elks is distinctly American," it began, "... it condemns all things and all persons that are in any degree or any manner opposed thereto...." The resolution proclaimed implacable hostility toward all forms of dangers and doctrines that threatened free institutions and the flag, including Bolsheviki, anarchists, and, of course, the IWW.

Reports concerning the IWW, carried on the news wires, in general were of two kinds. One brought the disturbing news that the radical union seemed to be in the ascendance again, gaining members and making trouble in the woods. Other reports told of actions being taken to combat the menace.

An IWW organizer was seized in his hotel room in Baker, Oregon, taken to the edge of town, beaten, and threatened with death if he returned.

In Everett the IWW requested permission to hold a parade on October 6 to generate public support for the campaign to release class-war prisoners. The sheriff and the mayor conferred, denied the request, then wrote Governor Hart asking him to send Company M of Centralia back to Everett because "it is feared that an attempt may be made to hold the parade regardless of the denial, and from the apparent public sentiment of the city it is feared that great disorder and riot may result from an attempt to hold such a parade."[4] Hart did not see fit to comply and the Centralia men were spared another tour of anti-Wobbly duty in Everett. Nor did the Wobblies attempt to hold the parade.

The most prominent class-war prisoner of the day was Thomas Mooney, convicted in San Francisco of throwing a bomb into a 1916 parade. Wanting to show their concern for him and others of their kind being held in various prisons, the Wobblies called for all workers to strike for a day on October 6. Many did, but none of the mills in Centralia was shut down.

The state Legion convention in 1919 requested every local post to offer its services to law enforcement authorities "for the suppression of disorders and riots or anything threatening the constitutional form of

Interior of the main hall in the Elks Club, Centralia.

government."[5] The post in Montesano, Centralia's near neighbor in Grays Harbor County, responded eagerly to this call to duty with a ringing offer of volunteerism which said, "Whereas there is a feeling of unrest in the country at large and especially in this county on account of the enormous amount of IWW ... literature . . . being circulated, and whereas our services may be needed at any time . . . to uphold that for which we as an order stand — Americanism — now therefore. . . ." The resolution went on to offer the Legion's services as might be required for the "suppression of sedition, to quell riots, or to be used in any way for the servants of good government."[6] Sheriff Jeff Bartell shared the Legion's belief that the Wobblies were capable of terroristic activity in Grays Harbor County serious enough to require men under arms to preserve order, and said he was ready to swear in the entire Legion post as special deputy sheriffs as soon as the Legion's membership drive was completed.

Such willingness to help in suppressing Wobblies told the public that trouble probably could be expected and that the local men who had gone off to fight a foreign enemy now stood ready to fight the enemy at home. Antiradical activities became so numerous that the Associated Press occasionally grouped reports of them in a "roundup." One in early November told of recent raids in New York, Detroit, Trenton, and Bridgeport, Connecticut. In New York alone, the report said, seventy-one raids had been conducted and five hundred prisoners taken.[7]

The *Seattle Union Record*, although a conservative paper compared to the *Industrial Worker,* still could not countenance what was going on. Its critical comments included enough references to Centralia to bring about what frequently resulted when local indignations were aroused — a meeting. Twenty-five local businessmen met and agreed to boycott the paper. What little advertising the *Record* was getting in Centralia would be reduced to nothing.

The few liberal labor and political leaders in the solidly Republican state — but no Wobblies — had a chance to plead their case at a high level in mid-September when President Woodrow Wilson, a Democrat, came west seeking public support for the League of Nations, which Congress would not support. A committee representing the Seattle Central Labor Council, the State Federation of Labor, and the Triple Alliance met with the president on a Sunday afternoon and presented a memorandum which included this:

> That there is a fundamental unrest among the workers of the United States is admitted by you, Mr. President .... The purpose of this meeting, as you admit, is to try to reach some conclusions as to a remedy for this unrest. ... Suppression and the methods employed under the emergency war measures, coupled with the inhuman and brutal treatment of those convicted and imprisoned . . . is a cause of the extreme bitterness expressed by the workers in their demonstration of unrest.[8]

The delegation told the president that many workers had been thrown into prison when their only offense was insistence on rights guaranteed them by the Constitution. The memorandum charged:

> During the war, the lumbermen of this state, in our nation's hour of need, attempted to raise the price of spruce from $40 to nearly $200 a thousand feet. They defied the President, the National Council of Defense, the State Council of Defense, the governor of the state, the public sentiment throughout the whole nation in their attitude upon the basic eight-hour work day and this very materially and effectively prevented the utmost efficiency in the war. We ask how long it will be before you, Mr. President, will use the power invested in you to grant amnesty to political prisoners. . . .[9]

The union men asked the president why the government was prosecuting "political prisoners" while failing to prosecute war profiteers. Wilson's responses to the group were not reported, since the meeting was closed, but news accounts did say he appealed for peaceable resolutions of labor's problems in the Northwest after hearing that a nationwide general strike in sympathy for the imprisoned Thomas Mooney was being planned.

By the end of summer, 1919, fifteen months had gone by since Centralia businessmen raided and demolished the local IWW hall on First Street. That raid turned out to be a successful repression. The focal point of IWW activities in Lewis County was eliminated and the members were scattered. It did not mean that there were fewer Wobblies in the area, only that they were not in evidence. They had no hall.

The new syndicalism law made it risky to hold open meetings, although going to jail was no disgrace for a Wobbly, and those who had been around for a while were used to being taunted, cursed, and even beaten. They felt nothing was to be gained by deliberately inviting more repressive actions.

Because of its industries and location, Centralia was something of a labor center in 1919. Seventeen unions made up the Central Trades Council, which had an estimated three thousand members. The Council felt sufficiently prosperous to announce in July that a thirty-thousand-dollar Labor Temple would be built.

The *Chronicle,* though antiunion editorially, saw fit to launch a weekly labor page which even carried news of a labor convention in Great Falls, Montana, attended by IWW delegates, where demands were made for withdrawal of troops from Russia and for recognition of the Soviet government. This convention was described as the launching of the "one big union" movement in America.

The Wobblies felt that they should not be pariahs indefinitely in a town otherwise so hospitable to organized labor. The other unions were building a temple. Perhaps the time had come when they could have a hall. The local Wobblies, the ones in Lewis County, were particularly eager to try again to establish a headquarters. They were not homeless wanderers like so many of the old bindle stiffs. Many were men who were born in the county, grew up admiring strong men who wore caulked boots, and took to the woods themselves in their teens, not aware that the camp conditions were poor, the pay low, and the bosses all tyrants until they read the IWW literature and listened to the older men, adept at complaining, tell about the bright future for workers when their day would come.

One of these was Britt Smith, born in Bucoda, a sawmill village beside the Northern Pacific tracks a few miles from Centralia. A round-faced, auburn-haired man of medium height, described in records of the law later as "sober, honest and reasonably industrious," he became a convert to radical theories and grew more radical as time went on. After two decades in the woods, living as loggers had to live, he was ready for the reforms that only the IWW was struggling for. He told Anna Louise Strong, gathering material as "Anise" for her blank verse sketches in the *Seattle Union Record*, "I have slept weeks at a time in wet clothes, working all day in the rain without any place to dry out. I have washed my clothes by tying them to a stake in the river, letting the current beat them partly clean. It was often the only place we had for washing."

Britt Smith, single and a firebrand Wobbly, was a logical selection as the local leader. He was named secretary and put in charge of organizing, collecting dues, and, very important, opening a hall that could be kept open, if that were possible. Smith was aware that employer hostility had not subsided. He read the newspaper reports about the Chamber of Commerce meeting on June 28 when, at the urging of George F. Russell, secretary of the Employers Association of Washington, F. W. Hubbard was authorized to form a local organization to deal with the radical labor element. But nothing more appeared in the paper about this move during the summer and in late August Smith set out to find space he could rent for a hall. It could not be in the main business district, of course, but should be near the railroad tracks, handy for traveling fellow workers. It needed to be large enough for sizable meetings and to provide the secretary with living quarters. Also the rent had to be cheap.

Far out North Tower were a cluster of the kind of hotels to be found near the railroad in most Western towns — two stories, false fronts, flush up against the sidewalk, with sleeping rooms just large enough for a bed, washstand, and chair. Loggers, making as much as three dollars a day, were among the main patrons of such hotels when they came to town on weekends or were between jobs because they had walked off or been fired. On North Tower were the Avalon, the Arnold, the Michigan House, and the Roderick, all close together near the corner of Tower and Second. The Roderick had a canopy extending over the side-

walk at the second-floor level, supported by turned posts. The hotel was fifty feet wide and had store space on the ground floor to rent. It consisted of a space sixteen feet wide and seventy feet deep, running from the sidewalk to the alley.

The Roderick was owned by Mr. and Mrs. James McAllister but operated by Mrs. McAllister, a strong-minded woman whose judgment her compliant husband did not question, and who had enough loggers among her patrons to have heard the Wobbly story frequently. She was sympathetic enough to take a chance and rented the vacant space in her building to Britt Smith on September 1. He moved in promptly.

A partition divided the long room about equally. The front thirty-five feet was the hall. The back part was Smith's living quarters. The hall was furnished with several benches and chairs, a table, a rolltop desk, and some bookshelves. It was heated by a stove. The space was intended for use as a shop and had tall display windows in the front and a double door recessed two feet. Well established in his new headquarters, Smith implanted a large IWW sign in the window and hoped for the best. This time, on the third attempt, a Wobbly hall in Centralia might survive.

September 1 was Labor Day in 1919 and the numerous AFL unions, eager for a show of strength, made the most of it. They staged what the press described as the "biggest parade ever held in Centralia." The teamsters, timber workers, coal miners, barbers, printers, carpenters, retail clerks, and railroad brotherhoods — but not the IWW — marched amid floats and bands. "It was Labor's Day," said the papers, "and Labor once more put Centralia on the map as a city of hospitality." Britt Smith could see some fellow workers marching in the parade. Some Wobblies were not above carrying two union cards.

Warren Grimm was considered an authority on the Russian revolution after his year of service in Siberia and was invited to make the Labor Day speech. He described what the Bolsheviks were doing in the Soviet Union and warned that America should be on guard against a similar threat from within — the Industrial Workers of the World.

Several days later when Elmer Smith went to Grimm's office on legal business, Grimm asked him what he thought of his speech. Smith replied that he thought it was "rotten" and did not agree with Grimm's antiunion utterances or his comparison of the IWW with the Bolsheviks. Smith reminded Grimm of the way Tom Lassiter had been handled, saying it was an example of the kind of "Americanism" he considered disgraceful. Grimm disagreed and defended the treatment given Lassiter.

Two days after the Labor Day festivities the *Chronicle* took note of what had taken place on North Tower. On its front page appeared this:

WOBBLIES RENT LOCAL BUILDING

Indications are that Centralia will again be headquarters for the Industrial Workers of the World who have secured a structure on North Tower as a meeting place.

The *Chronicle* went on to report, it being nothing for the city to be ashamed of, what had happened to the last IWW headquarters on First Street: "It was raided by citizens two years ago, the furnishings being piled in the street and burned."

In the next few weeks not much was said openly about the opening of the hall, much as it was taken to be an affront to a city that had made it completely clear on previous occasions that the IWW would not be tolerated in Centralia. Britt Smith and the other local Wobblies felt encouraged.

10

Appeals in Vain

The opening, for the third time, of an IWW hall was more than Centralia businessmen could bear. With that hated sign in the window —IWW — the Wobblies seemed to be flaunting their return, demonstrating that their presence was legitimate despite all that had gone before. They were being defiant. Something had to be done.

The logical person to do something was John Berry, sheriff. He agreed that a city with an impressive war record like Centralia's had to regard the presence of an IWW headquarters as a blemish that ought to be removed — but only by legal means. He opposed vigilante justice.

John Berry was almost a native of Lewis County. His parents took him there as a child in 1889, the year of statehood. He grew up to be a man of the law, serving first on the Chehalis police force. He married the principal of the state girls' reformatory school at nearby Grand Mound and was elected sheriff in 1912 and again in 1916.

The sheriff belonged to the Elks, like nearly everyone of any standing in the area, and listened with some alarm when friends in the lodge reported that something was going on. Meetings were being held in the club to discuss ways to close the IWW hall. The prosecuting attorney himself, Herman Allen, was attending these meetings, Berry was told, so he went to him. No need for anything underhanded, Berry said. Just issue a complaint declaring the hall a nuisance and in violation of the law in some way, and he would take some deputies and run the men out, knock down the sign in the window, and lock the doors.

Allen wasn't interested. He told Berry he didn't have the authority to do anything like that. The sheriff knew better and went to the state attorney general to confirm what he knew. Still Allen refused to act.

Berry, still hoping to avoid trouble, then appealed to the county commissioners. Would they appoint a special prosecutor to do what Allen would not? The commissioners told him just what Allen had — that they didn't have such authority. Again Berry appealed to the attorney general and was informed that the commissioners could, if they wanted to, do just what he suggested. But they would not. "Johnny, you are unduly alarmed," the commission's chairman said to the sheriff.[1]

On October 1 the secret meetings culminated in what was virtually an open meeting in the Elks hall. Next day the *Chronicle* reported it:

ORGANIZATION TO COMBAT IWW

About 100 citizens, the majority of them businessmen, met last night and organized the Centralia Citizens Protective Assn. The purpose of the organization is to combat IWW activities in this vicinity. The membership is open to all citizens desiring to see law and order maintained.[2]

However, if the local Wobblies felt intimidated by a public warning that those who ran the town were out to get them, it was not evident a week later when they distributed handbills calling for all workers to join in a one-day general strike to protest the continued imprisonment of Tom Mooney in California and class-war prisoners everywhere.

This provocative action caused the *Chronicle* to snort indignantly, "In the name of high heaven what is Mooney to us or we to Mooney that we should stop production for even one day in sympathy for his predicament?"[3]

The organizers of the Citizens Association, seeking an ally, approached the Legion. The Legion's patriotism certainly equaled that of the Elks and the Legion nationally had taken a strong stand against all radicals, including the IWW. The Grant Hodge post, having no

Eugene Barnett, convicted as the one who fired the shot that killed Warren Grimm after witnesses, who saw him in the lobby of the Avalon Hotel during the shooting, did not testify at the trial.

hall of its own, met in the Elks hall or the Chamber of Commerce office and its members were well aware of the discussions about the local Wobblies. The Legionnaires agreed that the hall was undesirable, but it was not their responsibility to take action against it.

Seeking more public support, the chief organizers of the Protective Association — Hubbard, Scales, and Livingstone — called another meeting that was to be open to anyone who wanted to join. Notices of the meeting, to be held on October 20 in the Elks hall, were widely circulated.

On the evening of that day an estimated 125 men climbed the stairs to the third-floor hall. Hubbard, as the holdover chairman of the original group formed in June, presided. No time was wasted on speeches denouncing the IWW. The speeches were concerned

with tactics. Sheriff Berry had not been quiet about his frustrations with the county commissioners and the prosecutor. One of the commissioners was present and he was asked directly why legal action couldn't be taken against the hall. His excuse was the same: lack of legal authority. Police Chief Hughes also claimed to be helpless. He said the city and county attorneys told him there was no law to prevent the IWW from maintaining a hall in Centralia.

Hubbard, the seventy-three-year-old mill operator, was enraged by all of this. If he were the police chief, he shouted, the Wobblies would be gotten rid of soon enough.

The only written account of this meeting by someone present is in an affadavit made by D. E. Burrell in 1923. He was an employee of the Lincoln Creek Lumber Company at Galvin, four miles from Centralia. He was asked by his foreman, Bob De Haven, to represent him in Centralia. Burrell quoted the vigilante call for action that he heard: "The only way to handle the IWWs in Centralia is to do the same thing done in Aberdeen. Clean 'em up, burn 'em out." This, he said, brought an outburst of clapping and shouts of approval.[4]

Despite the inflammatory speeches at the end, the meeting did not prompt immediate action against the IWW hall. Instead two committees were appointed. One was to draft an ordinance that might get around the apparent legal obstacles. The other was to look for alternative solutions. It was chaired by Warren Grimm, assisted by William Scales and F. B. Hubbard.[5]

At the October 20 meeting the gathering also elected permanent officers for the Protective Association: Dr. Livingstone, president; Scales, vice-president; James Jenkins, secretary; and Hubbard, treasurer. Livingstone at that time was also the commander of the new Legion post. Two weeks later he resigned and Grimm was elected post commander. Scales was the chief organizer of the post.

The *Union Record*'s report of the October 20 meeting said Scales openly advocated direct action against the IWW hall, "declaring he did not believe any jury would find those taking part in a raid on the hall guilty of violating the law."[6]

The *Chronicle*'s two-paragraph report of the meeting included the news that "several plans for ridding the city of the radicals were advanced . . . the city authorities being censured for allowing the IWW headquarters to remain open. A committee was appointed . . . which, it is believed, will be effective in obtaining the ends desired."[7]

The Centralians felt righteous about the strong stand they were taking when newspapers applauded them. The *Tacoma News-Tribune* commented:

At Centralia a committee of citizens has been formed that takes the mind back to the old days of vigilance committees of the West, which did so much to force law abiding citizenship upon certain lawless elements. It is called the Centralia Protective Association and its object is to combat IWW activities. . . . It is high time for the people who do believe in the lawful and orderly conduct of affairs to take the upper hand. . . . Every city and town might, with profit, follow Centralia's example.[8]

The *Hub* added its bit, saying that if the city were left open to the Wobbly menace, it would soon be at the mercy of an organized band of outlaws bent on destruction. Then it asked the question, "What are we going to do about it?"

Whatever was planned to do about it was kept secret, but when the Legion announced plans for an observance of the first anniversary of the armistice, which would, of course, include a parade, Centralians remembered that it was from the ranks of a parade that raiders came to destroy the IWW hall in May 1918.

The ordinance proposed at the citizens' meeting was not submitted, if ever one was drafted. Officialdom in Lewis County, except for the sheriff, was plainly unwilling to take action. They were aware of the new laws. One specifically made it illegal for any property owner to allow persons who professed beliefs like those of the IWW to use their property. It could have been applied to the McAllisters, owners of the Roderick, and the Wobblies themselves could have been charged under the syndicalism law. These recourses may not have been given serious consideration because the conviction record under the new laws was proving to be poor. In case after case charges brought against men merely for belonging to the IWW either were dismissed or disproved in court, usually with George Vanderveer acting as the defense attorney. At the end of October Vanderveer boasted that not a single Wobbly was in custody in Washington, Idaho, or Montana as a result of the syndicalism laws. In Seattle the IWW was even successful in obtaining an injunction to prevent the mayor from using the syndicalism

law to close its hall.

Despite all this, the helplessness professed by local officials in Centralia, especially in an open meeting where vigilante action was openly discussed, leads to the conclusion that the officials actually preferred to have the Wobblies dealt with in the harsh ways always used by hall raiders and were deliberately standing aside so that such action could be taken.

Sheriff Berry was removed from the scene at this crucial time by an unexpected event. A young Negro committed a murder in a southern Lewis County community made up mostly of families from the hill country of the deep South. He fled to California where he was promptly apprehended. Berry heard about a plot. When the train bringing back the killer passed through the town of Toledo, the murder victim's neighbors would force it to stop, seize the black man, and hang him. Things like that were common where they came from. Berry wanted no lynchings in his county, so he hurried to California to escort the prisoner and was delayed so long by extradition proceedings that he did not arrive back in Centralia until after November 11.

As the press reported, any plans made by the Citizens Association were to be kept secret. There were no more open meetings and no more news stories about the activities of the association after October 21. That something was in the wind, however, was plain enough and the wind brought it to the ears of the Wobblies. In his account of the Centralia affair, Ralph Chaplin wrote that "Chief of Police Hughes told a member of the Lewis County Trades Council, William T. Merriman, that the businessmen were organizing to raid the hall and drive the members out of town. Merriman in turn carried the statement to many of his friends and brother unionists. Soon the prospective raid was the subject of open discussion. . . ."[9]

William Dunning, a member of the Trades Union Council, knew Grimm well enough to ask if he knew about the rumors that a raid was being planned. Dunning reported, "I told him the Trades Council had discussed it and we would like to know if he knew anything about it."[10] Grimm then asked him if he were a member of the IWW. Dunning said no. Then Grimm, in a brief discussion, told Dunning he considered the IWW and the Bolsheviki to be one and the same.[11]

Grimm, Livingstone, and Kresky were the Legion committee that went to the city commission with a proposal for a celebration of the armistice. They asked that a half holiday be declared. The request was given immediate and enthusiastic approval. The program, the Legionnaires announced, would include a patriotic parade in the afternoon, a banquet at the Chamber of Commerce in the evening, and a dance at the auditorium afterward.

When the Legion post met in the Elks hall two days later to make final plans, the possibility of a raid had become a common topic of casual conversation around town, and in the hall at the Roderick it was one of intense and frequent discussion.

Britt Smith was the acknowledged leader, but there were others as loyal to the IWW cause as he and as determined not to be intimidated by threats of mob action. Most were young. James McInerney, who was on the *Verona* the day of the dockside battle in Everett, was one of the oldest. He was thirty-five.

What could they do? the Wobblies kept asking themselves. The Legion and the businessmen and the Elks were as one against them, plotting something. They could give up — close the hall and try to get along without a place to meet. But that would be cowardly. It would amount to surrender. What were the other alternatives? Someone, and it may have been the Wobblies' only friend among lawyers in town, Elmer Smith, suggested an appeal to the people. Surely everyone did not share the animosity of the businessmen. Some could see the injustice of what was being proposed. Fair-minded people, properly informed, might intervene. The idea was accepted.

The appeal took the form of a lengthy statement, hurriedly printed as a leaflet in Tacoma and distributed door to door throughout the city. In this appeal the Wobblies could not bring themselves to use restraint and avoid the inflammatory adjectives and accusations that were characteristic of IWW literature, always considered offensive by those who assumed it was they at whom the accusers were pointing.

Centralians read that the "profiteering class in the city" was plotting to raid the hall. "The bankrupt lumber barons" wanted to do what they had done before in 1918. "Criminal thugs," "mobocrats," "pilfering thieves," and "patriotic profiteers" were making false charges. IWW members who "fought and bled for democracy they never secured" came home "to be threatened with mob violence by the law and order outfit that pilfered every nickel possible from their mothers and fathers while they were fighting in the trenches. . . . "[12]

The Wobblies could not restrain their rage. The leaflet accused the "profiteers" of holding secret meetings and "covertly inviting returned service men to do their bidding. They say we are a menace, and we are a menace to all mobocrats and pilfering thieves. Never did the IWW burn public or private halls, kidnap their fellow citizens, destroy their property, club their fellows out of town, bootleg or act in any way as law breakers. . . . Our only crime is solidarity, loyalty to the working class, and justice to the oppressed."[13]

Centralians read the leaflet, shook their heads in dismay and disapproval, and did nothing. This attitude puzzled some of the younger men at the hall. They didn't understand the depth of small-city abhorrence of radicalism. Some hadn't been around long enough. Sometimes men would check in at the hall, leave for a job, and not be back for months, or never come back. The IWW at all levels was loosely organized and its membership fluid. Members were not tied firmly to a local unit like members of a craft union. They came and went. When a dues stamp was pasted in a Wobbly's book, it signified his good standing wherever he was. Some of those on hand during the crisis in Centralia just happened to be there. Not all were even well known to one another.

A few — the local ones — were old friends. There was Mike Sheehan, at sixty-four the oldest Wobbly in town by at least twenty-five years. He boasted that he had been a union man for fifty years because he was allowed to join the butchers' union his father belonged to in Ireland when he was only eight. Unions became his life after he became a leader in the famous tri-city strike in Limerick, Waterford, and Cork in the '80s and was blacklisted afterward in so many places he joined the exodus of the Irish to America. Here he worked at a variety of occupations across the country before settling down in Centralia. John Lamb, forty-two years old, was another of the local Wobblies who had lived long in Lewis County and endured the hard life as a logger until he found he could make a living selling pills, salves, and various home remedies door to door. One of his five children, Dewey, joined the IWW, like his dad, but after arguments with him about the radical nature of the organization decided in September to drop out.

Two others — brothers widely separated in age — were Bert and Commodore Bland. Commodore, who was forty-three and who often went by his initials, O.C., had been married since 1903 and now supported a family of seven, the oldest sixteen and the youngest two, by working as a logger. He moved from one camp to another when the situation in one could no longer be endured or when another seemed to offer something better or at least different, able to go home only at the end of a shift on a Saturday. After joining the IWW he became a recruiter and an organizing activist.

One of those he recruited was his brother Bert, nineteen, a logger since he was sixteen. Bert commonly was called "Curly" because of his wavy hair. "Fourteen of us slept in a ten-by-fourteen bunkhouse over in Raymond," Commodore told Anna Louise Strong, "with our wet clothes steaming in the middle of the shack. The bad conditions drove me from camp to camp — twenty-two different ones in a single year — and only one of them had a bath."

An occasional visitor in the hall was Eugene Barnett, who lived with his wife and one child in a small house near the Monarch coal mine in the Kopiah district where the Smith family had its homestead holdings. His employer described him in later years as an industrious employee who "always mined a good grade of coal and kept his place well timbered and his track in good condition."[14]

Barnett's childhood was as unfortunate as those of the men who came from Ireland. Born in the hill country of North Carolina, his schooling was limited to one three-month and one five-month term. His mother taught him to read and write. When he was eight, his father hired out as a strikebreaker and he never forgot the plight of the strikers, camped along a river after being driven from their company-owned homes. He was put to work in the mines where he hid from inspectors because the minimum legal age for miners was fourteen. He ran away at eleven, became a regular miner, and by the time he was sixteen had worked eight years underground.

Barnett was a good-looking youth. Somehow, he told Anna Louise Strong, he was able to get a good-looking wife who encouraged him to "improve himself." They went to Idaho where he proved up on a homestead. During the war, when the government called for miners, Barnett responded and went to Centralia where he listened with enthusiasm to an IWW organizer who described the better life workers could expect once the one big union prevailed.

Centralia's largest building, on the top floor of which was the Elks Club, where meetings were held to discuss what could be done to rid the city of Wobblies.

Another native of the area who grew up to become a Wobbly was a heavyset, twenty-year-old blond Swede known only as "Ole" Hansen. He was a good enough fighter to gain some recognition as a semiprofessional boxer. He was described by his companions, after his ultimate disappearance, as a quiet, pleasant youth who loved the outdoors and was a good shot with his .22-caliber rifle. He showed his IWW card with considerable pride and tried to get others to join.[15]

One of the ex-servicemen in town at the time was Bert Faulkner, twenty-one, who went to school with Warren Grimm, Arthur McElfresh, and others who went in the service. He could have been one of those planning the parade rather than the defense of the IWW hall, since he was an ex-soldier too, but he was a Wobbly — and had been since 1917.

Loren Roberts was one of the youngest local converts to IWWism. The Roberts family lived in Grand Mound, a rural settlement just north of Centralia, and when the father died Loren felt obligated to leave school and begin work as a logger. Roberts's lifelong interest in guns stemmed from the several rifles and revolvers left by his father. It was a long walk from Grand Mound to Tower Avenue, but Roberts showed up frequently at the new hall and acquired a nickname: "Grand Mound."

Many besides the local members — the typical Wobbly transients — visited the hall in the tense days leading up to November 11 and listened to the anxious speculation about a raid. One of these was a reserved, intense man of twenty-seven who took up residence in a rooming house near the hall but kept a small set of law books in the hall.[16] He was Wesley Everest, a logger and sawmill worker since he was seventeen. He was a native of Newburg, Oregon, where his grandfather, David Everest, took out a donation land claim in 1850 after coming west in a wagon train that arrived at the Whitman mission site shortly after the Indian uprising. He helped move the remains of the Whitman massacre victims to permanent graves.

Wesley, the third-oldest of seven children, was fourteen in 1904 when a startled horse, pulling a buggy in which he and his mother were riding, set off at a frenzied gallop, overturning the buggy. Mrs. Everest was fatally injured. The father had died two years previously so the seven orphans were parceled out to relatives. Wesley was sent to a great-aunt, Mrs. O. B. Westfall. She and her husband operated a dairy farm near Portland. Nothing is known of his experiences there, but when he was seventeen the pay rate for loggers, $1.84 for the standard ten-hour day, was enough to lure him away from the farm.

He was soon recruited into the ranks of the IWW, embracing that organization's philosophy so enthusiastically that he became an organizer, sent into logging towns to recruit more members. In 1914 he was in Coos County on the coast of Oregon and was caught up in a vigilante purge of local labor activists and deported along with others by an antiunion committee backed by over two hundred persons from the business community.

In 1917 Everest was drafted and, because he was a logger, assigned to help man the new sawmills of the Spruce Division at Vancouver Barracks. The "sprucers," as they were called, were not all convinced, as their officers frequently told them, that getting out straight-grained wood to build airplanes was just as ennobling as fighting with guns in France. They were paid more than foot soldiers — regular civilian pay less army pay — but there was considerable dissension.

Everest, embittered by his treatment at the hands of vigilantes in the Coos Bay region, was so radicalized by the time he was inducted into the army that he could not bring himself even to salute the flag and as a consequence spent considerable time in the stockade that served as a guardhouse.[17] In the mornings Everest would be let out of the stockade at reveille when the flag was raised. Everest would refuse to salute whereupon he would be marched back to the stockade for

another day. When it rained, or when the men were away from camp, there was no flag to be saluted and Everest worked as he was supposed to, but he worked also at recruiting members for the IWW.[18]

Everest took more interest than most of the others in the rumblings about a raid on the hall. He probably attended a meeting held in the Elks hall in mid-October. C. D. Cunningham saw him coming down the stairs after such a meeting.[19] He was eligible for Legion membership and may have looked in on a Legion meeting, but in any event he could have listened, in the bar or elsewhere, long enough to have gotten the news —the raid was to come off on the day of the armistice celebration.

As the day neared, Mrs. McAllister, owner of the Roderick and landlady to the IWW, learning that the parade would pass her place, decided that it was time to make her own appeal for help. She went to Chief Hughes and asked how he intended to protect her property if the Legion or any others raided the hall. The chief was not very reassuring. He promised to do the best he could but said that if the businessmen came after the Wobblies, they wouldn't last fifteen minutes. He told her the businessmen just didn't want any Wobblies in Centralia.

Lack of any sympathetic response to his pamphleteering appeal to the public and rejection by public officials of any alternatives to vigilante action led Britt Smith to conclude that if anything at all were to be done to save the hall, it was up to the Wobblies themselves to do it. He went to Elmer Smith. If they decided to defend the hall, he asked, would it be legal? Or could they all be arrested under some law they didn't know about? The advice Elmer Smith gave was essentially accurate. Property owners have the right to defend against those who threaten to destroy it, just as a person has the right to defend himself against any danger. There was nothing legal about mob action. Certainly a body of men could defend what was theirs against those who would steal or destroy it. Britt Smith went back to the hall and reported this.

Loren Roberts also consulted Smith. In late October, when he was out delivering IWW handbills, he went to Smith's office and asked if it was really true that they could defend their hall. Roberts later said of the conversation with Smith, "He said in case the building was raided, if they broke down the door, it was just like a man's home. If someone comes into your home and

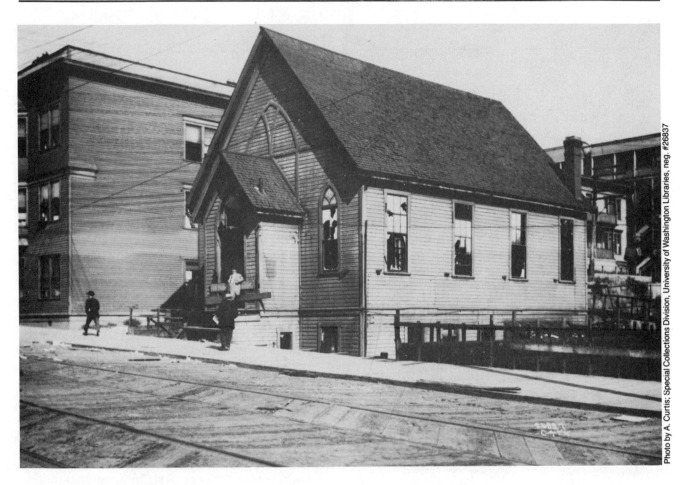

Photo by A. Curtis; Special Collections Division, University of Washington Libraries, neg. #26837

breaks in the door you have a right to shoot."[20]

What followed, based on this legal advice, was the best defense plan a group of fellow workers could devise, desperately hoping this time to survive another onslaught.

When he was in prison, Ralph Chaplin, the talented Wobbly artist, poet, and journalist, made friends with a fellow prisoner, a military aviator he identified only as "Captain Eddy." In long discussions he recited to Eddy the history of the IWW and what it had done and was trying to do. He explained how it was that the IWW leaders, including himself, were in prison. Captain Eddy thought about this, then concluded, "The Wobblies seem to have plenty of guts but no brains."[21]

Short on education might have been a fairer statement. Few working men of that era had much schooling, usually because of the necessity to begin working for wages as soon as they were physically able, or because schools were scarce and not regarded as

Wobblies held forth in this former church building in Seattle until it was raided, as IWW halls frequently were in the decade from 1910 to 1920.

particularly important by parents who themselves had little chance to go to school.

Only one of the Centralia Wobblies had more than a few grades of formal schooling and on November 11 he had been in town only two days, hardly long enough to comprehend fully what was going on.

He was Ray Becker, a young logger who arrived in Centralia from Raymond on about November 9. No evidence has been found that Becker, the educated one, found enough flaws in the defense plans to raise any objection to the decision finally arrived at, which was one Captain Eddy might have said confirmed his judgment — to defend the hall with arms and not make it known that they were going to do so.

11

Prelude to Tragedy

The celebration of the first Armistice Day in Centralia was planned only four days in advance. Members of the Grant Hodge post met in the Elks hall on November 7 and decided it would be "strictly a military day." They agreed to wear their uniforms. Everyone who had an American flag was to display it. And of course there would be a parade followed by a patriotic program.

Other Legion posts were invited to participate. Chehalis promised to send a hundred or more men, all in uniform. The line of march would be led by the Elks band followed by the Mexican border veterans, Spanish-American War veterans, Boy Scouts, Red Cross, Salvation Army, Elks lodges of both Centralia and Chehalis, and any others who wanted to march and show their patriotism. The Chehalis and Centralia Legionnaires would be the last of the marching groups. The parade route was north on Tower to Third Street, then back the same way to the high school, where H. E. Veness, described as a "speaker of rare ability," was to give an oration. A reviewing stand would be set up in front of the Holly-Mar store where men of the Grand Army of the Republic (Civil War veterans), too old to march, would sit.

The edition of the *Chronicle* reporting these parade plans contained an editorial quoting a ringing resolution adopted at the recent Elks national convention pledging "all lawful means to combat the IWW and kindred organizations." But lawful means were lacking in Centralia, or so city and county officials decided. There remained another way, used before in Centralia when action was called for and good men with right on their side were willing to act.

Raids on IWW halls in the Northwest were so numerous and effective that by the fall of 1919 few were left. In the war on Wobblies the opening of a hall in Centralia was regarded as a setback and so it was a surprise to no one, including the IWW, when plans to do something about it were openly discussed and reported. Unless law officers intervened, a raid was sure to come. It was only a question of when.

Raids were easy. No weapons were necessary. Raiders simply kicked in the door if it was locked, pushed any Wobblies on hand out into the street, then took everything that could be lifted and burned or smashed it. With a small hall like the one on Tower Avenue a raid could be over in minutes.

But when should it take place? The mass of testimony that resulted from the events of November 11 contained nothing to substantiate a belief that a raid was actually planned for Armistice Day. Yet the fact that the parade route was unprecedentedly long — all the way to Third Street before turning around, a route which would cause the parade to go past the IWW hall, located between Second and Third, going and coming — was often cited as evidence that Legionnaires decided in advance that a quick raid on the hall could be accomplished as a part of the patriotic events of Armistice Day. Parades in prior years had turned at First Street.

None but the most angry IWW writers actually charged that the Legion or the Elks as organizations plotted action against the Wobblies in Centralia. But in any planning that was done, Legion leaders were in the forefront. Dr. Livingstone, the Legion commander, was the chairman of the Citizens Protective Association and held the office of leading knight in the Elks lodge. Warren Grimm, who succeeded Livingstone as commander of the Legion post, was a committee chairman in the protective association. Leslie Hughes, the police chief, was chaplain of the Legion, and C. D. Cunningham was historian.

One who was sure the Legion as a body did not plot against the IWW in Centralia was Hollis Fultz, an

Olympia writer, Chamber of Commerce secretary, and politician who described what he saw and heard on November 11 in a history of the Olympia Elks lodge. Fultz wrote that after the war no one "took up the fight against this seditious organization (the IWW) more strongly than the Elks. And in no state was their help more needed than in Washington."[1] Fultz said he worked closely with Livingstone in Elks affairs and was convinced that the Legion did not plan in advance to raid the hall.

But as the day approached what anyone might be planning could not be made known. It would have been no more reasonable to announce that a raid on the hall was not planned than for a law-abiding person to declare that he was not going to commit a crime. One story, often told later, is that the matter of a raid was discussed when the Legionnaires assembled in the park just before the parade started and that a majority voted against it.

As November 11 approached, the Wobblies listened for some assurances that their hall would be left alone. They heard none. When their landlady, Mrs. McAllister, returned from a meeting with the police chief and told Britt Smith what he said, it was clear that the law was not going to provide any protection. If a mob attacked, the Wobblies would have to provide their own defense, if there was to be any.

As Armistice Day neared, the men discussed their plight, and their courage improved. They convinced themselves that the hall had to be defended. To abandon it or allow a mob to destroy it while they stood by and watched helplessly was not an alternative that appealed at all to men who were used to danger on the job, in the woods, and in the streets during strikes or demonstrations. Furthermore they felt challenged. The protective association, with its bold meetings reported in the press, seemed to be announcing its intentions to make an assault.

The Wobblies did plan a defense after a fashion. Four of their number explained this later, in statements that they were induced to make before a defense lawyer could warn them against saying anything that would support a charge that they had conspired in a diabolical plot to ambush and kill ex-soldiers as they marched past the hall. These four were Loren Roberts, Tom Morgan, Britt Smith, and Dewey Lamb, all too young or inexperienced to be aware of their legal rights when brought into the presence of the sheriff, the

Wesley Everest in uniform during World War I. He served in the Spruce Production Division at Vancouver.

Washington State Historical Society

prosecutor, and the police chief, and questioned with a stenographer taking down every word.

On Saturday night, two days before the armistice celebration, the Wobblies gathered in their hall to talk about what they were going to do. According to Roberts, Wesley Everest was the one who talked the most about a raid and seemed more wrought up about it than any of the others. Roberts said Everest "was the only desperate man in the bunch because he was a man who didn't give a damn. He was the only man there I believe of (that) disposition. He didn't give a damn whether he got killed or not."[2] When he questioned Roberts, Cunningham asked whether Everest had told the men in the hall that he attended a meeting of citizens in the Elks club three weeks previously. Roberts said no. What he did say, Roberts related, was, "When those fellows come they will come prepared to clean us out and this building will be honeycombed with bullets inside of ten minutes."[3] Britt Smith agreed. When the raid comes, he said, "there will be hell to pay on both sides."[4]

The excitement and apprehension generated by what was expected did not interfere with a scheduled gathering in the hall the next night, Sunday, when a general meeting, open to all, was held to hear John Foss, a unionist from Seattle, make an appeal for funds to help defend class-war prisoners. A "propaganda meeting" was the way it was described by James McInerney, who helped sell IWW literature — *The Revolution of Democracy, The Red Dawn,* and *Onward Sweep of the Machine Process* — to those who attended. An estimated one hundred persons were present, many of them not Wobblies.

After the meeting those who remained talked again about defense of the hall. The mob would come armed, Everest warned. They would be helpless if they didn't have guns themselves. It was no longer a question of whether the hall would be defended but how it was to be done.

They talked about guns. Who had guns? Britt Smith had a revolver. He had to keep cash on hand, he explained, and needed a gun in case of a burglary attempt. Loren Roberts had guns at home he could bring. Ray Becker had a pistol he bought in Raymond just before coming to Centralia. Wesley Everest had a .38-caliber automatic pistol. Some others had rifles.

No mention was made of an attempt to forestall a raid by issuing a warning that if raiders dared attack they would be fired on. Wobblies in a Wisconsin city had issued such a warning when they heard a raid was coming and as a consequence the raid hadn't taken place. Nor were detailed plans made for defending the hall. Strategy, what little there was, seemed to have originated with Everest and Britt Smith. But they had no authority to issue orders.

The hall itself was wedged between the Roderick Hotel lobby on one side and a variety store on the other. In a raid the attack likely would come from Tower Avenue rather than the alley. But a raid by men charging out from the ranks of the paraders was not what Everest, Elmer Smith, and others were led to expect. According to Tom Morgan, a raid was expected on Armistice Day, but the Wobblies thought it would be after the celebration events were over, probably after dark. "This here thing wasn't supposed to take place until after the parade," Morgan told Cunningham, "and after the speaking down there; there was supposed to be a speaking after the parade, if I understand it right."[5]

The way it was foreseen, a bunch of men —probably twenty or more — would come driving up, get out of their cars armed with guns and clubs, and go at the hall. The defense strategy was to catch them in a cross fire. Some defenders would station themselves in upstairs rooms of the rooming houses in the neighborhood where they could get a clear shot at anyone attacking the hall from the front. Just across Tower was the small Arnold rooming house with two second-floor windows facing the street. In the next block south, across Tower and next to the stable on the corner, was the larger Avalon Hotel with three windows on the second floor. North on Tower was the Queen rooming house.

The Arnold and the Avalon were the closest. Men hidden on their upper floors could pick off attackers like pioneers defending a stockade in an Indian raid. When it was over there might be some dead men in the street, but the hall would be intact and if the defenders were arrested they could plead self-defense, which was their right as Elmer Smith had assured them.

Even though a raid was not expected during the parade, it might come then, as it had in 1918 when men broke out of the Red Cross parade to raid the hall. The Wobblies decided they had better be ready when the parade came by.

Monday evening before the celebration Roberts

walked into town from Grand Mound, six miles away, and brought with him a rifle and a pistol. Unlike Everest, he was not in a mood for a fight. He considered backing out, he admitted later, but he was nineteen and this was the most exciting thing he had ever gotten into. He decided to stay.

Roberts remembered seeing Everest, Britt Smith, and McInerney in the hall Monday night and also a stranger named Davis — a large man with a thin, brown mustache. Some called him Jack, but his first name didn't stick firmly in anyone's memory and he went down in the records as "John Doe" Davis. Again Everest and Britt Smith did most of the talking at the Monday night gathering. They were adamant. If the hall was to be defended, they had to do it. A man named Sparks was there, Roberts recalled, and when Ole Hansen asked if he would go along with the defense, Sparks said he "wouldn't have anything to do with it and he was going home." Others counted themselves out, too, and left.

Roberts stayed overnight with Hansen in another neighborhood. "Next morning we started back to town again," Roberts related, "and I was about to back out for fear there would be trouble, but we went into town anyway."[6] At the hall they encountered Bert Faulkner, who knew Grimm and other Legionnaires since he was an ex-serviceman himself. He was reassuring. "You fellows don't need to be afraid of any trouble," Faulkner said.[7]

The stationing of men in upstairs windows was firmly decided on when Elmer Smith came into the hall the morning of the 11th. Britt Smith quoted Elmer as saying, " 'Britt, they are going to raid the hall. What are you going to do about it?' I said that if they started to raid the hall, we were here, and by that I meant we were going to protect the place."[8]

Britt Smith pointed to buildings across the street to show Elmer where men were stationed. The lawyer was in the hall only a few minutes and was heard to remark that he was going home to get his own gun and then go to his office just in case a mob tried to raid it too. In proceedings afterward Elmer Smith was never asked why, when he knew the Wobblies were armed, he did not go to Cunningham, Grimm, or other lawyers who would be marching and warn them.

Britt Smith, who felt responsible for organizing the defense as best he could, undertook to tell the few who had decided to arm themselves what they ought to do. But when he told Roberts to take his rifle and go to one of the upstairs rooms across the street, Roberts, nervous about the whole thing, bristled. No one was going to tell him what to do, he said. At that point he decided to team with Ole Hansen, who had a 250 Savage rifle, and Bert Bland, who had brought a 32-30 Savage. Roberts had his father's old .22-caliber high-power Savage rifle and a Colt revolver which he gave to McInerney. Asked if he heard Barnett say anything about a gun, Roberts replied that he "never heard him say anything about the raid."

It was agreed that the defenders should scatter around the neighborhood and someone suggested it might be well for some to station themselves on Seminary Hill (site of a short-lived Baptist seminary built in 1889) across the railroad tracks to the east, but Commodore Bland said he thought that was too far away.

Bert Bland, Roberts, and Hansen decided that Everest's room in the Queen would provide a good vantage point, but when they went there they found that to cover the hall they would have to lean far out the windows and would be easy targets for anyone firing from the street. Then they decided to go to a spot fifteen hundred feet away on Seminary Hill. It was distant but at least they could get away in a hurry if there were shooting, and not get caught.

Not only did the Wobblies deliberately refrain from letting it be known that they would be ready to shoot any raiders who might show up, they went to some trouble to hide that intention. Davis decided to use Commodore Bland's room in the Avalon and faced the problem of getting there without being seen carrying a rifle. He concealed the gun in his pants leg and started out of the hall, but he had to walk stiff-legged, and when some of the men laughed he came back. He pulled the rifle out, wrapped it in an overcoat, and made it down the street to the Avalon without being asked what he was carrying. Once in Bland's room, he started to examine the borrowed rifle, and it discharged, shooting a hole in the dresser mirror.

Davis reported this disturbing incident to Roberts, Hansen, and Bert Bland, who were having lunch across the street in the Union Cafe. Davis then went back to the Avalon to wait and others went to the hall to say they were going up on the hill. At the hall they asked for advice. When should they fire? Not until they heard shots down on the street, they were told.

Around one o'clock Bland and Hansen picked up a

suitcase containing their rifles at the Union Cafe and went to a place on Seminary Hill where they could get an unobstructed view of the hall. Roberts, carrying a knapsack containing two loaves of bread, crossed the tracks near the depot and went up the hill by another route to join his two companions. They found a hillside hollow where they could lie flat and settled down for what seemed to Roberts like a long wait.

Seven Wobblies chose to stay where the action would be, if there were any — in the hall itself. Four of these were willing to fight with guns if need be. The other three seemed to be unthinking, if not actually innocent, bystanders.

Wesley Everest was the one most ready for a fight. He was not a talkative man, according to the few fellow workers who came to know him, but in discussions about the IWW and the basic rightness of what it was doing, he was as unbending as the tall firs he felled as a logger. The more he heard about plans for a raid and the unwillingness of constituted authority to do anything at all to provide protection against vigilante action, even after it had been virtually announced on the front pages of the local newspapers, the more he brooded about the injustice of the Wobblies' situation, and the more determined he became that this time a stand had to be taken.

It would be dangerous. There could be a fight. Men might die. That did not deter him. In Everest's attitude there must have been some of the bravado that other men who are caught in hazardous situations admire. As Roberts put it, "Everest just didn't give a damn about anything." He had been denied a chance for war action, if indeed he wanted any. After being drafted, he was assigned to spend the entire war as a "sprucer." While others were experiencing the excitement of combat, the "sprucers" were in the woods logging or cutting cants in the government sawmills. Whatever his inner feelings, Everest was the one Wobbly most ready for action.

Beside him in the hall, holding a small revolver, was a relative stranger in town, Ray Becker, the nineteen-year-old minister's son, the rebellious youth who fled from the discipline of divinity school. His destiny, shaped by the events of that day, was to remain angrily defiant and resentful against Centralia and all authority for the rest of his life, most of which was spent in prison. Becker had not been in Centralia long enough to feel the intensity of the anti-Wobbly feeling there.

But he felt threatened by something when, with only a few dollars in his pocket and no job, he bought a revolver in Raymond just before going to Centralia. To stay in the hall and fight, if need be, he decided, was the courageous thing to do.

Tom Morgan, at eighteen the youngest Wobbly, was drawn into the Armistice Day affair by chance. He went to Centralia from Vancouver, Washington, Monday night, slept till nearly noon, and went to breakfast and then to the hall. There he found Britt Smith, McInerney, Becker, Sheehan, and the two Bland brothers talking excitedly about the expected raid. Barnett came in, sat for a few minutes, then left. "There's a guy with a lot of nerve," Morgan heard Smith remark, referring to Barnett.

Morgan saw Elmer Smith come into the hall, confer with Britt Smith briefly, then leave. It was only then, after noon on Tuesday, Morgan later contended, that he heard about the threatened raid.

Britt Smith had to stay in the hall. It was his home. And as the paid secretary of the local IWW unit, he was regarded as the chief of the local Wobblies. He had a revolver — a formidable .32-caliber Colt.

James McInerney was influenced by what he had seen and experienced in Everett. He survived the assault on the *Verona* and had the satisfaction of seeing bullets fell the sheriff and others who put Wobblies through tortures in Beverly Park. The Wobblies came out of that dockside bloodshed with some honor. A jury refused to convict. Now, facing another possible conflict, McInerney was armed with a .32-caliber revolver in a holster with a full ammunition belt, borrowed from Loren Roberts.

Mike Sheehan, the old man of the bunch, might have been willing to join the potential firing line. A rifle was available, but when it was put in his hands, it was so obvious that he didn't understand anything about using it that it was taken away from him.

Bert Faulkner was the seventh man in the hall. He was unarmed. His and Morgan's presence indicated that they, and possibly others, had no clear comprehension of the serious consequences of attempting to defend an IWW hall with gunfire. It hadn't been done before. The *Verona* confrontation did not involve a hall. The issue there was simply whether Wobblies in a body should be allowed to enter the city. The situation in Centralia seemed to be seen in the most simplistic terms: a bunch of men were expected to storm the hall,

just like the time before. But this time the Wobblies were going to show them.

O. C. Bland and John Lamb, two of the older local Wobblies, had homes on the edge of Centralia to the north. Lamb dropped into the hall frequently on his way to and from home and downtown. He heard discussions about defense. "Some of them said they wouldn't stand for them coming in and destroying their stuff without putting up a fight to save it," he told Cunningham on November 15.[9]

Bland and Lamb, walking home after the Sunday night meeting, made their decision. The hall ought to be defended and they would help. They rented a room in the Arnold, almost directly opposite the hall, and went there on Armistice Day. Bland took a rifle. Lamb went unarmed.

Eugene Barnett, who lived eleven miles out in the country, asked his wife to go with him into town the morning of the 11th but she said no. For one thing, a trip to town was a lot of trouble. When she went her husband had to go to the mine, half a mile away, get a push car, load the buckboard on it, hitch up the horse, and then drive the push car along a mile of track to the road. When he went alone, he just threw a saddle on the horse and rode off. He rode into town on the 11th and went to the hall where he heard the excited talk about defense preparations. He was told that Lamb and Bland were in the Arnold Hotel and Jack Davis was in the Avalon. Roberts, "Curly" Bland, and Hansen were up on the hill. Everest, Smith, and Becker had guns and would make a stand right there in the hall. The defense was ready, it seemed, and Barnett, with no gun, decided he did not need to join the defense force, nor to stay in the hall unarmed, like Sheehan, Morgan, and

Seminary Hill, where three Wobbly snipers stationed themselves, can be seen in the distance. This photo was taken at the intersection of Tower and Second streets looking east across the railroad tracks. The building at right was a stable. Next to it was the Avalon Hotel from which the shot that killed Warren Grimm was fired.

Faulkner, just to see what would happen. He could see from next door and that is where he went — to the lobby of the Roderick.

Uptown, the several hundred who were to march in the parade began assembling. It was an ordinary overcast November day, but not drizzling. Dale Hubbard, walking toward the park, passed the home of Ray Edinger, who was the son-in-law of Harry Bras, the outspoken editor of the *Chronicle,* and paused to help seven-year-old John Edinger with his efforts to push a lawn mower. He laughed at the boy, then walked on toward the park.

Ben Casagranda, an enlisted man, had come back from service overseas and opened a shoeshine parlor. He married and was living in an apartment on Center Street. His wife said she wasn't feeling well on November 11 and didn't intend to watch the parade. "You'd better go," her husband said. "This may be the last time you will see me."[10] Then he kissed her goodbye and left. Mrs. Casagranda recalled that "afterward, when I thought over what Ben had said, I became worried and finally decided to go downtown and ask him not to march in the parade. I hurried down Tower but I was too late. The parade was going by and I found that Ben was among the marchers."[11]

Warren Grimm, who would lead the Centralia marchers as the newly elected commander of the Legion post, started for the park with his army overcoat but decided it was too warm and gave it to his wife to take care of until after the parade.

Arthur R. McElfresh, who was a native of Centralia and the only son of Mr. and Mrs. Jess McElfresh, home from the war only six months, put on his uniform, sergeant's stripes on the sleeves, and took his place in the line of march with his Company M companions. He had survived fierce fighting in the Meuse-Argonne in September 1918, and now was embarking on a business career. Prigmore & Sears, who operated drugstores in Centralia, Olympia, and Chehalis, let him become a stockholder and made him manager of the Centralia store.

Adrian Cormier, astride a spirited brown horse, proudly took his position at the head of the Centralia men — the men of company M, the men back from France, the honored Legionnaires who were responsible for the new holiday.

By two o'clock the parade was moving — the band, the Boy Scouts, the color bearers, the Elks wearing their jaunty blue caps, a contingent of ex-marines and sailors, the Chehalis Legionnaires commanded by J. W. Murray, and finally the Centralia unit with Lt. Warren Grimm marching at the head. At the end, behind the Legionnaires, were several open cars carrying nurses, Red Cross workers, and citizens who just wanted to be in the parade.

Most of the spectators stood along the sidewalks in the town's main business section, but in the block where the IWW hall was located, scores of people gathered, on the sidewalks and in cars parked near by. Many remembered the Red Cross parade a year and a half earlier.

John Watt, one of the Centralia contingent, in later years guessed there may have been as many as fifty men in uniform that day who actually were members of the IWW. But if any of them knew the Wobblies had decided to make a stand and had guns ready to defend their hall, they didn't issue any warnings.

The parade moved north on the brick paving of Tower Avenue, the trombones and trumpets in the Elks band blaring away, with Dr. Livingstone, proudly wearing his army uniform, riding a horse as parade marshal. Upstairs in the Avalon, Jack Davis made sure the window would raise and kept his rifle out of sight. In the Arnold, Commodore Bland held his rifle and watched from the edge of a bed. John Lamb had no gun but just being there made him feel that he was a part of the hall's defense.

No Wobblies were among those watching from the sidewalk. The men stayed inside the hall, peering out apprehensively through the large window with the tall IWW lettering on it. The double wood-paneled door of the hall was closed and the lock catch set.

On Seminary Hill Bert Bland, Roberts, and Hansen decided to move a little closer to a place beside a large stump where they could resume a prone position and aim toward the hall, plainly visible past two vacant lots opposite the Roderick. They were uneasy. Shots fired from that distance were likely to be wild. They couldn't know who might be hit. If they shot at anyone in front of the hall, someone inside might be wounded.

On Tower Avenue the Wobblies watched closely as the parade moved north past their hall. Through the window they observed some of the marchers turn and "make faces" at them as they passed. One block north at Third Street, Dr. Livingstone reined his horse around and led the parade back down Tower so that for several minutes the parade was moving in two directions at once in front of the hall. The Wobblies kept particularly close watch on the uniformed veterans at the end of the parade. They marched four abreast, the Chehalis contingent first, then the men from the Centralia post. As they approached the vicinity of the hall, going back toward town center, Commodore Bland turned to Loren Roberts on Seminary Hill and expressed a fervent wish: "I hope to Jesus nothing happens." Instants later something did.

12

Terror on Tower Avenue

A hand held high. A shouted order. These set in motion the tragedy of Armistice Day, 1919, in Centralia. All of the parade was past the Wobbly hall except the Centralia contingent and several cars bringing up the rear. The Centralia group had fallen behind and a wide gap separated it from the Chehalis Legionnaires marching ahead. But when he reached the intersection of Tower and Second, with the men he led directly in front of the hall, Warren Grimm turned, held up his arm, and called out: "Halt, close up ranks!"[1] Almost simultaneously Lt. Frank Van Gilder blew a shrill blast on a whistle. Lt. Adrian Cormier, assistant parade marshal, wheeled his horse around to ask, "Why the stop?"[2] Why stop when it would seem that the lagging Centralia men should be ordered to speed up? The rest of the parade was moving on and the space between them and the Chehalis marchers was widening rapidly. Grimm never had a chance to reply, but others later explained the halt by saying it was ordered so that the spacing between the marchers could be evened out before they reached the reviewing stand.

Because of what happened within seconds after the order was given, the intent of the halt seemed to be to give the Centralians a chance to drop out of the parade, make a quick assault on the Wobbly hall, then resume the march, perhaps catching up with the rest of the parade before it reached the reviewing stand.

Some of the men talked about a raid as they marched south on Tower. One of these was Dr. Frank Bickford, at forty-nine a mature and respected medical doctor who was in the front ranks. When the order to halt was given, he decided that right then was a good time to do something about the Wobblies. He turned to others near him, volunteered to take the lead, and started for the hall. When he looked back and saw no one was following him, he hesitated. Then he heard "a commotion and hollering among the platoons in the rear."[3] Bickford moved on and saw others from the ranks just opposite the hall running ahead of him. They reached the hall's entrance before he did. Faulkner, standing at the window inside the hall, heard shouts of, "Let's go get them! Grab them! At them — get them!"

"A man at my right put his foot against the door," Bickford later testified, "and pushed it partly open." Faulkner heard and saw the glass in the door break and hit the curtain. At that dreaded instant, the shooting began. But such was the momentum of the raid that the shots did not stop it. The big windows were shattered and the double door smashed the rest of the way open. The gunfire from the hall signaled the other defenders. Davis from his second-story vantage point in the Avalon took aim. With his first shot, probably, he picked off Warren Grimm, although the argument was never settled as to where Grimm was hit — at the door of the hall, leading the raid, or standing at the intersection of Second and Tower. The bullet coursed downward through his chest and emerged at the tip of a left rib. Wherever he was, the bullet that hit him almost certainly came from the Avalon.

The three men stationed on Seminary Hill heard the popping of gunfire below and began to shoot, spraying bullets among the crowd of marchers and spectators on the sidewalks and in the street. O. C. Bland, in the Arnold, didn't get into the action. As men ran toward the hall, Bland jumped up from his seat on the bed and shoved his rifle through a window, and a piece of glass slashed a cut in the back of his hand so deep his friend Lamb was sickened by the sight.

In the hall, Faulkner, before he could turn to run, felt a bullet pass through the shoulder of his coat. Everest and Becker were standing behind him and not taking careful aim. They shot fast and then ran.

The gunfire took everyone by surprise except the

This picture, looking north on Tower Avenue, shows the corner of Second and Tower in the foreground. The Roderick Hotel is the second building on the left. The IWW hall was in the north one-third of the hotel on the first floor. The picture was taken after the November 11 raid when a canopy on the front of the Roderick was torn down.

Wobblies. Suddenly, from all directions at once it seemed, bullets were raining out and down on what till then had been a peaceful street parade. Men shouted and women screamed as they ran, some in one direction and then another, not knowing where the bullets were coming from. The scene was one of panic and confusion, and it was impossible later to reconstruct with complete accuracy what did happen because of variations in what witnesses remembered seeing and doing or thought they saw or did.

While those in the front ranks of the raiders, with the instinct of combat soldiers meeting resistance in an assault, continued their charge, others who hesitated or held back scattered, seeking shelter. Arthur McElfresh, C. D. Cunningham, George Barner, and others ran into the vacant lot adjacent to the variety store adjoining the hall on the north. Once there, McElfresh turned to peer around the corner of the building. A bullet from either the Avalon or Seminary Hill pierced his brain. As McElfresh fell, Barner caught and held him, helpless, as he died. Eugene Pfitzer was wounded in the arm by a bullet fired from the hall. Holding his arm, he loped down Tower to First Street where he found a person with a car to take him to the hospital. Bernard Eubanks took a bullet through the calf of a leg before he could get off Tower Avenue, and he hopped on the other leg around the corner of the co-op building.

The ex-soldiers who stormed into the hall found the front part of it empty. The firing, done only by Everest and Becker, while intense and rapid, was brief. It became evident to the Wobblies immediately that the attackers were not being driven off. They would come charging in, probably with guns blazing, and kill them all if they didn't flee. The men rushed to the back. On the back porch of the Roderick was a large cold storage locker. Four of the Wobblies squeezed into it to hide. Everest ran into the alley. Faulkner ran up a set of back stairs and tried to conceal himself on the roof of the hotel porch.

Two of the ex-servicemen, Ben Casagranda and John Watt, who had been marching side by side in the parade, ran toward the Roderick when they heard shots coming from down the street. Then, hearing gunfire from the direction of the hall, they turned and raced around the corner on Second Street. Everest, in a high state of excitement when he reached the alley behind the hall, turned south, and when he came to the alley's entrance on Second Street saw two men in uniform running toward him. He fired at both. Casagranda, shot through the stomach, fell on the sidewalk beside the co-op store. Watt was hit by a bullet that penetrated his midriff. Everest then turned and started north, pausing when he saw more uniformed men crouched in the vacant lot. Seeing him, C. D. Cunningham shouted, "Look out, he's going to shoot!" At that, according to Cunningham, George Barner "jumped straight up in the air." Everest quickly fired a single shot that hit no one, and then he started running up the alley.

The aroused ex-servicemen were not going to let the fleeing Wobbly get away. Several took after him, but let him keep a considerable distance ahead. None of the pursuers had a gun. Everest's route was westward, through three residential blocks with many vacant lots, stables, and sheds along the alleys, four-tenths of a mile between Second Street and the Skookumchuck River, flowing swiftly just before it converged with the Chehalis. Cunningham, one of the pursuers, had gone a block when he came to the home of a fellow ex-serviceman, Percy Draper, at Third and F streets. Draper was busy crating furniture and hadn't marched in the parade. Cunningham tapped on a window and asked if he had a gun. Draper, surprised, said no. Cunningham rushed off. A moment later another man in uniform knocked on his window. This time Draper went out on the porch and asked what was going on. Hobart Whitford said, "Hello, Percy, have you got a gun?"

"No, what's the matter?" Draper replied. Whitford, nervous and excited, didn't wait to reply but ran off to the north. Then Harold Genge, who had served with Draper in France, hurried up and asked for a gun and answered Draper's question, "Why, we raided the Wobbly hall and they killed Grimm and McElfresh."[4]

Dale Hubbard was able to find someone who handed him a pistol. He grabbed it and continued the pursuit, but when he caught sight of Everest and tried to fire, the pistol wouldn't work.

The fleeing Everest did not try to hide. He would pause, crouch behind a shed or fence and fire a shot at his pursuers, then run on. In a few minutes he came to the bank of the Skookumchuck, thick with trees and underbrush. He saw at once that he was trapped unless he could cross the river. He could not. The river was too swift and deep and he was burdened with heavy logger's clothes and boots. Everest crouched behind a stump near the water's edge and waited, gun in hand.

George Barner, Dale Hubbard, and Joseph Cole advanced cautiously toward him through the trees.

Warren O. Grimm.

Arthur McElfresh.

75

Hubbard moved out ahead, leveling the pistol that would not fire, and shouted at Everest to surrender. Everest responded with "defiant curses" and, when Hubbard kept coming, raised his gun and shot. Hubbard fell. Everest shot him again, and then again. That emptied his gun. Seeing him trying frantically to reload, the others rushed up. Everest reached for a long knife strapped to his belt in the back, but before he could draw it Barner was on him, grabbing his arms. Others followed, one kicking him in the head hard enough to draw blood.

Pulled to his feet, Everest, still defiant, resisted efforts to make him move. One of his captors took off his belt and looped it around the Wobbly's neck, using it as a leash on the long walk to the city jail nearly a mile away. Hubbard lay where he fell, gravely wounded but not dead. Soon a car and driver were found and he was taken to the Scace Hospital, the last of the Wobbly gunfire victims to receive medical attention.[5]

A trail of blood on the sidewalk leading past the Roderick to the corner at Second Street verified reports that one of the paraders, who was seen stumbling south away from the hall, bent over with his hands over his stomach, was shot in front of the hall. Some witnesses said this was Grimm. One who disputed this was Dr. H. Y. Bell, who was marching beside Lt. Van Gilder only eight feet behind Grimm when the order to halt was given. Immediately after the shooting started, he said he saw Grimm running south along Second, holding his hand over his stomach. Bell rushed over to him and asked if he had been hit. Grimm replied that he had an "awful pain in his stomach."[6] Grimm made his way to a shed behind Ax Billy's confectionery on the southwest corner of the intersection. Near this shed William S. MacKenzie was sitting with his brother-in-law, Clyde Tisdale, in an open Dodge touring car on the south side of Second, facing Tower. They saw Grimm, still standing, open his shirt to expose a wound later described as "big as an inkwell." He was helped into MacKenzie's car. Casagranda, dying or dead, was put in the car also. Then Watt, unconscious, was hurriedly loaded and the car sped off to the small city hospital, operated by Dr. Lee Scace.

Grimm was still conscious and able to walk when the car reached the hospital. The only thing he was heard to say was "for God's sake hurry up." He was helped into what passed for an emergency ward, but trauma of the kind he was suffering from was some-thing hospitals even in large cities were ill equipped to handle in 1919. Grimm's internal organs had been torn and ruptured and he quickly bled to death. Watt was more fortunate. He, too, had been hit in the middle part of his body, but the bullet missed arteries and organs. Neither of the men was opened surgically to determine if internal repairs could be made. Watt's two wounds — where the bullet entered and where it left — were dressed and he was left to rest. "I'll be out of here soon," he remarked, and in ten days he was.

While the dead and wounded were being tended and the one known Wobbly slayer being chased and captured, others among the ex-servicemen who escaped being hit poured into the IWW hall and the Roderick lobby to finish the raid.

They found no one in the front portion of the hall or in Britt Smith's quarters in the rear. This meant the Wobblies had gone out the back door. But had they all run off or were some waiting to ambush anyone who followed them? There was some hesitation about going into the alley, and it was during this time that Everest went south to Second, shot Watt and Casagranda, then ran back past the rear of the hall and headed north. He was shooting at anyone in uniform — all identified by him as enemies of the IWW — and he would have fired at anyone who came out the back door. The ex-servicemen, inside the hall, could hear the shots in the alley. When it was quiet, and after carefully peering out the rear door and seeing no one, several of the more courageous ventured out. No one was in sight. Inside the cold storage locker Mike Sheehan stuck his Wobbly card in a crack, ridding himself of what he knew would be incriminating evidence. McInerney unbuckled his gun belt and dropped it on the floor. He hadn't fired and had no intention of doing so now. The four men huddled in the dark of the box were frightened by the ex-soldiers, whom they thought were armed, just as those who were after them feared the Wobblies, whom they knew were armed. Faulkner was soon found on the roof of the porch. He indicated where the others were. Going over to the locker, one of the ex-soldiers called out, "Boys, if you don't shoot, I'll let you out." Sheehan did not need to consult with the other three. "There will be no shooting," he shouted back. The door was opened and the four men came out, surrendering meekly. They went willingly with a sizable unarmed escort to the city jail, and were there before Everest was brought in.

When Everest ran north, away from the hall, the shooting in that locality was over. Bland, Hansen, and Roberts fired as many as twenty shots from Seminary Hill, stopping when they saw frightened people frantically running in various directions and a crowd of men in uniform entering the hall. They knew the brief battle was over and they had better get away. In their haste they took their guns but left the suitcase, a box of soft-nosed bullets, field glasses, a coat, and an IWW songbook, all of which were found the next day. They hurried away eastward on a little-used road and went separate ways.

O. C. Bland, his cut hand wrapped in a towel, and John Lamb ran down the back stairs of the Arnold in the midst of the confusion and headed east across the tracks where they encountered Jack Davis, carrying the rifle he used in the Avalon. Davis walked with the two to Lamb's house. Bland set out to find a doctor and Davis asked Lamb if he would take his rifle and keep it for him, a request that Lamb immediately refused. Then Davis departed, taking his rifle with him, and vanished permanently from the Centralia scene. He was never caught.

Both the Blands and John Lamb and his son Dewey were well-known local members of the IWW. O. C. Bland and the two Lambs were arrested in midafternoon at Lamb's house.

Eugene Barnett, in the lobby of the Roderick when the raid started, threw off his coat, intending to join the fight. But when the shooting began, he stayed where he was. He was still in the lobby when the uniformed men came in. He recognized William Scales as one and afterward said that another, a navy man, was carrying a gun. He said he warned him to be careful with the gun because there was a woman — Mrs. McAllister — in the back. Barnett was not recognized then as a Wobbly and was not seized. He walked away unmolested and went uptown in time to see Everest brought in.

Once the building had been thoroughly searched, the Legionnaires proceeded to complete what had been their original objective — the destruction of the hall, the very least bit of retribution that could be exacted for what the wild Wobblies had just done. The men were enraged. Their commander had been killed and their comrades shot and wounded. In a state of excited fury they embarked on their mission of destruction, beginning by carrying out the furnishings and piling them in the street. Records from Smith's

Wesley Everest. He killed and then was killed at Centralia.

Special Collections Division, University of Washington Libraries, neg. #UW5754

desk, including the local IWW membership list, were handed to Prosecutor Allen, who happened to be standing across the street, watching. Then they pulled and heaved and tore down the roof that extended over the sidewalk and was supported by turned posts. Seeing this, Mrs. McAllister, afraid they were determined to destroy her whole building, hastily hung an American flag in the lobby window of the Roderick, identifying that side of the building as non-Wobbly territory. The depredations on the building then ceased while the men turned to a task that was ritual in IWW hall raids — burning the contents in a street bonfire. The fire blazed up. Nothing was saved. The crowd around, shocked by what had happened, looked on, not disapprovingly.

It was about a mile from the banks of the Skookumchuck to the jail on Maple Street, and as Everest and his captors moved along, the crowd following them grew. The story spread quickly. This was the Wobbly who shot Dale Hubbard in cold blood out on the riverbank. He had shot others too. Who was he? He was Smith, Britt Smith, the crowd was told, ringleader of the IWW. As the procession moved on through the residential streets, it grew into an angry throng, mostly men, feeling an impulsive need for revenge.

A troop of Boy Scouts who marched in the front part of the parade disbanded in the city park and went to the high school auditorium to act as ushers for the planned postparade program. When few others came, they left and went toward the center of town where James Gillespie, one of the scouts, encountered a woman "crying convulsively and screaming almost incoherently: 'They have killed him! They have killed him!' "[7] Gillespie ran on to Tower Avenue and saw the crowd bringing Everest in. "Everest was in the vanguard of a howling, sneering mob, brutally being pushed and shoved along by two husky truculent men," Gillespie later wrote. "He stumbled, was dragged and savagely jerked to his feet. His head was a bloody mass of welts from both men and women who dashed out sporadically from the curb to pummel him with their fists."[8] By the time the crowd reached the jail, someone had brought a rope and there were shouts of "Hang him!"

The captive Wobbly, still rebellious and defiant, endured the battering well enough to be able "to laugh in the face of the crowd around him."[9] The next day the *Portland Oregonian* reported that Everest, outside the jail, was defiant and hitched at his khaki trousers. He had lost his hat as he ran. 'You fellows can't hang me,' he gloated. 'I was sent to do my duty and I did it.' "[10]

Marjorie Ort, a seventeen-year-old apprentice news writer at the *Chronicle* at the time, remembered the scene as terrifying. A rope was tied around Everest's neck and the end thrown over a spike on a telephone pole in the alley in back of the *Chronicle* office, near the jail. Dr. Livingstone, just arrived on the scene after leaving the hospital where he watched as his friend Grimm died, was as angry as any at the Wobblies, but could reason well enough to know that a daytime lynching would be bad. Marjorie Ort saw him clamber up the foothold spikes of the pole where he began shouting to make himself heard above the clamor of the mob. "Don't hang him. Not here," he yelled. "Don't do something foolish."[11]

The appeals were almost too late. Everest was lifted by the neck and his feet were off the ground before Livingstone's frantic appeal to reason was heeded and he was let down. Quickly he was hustled across the street and pushed into a jail cell out of reach of the mob eager for a lynching. In the jail were the others who were seized in the rear of the Roderick.

C. D. Cunningham immediately began thinking about what lay ahead. He had been a prosecutor. These men would have to be tried. Evidence would have to be gathered and statements taken. Less than an hour after Everest was jailed, Cunningham went to see him. Still defiant, the Wobbly killer refused to talk.

The jailed men assessed their situation. They were locked up and in serious trouble, but at least they had survived. They had done what they had sworn to do — defend their hall — and now would have to face the consequences.

However irrational the whole affair, there could not have been any expectation by those in the hall that they would not be caught. But they would be caught defending themselves and their hall. Their cause, they were sure, was just. To their surprise, a little later, Elmer Smith, the attorney who assured them that they were right in deciding to defend the hall, was brought into the jail.

W. H. Graham, principal of the high school, was the leader of the Boy Scout group marching in the parade. He and others in the front part of the parade were well out of sight and sound of the violence at Second Street and didn't hear about it until after they had gone to the auditorium and waited for the others who didn't show up.

Graham, followed by some of the scouts, went to the city hall at Tower and Magnolia where he found a crowd gathering, excitedly discussing the frightening reports of an armed Wobbly assault on the Legionnaires. "What about Elmer Smith?" someone asked. He had been seen just a few minutes earlier at Tower and Pine. Men started down Tower on both sides of the street looking for him, Graham in the lead. He had known Smith as a teacher and didn't like him. Smith was a radical who opposed the war effort. Some parents objected to him being on the faculty. If he wasn't a Wobbly, at least he sounded like one and now, after what had happened, ought to be taken in.

Smith was found in his office, standing with his raincoat on, beside his desk.[12] Others were in the office with him. When Smith saw the crowd outside, he took off his coat and went to the door. What did they want? They wanted him to go down to the police station and give an account of himself.

Smith then stepped quickly from the door, saying that no one but an officer could take him away. He reached into his pocket for a small handgun. He moved back and forth before the door and window of the office, sizing up the gathering crowd outside. He was wary. What might they do with him? Mobs were unpredictable. One of the scouts had brought a rifle, not loaded, which was plainly visible to Smith. Graham made no threats, however, and finally Smith agreed to surrender his gun and go along with the principal. In the anteroom of the jail Graham told the police Smith ought to be held. He said he was a traitor who, in his own office one time, had said the United States had no business being in the war and that it was a capitalistic war to kill off the common worker.[13]

By this time anyone suspected of anything in connection with the Wobblies was being seized and held. The Wobbly horrors rapidly escalated into Wobbly hysteria. Smith was locked up.

The mob around the jail continued to grow and the intensity of its temper increased. Several times persons opposed to mob action attempted to get the throng's attention, urging the people to calm down and let the law take care of the killers. But the crowd remained angry and was in no mood to listen to conciliatory appeals. The anger intensified as the events of the afternoon became more widely known. Grimm, McElfresh, and Casagranda dead. Watt and Hubbard in the hospital, probably dying. Physter, Eubanks, and others wounded. Why, these Wobblies had committed a massacre, right there in Centralia! Get back at them, those milling about the jail muttered or shouted. Get even!

A mere raid on their hall, whether carried out or not, was considered no excuse for the slaughter of men wearing the uniform of their country, especially on the first anniversary of the victory they had won. What could these vicious Wobblies be thinking? Whatever it was, Centralians concluded, it was evil and frightening and for all they knew might presage something worse. Alarms and rumors of further terror and violence spread. It was war. Every known or suspected Wobbly had to be hunted down and locked up quickly before they could do any more harm.

13

Terror in the Night

Vance Noel, the only professional newsman on the staff of the *Centralia Chronicle,* was out of town on November 11. He went east on a family matter a few days earlier, remarking that he wasn't worried about news coverage while he was gone because nothing much ever happened in Centralia. When something did happen, it was up to Harry Bras, publisher, and Ray Edinger, his son-in-law, to write the news that suddenly focused the whole nation's attention on Centralia. Edinger was the *Chronicle's* business manager. The headlines on the story screamed the news and the city's outrage:

McELFRESH, GRIMM AND CASAGRANDA
KILLED BY THE IWW

FIVE MORE WOUNDED

SOLDIERS WHO DEFENDED OUR COUNTRY
SHOT DOWN ON THE STREETS BY IWW
AS THEY MARCHED DOWN TOWER AVENUE —
BOYS HAD NO CHANCE TO DEFEND THEMSELVES.
TOWN COWERS BEFORE SKUNKS.

The news story carried an ominous warning: "At the time of going to press the jail is surrounded by soldiers and citizens and if the IWWs contained therein are not hanged, they will be fortunate."

Bras and Edinger may not have been qualified reporters but their hastily written account summed up the situation accurately. Mayor Rogers and Police Chief Hughes sensed trouble. The crowd downtown and around the jail, growing rapidly as news of what happened spread, obviously was now a mob bent on vengeance. The clamor and excitement heightened when word came from the hospital that Hubbard had died and that Watt might not live through the night. That would make five killed. The sense of grief over the fallen, mingled with anger at the Wobblies and fear about what might happen next, put Centralia into a severe state of shock accentuated by feelings of sheer terror. Men went home for their guns and to tell their families to stay off the streets. When James Eubanks, friend of the Elmer Smith family and father of Bernard, who was one of the wounded, heard that Elmer was in jail, he went to the Smith home and, without alarming Mrs. Smith by saying she might be in danger, unobtrusively stood guard through the night.

The response was immediate when a call was issued for fifty men to meet at the Elks Club in ten minutes to organize for whatever might need to be done. In less than ten minutes, several hundred men swarmed up the stairs at the Elks Club, eager to be sworn in as deputies.

The prospect of mob action was enough to convince Rogers and Hughes they should summon help. Centralia needed the National Guard. A call was made to the Adjutant General at five-thirty, just as daylight was fading on Centralia's streets.

The irony of this was little noticed — outside guardsmen being called to guard jailed Wobblies in Centralia, the home of Company M, rather than Centralia Guardsmen being sent out as in past years to keep Wobblies under control elsewhere.

Company F of the Third Washington Infantry in Tacoma moved as fast as it could in response to the emergency. A train, hastily put together at the Union depot, was ready to depart as soon as forty men, each with full field equipment and one hundred rounds of ammunition, reported in. Guardsmen in Tacoma were summoned to duty by telephone and taxis were sent to the homes of those needing transportation. Captain Thomas L. Shurtleff was placed in command of a company of two officers and thirty-five enlisted men. Their train left for Centralia at 10:25 p.m., too late to prevent what the mayor feared might happen.

The long-dormant spirit of vigilantism was fully revived as night fell in Centralia. It demanded that something be done. The vicious killers should have a taste of viciousness themselves. Plans were laid. Word of them got around. Kate Robinson, secretary of the Chamber of Commerce, confided them to her friend Hollis Fultz, manager of the Olympia Chamber and a writer of "true detective" stories. He had raced to Centralia in a taxi when he heard about the shootings. Robinson told him to be on hand at the jail at seven o'clock "because the lights are going out and something will happen."[1]

Fultz was there. He saw several cars drive up with their lights out and park near the jail. Other motorists who turned into Pearl Street were warned to turn their lights off, and when one did not, the headlamps on the car were smashed.

Night patrolman Robert Jackson was on duty in the jail where Everest, Britt Smith, and the other Wobblies were held in two rows of small barred cells on either side of a central corridor.

Suddenly all the lights in the city went out. Someone pulled a main switch in the power distribution building adjacent to the jail. A Seattle newspaper report the next day said the vigilantes gained entrance to the jail by kicking out a panel in the wood door and reaching in to turn the key. Men entered and demanded that Jackson give them keys to the cells.

Fultz heard loud voices inside the jail and then a sound "like someone hitting a pumpkin with a ball bat." He saw one man half-carried, half-dragged out the jail door and shoved into the back seat of a car. The man was Wesley Everest.

From the crowd around the jail, estimated by reporters the next day at two thousand, came shouts of encouragement: "Lynch 'em!" The car carrying Everest, followed by several others, took off through the dark streets headed westward. Many others, curious about an awful event they knew was about to happen, followed also, Fultz among them. The death squad for Everest drove to the bridge over the Chehalis River at the western edge of town.

Bob Burrows, a farmer who lived near the bridge, provided the best eyewitness account, reporting, "The man was struggling between the men who held him. They worked without a word. I saw them stop not far from the end of the bridge near the city and throw a rope over the cross beam. The body went over with a

"Hangman's Bridge," over the Chehalis River, where Wesley Everest was lynched.

thud and then a shot was fired. Then more shots. I stood a distance away while perhaps twenty shots in all were fired close to the body."[2] Burrows said that one bullet went through the Wobbly's neck "close to where the noose had torn a gaping hole in the flesh." He said the lynchers went to their cars silently and drove away.

Afterwards, many of those who came to watch hurried back to the jail to see if any more were going to be seized and hanged. They found the crowds still excited, still milling about. "All night long the crowd wove back and forth in the Centralia streets," the *Tacoma News-Tribune* reported the next day,

swarming like bees about the entrance to the jail. They were rough men, angry, scornful men whose pockets bulged menacingly with the weapons they made small effort to conceal. There were many in uniform in that throng, both of blue and olive drab, and they were set, determined young faces with the light of battle in their eyes. Their buddies had been shot down by scoundrels worse than Boches and their hearts called for vengeance. Women, too, were among them . . . some with lips set and eyes flaming.

"Lynch them, lynch them!" urged one petticoated firebrand as she pled with passionate zeal with man after man in her mad effort to incite the mob to frenzied action. "Are you cowards? Would you let them shoot you down like dogs?" she shouted while under her whiplash tongue men straightened their shoulders, growled savagely, and promised her the vengeance she demanded.[3]

The mob around the jail was startled when photographers from a Tacoma newspaper took two flash

Everest's body was transported in a moving van to the cemetery where it was buried in a wooden box. Guardsmen went along to keep Wobbly prisoners, who dug the grave, from escaping.

pictures of the scene from the porch of the James Churchill residence across the street from the jail. The exploding flash powder sounded like bombs. No relieved humor was expressed when the cause of the noise was discovered. Instead the camera was jerked away from the photographer and his plates taken out and smashed.

Photographic records of Armistice Day in Centralia never turned up, although stories and legends about them are numerous. Pathe News was reported to have made a newsreel, but it was never seen. Assistant Attorney General Saunders in Seattle received a letter five days after the shootings from an Archie Henderson who said he stood across the street from the IWW hall and took a picture showing the men from the parade running toward the hall with its door still shut and the window intact. Later, he said, he was searched by soldiers at the depot and his camera confiscated but he was able to keep the film pack. He submitted the pictures to the *Seattle Post-Intelligencer,* he wrote, but they were not published. The letter was strongly pro-Wobbly in tone.[4]

The first assignment taken on by the posse hastily

organized at the Elks Club was to comb the city for more Wobblies who were involved in the violence, looking especially for the one who fired from the Avalon window. Officers said the man's name was known. The name probably was that of Eugene Barnett, a suspected Wobbly who was seen in town after the shooting, and subsequently the one accused of firing the shot that killed Grimm.

Barnett, after watching the excited throng gather around the jail when Everest was brought in, and seeing Everest's narrow escape from a daylight lynching, had concluded that no Wobbly was safe in Centralia. He climbed on his horse and headed for home. On the way he talked to farmer acquaintances, describing in bitter terms what he had seen in town. One of these, Barnett said later, went into town and told officials that Barnett was one of the Wobblies who had been on the scene.

The roundup of known or suspected Wobblies proceeded so fast that by late evening, after the lynching, the city jail was jammed with twenty-two prisoners, including Elmer Smith's two brothers and Tom Lassiter, the news dealer who was run out of town but came back.

Families of the slain men were distraught over the tragedy. A call was placed to William Grimm, Warren's brother, at the University of Washington. The call was taken by Lloyd Dysart, out of the army and again studying for a law degree. Dysart found Grimm, his fraternity brother, on the football field. They quickly borrowed a car and headed south over rough county roads, reaching Centralia about ten o'clock.

They found the city in turmoil. The downtown area was crowded with people, milling around, talking excitedly. A Wobbly had been lynched. The two young men were told that more were probably going to be lynched for they all deserved it. Dysart joined hundreds of others who drove to the bridge, shining car lights on the body of Wesley Everest, dangling in the shadows beneath the Chehalis River bridge, then went home. Judge Dysart had left instructions for Lloyd to put on his uniform, take his army pistol, and go to the Elks Club. There he found his father standing on a chair, pleading with the few among the hundreds jammed into the hall who would listen to him. When the judge saw his son, he said, "Lloyd, for God's sake help me control this mob." Most of the men in the hall were ex-servicemen still in their uniforms "and everybody was saying, 'Get a gun.' "[5] The judge said the National Guard was expected to arrive any minute and "we have got to keep this crowd in hand so nobody innocent is harmed."

A man described to Lloyd Dysart as the "ringleader" of the lynching a few hours before was pointed out to him. Then two men urged him to lead a group who would go down to the jail and "get some of those bastards and string them up."

"I told them to calm down and go home," Dysart related. "I said, 'You can't stir up anything more. You can't go down to that jail and start breaking in and taking anyone because you don't know who you'd be taking. You don't know who they are.' Finally the National Guard did arrive and that broke up any organization of another lynch party."[6]

Before he left the Elks Club Dysart was asked to form a posse that would search for Wobblies in the coal-mining region east of town. He agreed providing they wait until morning and that no more than fifteen or twenty men go along. He didn't want a mob.

The train bringing Company F from Tacoma arrived at 11:35 p.m. The soldiers were sent to the Chamber of Commerce office to wait while the officers conferred with Mayor Rogers and Assistant Attorney General Frank Christiansen in the city hall. The Guard officers were told about the lynching. In his report of the affair, Lieutenant Windsor of Company F said, "Conference with state, county and city officials developed the fact that the citizens generally were in a dangerous mood and that there was a strong possibility of further trouble unless great care was exercised in handling the situation."[7]

The danger point was the city jail but the Guard was not ordered to go there. The possibility of a clash between armed soldiers and civilians, many of whom were armed too, in an atmosphere of mob hysteria, worried the mayor and Christensen. They waited. Finally midnight came, and fewer clamors for another lynching were heard.

The news spread quickly that out-of-town soldiers had arrived. In the hours after midnight the crowds gradually dispersed, and as the noise diminished a feeling of massive relief came to the terrorized prisoners as they realized they were going to live through the night after all. They were told what happened to Everest. They listened for hours to the shouting mob outside the jail, lusting for another lynching. Now at last the worst was over.

Seventeen additional Guardsmen from Tacoma arrived and it was considered safe to assign them to guard duty at the jail. Other detachments were sent to five places where main roads entered the city with orders to examine all persons entering or leaving and to hold "all suspicious characters." Several men carrying IWW cards were caught in the next several hours at these outposts and turned over to the sheriff. Excitement erupted at one point when soldiers were fired on from a wooded area. The soldiers fired back and then searched the area but found no one.

The most frequently quoted accounts of the Everest lynching, none finally verified, accused the lynchers of emasculating him during the ride from the jail to the bridge. It made a likely story. The worst thing that can be done to a man, so the folklore of violence goes — the one irreversible punishment, a procedure used only on the most hated — is the hacking off of genitals. It is something done to a man by other men caught up in a mood of uncontrolled fury, yielding to the urge to bite and gouge like one animal attacking another. What the Wobbly killer had done that day was enough to arouse the worst animal instincts.

Emasculation was the fate of at least one Wobbly in Southern California. In the University of Washington library IWW picture file in 1983 was a photograph of a nude male body, lying on its back, legs spread to show what had been done. The feet of numerous onlookers, male and female, showed in the picture.

The report that Everest had been castrated gained credence that never diminished. It originated almost immediately and spread at least as far as Olympia by the next day.[8] Sixty years afterward a senior Centralian could point to a photograph of a prominent Legionnaire of 1919 on the wall of the county museum and say with assurance, "He did it."

A belief that neither he nor anyone else did perform such an act is best supported by the record of an examination of Everest's body in the Centralia jail. Since the investigator typed his report on a Tacoma police form, it can be assumed he was a member of that force, acting at the request of local police who did not have fingerprinting facilities. He wrote that no marks could be found on the body other than bullet wounds. He noted that the neck, still with a piece of rope around it, was cut. This report found its way into the files of Luke May, retained by the county and lumber operators. It was given no publicity, although it seems to constitute evidence that Everest was not castrated, and such evidence would have been useful in quieting the rumors of such an atrocity that began to spread the day after the lynching.

Whatever the facts, the report of the castration was generally believed because it was the kind of thing men acting outside the law, when an offender deserves punishment worse than the law allows, could be expected to do. So if Everest was castrated, hanged, and then shot, the reasoning went, it served him right. He was without doubt hanged and shot. If he was castrated, no matter. He was dead. Anyone who killed unarmed men as he did deserved the worst.

C. D. Cunningham had an explanation concerning the origin of the emasulation report. He said that when Everest's body was brought in and no one around the jail wanted to examine it for scars or other identi-

fying marks, a young man from Portland, in Centralia to solicit advertising for a Legion magazine, volunteered to cut off the bloody, wet clothes and search the body for marks. To impress or frighten the Wobblies in the jail the Portland man remarked in a loud voice that while he was at it, he would castrate him also. According to Cunningham, the imprisoned Wobblies either mistook what they heard as a report that he had been emasculated or started a rumor to that effect which was widely circulated.

No one element of the Centralia story received more attention than the report about castration. The verdict of those who have researched the records cannot be free entirely of reasonable doubt, but this researcher concludes that the reports, originating within hours of the lynching, were not a lie made up by Wobblies, for any Wobblies still at large on that fateful day in Centralia had fled for cover by nightfall when a mob was threatening to storm the jail. They were not in a position to start false rumors on November 12.

One of the legends that developed out of the chaotic events of Armistice Day concerned the supposed killing of another Wobbly. Eugene Barnett, who was not in jail the night of the 11th, wrote forty-two years later, "Fellow worker James McInerney saw him (Jack Davis) killed in the Centralia jail the first night of the rioting. He saw who did it. And loggers from Saginaw camp saw the body being covered with ashes and cinders later that night."[9] This report is counted as a legend because the report was not widely circulated, like the castration matter, and because there is no record of McInerney relating what Barnett quotes him as saying. But it is true that nothing from or about Jack Davis, who almost certainly fired the shot that killed Warren Grimm, was ever heard afterward by those concerned with the Centralia affair.

McInerney did say that the prisoners were mistreated in the jail. "I have heard tales of cruelty," Ralph Chaplin, writing in 1920, quotes McInerney as saying about that night, "but I believe what we boys went through on those nights can never be equaled. I thought it was my last night on earth and had reconciled myself to an early death of some kind, probably hanging. I was taken out once by a mob and a rope was placed around my neck and thrown over a crossbar or something. I waited for them to pull the rope, but they didn't. I heard voices in the mob say, 'That's not him,' and then I was put back in jail."[10]

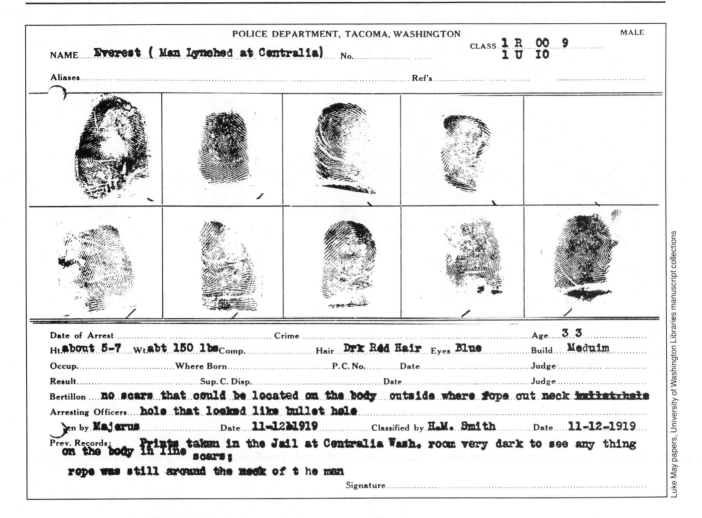

POLICE DEPARTMENT, TACOMA, WASHINGTON   CLASS 1 R 00 9   MALE
                                                    1 U 10

NAME Everest (Man Lynched at Centralia) No.

Aliases   Ref's

Date of Arrest   Crime   Age 3 3

Ht. about 5-7 Wt. abt 150 lbs. Comp.   Hair Drk Red Hair Eyes Blue   Build Meduim

Occup.   Where Born   P.C. No.   Date   Judge

Result   Sup. C. Disp.   Date   Judge

Bertillon no scars that could be located on the body outside where rope cut neck initialhals

Arresting Officers hole that looked like bullet hole

en by Majerus   Date 11-12-1919   Classified by H.M. Smith   Date 11-12-1919

Prev. Records: Prints taken in the Jail at Centralia Wash. room very dark to see any thing
on the body in line scars;

   rope was still around the neck of t he man

                                        Signature

Luke May papers, University of Washington Libraries manuscript collections

Chaplin makes a bare mention of the rumor that Davis was also lynched. If there actually was a second lynching, it is likely that the several investigators employed by the defense during the subsequent trial would have discovered some evidence of it.

In the days following November 11 a few men were heard to boast that they were among the lynchers of Everest, but soon the horror of what had taken place prevailed over any feelings of satisfaction at having gotten back at the Wobblies. A hush concerning the lynching and the lynchers became an accepted mandate in the always before quiet city after the newspaper editors undertook to assuage feelings of guilt by writing that what was done was fully justified in terms of morality and understandable in the light of what had provoked the action.

The *Centralia Hub* the next day commented, "No

These are the fingerprints of Wesley Everest and the report of an examination of his body by a man named Majerus on the day after the lynching. The body, brought in from the river by police, was dumped on the floor of the jail corridor where the Wobbly prisoners could see it. As the examiner noted, it was dark in the jail and difficult to "see anything on the body in the line of scars." If Everest was emasculated, the examiner either did not notice it or saw fit not to report it.

county official would admit that any lynching had taken place. No official wanted to be told of such action and it was generally understood that no effort would be made to learn the details or to bring any of those implicated before the courts."

When the weekly *Lewis County Advocate* in Chehalis came out two days later it said, "We cannot blame the lynchers when they forgot all else but the biblical injunction of 'an eye for an eye.' The Wobblies more than deserved what they got." The paper said the people showed "commendable reserve" in not hanging more of "the assassins."

The names of the lynch participants were widely known. Despite the attempt at concealment by turning out the city's lights, those who dragged Everest from the jail and hanged him from the bridge were seen and recognized by many, but no attempts to identify them publicly were ever made. Certainly no prosecution of them was ever attempted or even seriously considered by those in office.

Several lists of known or suspected lynchers were prepared in the course of defense efforts for the accused Wobblies. One list has more than fifty names on it. Not all the lists are the same. Julia Ruuttila, who undertook an independent investigation on her own in the 1930s, sought to identify the most likely lynchers by preparing a list of those whose names appeared on more than one of the early lists she found in Elmer Smith's files after he died. She showed it to Bob Burrows, the farmer who witnessed the lynching near his home, who told her, "You've left two names out."[11]

14

More Terror in the Aftermath

On the day after — November 12 — Centralia's leaders looked about them and made an agonizing summary: Four of the city's war heroes slain. Another seriously wounded. One Wobbly dead. Scores more in jail. The IWW hall destroyed. The National Guard in town to maintain order. Fugitives known to be involved in the shootings still at large. Inquests to be held. Proper funerals for the martyrs to be arranged. Some of the assassins in jail. Cases against them to be prepared. The townspeople carrying guns or afraid to leave their homes. The body of the man who was lynched to be disposed of. The town full of newspapermen. The whole country in an uproar over what happened in their normally peaceful city.

The most urgent duty was to pursue the murdering Wobblies who had gotten away. Search posses went to work. When Lloyd Dysart showed up at the depot at dawn, he found waiting, not the twenty-five or so he had specified, but a hundred armed men eager to join the hunt. "They were out to get blood if they could," he related later. "They were after that. They wanted it. And there I was — the leader, the head of all that mob. . . ."[1]

The posse boarded a train that headed east on a logging line. At Kopiah a railroad yard worker was told that a Wobbly hunt was on. He said the only Wobbly around there was Eugene Barnett, who lived in a little cabin back against the hillside. The posse members leaped off the rail cars eagerly and headed for the cabin, sitting in an open space in a thickly wooded area. Barnett saw them coming. To him the posse was a mob — a dangerous mob. He grabbed a rifle and a revolver and fled out the back door into the woods.

As Dysart and one other posse member moved out ahead and walked cautiously across the open space toward the cabin, Mrs. Barnett opened the door and stood on the threshold, holding her child. Was her husband there? No, she said.

Dysart and his companion looked back. None of the others came out from the cover of the woods to follow them. They decided to go on alone. Each ran for a blank place on the cabin wall on either side of the door where they couldn't be hit by shots from inside the house. Then, motioning Mrs. Barnett aside, they raised their guns, looked in the door, and entered. Hearing no shots, the rest of the posse, emboldened, ran up and helped search the house, including the attic. In the backyard they found a bitch dog tied up and two pups whimpering along a path leading to the woods. They released the dog and she loped off toward the woods with the posse running after her. The dog led them straight to Barnett, lying in underbrush on a ridge overlooking the cabin. He let himself be taken without resistance.

With one wanted Wobbly captured, the triumphant posse boarded the train and headed back to town. On the way, the men, impressed by Dysart's show of courage, agreed that he was the one to coordinate all other search efforts and bring order to the disorganized manhunt.

Back in town, with Barnett locked up, Dysart found that groups of mostly uniformed ex-servicemen were meeting trains and searching all who got off. Self-appointed small posses patrolled the streets. One of these was informed that an individual in the Wilkins poolroom and employment office was heard making critical remarks about the way the Wobblies were being handled. Immediately, posse members charged into the Wilkins and ordered the hundred or so they found there to line up with their hands held high while they were searched one by one. Sixteen with IWW cards were arrested.

The police deferred to the Legion men and stepped aside, letting Dysart, although still a college student, take over as leader of the law and order forces. He accepted the task, although as a law student he realized he was acting entirely without authority.

Dysart set up a clearing desk in the city hall where any posse, before it left on a mission, was supposed to state its objective and give the source of the information it was acting on.

Everest's body had dangled from the Chehalis River bridge through the night, a gruesome attraction for hundreds who came to see how some of Centralia's citizens had obtained a measure of bloody vengeance outside the law. Shortly before dawn someone cut the rope. The body splashed into the water, floated, and drifted downstream until it caught in an eddy.

At the jail, Mary McAllister, infuriated at being held at all and worried because her hotel, the Roderick, was left unguarded, remarked that it was a shame Britt Smith was wearing his best clothes when he was thrown into the filthy jail. This was heard by Prosecutor Allen, and he, surprised, led her into the cell block where she pointed out Britt Smith. Then she heard Allen call out to others in the front part of the jail, "Boys, it looks like we got the wrong man." It was not Britt Smith, the supposed ringleader, who was dragged out in the dark and hanged, as the lynchers intended; it was Wesley Everest.

Notified that the body was floating in the river, Allen called C. O. Sticklin, one of two local undertakers, and asked him to retrieve it. Sticklin refused. Allen called the other, Edward Newell, who said he would not have the body of such a man in his mortuary. Three deputies then were sent in a truck to pull Everest's body out of the river and do something with it. They found the body, loaded it in the truck, and then decided it would be well to let the other Wobblies see the price one of their number had paid for his crimes. They took the corpse, muddy and dripping, with the rope still around the gruesomely twisted neck, to the jail and dropped it on the floor of the corridor between the two rows of cells where all in the jail could see and smell it.

A hasty inquest was conducted by Coroner Livingstone before Justice of the Peace Charles P. Hoss.

No witnesses were called. The jury looked at the body briefly, then without delay issued a verdict. "We find that the deceased came to his death by gunshot wounds and by strangulation caused by persons unknown," they reported. Hoss accepted the findings without comment.

Four Wobbly prisoners were assigned the task of building a rough board casket. The body was dumped into it and the lid nailed shut. The casket was shoved into a moving van and the four prisoners were told they had to go along in another truck to dig the grave. A squad of Tacoma Guardsmen went with them to see that they didn't escape. The site of the burial is near the southwest corner of the Sticklin cemetery on the north outskirts of Centralia.

The *Hoquiam Washingtonian* reported the scene thus: "There were no prayers and no service of any nature when the body was lowered into the grave. Coroner David Livingstone, who had been marked for death by the IWW, was the only official present. The only spectators were a few newspapermen. No headstone, not even a plain board, was left above the grave to mark the spot. Centralia people, it was said, would not let such a marker stand."

Allen, in a gesture intended as response to any criticism that he was not doing his duty, made an announcement to the press on November 12 saying he would prosecute the men responsible for the lynching if he could obtain sufficient evidence. He also gave assurance there would be no more lynchings. "The boys have listened to the advice of the bar," he said, revealing that he knew who was involved, "and have promised to let the law take its course."[2] That course did not include any official effort to identify or bring charges against any of the lynch party.

Allen then gave his explanation of what happened

Headlines like these in the Tacoma News-Tribune *of November 12, 1919, the day after the shootings in Centralia, were published in all parts of the country and gave the public an inaccurate and distorted version of what had taken place. The drawing in the* News-Tribune *shows snipers shooting into the ranks of the servicemen from the roof and second floor of the Roderick Hotel, when in fact the only shots fired from that direction came out the door of the IWW hall. There was no confession of a "wholesale murder plot" by anyone. The fact that the entire front page of the Tacoma newspaper was devoted to the Centralia events indicates how sensational the "massacre" and subsequent developments were considered to be.*

THE NEWS TRIBUNE

24 PAGES TODAY

NIGHT EXTRA

36TH YEAR, NO. 39   TACOMA, WASH., WEDNESDAY EVENING, NOVEMBER 12, 1919.   PRICE 3 CENTS

I.W.W. CONFESSES WHOLESALE MURDER PLOT; PICK GUNMEN

Scenes at Centralia and Armistice Day Martyrs

At the right are the photos of the ex-service men who were shot down by hidden I.W.W.'s at Centralia Tuesday afternoon. Top, Dale Hubbard, right; Warren Grimm; below, Arthur Macelfresh. These sketches were made by Sam Armstrong, News Tribune staff artist, on the scene Tuesday night.

Guard Against New Lynchings at Centralia

CENTRALIA, Wash., Nov. 12.—(By Staff Correspondent)—National guardsmen and citizen deputies are guarding the jail in fear of another raid and lynching. Several I.W.W. prisoners were transferred to the county jail at Chehalis at 11:30. A posse of 40 determined men armed with guns and ropes left for Mendota at noon to raid the ranch of the I.W.W. attorney, Elmer Smith, where it is believed the slayer of Warren Grimm is in hiding.

The body of "Brick" Smith, who was lynched last night, was recovered from the Chehalis river today and taken to the Lewis county morgue at Chehalis.

By JACK QUINLAN
News Tribune Staff Representative

CENTRALIA, Nov. 12.—Murder in the first degree will be charged against every member of the I.W.W. arrested yesterday and last night in connection with the Centralia Armistice Day outrages in which four members of the American Legion, Warren Grimm, Arthur Macelfresh, Ben Casagranda and Dale Hubbard, were killed and three wounded.

ROUNDUP REDS IN TACOMA

On orders from Chief of Police Harry M. Smith every radical in Tacoma is being rounded up by the police and jailed.

Dead; Wounded

The dead as a result of the I.W.W. attack on paraders of the service men in Centralia yesterday are:

Warren Grimm, commander of the Centralia post of the American Legion.

Arthur Macelfresh, veteran of the Argonne battle.

Ben Casagranda, who fought with the 91st division in France.

Dale Hubbard, former soldier.

"Brick" Smith, leader of I.W.W., hanged by irate citizens.

Wounded:

Emery Coleman, John Earl Watt and Eugene Phitner, who marched in the Armistice Day parade.

CRY OF LEADER BRINGS VOLLEY

By JACK QUINLAN
News Tribune Staff Representative

CENTRALIA, Nov. 12.—"Brick" Smith, self-confessed "promoter" of the I.W.W. "Armistice Day" outrage in Centralia, dead—hung by the neck with a rope that is tied to a decayed piece of studding that projects from the old Chehalis river span outside the city limits.

AMERICAN LEGION RISES TO MEET I.W.W.

I.W.W.'s Fire on Bridge

SPIRIT OF VENGEANCE HANGING LIKE PALL OVER OUTRAGED CITY

Day Following Deliberate Slaying of Former Soldiers by I.W.W. Finds Citizens in Angry Mood; Prompt Reprisals to Avenge Deaths Is General Feeling

By ZILPA PHILLIPS

Dragged From Jail—Hanged

CONGRESS IS TOLD RADICALS MUST GO

the day before, saying, "The IWW expected trouble here yesterday and they prepared for it, but when the trouble failed to appear when the Armistice Day parade had about concluded, they decided to start it themselves."[3]

This photo was taken the day after the shooting and the raid on the hall. The windows and door of the hall were knocked out. A canopy extending the width of the Roderick Hotel over the sidewalk was pulled down.

The manhunt remained the center of attention for several days. The city and county jails were full, but there were still some known Wobblies who hadn't been caught. Fears of further violence persisted. Wobbly treachery had been demonstrated. Centralia wouldn't feel safe until all the radicals were locked up.

In pursuit of this commonly accepted objective, city officials printed an appeal and posted it throughout the area. It read:

Have you information of the whereabouts of an IWW? Any person having information, no matter of how little importance, concerning the whereabouts of members of the IWW or any information whatever concerning the outrage committed Armistice Day will confer a favor on the city officials if they will call at once at the city hall and give whatever data they may have to the chief of police.

Centralia paused in the stepped-up war on Wobblies long enough to pay as high a tribute as it knew how to the four servicemen slain on Armistice Day. Individual church funerals for Grimm and Hubbard were followed by a massive memorial service in the city's largest hall, the public auditorium.

The *Chronicle* described it as the

strangest funeral that the United States has ever witnessed and by far the most significant. . . . For the streets had the appearance of an armed city, grim and saddened, but resolute to stand the test and answer any call. Along the line of march were sentries with loaded rifles. They paced their beats about the auditorium itself. Centralia, and the American Legion, having once plumbed the depth of the red venom, were not at all inclined to take another chance. They had every reason to believe that the rabid enmity that turned slaughter loose in a peace parade would not scruple to violate the obsequies of its victims.

The auditorium was bare except for flags draped from the high white ceiling beams. The caskets of McElfresh and Casagranda, whose funerals would not be held until the next day, were side by side at the front of the hall.

Several thousand persons lined the streets to watch as the funeral procession moved slowly through the streets to the Mountain View cemetery. Most stores and offices posted notices saying that the hours of business had been interrupted "in honor of our heroes." Capt. Robert Longmire was the marshal of the

This is the Centralia jail where the Wobblies were locked up on the night of November 11. The photo was taken the next day when Everest's body was being loaded in a van. Guardsmen from Tacoma had been on duty throughout the night to protect the jail inmates from further vigilantism.

parade and Lt. Adrian F. Cormier was the assistant.

Because the staff of the *Chronicle*, busy getting out the paper, could not get away to attend the ceremonies, it held a short memorial service of its own in the newspaper office. The printers, members of the International Typographical Union, passed a resolution deploring the IWW's "dastardly deed." The Central Labor Council, also eager to dispel any notion that it had anything in common with the IWW, issued a statement denouncing the IWW and extending sympathy to the relatives of the shooting victims.

Proper tribute having been given, Centralia returned to its hunt for killers. Dysart's efforts to coordinate the searches were only partially successful. On November 15, two posses set out to check a report that fugitives were hiding in a cabin deep in the woods of the Hannaford District. In one of the parties, from Centralia, were John and George Stephens, Lou Carver, and Kenneth Clark. Among the four men in the other posse was John Haney, a Tenino farmer.

The day was stormy and cold and light was dim beneath the canopy formed by tall firs. The two groups, each unaware of the other's presence, stealthily approached the cabin from different directions, rifles ready to fire if a Wobbly dared show himself or open fire. Across a clearing, in brush near the cabin, the Centralia searchers saw a man, standing still. Immediately George Stephens shouted the prearranged challenge, "American Legion!" There was no answer. In-

stead, the man, who was John Haney, raised his right hand and took hold of the rifle he was carrying in his left. Stephens raised his rifle and shouted again, "Put up your hands!" Haney made no response. "Put them up!" yelled Stephens again. Then he fired. Haney dropped. When one of his companions came out of the shadows and went to him, another bullet from the Centralia posse ripped through his hat. With that, he and two others in the party turned and ran, convinced they had encountered an armed camp of Wobblies. "I went back down the hill, running from one tree to the next to avoid being shot," Ben D. King of Olympia said the next day.[4]

The Centralia posse retreated also, deciding they needed reinforcements before trying to storm what might be a Wobbly stronghold.

Stories of a battle in the woods between possemen and armed Wobblies spread quickly. Dysart said he was sure Bert Bland and Ole Hansen — two on their wanted list — were among those "who fought the posses this afternoon." He said a large force would leave the next morning to bring in the fugitives "dead or alive." When the large force did go back they discovered the tragic error.

Two days went by before the full truth of the mix-up was revealed. Those involved were reluctant to admit that such a thing could happen. As late as November 17 the *Chronicle* published a report saying that "fierce fighting" between Legion posses and IWW leaders had taken place at the head of Hannaford Creek, twenty-four miles from Centralia. The Wobblies were reported to be under seige. Then Haney's body was brought out and Centralia, learning the truth, had another shock to endure. Those involved in the tragedy were shaken. "To me the man standing in the thicket, with the storm whipping about him, was a hated IWW," John Stephens testified at the inquest. "Even now I cannot bring myself to believe that the man who dropped was not one of those we were hunting, though reason tells me it was one of our own comrades on the same mission."[5]

The jury returned a verdict of accidental death. At the end of the inquest, Bill Haney, twenty, one of twelve children in the family, said to members of the posse, "I don't blame you fellows. . . . You did your duty."[6]

The funeral for Haney was an attempt to admit him to martyrdom along with those who lost their lives on November 11 — a martyr who sacrificed his life for a good cause. The IOOF hall, the largest in Tenino, was the scene of the services. Centralia Legionnaires attended in a body and an honor guard of twenty uniformed men was posted. The pallbearers were in uniform. In his eulogy H. E. Veness reached one of his oratorical peaks, saying, "What gives vitality to Christianity? It is that it cost the blood of its founder. Even the race is renewed in the birth chamber by the shedding of blood. And always it takes the best. Socrates, Christ, Lincoln; our boys across the seas; our boys in Centralia; and now this man sacrificed as a vital contribution to the new step that some of us sense that mankind is even now taking."[7]

The funeral procession was a half-mile long. At the graveside, an army bugler blew taps. The slain Wobbly hunter was buried in style.

Bert Bland, Loren Roberts, and Ole Hansen remained the most wanted of the Armistice Day hall defenders still at large. Hansen successfully eluded the searchers and was never caught. Bland and Roberts, the other two Seminary Hill snipers, after parting with Hansen on a back road, went separate ways, but both undertook to hide out in the countryside around the

nearby communities of Rochester and Grand Mound.

Roberts slept in the open the night of the 11th, regretful that he had not followed his first inclination — not to participate in the attempted defense of the hall. It turned out much worse than he expected, as he tried to explain to his mother the next day when he was able to reach home without being seen.

Edna Roberts listened in anguish as her son told of shooting from the hill into the crowd in the street below. She had seen the newspapers — knew Loren was being hunted. She talked to him about giving himself up. He had to, she said. What else could he do? Roberts spent the night of the 12th at home, then the next day went into Centralia with his mother and surrendered. By this time Cunningham was taking statements from any prisoner who would talk, and he found Roberts the most willing talker of any.

Bland stayed free the longest, keeping out of sight, hoping desperately to avoid being recognized until somehow he could get far away and never be caught. He might have made it if he had been more resourceful in finding food. On November 16, after five days of worsening hunger, he made a daring move. He went to the Alex Jaaska store at Helsing Junction, southwest of Rochester, and ordered some groceries, saying he was a logger from a nearby camp.

Jaaska, aware of the manhunt, was suspicious. As he reached for the telephone, Bland nervously pulled out his revolver and backed out of the store. The storekeeper snatched his own gun from under the counter and followed him into the county road. Bland ran, then turned and fired. Jaaska fired back. Charles Hill, living nearby, heard the shots and came running with his gun. He shot at Bland also, but the young Wobbly escaped. His identity was established by a dental receipt he dropped on the floor of the store when he drew his gun.

Bland's next move was to enter the house of Jim "Curley" Mills, a few miles north of Helsing Junction, and demand food. Mills set food on the table and Bland ate "with ravenous haste." He finished and hurried away, heading west toward Independence, a depot stop on the western boundary of Lewis County. Some twelve miles northwest of that village he found an unoccupied shack where he hid.

Posses from Centralia responded promptly to the reports that Bland had been sighted and nearly shot near Rochester. Scores of armed men spread out over the area. On the 19th, members of one posse came to the cabin, approaching it slowly with rifles ready. Bland realized that escape was impossible. He walked out and surrendered.

Bland was described by his captors as being in "terrible physical shape, his boyish face seamed and drawn with the strain and stress of the hunted and the lack of food and shelter."

"Centralia took the news of Bland's arrest with a variety of savage joy," the *Chronicle* reported. "Of all the red murder suspects that have been at large since the killing, it has been Bland whom the searchers have favored with the bitterest hope that they would be in at his capture if he should fight instead of being taken. He is believed to know all there is to know about the Armistice Day assassinations and the plot to attack the American Legion."[8]

An inquest to determine the cause of the death of Warren Grimm, Arthur McElfresh, Dale Hubbard, and Ben Casagranda was convened by Coroner David Livingstone on the morning of November 13, two days after the shootings. This produced the first recorded statements of witnesses and is particularly significant because of the testimony of Dr. Frank Bickford, who stated that, when the parade halted and he was directly in front of the hall, he volunteered to lead a raid. The transcript of the inquest records what he said.

> He offered to take the lead if enough would follow. There were six or eight men in the lead, McElfresh was at the right of Dr. Bickford. Someone larger than McElfresh put his foot against the door of the hall and shoved. Immediately, a shower of bullets came through the door. The first volley consisted of from fifteen to twenty shots, after which everybody scattered. Dr. Bickford got down on his hands and knees and crawled to the corner of the building where he found McElfresh lying on his back. McElfresh was bleeding in the left ear, but Dr. Bickford found no bullet wound on his body. He put McElfresh in a car and started for the hospital with him, but he died on the way.[9]

The next day, the Associated Press carried a story which began with a startling summary:

> Testimony intending to show that the marching ex-servicemen started toward the IWW hall before shots were fired from the building or the Avalon Hotel opposite featured the coroner's inquest over the

bodies of the four former soldiers killed here last Tuesday, and is said to have been responsible for the failure of the jury in rendering a verdict to fix responsibility for the shooting.

The inquest jury found all four deaths were caused by gunshots fired by "persons unknown."

After the capture of Bland, posse activity diminished. Dysart decided he had to go back to school and turned his search leadership over to Frank Van Gilder. By then only fifteen searchers were still out, in addition to guards posted on trails.

Two days later, on November 23, a defiant challenge was received by the Legion posse headquarters. It came from one of the camps of the Mason County Logging Company, near Bordeaux to the north. "The men you want are here," read the message. "Come and try to take them out. We are organized and 90% IWW."

Legion posse men, by this time ready for anything, responded readily. Heavily armed, some two hundred of them boarded logging railroad flatcars and were pulled through the woods to the Bordeaux camp. They met no resistance and found no fugitives. They did discover that this group of loggers were indeed ninety percent loyal to the IWW despite the outburst of public sentiment against the Wobblies after the shootings.

One of the Mason loggers was nineteen-year-old Bert McDonald, who in later years became a prominent Olympic Peninsula logging operator. He described his experience thus:

> We came in from work at noon without knowing what the papers had said and found an ambush with about two hundred ex-soldiers armed to the teeth, led by Prosecutor Cunningham. They held kangaroo court and decided that another fellow and myself were the ringleaders. I was a smart-aleck kid who thought everybody had their rights. They taunted us in every way — tried to get us to sing "The Timber Barons say you will get pie in the sky when you die." They assured us we would get fifteen years. They also offered us a chance to escape with two hundred yards' head start before they started shooting. . . . After lunch we were loaded on flatcars, just two of us to start with, then we picked up four others from the other camps. By this time I began to take it serious and was thinking about the mob who would greet us at Bordeaux and again at Centralia where we heard they were shooting and lynching Wobblies. So I decided it would be better to escape.

I was sitting with my legs over the edge of the flatcar and we came to a long trestle. I felt I was quick enough to jump off and disappear in the brush before they could stop the train. But first I looked around and saw a fellow with a gun a few inches from my back. I decided to stay with the party.

At Bordeaux the big crowd were mostly newspapermen and curiosity seekers. At Centralia they were very hostile and threatened to string us up. They threw us in the can, about twenty of us . . . in a small room. Across the hall were the others who were to spend most of their lives in jail. After four days I got sick from lack of sleep. Commissioner White came out from Washington, D.C., and had me released. . . . That is how I learned about justice and constitutional rights.[10]

15

Rampant Hysteria

The first news accounts of what happened in Centralia were sketchy and incomplete. Headlines on these stories shouted the shocking news: "FOUR LEGIONNAIRES SLAIN BY THE IWW." They did not explain or ascribe a motive for the slayings. News handlers outside Centralia did not know on November 11 or the day after that the Wobblies fired in an attempt to protect their hall against a long-planned raid. That circumstance was not reported for at least twenty-four hours, and then in only a few publications and in ways that raised doubts and questions. The American public initially could only believe that the attack by the members of the IWW on the servicemen marching in observance of the first anniversary of their victory was nothing more than an unprovoked act of sheer terrorism.

This did not seem at all implausible. Wobblies were known to be roughnecks who struck, sabotaged, caused trouble on street corners, were disloyal, and used guns at Everett. It was not considered out of character for them to be rash enough to fire on servicemen in a parade. Their reputation was such that it was easy to believe the worst. Nor was there any sympathy expressed for the one Wobbly who was seized, smoking gun in hand out by the Skookumchuck, and later, in the dark of night, hanged from a bridge.

Wobblies all across the country suffered as a consequence of the way the Centralia violence was reported. Pent-up anger against the radicals was released. Finally they had done something so bad that no one could be critical of recriminations.

On the night of November 12 the Los Angeles headquarters of the IWW was raided and wrecked by club-carrying uniformed servicemen. Numerous radicals were injured.[1]

Near Walla Walla, Legionnaires descended upon two construction camps and forced 120 men to line up with heads bared and arms lifted high while they repeated an oath of allegiance. Four with IWW cards were taken to jail. When news from Centralia reached Portland, enraged ex-servicemen went into action. They charged into a meeting being held at the hall of the Council of Workmen and apprehended fifty-seven men. Later twenty-seven of these were indicted by a grand jury on charges of criminal syndicalism. IWW halls in Aberdeen, Astoria, and elsewhere in the Northwest were raided and closed on November 12. Wobblies by the hundreds were rounded up, taken into custody and jailed.

In Seattle the Centralia affair set off what the *Post-Intelligencer* described as a "campaign of extermination." By midnight on November 12 four IWW meeting places had been raided and thirty-eight Wobblies taken into custody. Detectives sought to connect Seattle IWW leaders with "the Centralia plot."

Only in far away Cincinnati did Centralia-inspired vigilante action meet with any official disapproval. There Mayor John Galvin censured members of the Legion who raided the headquarters of the Socialist Party and burned what they considered to be radical literature. He denounced the raid as "mob rule."

U.S. Attorney Robert C. Saunders, who for years exhibited symptoms of the "Wobbly horrors" at least equal to those that afflicted any lumber executives, was flabbergasted, bad as he knew the IWW to be. The radicals were guilty of an outrage worse than anything he ever feared or imagined. He sprang into action.

First he sent out instructions to law enforcement officers throughout the Northwest. Arrest every IWW suspect who can be found, whether he carries a card or is known to be a member, and hold him for federal investigation. Next he began sending frenzied reports to his superior, Attorney General A. Mitchell Palmer. In one message he warned that "the gravity of the situa-

RAIDS! RAIDS!! RAIDS!!!

Telegrams are coming in from all parts of the country telling of raids, of halls and offices having been closed, of furniture, office fixtures and typewriters having been destroyed. Many tons of literature has been confiscated or burned in bonfires; members have been badly beaten and hundreds of them thrown into prison. They have met with the same savage cruelty as perpetrated under the old Russian regime of pogrom when Cossacks committed the foulest and most vicious crimes against the Jews.

Here in the United States of America it matters not what an individual's religion may be, his color, his nationality, or the industry in which he is employed; if he is an I. W. W., he has no rights that profiteers or politicians are compelled to respect.

This most recent outrage began at Centralia, a small town in the State of Washington, where a number of large lumber companies have their local headquarters. An Armistice Day parade had been arranged. The paraders marched past the I. W. W. headquarters, turned and counter marched, and when nearing the end of the parade it is said that twenty-five or thirty men broke

tion from the federal standpoint cannot be exaggerated. The Centralia murders were clearly not individual but wicked assassination . . . and intended to obstruct all federal military activity by subjecting ex-servicemen to fear of assassination after discharge. . . . "[2] Saunders outlined to Palmer what he proposed to do: Seize all IWW records, literature, and paraphernalia; arrest all Wobblies and prosecute them.

Washington's attorney general, L. L. Thompson, was equally agitated. He appealed to Palmer for federal intervention, saying, "IWW situation demands action. Several hundred members now held on open charges and public sentiment greatly inflamed."[3] He asked that the Wobblies be prosecuted in federal courts because federal laws on conspiracy were more stringent than state laws. Palmer, three thousand miles away, was not moved to panic. He regarded the reports he received from Washington State as intemperate.

Newspapers — then the only means of daily communication — eagerly joined the general angry, patriotic uproar. The spirit of Everett's Beverly Park prevailed. Get the Wobblies. Convict them or hang them. Close the halls. Arrest anyone with a Red card. Smash the IWW once and for all.

The press on the scene, the newspapers of Lewis County, had to do more than rant. They knew the circumstances — what had brought on the violence. And they knew that their readers knew. So the big story was handled somewhat gingerly and the editorial comments undertook to express what the local editors

This is part of an IWW flier circulated after the Centralia violence and a wave of hall raidings swept the country.

considered to be the local public reaction, as small-city newspapers customarily did.

Two occurrences presented difficulties for the Centralia editors. One was the lynching. The all-night turmoil around the jail with the mob screaming for blood was not a journalistic concern. That could be ignored. The lynching itself could not.

The other troublesome occurrence was the unbelievable thoughtlessness of Dr. Bickford when he testified at the inquest that Legionnaires kicked in the door of the hall before the shooting started. This could be interpreted as an accusation. It made the good men in uniform appear to be aggressors who were fired on for some reason other than murderous villainy.

The *Chronicle,* trying to justify the lynching, said, "The episode of last night is but the natural result of a red-handed revolutionist getting his just desserts without loss of time or the painfully slow processes of the law. The man's guilt was unquestioned. . . . "

The paper even implied that the lynching might not and maybe ought not be the last. "What will be the fate of the captured conspirators only time can tell," it declared, "but there must be no travesty to justice as happened to Everett IWWs three years ago when . . . the murderers were tried in Seattle and finally released." The "apparent" infringement of the law, the lynching, concluded the *Chronicle* editor, "was the essence of

The IWW hall in New York was raided four days after the Centralia violence.

law and order. The man was self-convicted and the law-abiding committee was determined that no technicalities of law would in this case defeat the ends of justice. The people are tired of temporizing with a class of human beings whose evident intention is revolution. The end justified the means."[4]

The *Lewis County Advocate* in Chehalis admitted that "freedom-loving citizens deplore the use of mob force" but added that "we cannot blame the comrades of the slain patriots when they forgot all else but the biblical injunction of an 'eye for an eye' and took the

avowed leader of the Centralia murderers and hung him by the neck until dead. He more than deserved what he got and it was a commendable exhibition of reserve on the part of his executioners when, after they were inside the jail and had a dozen others who were mixed up in the crime at their mercy, they did not take them all out and hang them with their leader."

As for Bickford's damaging inquest testimony, the

local press tried to explain it by saying he admitted to being a little hard of hearing. Certainly the shots were fired before the men pounced on the hall. Bickford simply did not hear them.

Except for Allen saying "the boys" listened to him and there would be no more lynchings, officials remained silent on the subject, then and afterward. "No county official would admit that any lynching had taken place," the *Hub* reported. "No official wanted to be told of such action and it was generally understood that no effort would be made to learn the details or to bring any of those implicated before the courts."

One Chehalis citizen was quoted by the *Hub* as saying that "if any man on the street spoke up in defense of the acts of the IWW he would knock him down. . . . This sentiment seems to be reflected generally," the paper added.

The Centralia episode, lynching and all, and horrible though all professed it to be, did provide an opportunity for satisfying expressions of "we told you so's" concerning the Wobblies. Editorial writers were unrestrained in their condemnations and righteous assertions that now nothing should stand in the way of bringing the long war on Wobblies to a final end.

"For months the hell's spawn of the IWW have been preaching their hideous doctrines throughout the Northwest without let or hindrance," cried the *Tacoma News-Tribune*. "Their glib tongued orators have been ranting from soap boxes, shouting murder, sabotage and bolshevism. They have been deliberately corrupting the minds of the young and impressionable and filling their souls with lies and class poison . . . ." The *News-Tribune* called for speedy justice for the Centralia prisoners "to permit these murderers to receive the ultimate penalty of death which they so richly deserve."

Newspapers elsewhere in the nation were only a little less shrill. The respected *Washington Star* said, "No other single act of violence ever committed in a state of peace in this country has so stirred the patriotism of the people, has so appealed to their loyalty, or so aroused their determination to fight the radicals who are seeking to overthrow our institution. . . . "

The blood lust for revenge heard from the jailhouse mob on the night of the lynching came out in print. Wrote one Grays Harbor citizen to the *Aberdeen World*, "Let our physicians and surgeons ignore them in their hours of sickness and death. Bar them from all kinds of labor and let them feed upon each other; refuse them admittance to our schools and churches. . . . Let the merchants refuse to sell them merchandise. . . . Brand as a shyster any lawyer who defends them and bar him from any further practice before the bar of justice."[6]

What the Wobblies did in Centralia roused Legionnaires like the call to arms in 1917. "Eleven thousand ex-servicemen of Washington, in seventy-five posts of the American Legion, stand ready to assemble under arms and to fight to the last ditch to wipe out once and for all the bolshevism in this state," declared E. A. Kleebs, state adjutant of the Legion.

Expressions of mass indignation poured into the office of Gov. Hart, demanding action "to rid the commonwealth of its enemies who are undertaking to destroy it." Congressman Albert Johnson, whose district included Centralia, added to the chorus, contending that the shootings were a revolutionary act motivated by class hatred.

Gen. John J. Pershing, as much a hero one year after the 1918 victory as George Dewey, Ulysses S. Grant, or even George Washington were after the nation's previous military triumphs, expressed his outrage, saying, "Too drastic measures cannot be taken to rid the country of the class of criminals who inspire or commit such crimes."

The Centralia hysteria extended inevitably into politics. "This detestable outrage," thundered Sen. Miles Poindexter, a vocal Republican, "is the fearful penalty which Centralia has paid for the over-lenient policy of the national administration toward anarchists and murderous Communists."

But what the press said about Centralia in the days after November 11 was not entirely all of a kind. Joseph Pulitzer's *New York World*, in its lead editorial two days after the shootings, expressed disgust with the Centralia-inspired hysteria that brought on wholesale arrests of men who were not even near Centralia on Armistice Day. "What the State of Washington plainly

Three of the arrested Wobblies were believed to have criminal records. Luke May, retained by lumber companies and Lewis County to help prepare a case against the accused men, sent this circular to Northwest law enforcement offices. Only one had a record — Ray Becker, who gave the name of Ralph Bergdorff when he was arrested in Spokane for breaking out of jail in Bellingham, where he had been held on a draft evasion charge.

CONFIDENTIAL TO OFFICERS
DO NOT POST

The three men whose pictures, description and finger print classifications appear below are awaiting trial for first degree murder. They are all radical I. W. W's. Any information regarding them should be sent to the undersigned immediately.

Michael (Mike) Sheehan alias Mike Shannon. Sab cat around Spokane during wobbly trouble. 5 ft. 10 inches, 200 lbs., grey hair, grey eyes, heavy build, ruddy complexion, 55 yrs. old, Irish.
Finger Print 1 U 00 9
2 U I0

James McInerny, alias James Mack, has been active all over northwest. 5 ft. 11 in., weight 175 lbs. Hair dark brown, medium complexion. Age 34.
Finger Print 29 — I 14
19 — I

Ralph Bergdorff, alias Ray Becker. Height 5 ft. 7 in., weight 140 lbs. Medium complexion, medium build, hair dark brown, hazel eyes. Age 23.
Finger Print 1 u 00 18
3 — I

REVELARE INTERNATIONAL SECRET SERVICE, Inc.

L. S. MAY, President

Represented in all principal cities of United States, Canada and Orient

Send information regarding this circular to Executive Offices,

415 TO 421 LYON BLDG., SEATTLE, WASHINGTON

WANTED

Information Concerning Whereabouts of
Wm. H. COLLINS

Description: Height, 5 Feet 8 Inches; Age 42.

Notify Sheriff of Lewis County; Chief of Police, Centralia, or American Legion, Centralia, Washington

Chronicle Print Centralia, Wn.

needs," admonished the *World*, "is an administration that has brains enough to deal with a murder case according to the process of law. It is not a crime to be a member of the IWW.... Nor is it a crime in itself to be a Bolshevik." Shocking as they were, the *World* went on to say, "the Armistice Day murders at Centralia were not rebellion or revolution or sedition, or anything but plain murders. There is testimony now which goes to show that they were not even premeditated, but resulted from a conflict between members of the IWW and some of the marchers in the parade who fell out of line and attacked the IWW headquarters...."

Organized labor, meaning the AFL, never had much affection for and certainly no affiliation with the IWW. But both had common foes who were quick to use the Centralia affair as proof that all labor organizations were inherently bad, as employers and much of the press had been saying all along.

The AFL had a press of its own, the *Seattle Union Record.* In the November 12 issue it gave assurance that "organized labor has had no connection with nor has it any sympathy for the perpetrators of the violence in Centralia no matter whom they may be, and from the facts at hand both sides have earned the severest condemnation of law-abiding people."

But its editorial reaction was in marked contrast with that of other newspapers when, on page one, it proclaimed in large type:

DON'T SHOOT IN THE DARK
VIOLENCE BEGETS VIOLENCE
ANARCHY CALLS FORTH ANARCHY

That is the answer to the Centralia outrage.

And the reason for it is found in the constant stream of laudation in the kept press of un-American illegal and violent physical attacks upon the persons of those who disagree with the powers that be.

The rioting which culminated in the death of our returned servicemen at Centralia last night was the result of a long series of illegal acts by these men themselves and the acts which no paper in the state was American enough to print, except the *Union Record.*

The man who fired shots from the Avalon Hotel was identified as "John Doe Davis." He was probably William H. Collins, shown in this "wanted" poster issued shortly after the violence. He was never apprehended.

The Wobbly side of the Centralia story did get out quickly enough to reach the Butte, Montana, *Bulletin*, an IWW paper, in time for its November 12 edition, and since the Centralia defenders were locked up, dead, or in hiding, there is a possibility that the *Bulletin* was called by one of the two who got away — Hansen or Davis. In the best tradition of angry Wobbly journalism, the *Bulletin* commented:

The thugs of the lumber trust were riding behind the uniform and the name of the American Legion in Centralia. . . . The lumber barons have recruited dozens of General Disque's spruce heroes for the noble work of crushing organization. It is apparent to everyone not blinded by prejudice that the members of the IWW in Centralia were faced with the alternative of becoming nonresident victims of the white-collar mob or of dying fighting. . . . There is not the slightest doubt that the parade yesterday stopped at the headquarters of the IWW in agreement with a prearranged plan to clean out the premises and that the story carried by the capitalist press is a gross and willful misrepresentation of the facts sent out from Centralia by some tool of the lumber interest.

A cartoon in *New Solidarity,* published by the IWW in Chicago, showed an American Legion member saluting a fat figure in a swallowtail coat and top hat, with Wesley Everest, wearing an army uniform, hanging from the limb of a tree. The Legionnaire is saying, "Sir, I hung my buddy for you."

The *Seattle Union Record* was edited by E. B. Ault, an intelligent, articulate labor journalist. On his staff was the daughter of a Seattle minister, Anna Louise Strong, a firebrand lover of all liberal causes who was attracted to anything radical like a Wobbly to a street fight. She went on to make a career of being a radical and was one of the first Americans to be admitted to Russia after the revolution. She ended her years in the People's Republic of China.[7]

The Union Record editorial on November 12, which urged that passions not prevail until the full truth about Centralia were known, was generally regarded as pro-Wobbly propaganda. Await the truth? What truth? There was no question about the truth. It was quite evident. Four servicemen were killed. The Wobblies did it.

But Ault, despite his lack of affection for the IWW, saw the makings of a great injustice in the aftermath of Centralia. Two days later he collaborated with others in drafting a strong resolution repudiating violence as a means of attaining desirable ends and undertaking to set the facts straight. It said:

> 1. The tragedy was the culmination of a series of outrages perpetrated by lawless bands of Centralia businessmen.
>
> 2. . . . The parade halted in front of the IWW hall where the more hot tempered members of the column were urged to maintain their ranks and not invade the hall. . . . A window was smashed before any shots were fired. . . .
>
> 3. . . . Out of the ravings of a man about to be lynched, the prattlings of a boy just turned sixteen (presumably Roberts) and the vituperations of an aged woman whose furniture had just been destroyed by a mob (Mrs. McAllister), the prosecuting attorney intends to build a conspiracy which will send every man in the hall to the gallows. . . .
>
> In view of these facts and the further fact that every effort is being made by the kept press of this city . . . to mislead and inflame the public mind and use the incident to arouse the mob spirit everywhere, we call upon all true Americans to arouse themselves to combat the suggested violations of the law and to see that every principle of our Constitution be upheld and kept inviolate.[8]

The *Post-Intelligencer's* deep-seated prejudices against labor were aroused as never before by this statement. Its heaviest editorial artillery was brought out on page one on November 14 to blast labor with the worst accusations that could have been made against it — that it was soft on the IWW:

> Frankly we charge that organized labor in Seattle and in the state has given aid and comfort to the IWW and every anarchistic organization in the state.
>
> Organized labor has insisted with full voice that every IWW should have the fullest protection of the last letter of the law in their attempt to destroy the law.
>
> Organized labor has contributed its funds, hired its lawyers, paraded, and pamphleteered in defense of every assassin bearing an IWW card who has been brought to the bar of justice . . . but never has organized labor gone on record as deploring the activities of the IWW; never has there been one offical word of discouragement or disapproval. Organized labor has officially stood in silence before every revolutionary activity of the IWW and other Reds and has only spoken in their defense. . . .

This attack was too much for A. M. Short, president of the Washington State Federation of Labor. He sent a telegram to Attorney General Palmer saying the "dangerous state of public excitement that menaces the peace of this community" was being inflamed by exaggerated editorials in the Seattle newspapers. "The tragedy that occurred at Centralia," he said, "in which four returned servicemen were foully murdered by insane members of the IWW has aroused a feeling of revulsion everywhere and particularly in the ranks of legitimate labor." Short's telegram urged the attorney general to stop "this vicious labor baiting or close both papers (the *Times* and *P-I*) temporarily in the interests of public peace."[9]

But it was not the large dailies that were closed in the hysterical aftermath of Centralia; rather, it was labor's own paper.

Seattle still had not gotten over the shock of the general strike eight months earlier. The *Union Record* was involved in that strike. It had never openly supported the IWW but it sympathized with their plight in Centralia, especially when Tom Lassiter, the half-blind newsdealer, was expelled for daring to sell the *Union Record* and other labor papers. What the *P-I* said about organized labor being too friendly with the Wobblies expressed the feelings of leaders in Seattle just as the *Chronicle's* emotional outpourings reflected those of the establishment in that city. So intense were feelings generally in the days after the shootings that any printed suggestion that the Wobblies were not black with guilt could not be tolerated.

Saunders was the local federal law enforcement officer and he was expected to do something about a newspaper expressing opinions as outrageous as those appearing in the *Union Record.* The pressure for him to act was strong and on November 14 he told reporters, "We are going by every legal means to have a cleaning out of such publications. There is no room for them in this country. . . . The government is in deadly earnest. . . . I think the *Union Record* is open to prosecution."[10]

After wiring the attorney general again, quoting the "intemperate language" of the *Union Record* editorial, he obtained search warrants for a raid. Saunders wanted the recognition he felt he deserved for taking courageous action in time of crisis and so invited the newspapers and a newsreel company to send reporters and photographers to accompany him while he did his duty. They responded with enthusiasm. With several U.S. marshals at his side, and trailed by the press, Saunders descended upon the shabby offices of the *Union Record,* arrested editor Ault on a charge of violating the federal espionage act, and confiscated all papers found in desk drawers and filing cabinets that looked as if they might support accusations of disloyalty or subversion. Then the party moved to the plant of the Equity Printing Company where Walker C. Smith, then editor of the *International Weekly,* was also arrested. Files, records, and subscription lists there were seized also.

Thus, in the name of the United States of America, the First Amendment notwithstanding, two previously acceptable publications were forbidden to publish pending a determination of the guilt or innocence of those who expressed opinions in their pages. The public reaction to the press suppression was one of approval. The nonlabor Seattle papers, of course, were delighted. Saunders was proclaimed a hero.

Organized labor was enraged. The Machinists Union, 3,200 strong, and the Central Labor Council of Tacoma were the first to protest with strongly worded resolutions. The Seattle Central Labor Council named a committee of fifteen which went into session immediately. It issued an appeal for funds to fight the closures and called on Samuel Gompers, president of the AFL, to intercede. He did, asking Palmer to make an investigation.

While Palmer was investigating, an extremist right-wing paper in Seattle, the *Business Chronicle,* temporarily took the spotlight off the *Union Record* with an editorial that outdid anything the radical press had published in using inflammatory language. Written by the editor, Edwin Selvin, this editorial was reprinted in paid advertisements appearing in the *Tacoma Ledger,* the *Seattle Star,* and the *Post-Intelligencer.* It read:

> We must smash every un-American organization in the land. We must put to death the leaders of this gigantic conspiracy of murder, pillage and revolution. We must imprison for life all its aiders and abetters of native birth. We must deport all aliens. The IWW, the Non-Partisan League and so-called Triple Alliance in the State of Washington, the pro-German Socialists, the closed shop labor unions, the agitators, the malcontents, anarchists, syndicalists, seditionists, traitors, and the whole motley crew of Bolshevists and

> near-Bolshevists must be outlawed by public opinion and hunted down and hounded until driven beyond the horizon of civic decency. The administration in Washington has made a mess alike of the affairs of the world and the affairs of the American people. It is simple truth to state that the federal government in the hands of the present administration is responsible in greater degree than any other single agency for the present chaotic and menacing condition.[11]

The publishers of the newspapers that printed the advertisement containing the Selvin editorial claimed to be as horrified as anyone when they saw it, and hastened to repudiate it in their next day's editions, saying it had gotten by without anyone above the level of the advertising staff seeing it. Nevertheless it was printed and it gave the owners of the closed *Union Record* more evidence to support their claim that they were being made victims of press-incited hysteria.

William Short, president of the State Federation of Labor, wired the attorney general, quoting the Selvin editorial and pointing out that the AFL, which Selvin had called the "un-American Federation of Labor," included many who were members of the administration party — Democratic. In the telegram he said, "The article is replete with a denunciation of the national administration and of President Wilson who are equally responsible with organized labor. It insists on the leaders of labor being murdered and the movement exterminated. The article is inciting riot and is treason in its rankest form and menaces the immediate peace of the community. . . ."[12]

The publication of the Selvin editorial by the *P-I* was something of a "last straw" for the printers in the newspaper's composing room. They met, drafted a strongly worded resolution condemning their employers, and then, to the astonishment of readers, were able to print the resolution in the *P-I.*

The resolution said the union had been

> patient under misrepresentation, faithful in the face of slander, long suffering under insult; we have upheld our agreements and produced your paper, even though in doing so we were braiding the rope with which you propose to hang us; day after day we have put in type, stereotyped, printed and mailed calumny after calumny, lie after lie, insult after insult. . . . We have even meekly witnessed your unfair and reprehensible campaign of falsehood and ruin resulting in the suppression of the last medium of honest expres-

sion for our cause in Seattle, not only denying our brothers the means of livelihood, but denying us a far greater boon — the American right of a free press. So long as these things appeared to be a part of your unfair fight against organization — our organization and others — we have been able to endure them in the hope that at last truth must prevail. . . .[13]

The resolution concluded by saying that the Selvin editorial which the *P-I* printed was too much. In it "your hatred of opposition, your reckless policy of appeal to the passions of citizenry, reached depths of malice and malignancy hitherto unbelievable. . . ."[14]

Management of the *P-I* appended two paragraphs to this resolution before it was printed, explaining that the objectionable Selvin piece had not been approved by management before it appeared in the paper.

Shocked readers of the *Post-Intelligencer* concluded that *P-I* management must have been forced to publish, under some kind of duress, the vitriolic denunciation of itself. The *P-I* editors hastened to explain the next day that this was not so. The resolution was published, they said, to show what they had to put up with in getting out a newspaper in such times.

Meanwhile the pressure applied in Washington, D.C., on behalf of the *Union Record* took effect. Saunders was told to take the locks off the doors of the closed publications and tell the owners that publication could be resumed.

But this did not end the *Union Record's* troubles growing out of the Centralia case. As soon as publication was resumed, the Seattle postmaster barred it from the mails, and an appeal made to U.S. District Court Judge Edward D. Cushman was denied.

Organized labor warmed up to the fight. On November 25 Saunders wrote the attorney general that "as forecast . . . in my letter of the 14th the local fight around the *Seattle Union Record* and its rights is now between the government on the one hand and the AFL on the other. . . ."

C. B. Blethen, editor of the *Times,* was enraged by the decision to let the *Union Record* resume publication. "Permission to resume means extraordinary encouragement of Red radical anarchy," he wired to the attorney general. "If *Union Record* resumes publication riots are almost certain to follow. In addition influence of loyal press will be completely smashed. For God's sake do not permit this triumph of Bolshevism over Americanism."

The messages from Saunders and Blethen made less of an impression on members of the Wilson administration in Washington, however, than did messages from leaders in organized labor and prominent Democrats in Washington.

George E. Ryan, chairman of the Democratic State Executive Committee, wrote to Joseph R. Tumulty, secretary to President Wilson, to say that organized labor was greatly upset by what had happened, and especially so because the *Union Record's* competitors were invited to be witnesses to its closing. He said the *Tacoma Times* even published a report on the raid before it took place.

Ryan told Tumulty that inflammatory articles in the *Times* and *P-I* caused industrial unrest and possibly had something to do with the murder of American soldiers in Centralia. He enclosed a reprint of the Selvin editorial. Ryan also told of the shooting of John Haney, saying that the Seattle papers did not publish the news of the mistaken shooting "until public feeling had been worked up to a point where murder of innocent men might have resulted."[15]

The federal grand jury met early in December. Saunders predicted that the editors of the *Union Record* as well as Selvin would be indicted. But the grand jury returned indictments only against Ault; George P. Listman, a member of the board of directors of the Union Record Publishing Company; Frank A. Rusk, president of the board; and Anna Louise Strong. Listman had been an unsuccessful candidate for the Seattle school board in an election held the day before the grand jury returned the indictments. The jury foreman was the chief opponent of Miss Strong when she was on the school board. Those indicted were charged with violation of the federal espionage act of 1917.

Numerous appeals were received by Palmer not to prosecute Miss Strong. "The prosecution of a person of her type would be an advertisement to the world that the days of free speech are over," wrote Hubert C. Herring, D.D., secretary of the National Council of the Congregational Churches of the United States. Another wrote that she "is a cultured, high minded and very capable young woman."

Newton D. Baker, secretary of war, received an appeal in behalf of Strong from Dan F. Bradley, pastor of the Pilgrim Church, Cleveland, saying: "If Anna Louise in her writing has gone beyond the proper bounds of freedom, it may be because of her association and the tense atmosphere of the State of Washington where one is tempted to be either a near Bolshevik or a rabid reactionary like the distinguished Senator Poindexter. . . . "

After the Democratic leaders of the state pressured Tumulty, the Department of Justice was persuaded to be lenient. The charges against the indicted journalists were dropped.

Even Saunders relented, but it took a long time. Four months later he could write to the attorney general and concede that the court was right in dismissing indictments. He added, "A further consideration is the condition of the public mind after a cessation of active hostilities."[16]

16

A Town in Turmoil

Calm was slow in coming to Centralia after its day and night of horror. Each day brought more incidents and rumors, keeping tensions alive and creating new apprehensions about what might happen next. The spotlight of nationwide attention added to the discomfort of the community. Centralia, an ordinary American town, proud of its growth and accomplishments, suddenly was no longer ordinary. Something terrible had lifted it into the spotlight of public attention. And it wasn't over. No one could tell what the ultimate consequences might be.

Most comments which appeared in newspapers were sympathetic. Centralia, they said, had been victimized by the IWW. But not all said that. Some reports carried implications of shame.

The Haney killing was a shock but the manhunt later was rewarded by the capture of Bert Bland and the forcing of Loren Roberts out of hiding. Each day more suspicious-looking working-class types were brought in by the posses to be jailed and examined. As the jails filled and the workers fled, however, the number of seizures declined. On the night of November 14, three days after the violence, only forty men were brought in and fifteen of these did not seem menacing enough to lock up. The city and county jails were jammed by then, mostly with men being held without charge. Stories of what they had to endure drifted out to the citizens, who were uncomfortable that many not involved in the Armistice Day affair were being treated harshly in their own town.

Laura Smith, Elmer's wife, did not know until the next day, November 12, that Elmer had been arrested. When he failed to return home, she could only speculate fearfully about what might have happened. Like many other wives of someone known to be a Wobbly or even a friend of one, she was afraid to leave the house. She learned of Elmer's fate when her sister-in-law, Mrs.

James Smith, came to the house on Wednesday with the news that both their husbands were in jail. They went together to see them but that day of turmoil was no time for jail visits. They were turned away.

Reports from the hospital on November 13 said John Watt hovered between life and death all night and through Wednesday, then showed signs of improvement. Eventually he recovered.

On the night of the 14th lights went off all over the city again, bringing the same thought to all — another lynching. Some rushed out and headed for the jail, hoping to get in on the excitement, and there was some disappointment when it turned out to be an ordinary power failure.

Armed men in uniform continued to guard the entrances to Centralia and Chehalis. On the night of November 14, C. A. Godfrey, an employee of the Doty mill, did not respond to three successive challenges as he was returning home from an evening visit out of town. A nervous guardsman, assuming he was confronted with an enemy, raised his rifle and fired. A repetition of the tragic Haney shooting was avoided when the bullet hit Godfrey in the shoulder.

After the mob action on Tuesday night townspeople were ordered to stay off the streets after dark. Later this curfew was modified to 11:30. "Loafers after that hour will be subject to arrest," decreed the mayor.

In that first week Centralia came to realize that the Wobbly difficulties were by no means over and that no one could expect pleas of guilty by the men caught with guns in their hands while servicemen lay dead in the streets, nor even for a quick trial and certain convictions. None but a few fanatics, and the radical press in Seattle, dared suggest that responsibility for the violence lay anywhere except with the IWW.

The Wobblies by 1919 were seasoned veterans of what they called class-war conflict and were skilled at pamphleteering and other means of bypassing the newspapers to reach the public. What the public began to hear was that the radical sources were telling a different story from the one in the public press. Yes, they said, four servicemen were killed by Wobbly gunfire. But no, it was not terrorism. It was a group of men defending their meeting hall against mob violence.

Centralians were unwilling to concede that there was any truth in this. A defensive posture gradually took form, as if by common consent. It was a posture the battered city was never to back away from. It had to do with the few seconds before and after the shooting began, and with a tight-lipped silence about the lynching and any intentions the city had concerning violent expulsion of the IWW. No matter what Dr. Bickford said, it was concluded, he was wrong. He had to be, for otherwise the Wobblies would have substantiation for their claim that they were defending, not attacking, and fired only after an assault had begun. Any suggestion that the Wobblies were not entirely to blame was dismissed as impossible and intolerable. What Centralia must say to the world, in court and out, was that the Wobblies in their town hatched a cruel conspiracy which had as its aim the commission of a barbarous act of terrorism. The Legionnaires were simply innocent victims and the accused Wobblies were guilty. All this most Centralians believed, in full sincerity or not, and from this belief there was no deviation in all the turmoil of the closing battles and skirmishes of the Wobbly war.

It was the kind of war every respectable person was expected to join and support, establishing beyond doubt the guilt of the killers, sending them to their punishment, and refuting the lies the IWW was circulating about Centralia and what had happened there.

Few dared dissent from this posture. So it made headlines when N. B. Coffman, Chehalis banker and prominent layman in the Episcopal church, startled a mass meeting in Portland on November 15. As the news report stated, "He indicted the church and laid to it a large share of the blame for the outbreak in Centralia." "We cannot be Jekylls and Hydes," Coffman said. "We cannot be one thing in church and another in business. We cannot have two standards — one for church and another in business. No man can be a Christian who exploits his brother man."

While his audience was pondering this apparent reference to the way loggers were treated, Coffman got

back on track by adding that "we are valiantly going to fight this demon of Bolshevism."

Others who may have had misgivings about where responsibility for the tragedy of Armistice Day lay remained silent. Some who could give testimony that might help the Wobblies in court determined not to give it, as some admitted in later years when they felt free to speak.

As the turmoil of the first few days diminished, the attention of official Centralia and Chehalis turned to the problems of prosecution. The jails were full of men whose only offense was their affiliation with the IWW, but overshadowing them were the eleven involved in the shootings — the "guilty eleven" — who, much as they might not deserve it, had to be given a fair trial. For this the prosecutor needed help. Fortunately help was at hand in the person of C. D. Cunningham, a former prosecutor and now a seasoned lawyer and a Legionnaire who marched in the parade and was on the scene when Everest shot Hubbard. He was obviously the one best fitted to prepare a case that would get the Wobblies through the court and to the gallows as quickly as possible. He was retained by the county as special prosecutor for a fee of five thousand dollars.

The jailed Wobblies began thinking about their defense as soon as the Tacoma guardsmen took up station outside the jail so they would be spared Everest's fate. They would get a trial. Who would be their lawyer?

The Lewis County Bar Association called a meeting at which it was soon agreed that none of its members would ever take a Wobbly as a client. Instead it was now the duty of Lewis County lawyers to help the prosecution. Volunteers were called to help with the work of preparing complaints. A. A. Hull, H. E. Donahue, G. O. Thacker, J. M. Ponder, and O. J. Albers stepped forward to take on this assignment with no remuneration expected.

The firm of Vanderveer and Pierce in Seattle began to specialize in IWW defense cases after it successfully defended the Wobblies accused in the Everett dockside shootings of 1916. George Vanderveer was in Chicago when the Centralia trouble occurred, defending the top-ranking IWW members accused under wartime acts of disloyalty and subversion. Ralph Pierce was trying a case in Pasco, but could get away immediately. He boarded a train for Centralia and the Legion, forewarned that he was coming, sent

Elmer Smith

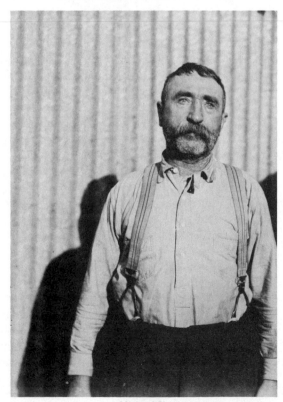

Michael Sheehan

two men in uniform to meet it and inform him that he couldn't get off. They stayed with him when the train went on to make sure he didn't get off in nearby Chehalis. Pierce had to ride on to Castle Rock where he got off and caught the next train going back. When it stopped in Chehalis, the same two uniformed men got on and again kept him from debarking in Centralia.

Pierce finally did get to Centralia on November 17 after telegraphing Herman Allen, complaining that he was the victim of a conspiracy to keep him from seeing the men he would be representing in court. Pierce did not see the prisoners soon enough to caution them about giving statements. Before he arrived, Cunningham and Allen pulled most of them out of jail, one by one, to be questioned with a court reporter present. As a consequence some of them, disregarding Cunningham's reminder that anything they said might later be used against them, answered all questions with complete candor, especially Loren Roberts and Tom Morgan. They related, in as much detail as they could remember, just what happened in the days leading up to Armistice Day, and what happened on that fateful day.

Statements were taken from John Lamb, O. C. Bland, Dewey Lamb, Roberts, and Morgan.[1] An attempt to get McInerney to talk failed. He had been through the Everett trial and was wary. He knew he had a right to see a lawyer and stubbornly refused to reveal anything except his place of birth and how long he had been a Wobbly. Roberts was such a willing talker that he was taken to Olympia after his first interrogation, presumably to keep him from being dissuaded by the other prisoners from making further revelations. There he was questioned a second time, with his mother present. Morgan also gave a repeat performance.

Excerpts from these statements were published with some glee in the newspapers and called "confessions." This was not entirely inaccurate in Roberts's case, since he described in detail how he and Bland and Hansen shot into the servicemen from Seminary Hill. Roberts talked freely either out of ignorance of criminal procedures or at the urging of a mother who believed that telling the truth was always the best policy. In the weeks that followed Roberts came to be declared insane by the defense attorneys, and whether he was or not, he began to act as if he were.

Morgan was labeled a "stool pigeon" by the IWW for talking openly with the prosecutors after getting assurance that he would not be prosecuted if he helped build a case against the others. He gave two statements, obviously in the expectation that he, alone among those in the hall when the shooting occurred, would not go to trial.

Pierce was allowed to see the prisoners one at a time and emphasized to each that nothing should be said to support a contention that the shootings were planned in advance. Any such admission would constitute evidence of a conspiracy and conspiracy to commit murder was a very serious offense indeed.

Both sides then began preparation for what was sure to be a lengthy and difficult trial involving hundreds of witnesses. Those who would testify for one side or the other had to be found and interviewed. This called for extensive undercover work. Not many witnesses were willing volunteers and some, as investigations in later years revealed, refused to talk to anyone, in or out of court, about what they had seen. The Wobblies were dangerous men. Anyone who testified against them in court might be subject to reprisals. Others who knew their testimony would support the contention of the Wobblies that they fired only at men attacking the hall didn't want to appear as Wobbly sympathizers. It was better just to keep quiet.

The prosecutors had more success than the defense in the witness hunt. The investigative firm of Luke May in Seattle had been used for several years by lumber industry employers to keep them informed about union activities. Now it was retained by Lewis County. May's operatives were put to work lining up witnesses. The IWW also had undercover agents who could question a prospective witness without revealing which side they were on.

While the lawyers were busy with these preparations, some citizens, still in a state of fear and anti-Wobbly frenzy, sought new ways to get at their foes. Governor Hart received a petition from Montesano calling for a special session of the legislature to pass more stringent laws aimed at suppressing the IWW. The governor replied that laws already passed, notably the antisyndicalism law, were sufficient. What was needed, he said, was more vigorous prosecutions under the new statue which "makes membership . . . in the IWW a felony." The Montesanans were not reassured. If the existing laws were adequate, they asked, how could the tragedy in Centralia have happened?

Hart came up with a new anti-Wobbly scheme. He

Eugene Barnett

Loren Roberts

John Lamb

Britt Smith

would set up a state Loyal League organization with branches in every county. These vigilantes would undertake to rid the state of the IWW "and other enemies of the government." Hart appointed William Scales as Lewis County's representative on the state organization.

Lewis County acted promptly. On November 17, six days after the shootings, the Elks Club in Chehalis was packed by citizens eager to join the new Loyal American League. A call for contributions was made to help pay the costs of the manhunt and the prosecution. Response was immediate and generous. The money came in faster than it could be counted, and when finally it was, the secretary, Virgil Lee, reported that more than a thousand dollars had been collected.

The Grant Hodge post had time finally on November 22 to hold a meeting at which it voted support of the Loyal Legion. The Legionnaires were informed then that state authorities were requesting them to stop bringing in IWW suspects who were not connected in some way with the "massacre" and instead to concentrate on obtaining convictions of the accused men and testing the effectiveness of the criminal syndicalism act against those whose only offense was possession of a red membership card.

After learning from the several talkative Wobblies just what did happen, Cunningham and Allen planned their strategy. It was not a simple task. Of the four men slain, one was certainly killed by Everest, now dead. One of the others, Ben Casagranda, was shot, along with John Watt, around the corner from Tower on Second Street, almost certainly by Everest also. That left Grimm and McElfresh. According to some witnesses Grimm was at the door of the hall when he was hit. Probably this was not true. The bleeding from his abdominal wound was internal, so the trail of bloodstains found on the sidewalk leading from the hall door to the corner could hardly have been left by him. Probably it was made by Eugene Pfitzer, who was shot in the arm. Grimm was at the head of the column, near the center of the intersection of Tower and Second, when the Centralia contingent halted. He was a logical target for a sniper in the Avalon Hotel. Roberts told Cunningham that Jack Davis went there with a rifle. But Davis eluded capture. Was there a second sniper in the Avalon? After questioning several witnesses, the prosecutors concluded that there was and that he was Eugene Barnett.

So Cunningham and Allen decided to base their case on the murder of Grimm only and to charge that all the Wobblies involved were guilty because they conspired to commit that particular murder. If by some fluke this couldn't be proven satisfactorily, the men could then be tried for the murder of McElfresh, who was felled by a bullet from Seminary Hill.

George Vanderveer, in Chicago appealing the conviction of high-placed Wobblies there, received an urgent request to go to Centralia. Because his Chicago clients were released on bail pending the outcome of their appeal, Vanderveer could get away to take on another defense case. So he headed west, and the more he learned about the circumstances of the Centralia case the better he felt about it. It should provide a chance for another spectacular victory. Evidence of oppression against the IWW was abundant. The hall in Centralia was raided and had been raided before. The conspiracy of businessmen to raid the new hall was even reported in the newspapers. Vanderveer felt sure he could convince a jury, as he had in the Everett trial, that the Wobblies were not aggressors and should be acquitted because they were acting in defense of their lives and property. Furthermore they were victims of anti-Wobbly persecution that had gone too far in the Northwest. A fair-minded jury should have sympathy for their plight.

The *Chronicle* noted on November 23 that the "Centralia police are still under complete control of the American Legion. A special committee of the post, headed by Lt. Van Gilder, directs all investigations of Wobblies arrested and organized the manhunts." A. J. Kresky assumed the post of commander, succeeding the slain Warren Grimm. He reported, with approval, that the Portland Legion post was demanding a restoration of the death penalty in Oregon as a consequence of the Centralia killings.

Anticipating an expensive trial, the lawyers for the prosecution let it be known that available public funds would not be adequate to pay the costs of prosecuting the Wobblies in the intensive way they deserved. This provided another opportunity for aroused citizens to demonstrate their support for those fighting the Wobbly war.

Grant Hodge officers sent off an appeal to Legion secretaries in every state, asking not only for funds but for publicity and support of legislation to curb the IWW. By December 1, $3,832 was received in response

Commodore Bland

Ray Becker

to the appeal. Contributions were encouraged when Police Chief A. C. Hughes reported that "black hand letters continue to pour in to him and others working on the case." Both Centralia newspapers gave as much space and attention to the fund-raising activity as they had to the wartime Red Cross drives. They published the names of contributors and the amounts given, even down to one-dollar donations. The Centralia Elks gave the most — five hundred dollars.

Some of the funds were used to counter IWW propaganda. H. E. Veness, the city orator, and L. L. Thompson were sent on a monthlong speaking tour through parts of Oregon and all of Eastern Washington. Their assignment was to assure audiences that the IWW was lying when it said the raid on the hall began before the first bullets were fired.

The *Oregonian* in Portland printed this excerpt from Veness's speech:

"It's a lie! It's a lie! It's a lie!" With these drastic words H. E. Veness, accredited representative of the Grant Hodge post, Centralia Legion, threw down the gauntlet to the IWW in the campaign of misrepresentations which this un-American element has spread concerning the Centralia outrage on Armistice Day. . . . "Everything the Wobblies say about the Centralia affair is a lie and I can prove it," he emphasized. "When the Wobblies said that these brave young soldiers started that attack, I say it's a lie! When the Wobblies say that members of the Legion had threatened days before to close the IWW hall, I shout it's a lie! When the Wobblies through their outrageous newspaper printed in Chicago say that the body of the IWW who committed suicide in Centralia that night was taken to the county jail and hung up for those inside to view it, I say again it's a lie."

Suicide? That is what Portland people read, assuming it must be true. It was in the *Oregonian*.

The *Spokesman-Review,* after Veness made a fund-raising visit to Spokane, commented: "Not a few good Americans, in their eagerness to be fair and impartial at all times, are prone to jump to the conclusion that the wrong was not all on the side of the IWW snipers. The speakers from Centralia who visited Spokane and other cities perform a great service by clearing away such misapprehensions."

The Loyal Legion printed membership cards for men who swore their patriotic loyalty. Employers were urged to insist that anyone seeking work show

the card or be told to leave the county. Nonconforming employers "will find a powerful sentiment to contend with," said the Loyal Legion spokesman, Dan. L. Bush, a Chehalis newspaperman.

The Loyal Legion also undertook to instruct the prosecutor, the sheriff, and Robert Saunders in the proper ways of dealing with Wobblies. A committee consisting of N. B. Coffman, J. P. Hurley, J. H. Johnson, J. deForrest Griffin, and Bush laid out their instructions which in summary said:

1. No bail for the Wobbly prisoners. Give them a speedy trial.

2. Do not be hasty in releasing prisoners being held without charge, but give all concerned plenty of time to build a case against them.

3. Make sheriff's deputies of those ex-servicemen who were most effective in the great manhunt.

In Bucoda, a sawmill town a few miles north of Centralia, the citizens held a patriotic mass meeting on November 22 to form a new anti-Wobbly Citizens Club. The speaker at this meeting was Judge John M. Wilson of Olympia, who was later to preside at the Wobblies' trial. The tone of his speech made a few headlines because it injected a discordant note into the chorus of anti-Wobblism heard throughout the region. Wilson said unrest in the industrial world could be blamed on the conditions under which laboring men were forced to work and because so little had been done to Americanize foreigners. Noted one newspaper several days later, "He assailed the employer who in his eagerness to make money left unheeded the conditions under which his men worked."[2]

The three elected commissioners of Centralia — Mayor T. C. Rogers, W. W. Dickerson, and J. S. Saunders — were unwilling to wait for a trial before drawing their conclusions about the case soon to be tried. On November 24 they felt moved to enunciate an official finding, which was printed on the city letterhead and widely distributed. Among their findings:

The attack was unprovoked and without justification or excuse. . . . The plot to kill was laid two or three weeks before the tragedy. . . . Conferences were held in the IWW hall to lay plans for the murders. . . . From the nature of the firing it is evident there was a preconceived plan to kill ex-servicemen of the U.S. Army. . . . Thus is laid bare a treasonable plot conceived in hatred and vengefulness which for diabolical plan and execution is without parallel in the history of the

United States. When the enormity of this atrocious, dastardly and traitorous deed became known, all patriotic people in the Twin Cities of Centralia and Chehalis and vicinity arose as one man and joined in a determination to bring the guilty parties to prompt trial. . . . Comrades of the American Legion joined the officers of the law in hot pursuit. . . .[3]

The statement made no mention of the lynching.

Ministers had their say also. One sermon, by Rev. W. J. Sharp, pastor of the Presbyterian church in Centralia, was considered good enough to be reported. First, he said, it should be seen that the IWW is

engaged in war on the United States. . . . They have followed guerilla methods and have enjoyed immunity. Wrecking machinery, defiling food, spiking logs, sowing seeds of sedition and obstructing the draft are only acts of war milder than open attacks on loyal citizens. . . . The Centralia boys who were murdered may be truly the saviors of their country as their deaths have finally awakened the nation to the peril threatening it. How shall we blot out this IWWism? First of all let us have the surgeon's knife. Let us cut out this cancerous growth. If we have laws, then enforce them. Apprehend every murderer, send them to the gallows. That is God's law and it is necessary for our self preservation today.[4]

The county commissioners were given an opportunity to do something more than excoriate the Wobblies when the wives of John Lamb and O. C. Bland appeared at one of their meetings to say they were destitute and entitled to public help under a law providing aid for families whose husbands were unable to work. The Blands had seven children, but the commissioners could not be concerned with their plight. The two women were all but thrown out of the courthouse. "The wrath of the commissioners was loosened on the women," reported the *Bee-Nugget,* "and the women were very firmly assured that there was nothing doing whatever. But the commissioners are prepared to go the limit on whatever funds are necessary to prosecute the band of criminals charged with the November 11 killings."

The Wobblies were in jail nine days before they were arraigned before Judge W. A. Reynolds. They were all accused of conspiracy on the slaying of Warren Grimm and charged with murder in the first degree. Pierce entered a plea of not guilty in behalf of the men and asked for a change of venue, saying it would

Bert Bland

J. C. McInerney

be impossible in a county so much stirred up against the IWW to find twelve persons who would carry no prejudices into a jury box.

This was a severe disappointment to the local people, who were counting on having the trial right at home in the Chehalis courthouse. For one thing it would be an exciting event, and it would bring a lot of people into town and be good for business.

Judge Reynolds, however fair-minded others might claim to be, conceded that he was not sufficiently free of prejudice himself to hear the case and disqualified himself. Judge George D. Abel of Grays Harbor County took his place.

The prosecutors then took unusual measures in an attempt to prevent the change of venue. They obtained 350 signatures on printed affidavits saying:

> Your affiant has read in the newspapers or heard concerning a certain riot or murder in Centralia on the 11th day of November, 1919, wherein it is claimed that four soldiers were killed and several others seriously wounded, but your affiant has formed no opinion as to the guilt or innocence of the particular defendants above charged; that because of the commission of said crime there was more or less excitement in Centralia and Chehalis; that there is no prejudice, so far as your affiant knows, against said defendants . . . and in any event there is no more prejudice against said defendants in Lewis County than in any other county, if any prejudice exists at all. That your affiant believes that said defendants can have a fair and impartial trial in Lewis County and that the ends of justice would be served if said defendants are tried in Lewis County, where, it is alleged, said crime occurred.[5]

F. B. Hubbard was among those who signed one of the affidavits. In addition the prosecution obtained 153 other individually prepared affidavits arguing that there was no more anti-Wobbly sentiment in Lewis County than in any others.

Also filed was an affidavit from Edgar Reinhart, reporter for the Associated Press who covered the whole Centralia affair, starting with the inquest. The IWW had spread a report that Reinhart was run out of Centralia on November 12 because he reported the inquest testimony of Dr. Bickford. His story did report that testimony but his affidavit gave assurance that his relationship with the people of Centralia was cordial and that at no time had he been threatened, terrorized, or replaced by another correspondent.

Pierce's motion for a change of venue had support as well as opposition. A petition signed by 315 persons favored the change and protested charges filed against Elmer Smith and Bert Faulkner, saying they were respectable citizens who had no connection with the shootings. This petition demonstrated that while many were intimidated enough not to dare let themselves be identified as anything but hostile to the IWW, three hundred at least were willing to express sympathy for two of the accused.

Pierce's evidence of prejudice against the Wobblies in the county included the commissioners' rejection of help for the Lamb and Bland families and the unanimous refusal of Lewis County lawyers to act as attorneys for the Wobblies.

Judge Abel looked over the affidavits, listened to the various arguments, and then agreed that the trial ought not be held where the flames of prejudice burned so bright. He denied the request that the trial be moved to Olympia or Tacoma, saying that the jails in those places were just as crowded as in Lewis County, and ordered that the trial be held in Montesano, in the courthouse of his own county, adjacent to Lewis on the west.

17

Montesano Justice

November, 1919 — the grim, tragic month for Centralia — was followed by a December that brought punishing cold of a kind Western Washington seldom experiences. Even freezing weather is uncommon in the valley of the Chehalis but in the last month of 1919 temperatures dropped into the twenties and kept descending until, on the 12th, a low of twelve degrees below zero was reached. Snow piled up in the streets a foot deep. Pipes froze and schools and businesses were closed. Then the power plant ran out of coal and electricity was shut off.

During this ordeal preparation for the trial of the accused Wobblies, huddled in chilly cells of the poorly heated county jail in Chehalis, proceeded slowly. One delay involved two ill-conceived efforts to prevent George Vanderveer from acting as the defense attorney. He would be a formidable foe in the courtroom, the prosecutors knew, and none among the few other attorneys in the state who would defend Wobblies in court could come close to matching his abilities. It would be well to get him out of the way. First an attempt was made to set him up in a situation that could be grounds for disbarment. IWW headquarters in Chicago sent him an express package containing IWW books, pamphlets, and other literature for use in defense cases. When it arrived in Seattle the police were notified. The package was delivered to his home at 721 Ninth Street. When Mrs. Vanderveer signed for it, the antiradical detail of the police, which had been waiting nearby, rushed up and seized the package. Here was the evidence, said a triumphant assistant prosecutor, that Vanderveer was himself a Wobbly and so certainly should not be allowed to practice law. Vanderveer was out of town but when he returned he was able, after a heated argument, to convince the court that he had not asked for the consignment of contraband printed matter; it was sent to him without his knowledge.

A little later, after a trial in Portland, the star Wobbly attorney went across the Columbia River bridge to Vancouver, where he stopped at the Clark County jail to confer with another man accused under the new syndicalism law. The jail door was locked and no one would respond to his knocks so, after some shouting, his client came to a window and conversed with him through the bars. On his way out of town a sheriff's deputy stopped the lawyer and said he was under arrest. "What's the charge?" Vanderveer asked. Conversing with a prisoner without permission of the jailer, he was told. "Where's your warrant?" he demanded. The officer had to admit he hadn't had time to get one. Vanderveer drove on, but a warrant was served on him in Seattle later and he was ordered to stand trial.

In the meantime his Vancouver client was tried and acquitted. Then when Vanderveer's case came up, he informed the judge that since his client was an innocent man, as his acquittal proved, what he had done was no crime. He had been merely talking through the window to an innocent citizen.

The court was unimpressed with this argument and found him guilty. Thus challenged, Vanderveer appealed to the Supreme Court and decided to have some fun while at it. He cited a case dating back to 1878 in which a man, while awaiting trial on a burglary charge, escaped jail. He was recaptured, tried on the burglary charge, and acquitted. Then he was tried on the jailbreak charge and convicted. Vanderveer included in his appeal a long piece of doggerel verse written by a newspaperman arguing on behalf of the convicted man, arguing that since his freedom had been taken from him wrongfully when he was jailed, he could not be punished for having regained by running away what had been taken from him wrongfully.

The Supreme Court was not willing to overrule

The trial judge, John M. Wilson.

Vanderveer's conviction on the basis of his whimsical arguments, but it did declare the trial court in error because it rejected an earlier motion for the judge in the case to disqualify himself because of prejudice.

These attempts to keep Vanderveer from defending the Centralia Wobblies only intensified his determination to stay with the case and try to get justice for men he believed to be victims of mass hysteria.

The movement of the Centralia prisoners to Montesano, forty miles away, began on December 3. Sheriff John Berry and three deputies escorted Bert Bland, John Lamb, James McInerney, and Eugene Barnett to the two-story brick jail behind the stately courthouse on the hill above the railroad station. The next day the other seven prisoners were transferred. Loren Roberts, Ray Becker, Mike Sheehan, and Britt Smith were kept separate from the others in the jail, because, surmised the local press, "of the confessions it is said they have made." They were confined in one side of a cell block on the first floor. The other seven were locked in adjacent cells on the second floor.

The *Montesano Vidette*, whose editor, Dan Cloud, was as outspoken a Wobbly-hater as any, undertook to sum up local feelings about the trial:

Montesano is not elated over the decision to bring the trial here. . . . The case will attract many visitors that Montesano will be proud to entertain, but on the other hand it is likely it will attract a lot of the Wobbly crowd who are not welcome but may not be denied. It is considered probable the state may send some soldiers here to see that order is maintained, though Montesano is not inclined to doubt that local officers would maintain it without outside help. Sheriff Bartell has gone through two Wobbly uprisings in this county.[1]

In his next issue the *Vidette* editor commented on the report that several mothers and wives of the defendants were seeking places to stay in Montesano during the trial. "We do not want to preach hard heartedness nor hatred," the editor wrote in his editorial, "but it will be no kindness to make room in Montesano even for innocent mothers or wives of these men, much less women who are friends. . . . Furthermore there are women spies in such organizations as the Wobblies, and even mothers and sweethearts have acted as spies from time immemorial — as spies and worse. Neither women nor men are to be trusted if their friends are Wobblies."

Cunningham and Allen, after studying the statements several prisoners had made, and knowing how Vanderveer performed in a courtroom, decided they needed more help. S. B. Christiansen, an assistant attorney general who was familiar with the case, was asked to join the team and he did. The most highly respected lawyer in the county where the trial was to be held was W. H. Abel. Any jurors selected would likely be aware of his integrity. His presence at the prosecution table would be helpful in getting convictions. So he was retained by Lewis County, like Cunningham, as an assistant prosecutor for a fee of five thousand dollars. This meant that his brother, the judge, had to disqualify himself and another judge appointed to try the case.

Govenor Hart appointed Judge John M. Wilson of Olympia. Wilson had mourned oratorically over the four slain servicemen at the Elks memorial services in Centralia shortly after the shootings but the governor did not consider that a significant display of prejudice against those responsible for the mourning.

Wilson hurried to Montesano, arriving the day before Christmas. The same day Vanderveer talked to Tom Morgan, still in jail in Centralia, in an attempt to find out what he had told Cunningham and Allen that apparently was going to keep him from being prosecuted, and what he would say on the witness stand if

The courthouse in Montesano where the trial was held.

called. Then he went to Montesano for the arraignment of the eleven men he was to defend. Realizing how much preparation had to be made, Vanderveer asked for a stay in the proceedings until January 22. That would give him a month to get ready for the trial. Wilson refused. He gave him three days and one of those days was Christmas. Vanderveer did win one concession when Wilson allowed him to confer privately with all his clients together.

Then, for the first time, the men who had resolved to defend their hall without realizing what might be the consequences were brought together in one room and told by an attorney they could trust just what the consequences of their rash action might be. They could all be hanged. If they were to escape that — if they were to have a chance of acquittal — they would need to testify in their own behalf, something the law could not make them do. Their defense could not be that they were not responsible for the four deaths. Wobbly guns, by whomever fired, did the killing. Their defense must be that they were acting individually, each one on his own, trying to defend themselves and the hall, and that there was no concerted plan for defense and certainly no conspiracy. Vanderveer talked to the men for two hours. They listened carefully and asked many questions. The seriousness of

The front of the courtroom in Montesano where the trial was held.

their plight was impressed upon them. But their hopes of going free were raised by Vanderveer's reassuring ways. Quite obviously he was going into this case to win, and if anyone could do that, he was the one.

When the conference was over, the men went back to their cells to endure a dismal jail-house Christmas. Judge Wilson, Vanderveer, and the other lawyers went home.

The Wobblies' lawyer quickly sensed that little had been gained by the change of venue from Chehalis to Montesano. The anti-Wobbly sentiment in the Grays Harbor lumbering area was just as intense as that in Centralia, making the task of assembling an unprejudiced jury there just as difficult. So he decided to seek another change of venue, to Seattle, preferably, or Tacoma, where there would be more potential jurors who could be expected to understand that the Centralia men had been driven to take up arms by employer oppression.

Montesano was the equal of Centralia in its hatred of anything that bore a Wobbly taint. By common agreement none of the citizens who had rooms to rent would make them available to anyone connected with the defense or the defendants. No one disputed the *Vidette*'s recommendation that not even the wives or mothers of the despised killers be accommodated.

The closed-door policy was not completely ef-

fective, however. William Allen, a realtor, did not pass up an opportunity to rent the vacant former Moose Lodge on Main Street to Elmer Smith's brother for use by IWW witnesses and others on the Wobbly side who couldn't find lodging elsewhere.

Montesano was not unhappy about the trial and the excitement and business it would bring. Local businessmen readily signed an affidavit saying that certainly a fair trial could be held in their city. In his arguments supporting a motion for another change of venue, Vanderveer made a strong point of the local anti-Wobbly sentiment, not only in Montesano but elsewhere in the county. He cited his inability to find a room in Montesano — being told that the Legion had all the rooms reserved. He pointed to the vitriolic editorials in the Montesano and Aberdeen papers, virtually demanding convictions. Then there were the pamphlets. The county was flooded with them. In one mail would come a tract damning the Wobblies generally and the eleven men in the Montesano jail in particular. This would be followed by another from the Wobbly side, claiming the oppressed workers deserved sympathy, not oppression.

The flurry of pamphlets began with the city of Centralia's official version of what happened on Armistice Day. This provoked a four-page flier ridiculing the contentions of the city leaders. If it were true, it said, that ten men stationed themselves at various points and fired without provocation on people marching in a parade, why did they do it?

> To assume that 10 or more men did act in such a manner and without provocation leads to the further query: How did 10 men come together in the first place and agree as they must do, to shoot from places of concealment at persons whom they never saw before? Is it possible for 10 sane men, without motive or provocation, to gather and plot a killing? Absolutely impossible. The only answer that presents itself to this ridiculous situation is that the men must have been violently insane. But reason rejects this answer by asking: How could 10 insane men come together and organize a plot that demands sane and orderly consideration? It might be possible for one insane person to commit such an act, but for 10 — never.[2]

Then followed a dissertation on the reasons the Centralia Wobblies were sure their hall would be raided. This pamphlet provoked a rebuttal. It stated that "the unprovoked murders in Centralia appear to have been intended as a warning that the IWW were determined to revolt, just as the sinking of the *Lusitania* was an advertisement of the Germany policy of frightfulness. . . . For the result of a minority resorting to arms when the task of converting the majority is hopeless there is only one precedent in the nation's history — the firing on Fort Sumter. . . . The motive was to give warning that the IWW have guns and that they are not afraid to shoot."[3]

This anonymously produced pamphlet was followed by another which declared that "the jury that will decide the fate of the accused murderers in Montesano will not deal with logic, but with facts, and the greatest of these facts is that the IWWs did attack the soldiers . . . and the motive was their natural aversion to all that stands for law and order."[4]

Still another anonymous flier accused the Wobblies of "spreading a vicious propaganda of misrepresentation in an endeavor to create public sentiment in favor of the accused Wobblies." It said Grays Harbor County was being flooded with thousands of circulars designed to create false impressions in the minds of prospective jurors, "such as the barefaced lie that the IWW hall was attacked by the servicemen." This pamphlet said it was "the duty of every juror as an Ameri-

George Vanderveer, defense attorney.

can citizen, to cast his ballot for conviction and maximum punishment and thus sever a few heads of a many-headed monster that is eating at the heart and vitals of the nation Centralia's Armistice Day victims fought to save. For a juror not to cast his ballot would be as traitorous an act as the Armistice Day Massacre itself. It is his duty to fearlessly cast his ballot in the face of these IWW threats. . . ."[5]

This kind of printing press vigilantism was too much even for a judge who was not without his own prejudices. On January 7 he agreed with George Vanderveer that a second change of venue was in order. He not only agreed, but he explained why. Montesano, he said, could furnish "absolutely no police protection and no assurance of any adequate means of serving the orders of the people of the community during this trial."[6] Wilson was empathetic, adding: "I have come to the conclusion . . . that this case ought not be tried in this county."

If not in Montesano, then where? Fearing that Wilson would favor his own county, Thurston, where

Olympia was the county seat, Vanderveer set out to gather evidence that anti-Wobbly sentiment was too prevalent there also for a fair trial to be held. He sent an undercover agent who posed as a Wobbly-hater to get signatures on a statement that proclaimed the IWW to be an un-American and seditious organization. The agent even solicited money for a fund to fight the radicals. This raised suspicions and he was jailed and had to discard his disguise to get released. He then interviewed the Thurston County sheriff, the mayor of Olympia, and the proprietor of a hotel, hoping to get statements showing anti-Wobbly bias. His motives were apparent, however, and he was able to gather little real evidence that Olympia would be as bad a place as Chehalis or Montesano for the trial.

In his summation of arguments before Judge Wilson, Vanderveer said that even though public sentiment was very hostile toward the defendants all over the state, it was least pronounced in the larger cities "where people are less provincial in their habits and are interested in other and larger matters and less concerned about local events. . . ."

Then to everyone's surprise, Judge Wilson changed his mind. He reversed himself, saying "the court" was unfortunate in making the statement it did in the hearing in which he ruled out Montesano. "It has erred," he admitted. The former ruling, he said, was based on law governing civil cases, not criminal. In a criminal case grounds for a change of venue consist only of prejudice on the part of a judge, "or to excitement or prejudice against the defendant."

When Wilson read this part of his decision, Vanderveer jumped up. "Excitement or prejudice!" he exclaimed. They envelop all of southwest Washington like the snows of the frigid winter that still held the region in its grip, he continued. Prove it, Wilson demanded, peering down from his high seat in the courtroom. The Wobblies' attorney had been concentrating on affidavits of prejudice from Thurston County, it never occurring to him that he would need any from Grays Harbor County which Wilson had at first ruled out. Caught unawares, Vanderveer pleaded for time to get support for his contention that there was too much excitement and prejudice in and around Montesano to allow a fair trial.

The eleven prisoners were brought into court and assembled before Wilson's bench. They testified, one by one, that they were sure that they could not get a fair trial in Montesano. Wilson was unmoved. He reminded Vanderveer that he had no affidavits to support his contention of prejudice. That brought on a lengthy and impassioned speech, the gist of which was that there was so much prejudice in the community that no one would sign any kind of affidavit which was intended to help the defendants.

Vanderveer quoted the judge's own remarks made the previous Saturday when he granted the second change of venue. Wilson remained unmoved. He did permit witnesses to be called. But witnesses who would say anything to help the Wobblies were scarce. Oliver Smith, who told the court he came to court against his will, did admit he had heard some anti-IWW sentiment expressed in the community. But under cross-examination he could remember hearing such remarks only from Charles Clemons, a prominent timber owner, who was heard to say he would like to furnish Vanderveer a room and put dynamite under it. The editor of the *Vidette* also was called after Vanderveer read aloud some of his most excited exhortations. Cloud calmly expressed the opinion that yes, the men could get a fair trial in Montesano. Another citizen, who admitted he was a socialist, testified that a fair trial would be unlikely.

At the conclusion of the hearing, Wilson declared that his ruling would stand. There would not be a second change of venue.

(Interviewed by the author in 1959, Wilson, then ninety-three, explained his decision. Olympia was too crowded a place for a trial of that kind, he said with a faint smile, and both Tacoma and Seattle were unacceptable because they were "hotbeds of the IWW.")

Vanderveer was crestfallen. He knew the ways of juries from long experience. He knew how prejudice affected deliberations in a jury room and that prejudice against the Wobblies was rife in the area. In that atmosphere would a jury dare vote for acquittal no matter how strong the case for the defense might be? It seemed unlikely. The public mood was to convict, punish, get even. Vanderveer made a prophetic statement: "No verdict can come out of Grays Harbor County for which the public can have any respect."[7]

If only the men could be tried as individuals, rather than together, he then concluded, they would be less likely held responsible for the sins of the Wobblies in general as well as for the killings in Centralia. He moved for separate trials. The motion was quickly denied. An appeal to the Supreme Court on this point proved futile also and so, at last, the stage was set. The eleven men would go on trial in the courthouse in Montesano, all charged with first-degree murder in the shooting of Warren Grimm. No mention was made of the other three slain servicemen or of the defendants' affiliation with the Industrial Workers of the World. The prosecution wanted a straightforward trial for murder under the law which would enable a jury to ascribe guilt to a group when it could be proven that the group conspired to commit murder. Judge Wilson set out to conduct the trial, or to attempt to, under the strict parameters of that charge.

18

The Antagonists
Take their Places

National attention focused on Montesano once that rural county seat town was selected finally as the place of trial. For two months millions had been reading about the sensational case. Now they read that the eleven dastardly Wobblies responsible for the deaths of four war heroes would soon be in court where they would get their just due.

The public was aware that in Chicago the national IWW leaders, traitors all in the view of patriots, had already gotten their due — long prison sentences. The law was catching up with the radicals. Many states now had laws criminalizing every aspect of the IWW. The word "syndicalism" was not widely understood but it had a sinister sound, like a dread disease, and so syndicalism laws were welcomed as an antitoxin against something evil. The war on Wobblies was being won. And now, in Washington State, the worst of the bunch — the killers — could be punished.

Such views were not shared by everyone, however. Detailed accounts of the Armistice Day events in Centralia and the occurrences in preceding months were spreading. The liberal magazines were picking them up. Some editorial writers were raising questions. And the labor press, without openly embracing the Wobblies, began to see antilabor overtones in the Centralia case, especially after the change of venue reversal. Concerns were expressed that not just the Centralia Wobblies would be on trial in Montesano. All of labor had something of a stake in this case. Lynchings and courtroom railroadings were tactics that could be used against others.

The young American Civil Liberties Union began taking an interest after a report by Professor T. S. McMahon of the University of Washington was pub-lished in the November 29 issue of *Survey*. Subsequent similar reports appeared in the *New York Call*, the *Butte Daily Bulletin*, the *Milwaukee Leader*, the *Portland Telegram*, and other papers. These, plus appeals from IWW partisans, convinced ACLU leaders that here was a fight they should get into.

The ACLU quickly published an eight-page pamphlet entitled *The Issues in the Centralia Murder Trial*. It said the Centralia confrontation "was the result of long and bitter industrial warfare between the lumber trust and the lumber workers of the Northwest. It is a case of national significance because of the industrial issues involved, the claim of the defendants to the right of self-protection by arms, and the exceeding difficulty of securing a fair trial." The pamphlet concluded with an outright appeal for help. Send money to the IWW defense fund, it urged. Write letters to the editors of newspapers. Help distribute the ACLU pamphlet — five cents each or three dollars for a hundred.[1]

The IWW leadership set out to raise a defense fund for the Centralia prisoners immediately after Armistice Day. Herbert Mahler, former secretary of the Seattle IWW local, was placed in charge, as he had been when the Everett trial was in preparation. He established defense committees for money-raising purposes wherever the IWW had local strength, and this gave rise to rumors, repeated by Legionnaires when they also began fund-raising, that the IWW was amassing a war chest of $100,000 to help them with the trial at Montesano.

IWW headquarters also contributed copious amounts of propaganda aimed at breaking down the commonly held belief that the men were murderers rather than underdog class-war victims. George Williams, treasurer of the Northwest District Defense Committee in Butte, in one of his pamphlets declared that "the Centralia case will be the most important one in the annals of labor. Lurking behind the murder charge . . . lies the real issue. . . . This issue has nothing to do with the murder charge; it has to do with Life itself. . . . Behind these ten workers every member of the working class, every lover of industrial democracy, must array themselves. . . ."[2]

William D. Haywood added his influential voice in another pamphlet, *Workers, Judge for Yourselves about Centralia*, arguing at length that the Centralia men were no more guilty than was he when he was tried in Idaho on the charge that he hired the man who assassinated Gov. Frank Stuenenberg.

The American Legion, and particularly the Grant Hodge post in Centralia, took responsibility for raising funds for the prosecution. Although the actual attorneys' fees were paid by the county, money was needed for other aspects of the case.

In a bulletin sent to all Legion posts in the state, the commander of the Department of Washington warned that the IWW was planning to raise $500,000 and in Montesano was getting ready to create "such a feeling of terrorism among the people that a fair trial cannot be secured." He didn't recommend an assessment of members, however, even though the national commander of the Legion, after receiving a plea for help from the Grant Hodge post, wired the Washington state commander suggesting a twenty-five-cents-per-head assessment on all state Legionnaires to assist the prosecution fund.

It remained for employers to raise most of the money needed for all-out efforts to convict the Wobblies. At a meeting of the West Coast Lumbermen's Association on December 23, presided over by F. B. Hubbard, a contribution of one thousand dollars to the Grant Hodge Legion fund was approved. Lumber mills throughout Western Washington made individual contributions.

The Grant Hodge officers, who received nearly a thousand telegrams of sympathy and concern after Armistice Day, extended their money-raising efforts by sending letters of solicitation to Legion posts around the country. This prompted the national Legion to wire the Washington state commander saying that such solicitations by individual posts were improper. The state commander replied that the Centra-lia post was just a little overzealous and would stop raising money by mail. He added that "the Centralia post turned down an offer of $50,000 from wealthy business concerns in this state."[3]

A considerable amount of the prosecution funds was used to pay Luke May, who sent several undercover agents, some posing as Wobblies, to Centralia and Montesano to discover what the IWW was up to that might make trouble for the prosecution. May charged twelve dollars a day plus five dollars for expenses for each of his operatives. Five Lewis County lumber companies paid May one thousand dollars each in the first half of 1920.[4] The operatives, in their written reports, included rumors and gossip as well as facts. One reported that Fred Leech, an organizer for the Timber Workers Union, told him that Hubbard, before Armistice Day, had offered the American Legion five thousand dollars if it would break up the IWW organization in Centralia and wreck its hall. Leech also said that none of the Legionnaires on Armistice Day was armed and that Elmer Smith was arrested only to keep him from helping with the defense of the others. There was no real intent to convict him of murder.[5]

May billed the county for such services as sending out a circular to law enforcement offices throughout the Northwest containing pictures of Michael Sheehan, James McInerney, and Ralph Bergdorf, asking whether any had been in trouble with the law before. It turned out that none had, except Becker (Bergdorf) who refused to register for the draft in Bellingham. With his circulars the enterprising May enclosed a pamphlet advertising the services of the Revelare Secret Service, the name of his company.

Apprehensions among employers and the prosecution about what the Wobblies might do in the weeks after Armistice Day accounted for the elaborate effort to infiltrate the IWW and obtain advance information about whatever the radicals might be plotting. May's agents found that Wobblies were arriving in Centralia with defense money collected in Kelso, Astoria, and other places. This was considered evidence that the Centralia Wobblies had widespread support that might be growing.

During this period fear and hatred of the Wobblies on a national basis did not diminish. The jails were kept full as police and prosecutors used the new syndicalism laws to suppress and silence radicals. Judge R. M. Webster in Spokane devised a new tactic.

Bill Sheehan, left, son of Mike Sheehan, originally one of those charged with murder, helped as an investigator for George Vanderveer, right, in the preparation of the IWW's case.

Washington State Historical Society

Confronted with sixty-six men accused of what was now a crime — belonging to the Industrial Workers of the World — he issued an injunction prohibiting them from remaining members of that organization, from distributing its literature, and from advocating or teaching any of its doctrines. Fair-minded individuals shook their heads in dismay. An injunction, of all things, against the exercise of free speech!

Some bounds on intolerance were drawn in one remote place in Washington. In Friday Harbor on San Juan Island the two proprietors of the local newspaper were arrested on a charge of publishing an editorial that was an incitement to violence. "It seems deplorable to advocate mob violence," the editorial said, "but when such outrages as the recent troubles at Centralia occur, it seems this is the only course to take. The time is coming when every man caught with an IWW card in his possession will be given an application of tar and feathers. . . . The quicker the community makes it so hot for them that hell will not be a comparison, the quicker much of our industrial unrest will cease." The prosecutor who filed the information against the two country-weekly publishers said he could find no Wobblies in his district preaching violence, yet here were two businessmen in the peaceful San Juans advocating vigilante brutality. Tolerance of intemperate editorial roaring against the IWW, this incident demonstrated, did have some bounds.

Late in January George Vanderveer, having been rebuffed in all his legal manuevers — to get a second charge of venue, to appeal the decisions, to have separate trials for his clients — had to agree it was time at last to begin the trial.

The trial was widely expected to determine much more than the guilt or innocence of men charged with murder since all of them were members of an outlawed organization, the IWW. If the IWW had any right to exist, then some heed need be given the contention that the Tower Avenue hall was being defended. But if the IWW was really the abomination the law now declared it to be — if it were really illegal even to be a Wobbly on Armistice Day — then that defense posture was invalid. The hall should not even have been there. It was not something that justifiably could be defended. It was outlaw. Wobblyism in toto was outlawed. Thus the men were operating outside the law no matter what their motive in shooting the servicemen. They killed, so this line of reasoning went, and they were guilty. For the jury to find otherwise would be to repudiate what was now the law of the land. It would be to declare the unthinkable — that members of the IWW had the same rights and freedoms that other Americans enjoyed.

Such was the reasoning that was prevalent in Grays Harbor County and elsewhere as the day of the trial approached. Convictions were considered certain, but even so there was widespread apprehension among those who considered the Wobblies dangerous because of their sheer numbers. It was, in a true sense, a kind of brotherhood and its members looked out for one another. This was evident from the response to the Wobbly appeal for funds. While the prosecution money came from corporate and public bank accounts, the defense money came from men working for as little as three dollars a day. The thousands of red-card carriers in the country did not accept the contention that there was no issue in the trial except the slaying of four men who came to raid their hall. It was a chance for a jury — just possibly a fair-minded one — to rule that men were not automatically guilty in court just because they were Wobblies. The prejudices against them, they knew, would make it difficult to have a fair trial, but still there was a chance. The odds were against them, but then they always were, and they had to fight.

Whatever the nature of it, the trial was to be openly public. Permission to take photographs in courtrooms was to become a burning free press/fair trial issue in later years, but in 1920 it bothered Judge John Wilson not at all. He readily acceded to the request of newsreel cameramen that they be allowed to set their bulky cameras in the aisles to take motion-picture shots of the trial's opening.

The courtroom itself was larger than those in most small county courthouses. It was one of two of identical size on the second floor of an imposing structure with tall white columns supporting a classic Grecian roof at the entrance. In the courtroom, with spectator seats for two hundred, the wall behind the bench then, as now, was decorated with two large colored murals. One, bearing the caption "Transgression," shows an idealistic figure seated among the broken columns of a temple. The other, titled "Instruction," shows a feminine figure holding a tablet on which were graven the numbers of the ten commandments. She is tutoring a child. An inscription between the two reads, "Justice — the hope of all who are just; the dread of all who are wrong."

Behind the courthouse, connected by an enclosed overhead walkway, was the three-story brick jail. There the Centralia prisoners waited and were far from content. They seemed to have agreed that James McInerney, the Irishman of mature years, would be the spokesman and that no one else would talk to outsiders about the case. He said little. At one point they decided to talk to no one at all and for several days all remained mute. Another time they defied the jailers by throwing food through the bars onto the floor, saying they wanted something for breakfast besides mush.

Jail visitors — and none but attorneys were allowed in — were searched and then could converse with prisoners in a small room where a prisoner was locked in on one side and the visitor on the other. A fine screen seperated them. This jail, like most others in the state at the time, was filled with Wobblies awaiting trial under the syndicalism law.

Three days before the trial began a *Vidette* reporter was allowed to visit. Britt Smith, Mike Sheehan, and Ray Becker were on the second floor. He found them playing cards. The reporter asked for Smith, considered to be the leader of the group. Wrote the reporter,

His thick blond hair was parted in the middle, and he smiled as he told of his jail life. "We get pretty good treatment here," he said. Becker talked freely but said nothing about the case. Sheehan, the oldest of the eleven, said nothing. Loren Roberts has light brown hair, shifty eyes which convey a weird expression. He talked freely until questioned about the case and refused to say anything further. On the third floor were the remaining seven. Bert Bland, it will be remembered, put up a fight before he was captured. His dark wavy hair and large blue eyes tend to make him rather handsome.

"There is not the slightest doubt in my mind," said Elmer Smith, "regarding the outcome of the case. I know that every one of the eleven will be cleared. As for myself I was in no way connected with the affair."[6]

Montesano became a crowded town days before the opening of the trial. Any resident with a spare room could rent it for two dollars a day and many were occupied by two men, each paying two dollars. Restaurants were few so some families took in boarders. The overflow found housing in Aberdeen, ten miles to the west. A bus ran between the two towns.

Thirty-four special deputies, mostly Legionnaires, were sworn in by the Grays Harbor County Sheriff to help patrol Montesano's business district and guard the jail and courthouse. They worked in shifts of eight, day and night.

The Legionnaires suspected that the Wobblies would follow their customary tactic of packing a courtroom when any of their members went on trial, so decided to use that tactic themselves. Ex-servicemen were recruited from several towns to attend the trial in a body. For this they were paid four dollars a day and provided with sleeping quarters and meals.

This would be most effective, C. D. Cunningham concluded, if they could wear their uniforms, but he was not sure this would be allowed. He queried the local congressman, Albert Johnson, who wired promptly from Washington, D. C., that Congress had passed an act permitting ex-servicemen to wear their uniforms in public provided they had a red chevron sewed to their left sleeves. So the four-dollar-a-day spectators wore uniforms.

Lt. Walter Crawford of Mt. Vernon, Washington, was placed in command of the Legion contingent, and army cots and blankets as well as rifles and pistols were provided from Camp Lewis near Tacoma. The mess hall was in the fire station from which the hose carts had been removed. The hired Legion spectators came from Tacoma, Centralia, Chehalis, Bellingham, Port Angeles, Aberdeen, Hoquiam, Mt. Vernon, Anacortes, and Bremerton.

The Wobblies could not pack a court any longer, however, without risking mass arrests. Their undercover agents occupied themselves with information gathering and locating witnesses. One, F. Kaffre, was sent to Centralia with an assignment: find loggers who would admit they had been threatened with loss of their jobs if they didn't donate to the Legion fund and who would so testify at the trial. He found three who agreed to be witnesses, but most said if they dared testify for the defense they would never be able to get another job in that part of the state.[7]

Conservative AFL labor leaders in the Northwest sensed that all would not be well at Montesano. Putting uniformed men in the courtroom obviously was intended to intimidate the jury. The Wobblies, for all their irrationality, deserved a fair trial, they concluded, and so they conceived the idea of sending a jury of their own, made up of working men, to sit through the trial and render a verdict at the same time the official verdict came in.

A six-man "jury" was selected. They were: John O. Craft, Metal Trades Council, Seattle; Paul Mohr, Central Labor Council, Seattle; W. J. Beard, Tacoma Labor Council; T. Meyer, Everett Labor Council; William Hickman, Portland Labor Council; and E. W. Thrall, Centralia Brotherhood of Railroad Trainmen. They took their assignment seriously, sitting through every session of the long trial.

The major papers of the Northwest sent reporters with instructions to file daily reports. Edgar Reinhart of the Associated Press took a room in the same residence where Frank Christiansen, one of the prosecutors, found housing. The other two national news wire services were represented by Clem J. Randau, United Press, and Fred H. McNeill, International News Service. Ben Hur Lampman was sent by the *Oregonian*. David Hazen came from the *Portland Telegram* and Carter Brooke Jones from the *Seattle Post-Intelligencer*. Others covering the trial were Roy A. McMillan, *Tacoma News-Tribune*; Ora Willis, *Seattle Times*; Ruth Dunbar, *Tacoma Ledger*; Russell Mack (future congressman), *Hoquiam Washingtonian*.

In addition to these — all accused by the labor press of bias against the Wobbly defendants — were a few who could be counted on to report with bias from the other side. The most prominent of these was John Nicholas Beffel, writing for the *New York Call* and various labor papers. Ralph Chaplin, artist, poet, IWW member, and inveterate champion of radical causes, covered the trial for the labor press also. Afterward he holed up in a Seattle hotel room to write one of the two classic prejudiced accounts of the Centralia case. Titled *The Centralia Conspiracy,* it ran to 143 pages and was so much in demand that successive editions were published. The other classic, *Centralia, Tragedy and Trial,* commissioned by the Legion, was written by Ben Hur Lampman. He used only 78 pages to tell the Legion's side of the story.

The *Montesano Gazette,* of course, was represented by its co-owner and editor, Dan Cloud, who was so delighted to have important colleagues in town that he persuaded officers of the Ivanhoe Lodge, Knights of Pythias, to make their lodge hall available to the visiting writers for recreational purposes. The janitor opened the place every day at five o'clock and built a roaring fire in the stove, and there the reporters gath-

Seven of the defendants: (standing) Bert Bland, John Lamb, Britt Smith, J. C. McInerney; (kneeling) Commodore Bland, Ray Becker, Eugene Barnett.

Special Collections Division, University of Washington Libraries, neg. #6636

ered after filing their stories with Western Union. Cloud declared it to be the "Montesano Press Club" with himself as president and secretary. He handed out printed membership cards. The members awarded him the "Palm for Vituperative Vindictiveness" when George Vanderveer, after his last futile argument for a change of venue, called an editorial by Cloud the most inflammatory piece of writing yet produced by newspapers seemingly vying with one another in denouncing the IWW. The night before the trial ended the Knights of Pythias bestowed upon Cloud the rank of third degree and the ceremony was followed by a banquet at which the "press club" members presented him with a watch charm inscribed, "The Battle of Montesano, war correspondent, to Dan Cloud, Febru-

ary, March, 1920."

All this displayed a spirit of kindredness among those reporting the trial for the public press and a total absence of any disapproval among the newspapermen of Cloud's brand of "vituperative" journalism that cried out in print for vengeance against the Wobbly defendants even before the jury was selected.

There was no "air of excitement" in Montesano on the day before the trial opened, the *Post-Intelligencer* reported. The preparations had dragged on for two and a half months and emotions had cooled somewhat. But tensions preceding the coming courtroom combat ran high. It was common knowledge, the *News-Tribune* reported, that nearly everybody in Montesano was carrying a gun.

The *Industrial Worker* presented its version of the scene thus: "Montesano is crowded with gunmen, stool pigeons, newspaper reporters and the morbidly curious, and more are coming in every day. Every train brings ex-servicemen. It is thought that a large number of these men are friendly toward the defendants while others are obviously there for no other purpose than to take advantage of any chance to make trouble."

19

The Opening Curtain

On the premise that justice delayed can be justice denied, the Constitution guarantees a speedy trial to anyone accused under the law. In the Centralia case the trial of the accused did not begin until January 26, 1920, two and a half months after the violent events of Armistice Day, but the delay was not deliberate. At first little could be done until Centralia could settle down, could make sure the unexpected battle in the Wobbly war was really over so the outside troops could be sent home and citizens could venture out unarmed. Then came the big freeze. The city was paralyzed for a time by the cold. There followed the ultimately futile maneuvers of Vanderveer to have the trial moved away from the hostile tensions in Grays Harbor County. Hundreds of persons had to be tracked down and interviewed to find witnesses whose testimony would be helpful to one side or the other. Accommodations had to be found for the judge, the lawyers, the jury, the press, the Legionnaires hired to sit in the courtroom, and at least some of the key witnesses. A long list of veniremen — potential jurors — had to be prepared and those on it called for possible duty. It all took a lot of time.

Trials of a number of persons together for one crime were not unprecedented but they were uncommon until ways were found to take Wobblies to court in groups. A notorious precedent, unmentioned in the Centralia proceedings, was the Haymarket trial in Chicago late in the previous century when a group of persons identified as anarchists — radicals fully as much despised in the 1880s as the IWW was a half-century later — were convicted of first-degree murder in the death of a policeman who was killed by a bomb thrown by an unidentified person protesting the breakup of a public meeting by uniformed officers.

Acquittals of accused radicals were rare in America, but in the Everett trial the accused Wobblies did escape conviction. Vanderveer prevailed in that trial and he was sure he had a chance to do so in this one. Animosity toward the IWW was not so universal that all juries could be counted on to convict.

The Centralia prosecutors were quite confident they could get convictions, but that would not be enough. They wanted first-degree murder verdicts, preferably followed by sentences of death. Because of the dispute, never finally settled, about who was the aggressor — the raiding Legionnaires or the gun-firing Wobblies — it could not be concluded that a jury, even in Grays Harbor County, would certainly come in with a verdict that called for hanging. The case would require careful handling; hence the hiring of not one special assistant for the prosecutor but two — Cunningham and Abel — reinforced by lawyers from the attorney general's office.

Standing alone against this corps of lawyers was George Vanderveer, smart, energetic, thoroughly versed in criminal law, and carrying within him a deeply felt sense of brotherhood with all those he saw as victims of oppression by the established order. He fought as hard in trials where he was paid little or nothing as in ones where the compensation might be adequate, as he expected it to be in this case because of the national fund-raising effort.

Vanderveer arrived in Grays Harbor County a few days before the trial opened and this time was able to get the Savoy Hotel in Aberdeen to provide him a room and one next to it for Kitty Beck, a slender woman with black hair and a dark complexion who loved him and lived with him while he resisted his wife's appeal for a divorce. Vanderveer shunned divorce as something scandalous. Beck registered, one of Luke May's operatives noticed, under the name of "Mrs. Irwin." The operative furnished May with a floor plan of the hotel and noted that Vanderveer had the locks changed on

W. H. Abel, Montesano, retained by the county and employers to assist the prosecution.

both his and Kitty Beck's rooms.

The selection of the jury took ten days, an unusually long time. Only a few women were among the 150 persons subjected to searching questioning by both sides, and none were chosen. Vanderveer complained to the judge that the prosecution had been busy trying to influence every possible juror before he was called for questioning and that women among the talesmen were visited by committees who told them the jury box in a trial of this kind was no place for decent women.

Most of those called did not want to serve. In one day fifty-nine of sixty-nine persons summoned for questioning asked to be excused and were. The *Vidette*, commenting on prospective jurors being asked whether they believed in capital punishment, made its own views plain, saying, "The men guilty of the murders at Centralia should be hanged. . . . Shocked by the crime, we want vengeance, or, if we are a little better than that, we want punishment."[1]

As the questioning proceeded and a large majority of those summoned admitted some degree of prejudice against the IWW, Vanderveer, in the faint hope

that the judge might agree, moved again for a change of venue, saying the attitude of scores of persons questioned was proof that his clients could never have a fair trial in Montesano. Judge Wilson could not agree.

A few of those called were examined for as long as two hours. Vanderveer kept probing for evidence of anti-Wobbly attitudes, causing Judge Wilson to remind the defense lawyer that men, not the IWW, were on trial. He said hatred of the IWW did not disqualify a person for jury duty provided the hatred did not extend specifically to the eleven men accused.

While the jury selection proceeded, a trial in Tacoma of thirty-six Wobblies charged under the antisyndicalism act with being members of the IWW ended in conviction. Vanderveer's associate, Ralph Pierce, was the defense attorney in that case.

By February 5 ten jurors finally were agreed upon and Vanderveer still had one peremptory challenge to be used in disqualifying a person for no stated reason. After conferring with the defendants, he waived use of this challenge and the last juror was selected. They were: E. E. Torpen, sixty-six, of Montesano, a retired farmer; U. G. Robinson, fifty-seven, of Hoquiam, a carpenter; Harry Sellars, forty-seven, of Elma, a laborer; Carl O. Hulten, thirty-nine, of Lake Quinault, a farmer; Frank Glenn, forty-five, of Brady, a farmer; E. E. Sweitzer, fifty-eight, of Oakville, a farmer; F. H. McMurray, forty-one, of Aberdeen, a teamster; W. E. Inman, fifty-three, of Elma, a rancher; Aubrey T. Fisher, thirty-two, of Aberdeen, a realtor; Edward Parr, forty-six, of Hoquiam, a logger; P. V. Johnson, thirty-four, of Aberdeen, a paver; and Samuel Johnson, fifty-seven, of Montesano, a fisherman.

Another day and a half were required to select alternate jurors. These were subjected to the same severe questioning as the first twelve. Influenza was approaching epidemic proportions in Montesano and it was likely that one or more of the alternate jurors would be needed. Special care was given to the selection of the first alternate, who turned out to be James A. Ball, a blacksmith.

This jury with one exception was made up entirely of men the Wobblies might consider "fellow workers." This was an initial victory for Vanderveer. He hadn't been able to have the trial moved to Tacoma or Seattle where there would be a better chance of getting a jury of men who, if not outright union sympathizers, at least would understand the problems of working men. But he was able to get a jury, right in enemy territory, comprised of men who were certainly not members of the employer class.

Now, with the jury sworn in, the trial could begin. In the high-ceilinged courtroom the judge sat behind a tall, raised bench, the jury box to his right. A railing extended the width of the courtroom in front of the rows of spectator seats. The defendants sat on a long bench inside the railing. Between them and the jury box was the lawyers' table with Vanderveer alone on one side. The attorneys for the prosecution were so numerous all could not find seats at the table. An extra bench was brought in. Besides Herman Allen, the Lewis County prosecutor, and J. H. Jahnke, assistant prosecutor, there were C. D. Cunningham and W. H. Abel, the special prosecutors; L. L. Thompson, attorney general; and Frank Christiansen and John H. Dunbar, assistant attorneys general.

Most of the accused Wobblies sat quietly through the long jury selection process, occasionally smiling when Vanderveer was able to win a point. One who behaved differently was Loren Roberts. He and Tom Morgan were the ones who had freely answered questions put to them by Cunningham in the days after Armistice Day and whose statements were labeled "confessions." Vanderveer knew the prosecution would lean heavily on these statements in presenting its case, so he devised a strategy. Roberts actually was or would be insane, incapable of making credible statements. Morgan gave his statement, it would be claimed, either because he was under severe duress after the night of terror in the Centralia jail or because he was promised immunity if he would cooperate with the prosecution. Morgan turned out to be the only one in the hall at the time of the shooting who was not prosecuted, lending credibility to the belief that he had, as the Wobblies charged, turned "stool pigeon."

Press reports noted that Roberts, the youngest of the defendants, did not display the poise of the others. "He squirmed, fidgeted and was as self-conscious as a small boy when confronted by a stern parent with some misdeed," the *Chronicle* reported. "Ray Becker, the next youngest, also lacked the bravado, whether assumed or natural, of the other prisoners. He sat during the entire narrative with his head hung down and his hand to his mouth."

One of Vanderveer's first moves was to request separate trials for Elmer Smith and Roberts — for

Herman Allen, Lewis County prosecutor.

Smith because he was not a participant and was not at the scene of the shooting, and for Roberts because he was insane. Wilson denied the motion.

A number of concerned relatives attended the trial at the outset, including the widow of the man whose slaying was being attributed to all eleven defendants — Mrs. Warren Grimm. She was accompanied by her sister, Mary, and her sister-in-law, Mrs. Huber Grimm. Sitting in another part of the courtroom were Mrs. C. Faulkner, mother of Bert; Mrs. Edna Roberts, mother of Loren; Mrs. Elmer Smith, Mrs. O. C. Bland, and Mrs. John Lamb.

The trial opened in traditional fashion with a statement by the prosecutor. Herman Allen talked for nearly an hour, describing the role he was attributing to each of the defendants in the violent drama of Armistice Day.

"Our position," he said in his opening statement, "is that the boys were standing in the street in military formation under the charge of their commander, paying attention to him, when he gave the command to halt and close up ranks and that they were marking time when they were fired upon."

Vanderveer interrupted Allen to ask whether the prosecution would "stand or fall" on the contention

The "Labor Jury": W. J. Beard, Central Labor Council, Tacoma; Paul K. Mohr, Central Labor Council, Seattle; Theodore Meyer, Central Labor Council, Everett; E. W. Thrall, Brotherhood of Railway Trainmen, Centralia; John O. Craft, Metal Trades Council, Seattle.

that there had been no attack on the IWW hall before the firing began. "In other words," Vanderveer continued, "it is equivalent to a statement that there was no attack on the hall, and the doors were not smashed in before there was any shooting, and you will be judged by it hereafter?" Before Allen could answer, Abel was on his feet. "We surely will," he declared. The Wobblies had a name for the large and smooth-mannered Abel. They called him "Oily."

Lieutenant Grimm, Allen said, was standing at the head of the Centralia contingent facing southeast when he was hit by a bullet fired from the Avalon Hotel.

The Wobblies plotted the ambuscade, Allen contended, but he offered no theory as to why. He said they met in their hall on Sunday night and made plans to place armed men in the hotels across the street and on Seminary Hill so the soldiers could be attacked from both sides of the street.

In his statement Allen said nothing about the Industrial Workers of the World — nothing about dis-

loyalty, sedition, or overthrowing the government, nothing about the reasons why the Wobblies were hated and feared. He had to avoid such references carefully lest he place some credence on what he knew would be the defense contention — that the Wobblies were defending their hall against an attack by citizen and Legion conspirators determined to drive the IWW out of Centralia as they had been driven out before.

Allen made plain that the state — the prosecution — considered this to be a trial for murder only, nothing more. The eleven men were charged with a conspiracy that led to the shooting of Warren Grimm. Only one shot killed Grimm, but all eleven were considered equally guilty in the firing of that shot.

Allen's opening statement was disturbing to Vanderveer. Quite obviously the prosecution's strategy was to draw a curtain over everything that occurred before Armistice Day and to insist that the jury make its judgment solely on whether the defendants were guilty of killing Warren Grimm, whatever their motive. This led him to make an unusual move. Rather than wait until it was time for the defense to present its case, he would make his opening statement now even though he had no notes or text prepared.

His strategy was to get certain facts before the jury without delay — to let the jury know right at the outset what he might not be able to present with testimony later on. He rose, started talking, and kept on talking for nearly two hours. What he said was considered by the IWW to be such a strong statement that it was printed and widely circulated.

First he delivered a dissertation on the IWW in general and the background of the Centralia violence that brought to the jury's attention the pre-Armistice Day events that the prosecution wanted kept from the jury. The central question, said Vanderveer, is, Who was the aggressor? The defense, he said, would stand or fall on the answer. He was sure that if he could show that plans had been laid, some openly, some secretly, weeks in advance of Armistice Day to rid Centralia of the nest of Wobblies on Tower Avenue, the jury would agree that the men were justified in preparing to defend themselves against an onslaught of violence exactly like that to which the Centralia IWW had been subjected in the previous year. And if he could show that the men in the parade made a rush toward the hall before the opening shots were fired, it would be apparent that the aggressor was not his clients but those who planned an attack and carried it out.

The state was trying to make it appear that it was not an IWW trial. But the IWW has to be an issue, he said, adding, "The IWW is at the bottom of this."

Then Vanderveer launched into a lecture on the beliefs and objectives of the organization, confident that the jury, even if it did not agree with the philosophy, would be understanding of the serious nature of the IWW program and the risks its members were willing to take in resisting efforts to destroy them.

He said the IWW

is the representative in the United States of the idea that capitalism is wrong; that no man has a right,

MONTESANO, WASH.

Begin trial of I. W. W. men for Armistice Day shooting -- First pictures of opening session of case in connection with shooting paraders in Centralia.

PATHE NEWS
18

The opening of the trial in Montesano was national news. Pathe News, a leading newsreel company producing current events films for movie theaters, sent a cameraman. These pictures show the jury and courtroom officials walking out of the courthouse and standing to be photographed.

Pathe News photos courtesy of C. Campbell Wyckoff

W. E. Inman, the last surviving juror, interviewed in
Oakville in 1960. He is shown here with a granddaughter,
Nancy Knight.

Vanderveer cited statistics showing that two percent of the people owned two-thirds of the wealth and that seventy-five percent of the workers were unable to send their children to school. The IWW, he said, advocated a program in which economic chance and social betterment went hand in hand.

Employers in Centralia, he claimed, were as alarmed as those elsewhere by what the IWW was attempting and therefore organized themselves into a militant force to combat the revolutionary efforts of the radicals. This attitude, he explained, accounted for the plans to close the IWW hall on Tower Avenue soon after it was opened.

The Wobbly attorney then described the meetings held in the Elks hall, the futile efforts to get the Wobblies run out of town by legal means, the raid on the old hall during the 1918 parade, and the attacks made on IWW units in Red Lodge, Montana; Bisbee, Arizona; and Tulsa, Oklahoma. The Wobbly war, though he did not call it that, was nationwide.

Toward the end of his talk Vanderveer indulged in flights of eloquence in an attempt to stir the emotions of the jurors, who listened solemnly as he spoke.

"They had appealed to the citizens, they had appealed to the officers, and some of their members had been tarred and feathered, beaten up, and hung, and they said, in thought (when the hall's door was smashed in), 'Patience has ceased to be a virtue. If the law will not protect us and the people won't protect us, we will protect ourselves,' and they did. And in deciding this case I want each of you, members of the jury, to ask yourself, What would you have done?"[2]

Vanderveer described in colorful detail the lynching of Everest, then added, "I exonerate the American Legion, as an organization, of the responsibility for this. For I say they didn't know about it. The day will come when they will realize that they have been mere cat's-paws in the hands of the Centralia commercial interests."[3]

He closed by citing a case most jurors were unfamiliar with — the pre-Civil War persecution of Elisha Lovejoy, an Illinois publisher advocating abolition of slavery, who was slain by a proslavery mob that also destroyed his printing plant. Whatever the verdict in this case, he said, the verdict ten years hence will be like that in the Lovejoy case. In a decade, he forecast, the Centralia Wobblies would be vindicated. His prophecy turned out to be less than accurate.

moral, legal, or otherwise, to exploit his fellow men; the idea that our industrial efforts should be conducted not for the profit of any individual but should be conducted for social service, for social welfare. So the IWW says first that the wage system is wrong and that it means to abolish that wage system. It says it intends to do this, not by political action, not by balloting, but by organization of the industrial or economical field precisely as employers organize. . . .

He went on to argue that industrial unionism was superior to craft unionism because a union representing all workers in an industry, such as steel, transportation, or lumber, was stronger than several smaller AFL craft unions. (This was fourteen years before belated acceptance of the industrial union principle led to the formation of what became the Congress of Industrial Organizations.)

"This plan," he declared, "is extremely distasteful to employers because it is efficient; because it means a new order, a new system in the labor world." He cited recent strikes in the steel and mining industries by workers organized as a unit who were able to shut down a whole industry rather than just parts of one.

20

Case for the Prosecution

Prosecutors Allen, Cunningham, and their several assistants had their case well prepared. They set out to show, first, that Eugene Barnett, leaning out an open second-story window in the Avalon Hotel, fired the shot that killed Warren Grimm; second, that his fatal shot was part of an armed conspiracy in which the other defendants were involved, and hence all were guilty; and third, that the Wobblies were plainly the aggressors. They fired into the ranks of the soldiers as they stood marking time in the street, not after an assault on the hall began.

They dared not bring in testimony about the organization to which the defendants belonged — the Industrial Workers of the World — lest they lend credibility to the contention that the men had a justified motive for using gunfire — defense of their hall against assault.

To set the stage, a model of the Second and Tower neighborhood, constructed by a cabinetmaker, N. Welter, was brought into the courtroom. A large map was displayed on an easel so witnesses could point to specific places — where they were standing when the action began, where the slain and the wounded were hit by bullets, where they fell, where cars were parked, and where others they saw were standing.

Numerous photographs taken at the scene afterwards were put on display. The whole arsenal of rifles and automatic pistols used or carried by the Wobblies was introduced in evidence. The sheriff had to admit that no fingerprints were taken from the guns. He and his deputies didn't know how to do it.

When a witness whose car was pierced by a bullet parked it outside the courthouse so the jury could inspect it, Vanderveer suggested that the jury be taken to the scene of the action in Centralia where they could see, for example, just how far the Avalon and Arnold hotels were from the hall, and how short the distance the raiders had to run in rushing from the edge of the street to the door of the hall. The prosecutors agreed that it was a good idea.

Wilson took the matter under advisement and later denied the motion on the grounds that the forty-mile trip to and from Centralia would have to be made by train, that it would disrupt the proceedings, and that it would attract a large crowd and expose the jury to comments that might not be admissible in court. Furthermore the duty of a jury, he said, is not to investigate or examine evidence on its own. Its duty is to evaluate evidence that is admissible in court.

Vanderveer was disappointed. He wanted the jury to see how the men in the parade had wrecked the hall and torn away the canopy of the Roderick Hotel.

The prosecution brought on scores of witnesses. Of most importance were those who identified a man seen leaning out a window of the Avalon with a rifle in his hands at the time of the shooting.

A. H. Carpenter and H. H. McDowell, owners of a garage across the street from the Avalon, and their bookkeeper, Elsie Hornbeck, were called. McDowell said he saw a gun sticking out the window of the Avalon and yelled to the others to look. Hornbeck, through the window of the garage, saw a man looking out the south upstairs window of the Avalon. "He had rather dark hair and a thin face," she said.

Cunningham questioned her:

CUNNINGHAM: Do you know Eugene Barnett?
HORNBECK: No, I do not.
CUNNINGHAM: Do you think you can glance over this row of defendants and see if you recognize the man who was leaning out the window?
VANDERVEER, interrupting: This is a good stage play.
ABEL: Well, it may be more than a stage play. I don't know whether the witness can do it or not.
VANDERVEER: I suppose you do not.

ABEL: I do not. The lady is a stranger to me.
HORNBECK: I think the one on the end.
ABEL: Just stand up Eugene Barnett, please. (Barnett stands.) You think this is the man you saw?
HORNBECK: The general appearance is the same.
ABEL: Now after Mr. McDowell said "Look, look!," what did you do and what did you notice?
HORNBECK: Well I looked every way up and down the street and I happened to look across the street and saw a gun jerked back in the window.
ABEL: Who had hold of the gun?
HORNBECK: I don't know.[1]

Hornbeck went on to say that a man she saw looking out of the north window — a different window from the one where the gunman was seen — was an older person not wearing a hat, with grey hair and no mustache. Under cross-examination she insisted that she had not been taken to the jail in advance to see Barnett and that no one had told her where he was sitting in the courtroom.

Vanderveer began his cross-examination:

Q. You say this is the man you saw. You know that this is a matter of life and death. Knowing that, will you say on your oath that that is the man you saw in the window?
A. No I will not. I said the general appearance was the same. He looks more like the man than any of the others.
Q. But you won't say he is the man you saw?
A. No.
Q. Will you say on your oath — look at me please — knowing the importance of this thing, that your oath means life or death, that in your opinion this is the man?
A. Yes.[2]

Under further questioning Hornbeck admitted she had in fact been shown a photograph of Barnett, although she did not remember when. She thought it was brought in by "one of the Legion boys" a couple of weeks after the shooting. Lieutenant Van Gilder and Frank Christiansen, she said, had been to see her to find out what she had seen.

Clarence O. Watkins and William Scales were the color bearers for the Centralia contingent in the parade. Watkins, describing the scene, said, "I heard a command 'Halt!' and I left the flag at rest. And just about this time I heard three shots — one shot and then a couple more." He was sure they came from the Avalon. "I noticed two shots that came very close to me. After the third shot I saw him bring his gun in and then look again with his face out the window. The window was raised about eighteen inches, I judge, and as he brought the gun in, he looked out as though he was looking for someone. Then I saw someone stagger across the street and fall. That was Grimm."[3]

Watkins said he went to the Chehalis jail to see if the man he saw in the window was one of those being held. Only one prisoner was brought out for him to see. It was Barnett. Watkins identified him as the man he saw shooting from the Avalon window in the few seconds between the time he dropped the flag and when he ran to take refuge behind an automobile. Asked what Grimm did when he was shot, Watkins said he started walking away at a fast pace, just ahead of him, then began to stagger.

Vanderveer questioned Watkins closely, attempting to show that in the excitement and confusion he might not have seen exactly what he described. The prosecutors frequently interrupted him with objections, irritating him to the point where he would snap back at both Allen and Abel. The judge was moved to intervene, saying, "I do not know what is the matter with you gentlemen this morning but you certainly must cut out this talk backwards and forwards."

Abel, angry by this time, turned toward Vanderveer and challenged him, "Shall we adjourn to the jail for a few minutes?"

Vanderveer replied contemptuously, "You are too old to fight me."

Abel responded, "Don't you ever think it."

"You always hollered for help before," answered Vanderveer. At this point the judge called a recess.

Later, when he was called back to the stand, Watkins admitted under further cross-examination that he was 150 feet from the window of the Avalon where he had seen the gunman.

Frank Van Gilder gave some of the strongest testimony for the prosecution. He said Grimm was about eight or ten feet into Second Street when he gave the command "Halt." After the halt he and Grimm were talking and Grimm told him he had committed a "great bobble" when, marching north, he had failed to give the order for "eyes right" as the unit passed the reviewing stand. While they were talking, Van Gilder heard "sounds like firecrackers" and bullets whistled past his ear.

Q. What direction was Grimm facing at that time?

A. Looking southwest.

Q. Looking toward Ax Billy's place southwest?

A. Yes, and while I was looking at him I noticed that something seemed to jar him, jarred him very heavily and he turned very pale. I asked him, placed my hand on his arm in this manner and I said, "Are you hit?" And he said yes. I turned around and noticed a machine stationed right over there, practically at Ax Billy's, and I said, "Go over to that machine and get to the hospital and get dressed up," and he started at a kind of slow trot or slow run. And he began to double over and put his arms across his stomach, and run kind of sideways.[4]

William S. MacKenzie and his brother-in-law, Clyde Tisdale, were sitting in a Dodge car parked on Second Street at the southwest corner of the intersection with Tower. They told of taking Grimm to the hospital. The wounded man said nothing on the way, Tisdale testified, but just as they arrived said, "For God's sake hurry up, boys, and get me in quick."[5]

Tisdale's testimony included this:

Q. Were the boys in the parade in formation at the time the shots started?

A. I think they were. I have never seen any break.

Q. When did the break in the ranks occur with respect to the first shooting?

A. Immediately afterwards.

Q. In what direction did the boys break?

A. Most of them broke around and behind this building.

Q. Would you say you could see back twenty-five or fifty feet north on Tower Avenue?

A. I don't think I could see that far.

Q. Then you don't know whether these men rushed this doorway or not?

A. I don't know anything about that at all.

(Tisdale, later a state senator from Pacific County, strongly sympathetic to organized labor, reluctantly admitted in a letter to investigators in 1939 that he had testified falsely in response to public pressure for a conviction of the Wobblies. He said he did not actually hear shots before the men in the parade broke ranks.[6])

Witnesses found it difficult to give precise, positive answers to questions about what they saw and heard in the confusion and panic that erupted when Tower Avenue was hit, like a thunderclap, by unexpected violence. Several men who were in the parade testified that Grimm was shot in the street and not at

Elsie Hornbeck, a witness for the prosecution, testified that she looked out this window and saw a man who looked like Eugene Barnett fire a rifle from the upstairs window of the Avalon Hotel across the street.

the door of the hall. One of these was Dr. E. C. Roberts, a dentist, who went to the witness stand wearing his army uniform. He said he was only five paces behind Grimm when the shooting started. "I stood still for just a minute and then when I realized it was shooting, I started down Second Street to get out of the way. Grimm was ahead of me and after I started to run I don't know where he was."[7]

Vanderveer was more interested in his appearing in uniform than in what he remembered. "Did you wear that uniform here to give greater weight to your testimony?" he asked.

Abel objected and the judge interjected, "The witness' appearance will be taken into consideration by the jury." Vanderveer wouldn't let up.

Q. Was it your idea that your appearance would be taken into consideration that you wore the uniform, doctor?

A. Well, possibly.

Q. Did someone ask you to wear it?

A. I don't remember.

Q. Were your members requested to wear uniforms in order that the value of their testimony might be enhanced by the appearance of the uniform?

A. Possibly.[8]

Another leading witness used in building a case against Barnett was Charles Briffett, superintendent of schools in Port Angeles who happened to be in Cen-

Pathe News

The Pathe cameraman was allowed to take pictures in the courtroom as the trial began. This shot shows Judge Wilson on the bench, and the backs of four defendants sitting on a front bench. On the white sheet in the background is a large map headed, "North Tower Ave. in the Vicinity of Second and Third Streets, Centralia." A basket, where numerous exhibits, including rifles and revolvers, were placed, can be seen at Judge Wilson's right.

tralia on Armistice Day. Shortly after the burst of shooting, he saw a man in the alley in back of the Avalon putting cartridges in a rifle while crossing Second Street in a northeasterly direction. Briffett said he was certain the man was Barnett.

The statements made to Cunningham and the sheriff by Loren Roberts and Tom Morgan shortly after Armistice Day were the basis for the prosecution's claim that the Wobblies plotted in advance to attack the men in the parade. Vanderveer demanded to see the statements, but he was put off. They had been mislaid and were not available, the prosecutors said.

Then Frank Christiansen took the stand and read the supplementary statement Roberts made on November 24, adding that six persons were present when Roberts was questioned and that he appeared to be completely rational.

Roberts himself was not called to testify but Morgan was an early witness for the prosecution. He said that he spent a half-hour in the IWW hall the night of

November 10. The next morning he was there again and saw Elmer Smith when he came in to talk to Britt Smith. Morgan said Elmer asked Britt if he was sure he had plenty of men. Then he said Elmer Smith remarked that he was going up to his office to protect it.

The most damaging part of Morgan's testimony was his description of the preparations the Wobblies made on the morning of Armistice Day — Britt giving instructions to go to the Avalon and the Queen and the Arnold; Britt saying that "it was kind of nice for an attorney to come in and tell them to do their duty"; Commodore Bland coming in with a rifle wrapped in an

Pathe News

The jury. C. D. Cunningham, seated center, looks out past the defendants toward the crowded spectator area.

overcoat; Bland and Sheehan saying they didn't want guns; Davis strapping a gun to his leg and trying to walk with it stiff-legged, then taking it out when the others laughed at him; Barnett leaving the hall before Davis; someone making the remark that if they should get caught nothing should be said about what was said or done in the hall; and McInerney "hollering over to the others" in jail to tell them to keep their mouths shut.

The Wobblies had already denounced Morgan as a stool pigeon. He was obviously willing to relate anything he heard or saw regardless of the effect it would have on the defense of his "fellow workers." Morgan even took the position that shots were fired before the paraders broke ranks.

> MORGAN: When the parade came past there, why when the soldiers came up by there, they stopped. And they were turned facing back to town and some of them were closing up and the others were keeping time.
> Q. What happened when the soldiers were closing up and keeping time?

A. There were some shots fired.
Q. Who fired the shots?
A. I could not say as to that, but they were fired from across the street.[9]

Vanderveer began his cross-examination by getting Morgan to admit that he twice refused to see him, Vanderveer, when he sought to interview him in the jail. Then he asked:

Q. What were you doing in the hall, Tom?
A. I was with Becker.
Q. The truth of the matter is you were an IWW and went there because it was the IWW hall.
A. The truth of the matter ain't.
Q. And they scared you into denying that you were an IWW?
A. They did not.

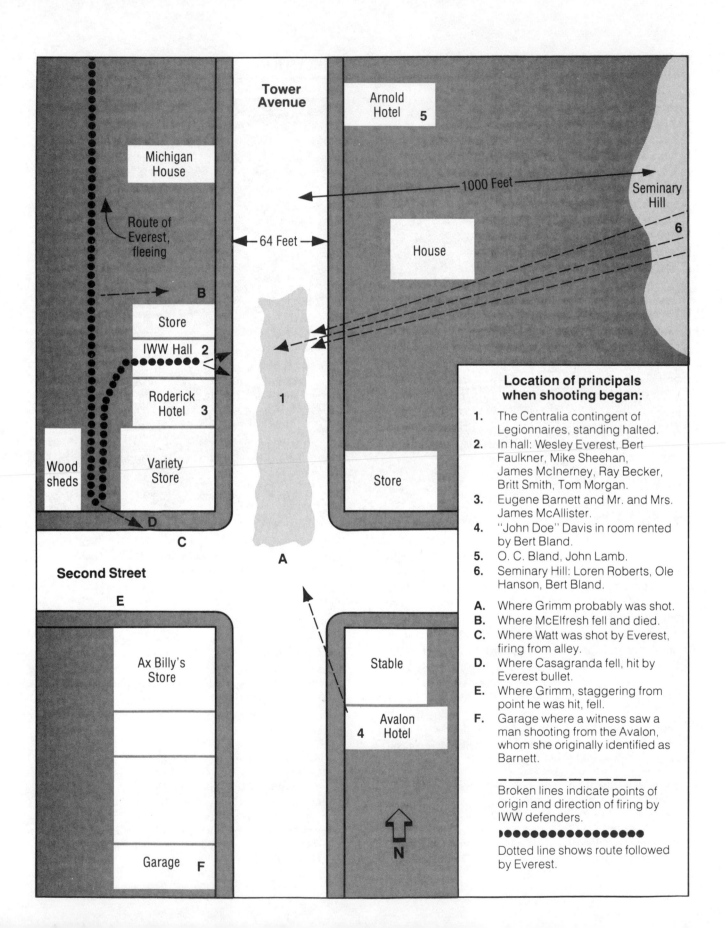

Tower Avenue

Michigan House

Route of Everest, fleeing

← 1000 Feet →

← 64 Feet →

Arnold Hotel **5**

Seminary Hill

6

House

B

Store

IWW Hall **2**

Roderick Hotel **3**

Wood sheds

Variety Store

D

C

1

A

Store

Second Street

E

Ax Billy's Store

Stable

Avalon Hotel **4**

Garage **F**

N

Location of principals when shooting began:

1. The Centralia contingent of Legionnaires, standing halted.
2. In hall: Wesley Everest, Bert Faulkner, Mike Sheehan, James McInerney, Ray Becker, Britt Smith, Tom Morgan.
3. Eugene Barnett and Mr. and Mrs. James McAllister.
4. "John Doe" Davis in room rented by Bert Bland.
5. O. C. Bland, John Lamb.
6. Seminary Hill: Loren Roberts, Ole Hanson, Bert Bland.

A. Where Grimm probably was shot.
B. Where McElfresh fell and died.
C. Where Watt was shot by Everest, firing from alley.
D. Where Casagranda fell, hit by Everest bullet.
E. Where Grimm, staggering from point he was hit, fell.
F. Garage where a witness saw a man shooting from the Avalon, whom she originally identified as Barnett.

――――――――――――
Broken lines indicate points of origin and direction of firing by IWW defenders.

●●●●●●●●●●●●●●●
Dotted line shows route followed by Everest.

George Vanderveer, defense attorney, standing before the map where witnesses pointed to places they talked about in their testimony.

Q. Then the truth is, the only reason you were there on those four occasions — Sunday, Wednesday, Monday night and Tuesday night — was because Becker was there?
A. Yes sir.

Morgan admitted he and Becker were acquaintances, not friends. They met only the day before Armistice Day. Vanderveer, who had been able finally to see Morgan in jail despite his objections, questioned him about the visit:

Q. Did you tell me in jail that you were charged with murder in the first degree and they had dismissed the case against you?
A. I did not.
Q. And didn't I ask you what they were holding you for? And you said, "Nothing."
A. I did not.
Q. Didn't I ask you if you had been in jail then about seven or eight weeks?
A. Well, you said that, yes.
Q. Asked you how long you were going to stay for nothing, did I?
A. I don't remember.

Vanderveer tried to question Morgan about seeing Everest dragged into jail but Judge Wilson would not allow it.
The questioning continued:

Q. You have been in jail since November 11. Are you going to be released as soon as this case is over?
A. I don't know.
Q. How long are you going to stay there, forever?
A. That is my affair.

141

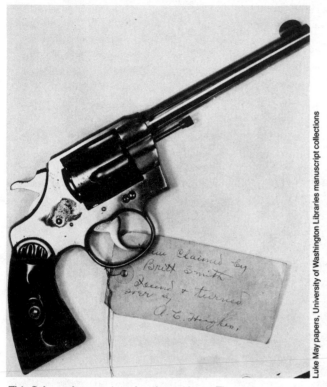

This Colt revolver was introduced as evidence. The tag says, "Gun claimed by Britt Smith."

Luke May papers, University of Washington Libraries manuscript collections

Q. You expect to be released as soon as this is over?
A. I can't say.

Then Vanderveer turned to the judge and said, "Your honor, we contend we will prove that this man was thrown in jail on that night; that he was subjected, as all the other prisoners were, to the horror of seeing a man brought in there, beat up and dragged out afterward and lynched, and there was . . ."

Wilson interrupted. He would not let Vanderveer say in front of the jury what witnesses were not allowed to say. But Vanderveer was satisfied. He had made his point, and the jury had heard.

The prosecutor himself, Herman Allen, took the stand to testify about a conversation he had with Bert Faulkner a week after his arrest. This gave Vanderveer an opportunity to ask Allen about his presence at the scene on November 11. He had been seen standing on the corner of Second and Tower while the hall was being torn apart after the shooting.

"What were you doing there?" he was asked.

"I don't know," he replied.[10]

Allen admitted that some pictures and papers taken from the hall during the raid were handed to him while he stood on the corner.

VANDERVEER: And at that moment a lot of people were wrecking the hall and burning books and, among other things, a set of the *Encyclopedia Brittanica* — a lot of books, desks, chairs and furniture outside the hall, were they not?
ABEL: I object. (Objection sustained.)
VANDERVEER: This witness is the prosecuting attorney under oath to enforce impartially and fairly the laws of the state. There is a law which punishes the willful destruction of property. . . . If he saw it and made no protest, it indicates there must have been a reason.

Wilson told Vanderveer he might bring that out later, but his ruling on the objection would stand.

To Vanderveer this was a show of partiality on the part of the judge that was intolerable. "I propose to inquire and ascertain before I have finished with your honor's ruling," he declared. "Otherwise I propose to leave this case. When I cannot conduct the defense of my clients' charge of murder and do it conscientiously under my oath I will not do it at all. Now I wish to know if I can cross-examine witnesses hereafter in matters affecting their interests."

Allen testified that he had interviewed all the prisoners and Morgan two or three times. He said Vanderveer had been allowed to talk to Morgan once and he thought that was enough.

Bernard Eubanks followed Allen to the stand to testify that he was running around the corner of Second and Tower when a bullet hit him in the right leg. Pressed to say whether he felt the hall was attacked before shots were fired he said, "I have not formed an opinion as to whether it was or not. Possibly it could have been and it is possible that it was not. I was not looking back to see."

On cross-examination, Vanderveer asked:

Q. Didn't you tell your father after the matter was over and while it was still fresh in your mind that the boys in the parade attacked the hall and got shot and while it was unfortunate it was their own fault?
A. I don't remember making any statement like that.
Q. You know your father claims you did, don't you?
A. No sir, I don't.[11]

(Bernard Eubanks, interviewed at his home in Oregon sixty-six years later, reiterated what he had said on the witness stand. He was looking the other way when the action began, started running, and was hit in the leg almost immediately.)

W. H. Graham, the high-school principal, took the stand to describe his part in the arrest of Elmer Smith, including Smith's display of a gun when he and others, including "six or eight Boy Scouts," confronted Smith in his office about forty minutes after the shooting.

Vanderveer asked Graham if he had ever heard Smith say anything he considered disloyal to the United States. He had. What was it? He had once said, while Graham was in Smith's office, that the U.S. had no business being in the war; that it was a capitalistic war; and that it was waged by capitalists to kill off the common workers.[12]

Vanderveer tried to get Graham to concede that this remark was made when Graham went to Smith's office to get help in preparing a questionnaire needed in his claim for exemption from military service, but Abel objected and the objection was sustained. Adept at getting around the frequent sustaining of objections, Vanderveer then asked Graham:

Q. So you believe it is traitorous for a man to have an opinion about the propriety of our going into the war?
A. Not necessarily.
Q. And you believe it is traitorous to the government for a man preparing a claim for exemption for military service to say he thinks the government should have kept out of the war?
A. Not necessarily.[13]

T. H. McCleary, Centralia's postmaster, was asked to explain a widely circulated story that men in the parade carried ropes, ostensibly to be used to hang Wobblies. "I was in the parade," he said. "I carried a rope. I found it in the middle of the street between Pine and Main. I picked it up and Mr. Rhodes took hold of it and it came apart. We had no idea to hang anybody with that rope."[14]

Lyla Tripp, a young woman who lived with an aunt on B Street, on the east side of Tower, contributed something to the prosecution's case against Barnett. When she heard the shooting she went into the alley near Second Street where she saw a man loading a gun as he walked.

Tom Morgan was one of the Wobblies in the hall who did not fire a gun. The others were prosecuted and convicted. He was not brought to trial after giving a detailed statement to the prosecutor that was labeled a "confession." The Wobblies called him a "stool pigeon" who turned against fellow workers in exchange for a promise that he would not be tried.

Q. What was he like?
A. He was short and walked slouchy-like and wore a brown coat and a dark hat, kind of peaked at the top. His eyes were blue.
Q. Blue eyes? Afterward did you go down to the Chehalis jail?
A. Well, that evening I was taken to the police station in Centralia twice. . . . It was about a week afterward that I was taken to the county jail.

Then she continued her story. After he saw her he walked faster and walked right down Second Street, turned and crossed Second, and went down B Street and out of sight. Then she said she saw another man, coming from the direction of Tower, carrying a gun and "kind of leisurely looking around."

Vanderveer knew that Miss Tripp would be asked to identify Barnett as the man she had seen in the alley, so, remembering the procedure used with Elsie Hornbeck, he had his clients change their usual positions on the defendants' bench.

Abel, noticing this, instead of asking his witness to

143

Luke May papers, University of Washington Libraries manuscript collections

Rifles and handguns surrendered by the Wobblies who were arrested in the Armistice Day shootings.

look at the defendants and identify one as the man she had seen, said, "Eugene Barnett, stand up."

The trick didn't work. Vanderveer leaped to his feet. "I object to any more of this kind of stuff," he shouted. Wilson sustained the objection and Tripp was not asked to attempt an identification. He knew, Vanderveer informed the witness, that she had been told before she took the stand that Barnett was sitting third from the right and during the recess he had the defendants mixed up. The jury heard him.

The solemnity of the proceedings was punctuated occasionally by a baby's cry. Warren Grimm's widow sat through the trial, holding her squirming eleven-month-old daughter. On another side of the court-

room sat Mrs. Elmer Smith, also with a baby daughter in her arms. When Laura Grimm was called to testify about the clothing her husband wore when he joined the parade, she handed the baby to her sister-in-law, Mary Grimm. "Dressed in black with a black velvet hat that accentuated the pallor of face," the press reported, "the witness took the oath and testified that she now resided with her parents in Spokane and had gone to view the parade and taken a seat in a Tower Avenue office to watch. In that office she received a telephone call to go to the hospital."[15]

Near the close of the state's case, Loren Roberts suddenly sprang from his place on the prisoner's bench and took a seat on the witness stand, smiling and looking as if he expected to be questioned. Judge Wilson quickly ordered him away. Roberts said nothing and returned to his seat. Several doctors testified about Roberts's state of mind. One of them, Dr. C. O. Ahlman of Hoquiam, said it would be impossible to feign dementia praecox successfully, though Roberts was trying. Dr. William House of Portland, who admitted he didn't like the IWW, said he was certain Roberts was faking. Two jailers testified that Roberts apparently had no delusions while confined in his cell.

The motions calling for the dismissal of charges against Sheehan, Becker, and McInerney, as well as Smith, having been denied, Vanderveer renewed a previous plea — that Smith be admitted to bail pending the outcome of the trial. "The man is an attorney," Vanderveer pleaded. "He is trying to assist me. I am laboring under a great many difficulties — alone in the case. I want his assistance. He has the right to be out where he can defend himself. . . ."[16]

Wilson's response was brief and decisive: "The motion to fix bail at this time is denied."

Then Wilson surprised everyone in the crowded courtroom by saying he had studied the cases cited in support of the motion to dismiss charges against Faulkner and had decided to grant it. The young Wobbly was taken aback. Was he free, really? "Yes," said the pleased Vanderveer, "go take a seat in the audience with your mother."

The other defendants, though envious of his good fortune, congratulated him with their smiles as he went back to the bench where his mother was seated. She moved aside, her face glowing, and motioned for her son to sit beside her. "I don't know just exactly how I feel," he said later. "I've been in jail so long that it seems like home to me."[17]

Wilson offered no explanation for allowing Faulkner to go free while requiring that others who did no shooting remain as accused murderers. He was young — just twenty-one. He was a local youth, not a transient like most of the others. His mother was there at the trial every day, anxiously listening. Whatever the reason, the judge, who was stern and unbending at all other times, was moved to compassion in the case of this one defendant.

Finally, on March 10, the last of 147 witnesses for the prosecution testified and the prosecutors rested their case. It would now be the defense's turn, although Vanderveer, with his aggressive tactics and probing cross-examination, had utilized the time given to the prosecution's case to make many points of his own.

The *Union Record,* several weeks after the trial began, observed that a "decided change in opinion concerning the case was noticeable among those attending the trial. Contempt for Vanderveer and his methods had changed to respect. Smiles could be seen when he scored a point." This change was attributed in part to the performance of the prosecutors. Allen inspired no admiration when it was brought out that he was on the scene and did nothing to stop the raid on the hall after the initial violence. The correspondents covering the trial, the *Union Record* claimed, were modifying their opinions. Now they were sure there would not be a first-degree murder verdict. The number of Legionnaires attending the trial, it was noted, had diminished. It was now March 10, six weeks after the trial began, and it was only half over.

21

The Defense

George Vanderveer began his defense presentation by telling the jury exactly what he intended to prove: first, that Eugene Barnett was not in the Avalon Hotel; second, that since Loren Roberts was insane, his statements could not be taken seriously; third, that Mike Sheehan was not in the hall before Monday night and so could not have been a party to any defense preparations; fourth, that a raid on the hall had been planned in the Elks Club by members of the Commercial Club and other businessmen and that those plans, plus the fact that the IWW hall was raided the previous year, fully justified the defendants' expectation of a raid and preparations made to defend themselves; and fifth, that the raid started before guns were fired and that Warren Grimm had been one of the raid's leaders.

Persons charged with criminal offenses cannot be required to testify at their own trials and usually do not, but in this trial Vanderveer called all except Roberts and Becker to testify. Roberts could not be called because, under the defense strategy, he was considered insane. Becker's situation was quite different from that of the others. He was in the hall with a gun, which he fired, but most of the firing was done by Wesley Everest.

The defense position was that Grimm led the raid and was shot by someone in the hall. Best to attribute that shot to Everest, who was dead. And best to keep Becker off the witness stand and avoid risk that under cross-examination he could be identified as the one who shot Grimm, if, indeed, Grimm was near the hall door when the shooting began.

The first defense witness was the number-one accused — the one identified by prosecution witnesses as the lean-faced man they saw leaning out of a window of the Avalon with a rifle in his hands — Eugene Barnett. Since the prosecution was basing its case on just one slaying, and since Barnett was the one identified as the slayer, the defense could undermine that strategy if it could firmly establish Barnett's alibi — that he did not go near the Avalon hotel and that he was being mistaken for one of the Wobblies who did go there with a rifle — the one who got away, John Doe Davis.[1]

Barnett on the stand, reported the *Chronicle*, was unabashed and positive in his answers, "frequently tossing sharp retorts at the state's counsel during cross-examination." Barnett said he knew nothing about the proposed defense of the hall; that he was in the lobby of the Roderick throughout the firing; and that he never had possession of the .38-caliber rifle with which Grimm was slain.

Barnett described the storming of the Roderick lobby by Legionnaires while he was still there. One was carrying a gun so he shouted at them to be careful because there was a woman in the back (Mrs. McAllister, the proprietor).

Barnett did not identify one of the Legionnaires he saw in the Roderick, as he did later, as William Scales, and Scales unaccountably was never summoned as a witness by either side to affirm or deny that he had seen Barnett in the Roderick.

Barnett was kept on the stand for several hours, readily answering all questions and welcoming a chance to express his views, which included a total lack of remorse over the deaths of the four servicemen. He said that they had gotten what was coming to them and added, "The authorities refused to enforce the law and let the businessmen go ahead with their plans to raid the hall."

Several witnesses, including John Mahar, an eleven-year-old boy, told of seeing Barnett on Armistice Day, riding his horse into town unarmed, riding home in the afternoon, his horse at a walk, wearing the

The eleven men who were tried for the Centralia killings. Top row: Loren Roberts, James McInerney, Britt Smith, O. C. Bland, Bert Faulkner, Ray Becker. Bottom row: Mike Sheehan, John Lamb, Eugene Barnett, Bert Bland, Elmer Smith.

distinctive clothes of a cowboy — chaps and a broad-brimmed, high-peaked hat.

S. A. Hand, proprietor of a secondhand store near the scene of the action, saw Barnett walking south on Tower about ten minutes after the shooting. Hand was one who immediately recognized the proportions of the tragedy that had occurred and was so overwhelmed he was in the back of his store, crying, he testified, when a number of excited persons came in to tell him what they had seen.

The trial proceedings were interrupted when Vanderveer was subpoenaed to go across the hall to testify in what had come to be known as the "Montesano sideshow" — the trial of eleven other Wobblies charged under the syndicalism act. He was the last witness for the defense. Ralph Pierce, his partner, who was defending the accused men, wanted someone who could make an eloquent statement about IWW philosophy. His only hope for acquittal lay in convincing the jury that the syndicalism law was unjust in making mere membership in the IWW a crime.

When asked if he were a member of the IWW, Vanderveer said regretfully, no, the union wouldn't have him. He was not a wage earner. Then he remarked that the Wobblies looked upon lawyers as useless institutions, a comment that produced an intended laugh. But did he believe in the IWW philosophy? "I certainly do," he replied.

The Issues in the Centralia Murder Trial

Ten lumberjacks and one of their lawyers went to trial in January at Montesano, Washington, charged with murder as a result of the killing of five ex-service men in the Armistice Day parade at Centralia.

The fight was the result of long and bitter industrial warfare between the lumber trust and the lumber workers of the Northwest. It is a case of national significance, because of the industrial issues involved, the claim of the defendants to the right of self-protection by arms, and the exceeding difficulty of securing a fair trial.

Published by the
AMERICAN CIVIL LIBERTIES UNION
138 West 13th Street, New York City
February, 1920

241

The cover of a pamphlet produced in February 1920 by the American Civil Liberties Union. This pamphlet astonished numerous persons who had formed opinions about the Armistice Day violence from news accounts which said little or nothing about the causes of the affair or the motives of the Wobblies in defending their hall.

From the witness stand, Vanderveer gave a dissertation on the history of the IWW and the reforms it advocated to improve the lot of the working man in logging camps and elsewhere. But the Grays Harbor jury, perhaps influenced by what was taking place on the other side of the courthouse, did not feel it was a time to show any leniency toward any Wobblies. All eleven were found guilty.

Another interruption in the trial occurred when one of the jurors, James Parr, fell victim to the flu. He had just been replaced by one of two alternate jurors, James Ball, when three other jurors went to bed with the ailment that had become epidemic in Montesano. An infirmary and dormitory for the sick jurors was set up in the firehouse where the Legionnaires were quartered, an arrangement that had the approval even of Vanderveer — anything to prevent a mistrial, which could be declared if the jurors didn't recover within a reasonable time.

On the fifth day of the court's enforced recess an extraordinary thing occurred. The United States Army was called in. To the astonishment of the whole town a train pulled into the Montesano depot on March 1 and eighty fully equipped soldiers of the Thirty-fifth Infantry regiment from Camp Lewis disembarked and marched to an open space behind the city hall where they set up camp. The resulting excitement was intense. What did it mean? Why were they there? Who called for them?

Judge Wilson was one who wanted answers to these questions. The "Labor Jury" demanded them as did Vanderveer, who realized immediately the effect armed troops near the courthouse would have on the jury. The jurors could only conclude that the Wobbly threat must have gotten so bad that troops were needed to stand guard.

Prosecutor Allen answered one of the questions. It was he who asked the governor for the troops as a "precautionary measure." Governor Hart, ever ready to believe the worst about the IWW, was quick to comply. He telephoned Lt. Gen. Hunter Liggett, commanding the Western Department of the Army in San Francisco, who without hesitation ordered Maj. Gen. John T. Morrison, commander at Camp Lewis, to assign troops to Montesano. Allen met with the Labor Jury to say that the troops were necessary because of rumors that the IWW was planning armed intervention to enable the ten defendants to escape from jail and avoid the certain fate that awaited them if they remained — conviction for murder.

The Labor Jury, as it was called, made up of a wide cross-section of labor, was incensed. Its members sent wires to their respective unions urgently requesting that some action be taken to get the troops withdrawn. "Troops not needed," they declared. "Are here to create atmosphere."

The absurdity of the rumors was apparent even to Allen, who was quoted the next day as saying, "We have reason to believe that most of the rumors of impending trouble are idle and unfounded. At the same time it is certain that no harm can be done by taking the proper steps to anticipate and forestall any possibility of serious friction. . . . The troops' presence in Montesano will be in the interests of the defense as well as the prosecution."

Wilson commented publicly that it seemed strange that such action would be taken without consulting the trial judge or the local peace officers. The sheriff had not been asked if he and his numerous deputies were incapable of preserving order during the trial. Wilson ordered Allen to provide him with the information on which the call for troops was based. Then, indicating his initial disapproval, he ordered that none of the soldiers be allowed in the courtroom or even the hallways of the courthouse.

Vanderveer was more furious about this setback than any of the others he had encountered. He considered it a trick on the part of the prosecution to influence the jury, to create tension, to generate fears that more Wobbly violence of some kind was possible, and to make more apparent the necessity to put the Wobbly killers away before any more harm was done.

The presence of the troops could not be kept from the jurors even though they could not talk to anyone or read the newspapers. Some were to admit in later years that the bringing in of troops did have something of the effect that the prosecutors intended. The region was gripped by fear when the violence occurred. Why it happened and what led up to it was of little concern compared to the reality of a deadly rain of bullets from several different directions into a street crowded with people. It was this fear that sent the posses out to round up as many of the "enemy" as could be found. It was fear that caused men to start carrying guns under their coats and women to be afraid to leave their houses at night. The jurors were aware of all this —

everyone in the region was — and so when troops appeared on the scene it had to be assumed it was for good reason.

When the trial finally could resume Vanderveer immediately addressed the court:

> Before we proceed I feel that the court ought to decide whether (the trial) is going to be conducted as a lawsuit or as a drumhead court martial. If it is decided to make it a court martial, I am going to withdraw from the case. . . . If it be as thought in having these troops brought here to create the impression that the IWWs are a lawless, murderous organization and if it be its purpose to create in the public mind a belief that everything charged in this case is true, and (to deceive) the jury (for) they are bound to hear the bugle calls all over the city and they can draw only one conclusion. Now if that be the purpose (Allen) deserves to be punished for contempt.

If Allen sent out a report that the IWW was considering a jailbreak, he added, that certainly was contemptuous conduct.[2] His voice rising, he continued:

> I will not lend myself to a judicial farce no matter what the penalty might be. I will not do it. I have tried many of these cases. I tried a case in Everett where seventy-four men were accused of murder. Not only was there no disorder, threat of disorder, jail break or anything, but those men were time after time paroled in my custody as these men here could be.
>
> We have had to fight everywhere from the 11th day of November until now. We have had to fight prejudice more than facts. Today I fear prejudice more than I fear the evidence . . . and I ask Mr. Allen why he did it, upon what information he acted, what his reason was, what his idea, his thought, his purpose, and I was told virtually that it is none of my business. . . . The presence of these troops is an insult to American institutions, an insult to this community, an insult to the men on trial for their lives, an insult to me, to this court and to everybody.[3]

Abel then said he had confidential information concerning the need for the troops that he would share with the judge. The two conferred but the "confidential information" remained just that. It was never made public. On the morning of February 27 Judge Wilson issued his ruling:

"The court has come to the conclusion that inasmuch as the troops were brought here without any action on the part of the court and inasmuch as there is

a showing which might be construed to mean a reason for the action, the court will not take the responsibility of requesting the removal of the troops."[4] Major Arthur Casey, commander of the troops, met with Wilson and told him the soldiers were in town only to provide readiness in case of an emergency when local authorities might need help.

Vanderveer was not placated. "I refuse to lend myself in any way to a proceeding which I believe is designed to stir up and manufacture prejudice against my clients," he thundered. He demanded to know what anyone was afraid of. If there was cause for fear, he said, he had a right to know about it.

Abel responded by recalling that when Vanderveer was arguing against holding the trial in Montesano, he claimed there would be breaches of the peace — that the Legion and the IWW would be there, and there would likely be clashes.

Vanderveer remained adamant. "Let us not forget that . . . the inevitable result of the presence of these troops will be that the jury will ultimately get, and the public already has gotten, the impression that there exists an IWW menace here of the very kind that is on trial in this case."[5]

Wilson waited for Vanderveer to run down. When he stopped speaking, the judge asked, "Are you ready to proceed?"

Though bitter and disappointed, he had to say yes. He couldn't withdraw. He couldn't leave the men with no one to defend them. "My clients seem to feel," he said, "that we have no alternative but to submit, which we will do, but not meekly."

The jury, kept out of the courtroom while the troop matter was discussed, was then called back.

Vanderveer was not entirely displeased with the way the trial was going at this point. Although the judge sustained most of the objections to his attempts to introduce evidence showing that a raid on the hall had been planned if not definitely scheduled, he was able in various ways to make sure the jury learned that the gunfire was in defense of the hall and not an irresponsible act of terrorism.

In a letter to Roger Baldwin, director of the American Civil Liberties Union, Vanderveer wrote: "We will be able to establish that the Employers' Association of this state planned this occurrence. . . . I can prophecy with assurance that there will be no convictions, although it is possible at least one juror is under the direct control of the prosecution."[6]

The time came for Elmer Smith's eagerly awaited testimony. He told his story. On November 11 a man named Burness came to him and said he had positive information that the hall would be raided that day. He went then to the hall and conferred with Britt Smith.

"My sole objective in going to the hall was to tell them it was to be raided," Smith said. He added that he feared any raid would be followed by the lynching of its occupants, or tarrings and featherings. Under cross-examination he admitted that he had said, "Boys, are you ready for the raid?" and that he did not warn Britt against the use of guns.[7]

Mike Sheehan, at sixty the oldest of the defendants, and still a citizen of Ireland, took the witness stand to say that he came in from a logging camp and went to the hall for the first time on November 10. He heard remarks about an expected raid, but his main concern was talking with fellow Irishman James McInerney about the visit to Tacoma of the Irish statesman, Eamon DeValera. Although he was in the hall when the action took place, Sheehan considered himself an innocent bystander.

McInerney, veteran of the *Verona* slaughter in Everett and the Centralia IWW hall destruction in 1918, took advantage of his time on the witness stand to let the jury know what the Wobblies thought might happen if and when the expected raid was made. "We thought they would come down and club us up and tar and feather us and hang some of them," he said.

> Q. And wreck the hall?
> A. Yes, wreck the hall.
> Q. Why would you think they would wreck the hall?
> CUNNINGHAM: Objected to as incompetent, irrelevant and immaterial.
> COURT: Objection sustained. [8]

The testimony of the Bland brothers, according to the *Chronicle*'s reporter, caused a "profound sensation — the most astonishing development since the start of the trial."[9]

Vanderveer had not intimated that the defense would admit shots were fired from outside the hall. But here was Bert Bland describing how he and Loren Roberts and Ole Hanson stationed themselves on Seminary Hill and fired into the crowd in front of the hall on Tower Avenue; and Commodore Bland admitting he took a rifle and went to a room in the Arnold

In the midst of the trial a contingent of soldiers from Fort Lewis arrived in Montesano and camped near the courthouse where they could be seen by the jury and prisoners. The judge would not allow them inside the courthouse itself.

with John Lamb where he sat waiting for the expected raid to start. He fired no shots, he claimed, because he cut his hand badly when he broke a window.

Bert Bland said he was friendly with both Warren Grimm and Dale Hubbard and neither he nor any of the others had any reason for wanting to kill any of the ex-servicemen.

Bert Faulkner was now a free man, more willing than most of the others to tell every detail of his experience on Armistice Day. He said he was standing at the window of the hall, looking out, when the paraders stopped in the street outside. "I heard someone say, 'Let's go get them', or words to that effect," he reported, "and I judge it was one or two seconds before they hit the pavement and they said 'at them, get them' and 'grab them,' and just at that time they were breaking the window."[10]

Faulkner told the court that he was about eight feet from the window. The broken glass came through and hit the curtain. "At the time," he said, "it sounded to me like they threw a sack of wheat or spuds against the door. Just like a man hit the door with his knees or his shoulder."[11]

When the shooting started, Faulkner said, he was standing between the man who was doing the shooting (Wesley Everest) and the door. He reported that a bullet fired from behind him ripped through the shoulder of his overcoat.

Elmer Smith, recalled to the stand, testified that he was not discharged from the Centralia High School, as his detractors had charged, but taught for the full year of his contract and was in fact reelected for another term at an increase of ten dollars a month, but declined to accept.

This produced a rare thing — an apology from a newspaper. The *Vidette,* which was one of the papers that had reported Smith was discharged for refusing to take an oath of allegiance, said this must be wrong for otherwise Smith would not dare deny it under oath. It was something that could be easily proven.

"The *Vidette,*" its editor wrote, "without solicitation, wishes in justice to itself as well as to Smith, to correct its error. We would not, and did not intentionally add to the disrepute of any prisoner by publishing any falsehoods."[12]

Those who were sure Loren Roberts was faking insanity began wondering after his jail mates described his conduct. Britt Smith testified that Roberts claimed he saw a funeral march outside his door one night and thought an undertaker had buried him. Roberts told Bert Bland that some kind of a talking machine in the jail kept repeating, "You are guilty, yes, you are guilty, you killed them, you killed them, we will fix you, you will confess, you can't help it." Roberts told Smith this was repeated over and over and it was driving him crazy.

Testimony brought out that Roberts thought Vanderveer was Col. Bryce Disque, the 4-L chief, who had a lot of nerve coming to Montesano and masquerading as a defense lawyer.

Jackson Hardy, who had shared a cell with Roberts, was called, and was asked, "What do you think about his mental condition?"

He answered, "I am not an expert. I don't believe I am overly bright myself, but I think I have got it on him a little bit."[13] He reported that Roberts did not seem sad. He was continually humming, Hardy said, and never talked about his case.

Loren's mother was willing to support the contention that her son was mentally ill. She testified that her own father had "lost his mind" and that two first cousins were mentally deranged. One went to an "insane asylum." She herself, she admitted, was "nervous" and her daughter was "nervous."

Arthur F. Calhoun, described as a specialist in nervous and mental diseases, and a member of the American Legion, was brought in to testify for the defense. He was a fraternity brother of Warren Grimm at the university.

Dr. Calhoun told of questioning Roberts with Vanderveer and another doctor present. Vanderveer, Roberts told Calhoun, was Colonel Disque. As for Calhoun, he was no doctor. He was a prosecuting attorney from Thurston County. Roberts told the doctor that his bed was "shocked with electricity at night" and that the courtroom was controlled by wireless.[14]

When Dr. House, who also was present, turned to Roberts and said, "I think you are faking," he smiled and replied, "Sure."

Calhoun, asked if he had seen faking before, said yes, but he was sure Roberts was not faking. Instead he was suffering from a type of dementia praecox.

Many witnesses admitted they were interviewed by Cunningham and Allen before they talked to other attorneys about the effect their courtroom testimony might have on the case. In not a few instances their testimony differed from what they had been recorded as saying in the early interviews.

Mrs. Mary McAllister, the sixty-eight-year-old proprietress of the Roderick Hotel, and a key witness for the defense, provided an example of this. After saying she had known Ben Casagranda since he was three years old, she was asked:

Q. Do you remember talking with Mrs. Casagranda the night of the shooting?
A. No, I did not talk with any woman.
Q. Don't you remember that she told you Bennie was shot?
A. No sir, nobody told me that.
Q. And you said "It serves him right, he had no business marching with the soldiers."
A. No sir.[15]

Then Abel asked whether, in her interview on November 14, in answer to his question, "Do you know whether or not the shooting started before they started to raid the hall?" she had said, "The shooting started just as soon as they started to run for it."

Mrs. McAllister pleaded confusion. Referring to the interview, she said, "There was so many crowded in there and they had me scared to death and I don't know what I put down."[16]

Now on the witness stand, under oath, she was positive in her assertion that the shooting did not start until the soldiers hit the door of the hall. Asked if she knew there was a man on the roof of the porch shooting, she said no, nobody was on the roof. The windows and doors were fastened and nobody could have gotten upstairs and climbed out on the roof.

The prosecution protested when Vanderveer questioned Mrs. McAllister about her attempts to get police protection for her property prior to Armistice Day. Such testimony, the prosecutors knew, would help support the Wobbly alibi for the shooting.

But Vanderveer worked around the objections. He brought out that Mrs. McAllister had gone to see the chief of police.

The chief asked her what was on her mind and she said a man had come to her and said her property was in danger of being broken up because she had the IWW as tenants. When she asked the chief for protection he told her there was nothing he could do legally because the IWW had not actually broken any law.

He mentioned nothing about being powerless to prevent a raid. Referring to that possibility, the chief said to Mrs. McAllister, according to her testimony: "As far as the Wobblies are concerned they would not last fifteen minutes. It might bring on trouble, it might bring on bloodshed; it might bring on hard feelings among the people and all sorts of trouble. That is what we are trying to prevent."

She said she asked the chief then if he could protect her property and he replied, "Yes, I will do the best I can. . . ."[17]

Cunningham moved to strike all of the McAllister testimony from the record and the motion was upheld, whereupon Vanderveer paraphrased aloud what his witness had said so that the jury would be sure to get the import of it. Then a recess was called. Afterward Judge Wilson changed his mind. The McAllister testimony could stand.

This was a setback to the prosecution because in subsequent testimony Mrs. McAllister was able to tell about a Legionnaire who had called on her in advance of the parade. She didn't know who it was but "she saw him afterward carrying out things, burning and wrecking everything."

Q. What did this Legionnaire who called on you say they would do?
A. He said they held a meeting at the park the night before. He said they were going to come up and clean them (the Wobblies) out and they took some sort of a straw vote on it and he said half of them decided to and half decided not, so they did not go, but he said,

"You had better look out, they will come up some day and clean you out good and clean."[18]

Mrs. McAllister said the Legionnaire objected most particularly to the display of the Little Red Song Book and other Wobbly material in the window of the hall. When he left she went to Britt Smith and demanded that he remove the material. He did.

Her husband, J. C. McAllister, also had trouble reconciling his early statements with what he was now saying as a witness. "I was in the office in the lobby of the hotel," he testified.

My wife was there and Mr. Barnett sat there in a chair. There was another gentleman, a stranger (who) just dropped in and sat there watching the parade. Mr. Barnett was there at the time the parade passed, I suppose about one and a half hours. He remained there when they started to tear the posts off from under the porch. Then he got up and said, "I better get out of here or I can't get out."[19]

McAllister was asked by Cunningham if, prior to the trial, he had said there was no one in the lobby but himself. The witness, who had by then become obviously uncomfortable and nervous, admitted that is what he told Cunningham and Allen the day of Grimm's funeral, but now said:

I didn't have any oath. He did not swear me and I didn't have to tell them. I told them I didn't see anybody. The reason I told them was because I was not sworn. I told them I did not want to be dragged into . . . I didn't want to be mixed up in it. My wife was down in the jail. . . . My place was all broken up. I didn't see anything going on outside the hall.[20]

One of the strong defense witnesses was Dr. Bickford, a quiet, dignified man, forty-nine years old, whose testimony at the inquest was widely considered so incredible he was disbelieved.

He did not change his story at Montesano. Yes, he said, the rush to raid the hall did begin before the shooting started. Bickford described the scene: Van Gilder commanding his platoon; Cormier on a horse that was scared and prancing around; men marking time and talking.

BICKFORD: I don't remember whether it was Van Gilder or Grimm, but one or the other of them began to talk.

Q. Did you hear what he said?
A. I heard most of it, yes.
Q. Had it anything to do with what happened subsequently?
A. Yes.
Q. Will you tell the jury?
A. He said "Eyes right as you pass the viewing stand. We forgot that when we went up Tower."

Then Bickford said he heard nothing actually that related to what happened next, but added:

A. I heard a commotion . . . and I turned and saw these platoons in the rear breaking ranks and scattering. Some were going toward the IWW hall, some were over in here, and some this way and some were going over there and the whole bunch was scattering and there were three men going toward the IWW hall.
Q. Had someone just about that time said anything to you about a raid?
A. Yes sir.
Q. Do you know who it was?
A. I do not.
Q. What did he say?
A. He simply made mention of a raid that had taken place about a year ago.

Describing his own action, Bickford said he went up to join three men who were going toward the hall. When they reached the hall door one of them put his foot against it and pushed.

Q. What happened?
A. It opened about that far (indicating with his hands).
Q. Did the glass break?
A. No sir.
Q. Had there been any shooting before that time?
A. I had not heard any.
Q. Did the shooting follow that?
A. As soon as he put his foot against the door and pushed, there was sure shooting.
Q. And you say a moment or so — how long was it before that you heard the men speak about the former raid on the IWW hall?
A. Well, as we marched back — up to that time I had not known that the IWW hall was there. But someone marching close to me made some remark which drew my attention to the hall, and I looked over this way and I saw the IWW signs painted on the doors or the windows. And he made a remark regarding the (1918) raid, and I remember that my answer was that I wasn't

in a raid at the IWW hall at that time, but I had read about it in the paper and heard about it. Then I spoke to him as we were marching and we were just talking and I said "if anyone wants to raid the hall," or I asked him if there was going to be a raid, and he said he didn't know. Well, I said if they want to raid the hall I will take the lead, if you want to go.[21]

On cross-examination Bickford explained that the conversation about a raid took place before the parade stopped in front of the hall. He did not know why the men were scattering but it might have been because there was a shot he had not heard since he was somewhat deaf.

The first shots he heard, he said, came through the door of the hall "because I was standing about four feet from the door and could see the glass fly as the bullets came through."[22]

Q. Did any of the soldiers break the door or break the windows?
A. He did not break in the windows. He pushed the door open, but the lock gave way . . . but the glass did not break while he was pushing the door in.

Bickford said he was the first physician to reach the hospital. He went in the car that carried the wounded McElfresh.

Vanderveer reinforced the Bickford testimony with a parade of witnesses who said much the same thing — that the attack on the hall began before shots were fired. In an attempt to discredit this line of testimony the prosecution resorted to the accusation of perjury tactic. By arresting witnesses on charges of perjury the prosecutors sought to impress the jury with their contention that the testimony was false.

Knowing how some witnesses would testify, arrest papers charging perjury were prepared in advance and were served with a flourish when the witness left the stand.

One of those served was Jay Cook, who told of seeing the attack begin and then observing a wounded man walk away from the front of the hall bent over and holding his stomach. Cook said he later saw the same man in the back of Ax Billy's establishment, the place where Grimm collapsed. His brother, Ray Cook, corroborated Jay's statement.

Another witness charged with perjury was a youth, Guy Bray, who testified that Frank Van Gilder and Grimm were within a few feet of the hall when the shooting started. Neither of the arrested witnesses was subsequently prosecuted.

Sheriff Berry and Vanderveer engaged in an arm-waving argument over the Bray testimony. Berry wagged an accusing finger at the lawyer, who slapped at his hand. Berry slapped back, knocking a cigarette from the counsel's mouth. Berry contended that Bray admitted he was promised bail if his testimony led to his arrest and that it would be furnished by Harry Smith, brother of Elmer.

The credibility of another witness produced a tiff between Vanderveer and the judge. May Sherman, also known as Bertha Hope, lived in the nearby Queens Hotel, was in touch with some of the IWW men, and went out on Armistice Day to see the expected trouble. She saw the "door smashed and the glass fly," and a heavyset man holding his stomach passed her on the sidewalk going south.

Under cross-examination she admitted that she might have said to a woman in the corridor outside the courtroom, "We will have evidence to meet anything they bring up."[23] The judge smiled, causing Vanderveer to erupt.

"Will your honor refrain from smiling," he demanded. "It is the most pernicious comment on testimony, whether your honor is conscious of it or otherwise, the making of that kind of comment on the evidence." The judge assured him that any smile was not intended to reflect his opinion of testimony.

The extensive efforts of the prosecutors in advance of the trial to shape testimony that would be given was revealed in the testimony of Forrest Campbell, a nineteen-year-old candy maker who was standing in front of the building across the street from the hall when the parade stopped. He said the men broke ranks and ran toward the hall, adding, "There were about two or three close to the door and the rest were after them. They were running. They ran into the door. I heard it crash. I heard shots from the hall. The crash came before the shots. McElfresh was one of the first to smash in the door."[24]

Campbell said that on the day after November 12, he was escorted to American Legion headquarters over the city hall where he was kept all afternoon, about six hours, relating what he had seen and heard. The prosecution tried unsuccessfully to block this part of his testimony.

When J. M. Eubanks, father of Bernard, one of the wounded Legionnaires, took the stand he was asked if his son told him after the shooting that the Legionnaires attacked the hall. A quick objection, sustained by Wilson, prevented an answer. Then Eubanks was asked about his attendance at the October Elks Club meeting where plans for ridding the city of Wobblies were discussed. At this point the prosecutors demanded a recess.

With the jury out of the room, Vanderveer argued that what Eubanks would say was pertinent because it supported the defense contention that the Legionnaires were the aggressors. He reminded the court that the prosecution in its opening statement said it would stand or fall on the issue of whether there was a raid. At that point Abel interrupted, "We never agreed to any such thing."

Vanderveer: "I knew you would quit agreeing to it some time, but I put you there then so plainly that you would be terrifically embarrassed in getting away from it. So long as that issue is in this case . . . we (must be) permitted to introduce evidence (concerning) a plan for a raid and that it was participated in by people who were in that parade. . . . Now are we permitted to show plans for a raid? . . . Are we permitted to show who was the aggressor? If so, this evidence is admissible."[25]

Abel responded in a confused fashion. He noted that not until that day had the defense contended that Grimm was a participant in a raid or that he knew of any plans for an assault. He conceded a willingness to let the defense prove that there was a raid and even that a plan was made at the Elks Club meeting for a raid, but then he said that really wasn't a pertinent matter because meetings to discuss the "Wobbly question" were common in Centralia, and "it is not admissible for the purpose of inferring . . . that a plan was arranged . . . to have a raid."[26]

Wilson, after a moment, ruled, "If counsel can show that at this meeting the question of a raid was discussed and anything was said by any of the speakers or persons there which extended to a plan for a raid upon this hall, I think he should be permitted to do so."[27]

Despite this, when the jury was called back and Vanderveer asked Eubanks to tell what the chief of police said at the October meeting, the prosecution's objection was sustained. But when Eubanks was asked to report what Hubbard said, he was allowed to answer. Hubbard, Eubanks testified, said that "if he was the police chief he would get rid of them within twenty-four hours."[28]

Abel, who earlier admitted that Cunningham was the attorney for Hubbard's company, and Cunningham himself, objected strenuously to Vanderveer's line of questioning, but were overruled. As a consequence the jury finally heard a full report on what was said at the much-discussed Elks Club meeting in October.

This was a victory for Vanderveer, though during the trial he lost far more of his arguments with the judge than he won.

He wanted to convince the jury that the IWW was the underdog — hounded, plagued, and persecuted. The judge wouldn't let Mrs. Barnett tell about the vigilantes coming to their place and capturing her husband. He wouldn't allow Ralph Pierce to say that he was not allowed to get off the train in Centralia when he came to act as legal counsel for the accused men.

The judge's patience often wore thin as Vanderveer hammered away with his arguments and made comments that bordered on the disrespectful. At one point Wilson said, "You are asking the court about things which are not before the court," to which the attorney responded, "That's the most ridiculous thing I have ever heard in my life and I am forty-four. . . ."[29]

After another exchange in similar tone the judge was seething. He ordered the baliff to take the jury out. When the jurors were gone he glared down from the bench and made a lengthy statement.

He said Vanderveer time after time had argued with the court's rulings, declaring them "silly" or "ridiculous." He had insisted on arguing about the rulings. Now, he cautioned, "I want to warn you for the last time that the next time you make a statement of this kind . . . you shall suffer the consequences which the law provides. . . ."[30]

The stern admonition had little effect on the brash attorney. "Your honor makes rulings incomprehensible to me," he declared. Then he went right back to the argument that the judge had interrupted, which concerned why O. C. Bland, on the stand at the time, should be allowed to tell why he had armed himself on the day of the parade. Wilson pounded his gavel and cried, "I will listen to you no longer!"

Undaunted, Vanderveer kept on:

The more you listen the more you will learn about the facts and the more nearly I believe you will understand

how to rule on them.
WILSON: I request that you be silent and proceed.
VANDERVEER: I would like to call your honor's attention to the fact that William Scales, a member of the American Legion. . . .
WILSON (interrupting): That has nothing to do with the question. Now will you please be seated and end the controversy.[31]

This time Vanderveer gave in. He stopped talking and sat down.

All the defendants made good witnesses in their own behalf. Press reports noted that they were forthright in describing their actions and their motivations and carefully skirted the prosecution's theme that they planned and plotted an attack on the parade.

Britt Smith was on the stand longer than any of the others. When first called he was asked to identify newspaper articles about meetings of Centralia citizens to discuss plans for ridding the city of the IWW. Cunningham, of course, objected. Vanderveer retaliated by saying he could prove the conspiracy to raid the hall involved the American Legion, that Grimm was its commander, and that "presumably" he gave the order for the raid. "We will prove that the shooting started from inside the hall," promised Vanderveer. "The man who did that was Wesley Everest. He had a .45-caliber army automatic and he shot out the front door and shot three of these men. . . ."[32]

For such evidence to be admissible, the court said, it must either show an "overt act" on the part of Grimm, or that he actually had a part in a conspiracy to raid the hall.

With Cunningham and Abel both objecting, Wilson ruled that the newspaper articles could be introduced. Vanderveer not only introduced them, but read them aloud. They included the October 20 *Daily Hub* story that was virtually a bugle call for action:

"Employers: Your presence at the Elks Club Monday evening at 8 o'clock to discuss the IWW problem is earnestly requested."[33]

Finding the judge in an agreeable mood, Vanderveer, after reading the incriminating news items, tried to introduce a photograph of the previous IWW hall that was raided and wrecked in 1918. But he had gone far enough. This time the judge sustained Cunningham's objection.

Britt Smith told his story — hearing from several that there would be a raid; going to the mayor's office and not finding him; suggesting to Mrs. McAllister that she seek protection for her building; printing and distributing a thousand pamphlets appealing for public support in not permitting use of force against the IWW; and concluding, after conferring with others in the hall, that a raid was inevitable and that their only recourse was to defend the hall themselves.

Abel produced a hand-drawn map and asked Smith if it was not intended to show where men with guns would be stationed, saying the map was found in the drawer of his desk. Smith denied that the map was a part of any defense plan.

At this point Vanderveer made one of his few objections — to the introduction of anything seized in the raid on the hall because such seizure was unlawful and unconstitutional. Wilson had to agree.

The defense faced severe difficulties in trying to prove that Warren Grimm was a participant in a conspiracy by townspeople or Legionnaires to raid the hall and that he was actually shot while leading the raid. The judge took the position that Centralia's historic antipathy toward the IWW, which could not be concealed, and the discussions about ridding the city of the IWW in the months and weeks leading up to Armistice Day, all hostile in nature, were not pertinent to this trial unless it could be shown that Warren Grimm actually did something that identified him as one who took part in whatever brought about the Wobblies desperate armed stand. In an attempt to modify this position, Vanderveer came to court one morning with law books under his arm hoping to win one vital argument with Judge Wilson.

He began by asking for a ruling on whether witnesses could be permitted to testify to certain remarks made to Grimm a few days before the parade regarding the matter of a raid. Holding up a law book, he said: "The law is clearly settled in this state. . . . A person being at a place where he has a right to be (and who) is not himself a trespasser or wrongdoer . . . has a right to resist force with force; he has a right to stand his ground; he is not required to retreat; he is not required to give warning; he has a right to employ as much force as the circumstances of the case . . . seem reasonable to justify." He read citations from other cases to support his argument. He argued that the evidence he sought to introduce was admissible "because if the shooting of Warren Grimm was absolutely justifiable, no matter who shot him or where he was shot from, all is admis-

sible, because every part of that testimony tends to show who were the aggressors. . . . Every part tends to show a conspiracy. If there is a conspiracy and one of these men was the aggressor and any of them got shot, it is excusable whether Warren Grimm was himself an aggressor or not. . . ." The Wobbly lawyer talked for an hour and a half, saying it was up to the court "to determine what an overt act is, (and for) the jury to determine whether it was committed."[34]

Vanderveer made a persuasive point when he asked the judge to suppose that Barnett had quarreled with Grimm, or was hostile toward the American Legion. Would those circumstances be admissible in this case? he asked. "Surely," he said, answering his own question, "so can we not prove hostility on the part of Grimm and the American Legion to these men and their organization?"[35]

When he finished Wilson responded at length. He said he did not mean that "counsel must first prove an overt act on the part of the deceased himself or must prove that a conspiracy existed in which the deceased was a party."

What was lacking, said the judge, were specifics. "Stories about meetings and what was said at them, picnics where Grimm might have been present, and attempts to show in a general way some collective effort to raid the hall. . . . The situation is entirely too general. There must first be shown a conspiracy in which the deceased was a party . . . and until that is shown . . . the court will not permit this evidence to be introduced and the offer is denied."[36]

As it turned out, Vanderveer was able to get some testimony before the jury, showing that Grimm was certainly anti-Wobbly, though no more so than most Centralians, but could not find or bring out irrefutable evidence that he was a participant in any decision to raid the hall.

Teenagers, who might be considered too nervous in a crowded courtroom to fabricate their stories, helped the defense. Glenn Dorsch, seventeen, testified: "I heard Cormier giving orders to halt. Then a couple of fellows from the rear shouted something. They started to run toward the hall. Just about the time they got on the steps, shots were fired."[37]

Richard Buzzard, sixteen years of age, testified that he saw soldiers leave the parade ranks and run toward the hall and that there was no shooting before the rush began.[38]

John Patterson, a Centralia mill worker, revived memories of terror on the night of Armistice Day when he was questioned.

Q. Were you arrested after the shooting?
A. No sir, I was mobbed. They came and stuck rifles in my nose. Five men came, one at the front door and one at the back door and one at each window.
Q. Are you an IWW?
A. No sir.
Q. What did they want you for?
A. That's it, they wouldn't tell me. They took me out, threw me into the car and took me down to jail.[39]

The ability of the Labor Jury to render an impartial judgment was shaken when, near the end of the trial, one of the union men, E. W. Thrall, was called by Vanderveer to corroborate the testimony of another witness. Under cross-examination Thrall admitted he helped the defense by finding at least one witness who would testify for the defense. But considering the allegiances of the labor jurors — each one representing a different union — their impartiality was suspect anyway from the start.

The last defense witness was Joseph Smith, who marched in the last platoon of the Centralia contingent. He testified,

When we came back we closed up to the required fifteen paces, and somebody said "Let's run now. They are stopped down there." . . . We were marking time. I said to them: "What do you want to run for now? You have the required distance." And at the same time I asked: "What about this eyes right? Where is this reviewing stand?" He said, "There is not going to be a reviewing stand. They are going to give the Wobbly hall the eyes right." We marched down the street a short distance and I seen the crowd break, seen them rush to the hall, kick the doors. It looked to me like it was about three platoons ahead of me. . . . It seemed to me as though they just shot right out of the ranks right against the door. They kicked in and they got the door about kicked in and then I heard — it sounded like a bunch of firecrackers and then several loud reports.[40]

Vanderveer called so many witnesses — 115 in all — that the proceedings became tiresome. The press reported that spectators seemed to be losing interest. A number of witnesses were called a second time, for rebuttal testimony, and the trial droned on. Finally the defense rested. Everyone was relieved. It had been a long trial — six and a half weeks — and, although at times interesting and eventful, mostly tedious. There was general eagerness to get to the end — the verdict. Now only the closing arguments and the judge's instructions to the jury remained.

Through most of the long trial the defendants, it was noted, appeared to be in generally good spirits, frequently laughing and joking among themselves. They were in serious trouble together and together they developed confidence in their claim of self-defense as Vanderveer brought out what they knew to be the truth of what they had done. To them it was inconceivable that the jury could believe they had conspired to shoot men in a parade without cause, or that they would be convicted, not because of the shooting, but because they were Wobblies.

Even so, toward the end of the trial those reporting the proceedings noted a change in their attitude. Any signs of bravado disappeared. With the end near, a realization of the seriousness of their situation had a sobering effect. "There is little sunshine or laughter in the last chapters," the unfriendly *Vidette* commented, "yet there is hope, looking at it from the eyes of the defendants."

22

The Verdict

March 13, a Friday, cold and rainy, was to be the last day of the trial. By 9:30 the four hundred seats in the courtroom were filled and hundreds who weren't able to force their way into the room stood jammed in the corridor outside and on the stairs. They came expecting to hear the closing arguments and possibly even the verdict if, as many anticipated, the jury reached an agreement quickly.

But Judge Wilson disappointed them. He announced at 10 o'clock that the court would not convene until 1:30. He was working on instructions to the jury and they were not ready. When finally he did have them finished it was 2:45. The crowd then seemed even larger than in the morning. The courtroom doors were left unlocked during the noon hour and those standing outside rushed in to take seats vacated by those going to lunch. Even some of the reporters and relatives of defendants were not able to get back in the courtroom. In the crush and heat of the hallways, the local newspaper reported, women fainted; "many others who finally got to the doors and were passed, after being searched for arms, entered in a bedraggled condition as if they had been nearly torn to pieces. It is estimated that about 700 persons got into the courtroom and the adjoining rooms."[1]

Before a criminal case goes to a jury the judge issues a set of instructions, defining precisely what the jury may and may not do. These are given to the jury just before it retires to begin deliberations. Vanderveer, a skillful writer as well as speaker, sought to influence the jury's thinking by composing some fifty suggested instructions he hoped Judge Wilson would adopt. Most of them, not unexpectedly, were rejected. Among them were these:

It is not unlawful to use force in a case of malicious trespass or other malicious interference with real or personal property.

A man may repel force by force in defense of his person, habitation or property against someone intending to commit a felony and if that assaulter is killed in the defense, it is justifiable homicide.

If the evidence showed Warren Grimm advocated or advised violence against the IWW, or helped organize any group to advocate or teach injury to the IWW, and if Grimm was shot it was justifiable homicide.

It is lawful for a person defending his property to conceal himself on or off the premises of his property.

The law accords to every person threatened with mob violence the right to stand his ground and use force.

The presence or absence of a motive on the one side or the other is a "most material and important circumstance in determining the question of who was the aggressor."

The instructions that were actually given to the jury by Judge Wilson, among them some others that Vanderveer suggested, included the following:

If the shooting of Warren Grimm was either justifiable or excusable, the defendants must be acquitted.

Unless it is found that the defendants conspired to kill Grimm and he was killed as a result of that conspiracy, the verdict must be not guilty.

If there is reasonable doubt that any one of the defendants was a party of any such conspiracy, he shall be found not guilty.

Jurors must not find defendants guilty out of fear that otherwise a crime may go unavenged.

If Tom Morgan appeared to have been influenced by a threat of punishment or promise of immunity from prosecution "you should view his testimony with grave suspicion". . . .

Confessions are to be received and considered with great caution. Any confession made by Loren

Roberts may be considered as evidence only against Roberts and not any of the others.

The absence of a motive for the commission of the crime charged may be considered as having a bearing on whether the defendants are guilty.

If there is a reasonable doubt about Barnett being in the Avalon, and if there is reasonable doubt that he was part of a conspiracy, he is to be found not guilty.

No person can be convicted of a crime "merely because of the kind or quality of his character or his private opinions. . . . The IWW is not on trial and the economic and social theories of that organization, whether subscribed to or not by the defendants, may not be allowed to prejudice you against the defendants."

The defendants cannot be found guilty of murdering Grimm merely because they are presumed to be guilty of killing Arthur McElfresh and Ben Casagranda.

In his longest instruction Wilson said that while persons have a right to defend their property with arms, the law does not allow the placing of armed men at outside stations to defend property. He went on to say that if the jury found that the IWW had stationed armed men in the Avalon, in the Arnold, and on Seminary Hill to repel a "raid or attack on the IWW hall," that action was unlawful, and if armed men so stationed shot and killed it "would be murder" and "each of the defendants would be guilty of murder."

Since the defendants freely admitted doing what the judge now said was unlawful, this instruction could be interpreted as a mandate for conviction.

If you find that Eugene Barnett . . . entered into the conspiracy having murder and violence as an objective and as a natural, reasonable consequence of such conspiracy Warren O. Grimm was killed, then it will be your duty to find Barnett guilty as charged whether he has been identified as being the defendant who fired the fatal shot or not and whether he was armed or not.

If you find that Elmer Smith did no more than advise the other defendants to resist and endeavor to repel unlawful assault by all lawful means, then you should acquit him, and I instruct you that if you have a reasonable doubt about the truth of such fact it is your duty to resolve such doubt in favor of the defendant and acquit him.

I charge you that as to the defendant Elmer Smith your verdict must either be guilty of murder in the first degree or not guilty.

In these last two instructions Wilson all but required that the jury acquit Elmer Smith. To say that he could not be found guilty of anything except first-degree murder was to say that he could not be found guilty of anything.

In a final instruction Wilson told the jury it was not responsible for fixing the penalty if any of the defendants were found guilty. That was up to the judge.[2]

The instructions given, Wilson asked the jury if it would sit for a night session to hear the closing arguments. Then it could begin deliberations the next morning. The jurors readily agreed.

Cunningham led off. He admitted he was biased since he felt deeply the loss of a personal friend when Grimm was murdered. He stressed the existence of an unlawful conspiracy by the Wobblies, saying it was illegal for them to station snipers across the street and on Seminary Hill and that any who knew about those snipers were guilty of conspiracy. He made an impassioned closing: "If these defendants are turned loose as guiltless, such action will mean that good government in the U.S. is at an end. It will mean anarchy and red murder such as I saw on the streets of Centralia on the 11th day of November, 1919."

W. H. Abel made the most impressive argument for the prosecution, according to press reports, which said his voice control was as great as Vanderveer's, his English as perfect, and that he was quite capable of dramatics. Abel demanded a verdict of first-degree murder, but not the death penalty. The real issue, he said, was not who was the aggressor but was there a conspiracy to defend the IWW by illegal means?

"Mr. Vanderveer," Abel said, "tells you that he is fighting for the underdog. But this is not so much a battle for the underdog as it is for the vicious and cruel. I fear that Mr. Vanderveer's voice has been raised more often in behalf of treason than in behalf of justice."

Vanderveer's speech was short for him — only two hours. As reported by the always sympathetic *Industrial Worker,* he "made one of the great speeches of history in his closing onslaught against the lumber interests." His theme was that the Wobblies were driven in desperation to make a last stand in their hall on Tower Street — driven by a hate-inspired conspiracy on the part of union-fearing industrialists who found an ally in the American Legion, whose members deplored the IWW's lack of loyalty and patriotism in wartime.

EXTRA   **EXTRA**

THE CENTRALIA DAILY HUB

Vol. 7, No. 140   CENTRALIA, WASHINGTON, SUNDAY, MARCH 14, 1920   10c A WEEK BY CARRIER

JURY'S VERDICT IS
GUILTY! SECOND DEGREE
ACQUIT SMITH AND SHEEHAN

Cunningham Makes Strong Argument

He had for seven years being the reporting guide business at Barnett's own testimony. Cunningham showed that Barnett acted perfectly in sympathy with the killing of service men. Barnett said he was not angry because workers had been killed, but that he was mad because of the attempt to lynch Everest. Cunningham also pointed to the

In the opinion of Cunningham, the state had shown Loren Roberts to be faking of insanity. He pointed out that not even Dr Arthur P. Calhoun, defense alienist, had claimed Roberts insane at the time of the confession. Dr Calhoun had testified, his confession appeared to be the statement of a normal and rather sane man.

lost control of the team. Just as the horse, going at a terrific speed, were about to plunge into a gulch at the right of the road, Miss Moore jumped as Tom Mix often had told her to do. His tutorship stood her in good stead. She knew that if she alighted in the wrong way she would probably break a limb at least so she doubled up

COURT HOUSE, MONTESANO, MARCH 13—(SPECIAL TO THE CENTRALIA DAILY HUB.)—SECOND DEGREE MURDER VERDICTS AGAINST O. C. BLAND, BRITT SMITH, BERT BLAND, JAMES McINERNY AND ROY BECKER WERE RETURNED BY THE JURY IN THE CASE OF TEN I. W. W.'s CHARGED WITH THE MURDER OF WARREN O. GRIMM. THE VERDICT WAS BROUGHT IN

He told the jury there was much it had not been allowed to hear. (The jurors were aware of this and at least one — Inman — said in later years that he found out more about the case in casual conversation around Centralia, talking to persons who had been spectators, than he learned sitting in the jury box.)

"There are only two real issues in this case," Vanderveer stated. "One is the question: Who was the aggressor? The other is: Was Eugene Barnett in the Avalon Hotel window when the affray occurred? We have proven by unimpeachable witnesses that there was a raid on the IWW hall on November 11 — a raid in which the business interests of the city used members of the American Legion as cat's-paws. We have shown that Warren Grimm . . . actually took part in that raid and was in the very doorway of the hall when the attack was made. . . . We have proven a complete alibi for Eugene Barnett."[3]

Emphasis was placed on the strongest point for the defense — the absence of any motive at all for the shooting except the defense of the Wobblies' hall against mob violence.

Vanderveer noted that the prosecutors were em-

phatic in asserting that this was not a labor trial and yet they were careful to ask defense witnesses if they belonged to any labor union or were sympathetic toward workers. He continued:

And when the answer was yes, they tried to brand the witness as one not worthy of belief. Their policy of thus browbeating working people . . . is in keeping with the tactics of the mob during the days when it held Centralia in its grasp; it searched homes without warrants; it spied on and denounced and threatened everybody who admitted having any sympathy with organized labor. . . . You kick a dog around long enough and he'll bite you. They kicked this dog too long. To me it is a shocking thing that an agreement among working men to defend their hall, their rights, their freedom of speech and assembly, could ever be held guilty of conspiracy. I say to you that if your verdict stamps this seal of approval upon raids, on mob law, this will indeed be the end of good government in this country — at least for the working man.[4]

The *Vidette*, reporting Vanderveer's speech, said that "at telling places he made his voice tremble with emotion and frequently wiped his eyes and those who

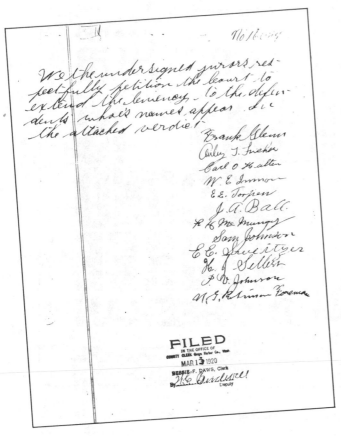

The jury's handwritten request for leniency handed to Judge Wilson with the verdict.

But on the other side of the scale of justice were the attitudes and actions of people in Centralia who quite obviously had driven the Wobblies to an act of desperation, however rash it turned out to be. The hall was raided. One of the defenders was lynched. Others were cruelly treated.

Affidavits signed by several of the jurors in later years mentioned the fear some of them felt when army troops were brought in. The soldiers could be seen by the jurors when they went outdoors for exercise. A bailiff told them the troops were called because of a report that a thousand Wobblies were camped in the woods near town, threatening an invasion.

Three jurors were reported to have been so fearful that they asked if they could have guns for self-protection. The bailiffs were armed. Inman, who had been a Texas Ranger before coming to Washington, said one bailiff, whom he had known in Texas, wore two guns and told him that if there were trouble, he could grab one of his guns and use it.[6]

The situation in which the jury found itself was not conducive to concentration on the evidence, to the exclusion of all other matters, as a jury is supposed to do. The trial took place in a county where severe prejudice against the IWW was everywhere evident. All the defendants, except Elmer Smith, were members of that organization at a time when other men were being given prison sentences merely for carrying red membership cards. The courthouse was in a town where the threat of more IWW violence, real or imagined, was so great a unit of the army had been summoned to protect it. And yet the jury was instructed to ignore the IWW in its deliberations.

All the jurors could be certain that if they voted for acquittal the result would be a public uproar of such intensity that they, the jury, might not live through it. Vigilantism could not be considered dead yet. On the other hand if they voted what the prosecution asked — conviction of first-degree murder — it would be grossly unjust, for no reasonable person could deny that what motivated the shooting was not lust to kill, but a desire to drive off a mob attacking the hall. It was a foolish stand, doomed to failure, but nevertheless it was done. And there was a segment of public opinion, minor though it might be, that considered the Wobblies justified in what they did. A first-degree murder verdict would arouse enmity also.

From what several jurors said afterward (in affi-

could see say there were actually tears."

When he finished, the trial was over. It was 10:30 p.m. It had been a long day. Everyone went to bed.

In their deliberations beginning early the next morning, the jurors, it turned out, were divided in their judgment in the beginning. At least three were for acquittal and two were adamantly in favor of finding the men guilty of first-degree murder. Harry Sellars, according to William Inman, said he "wanted to hang them all. He was awful pig-headed."[5]

The jurors argued all aspects of the case, discussing the matter of who was the aggressor and what motivated the Wobblies. The pressures to convict were numerous: public opinion strongly for it; the desire to punish for the murder of four ex-soldiers; fear of how their own personal safety might be affected if they voted for conviction, or if they did not. (Inman said he carried a gun for years afterward.)

davits) it can be concluded that the element of fear strongly affected their decision. They dared not acquit, and could not anyway since at least two jurors would never have voted for acquittal. A simple way out would have been to remain deadlocked. A hung jury would mean a second trial, but it also would mean that those voting for acquittal would be identified as IWW sympathizers. The jury in a second trial might be of a different mind. It might convict all of first-degree murder. A majority of the jurors did not want that.

So the twelve men argued, all through the day. At one point tempers flared to such intensity that Inman jumped on the table, which extended almost the length of the room, and "was going to kick (a fellow juror's) head off until the others pulled me off."[7]

The arguments continued through the afternoon. Then at 5:15 the sound of applause was heard in the jury room. But not until 6:40 was a bailiff summoned and told that a verdict had been reached.

By then many of the spectators had grown tired of waiting and left. The courtroom was not full. Among those who remained were Mrs. Barnett, who, like Mrs. Smith and Mrs. Grimm, was holding an infant in her arms; Mrs. Edna Roberts, mother of Loren; Mrs. O. C. Bland; William Sheehan, son of Mike Sheehan, who had helped Vanderveer as one of his investigators; and Mrs. T. W. Smith, mother of Elmer and Henry Smith.

The jurors filed in and took their places. The defendants, solemn and nervous, came in and sat down. The attorneys gathered. Only Cunningham was absent. Everyone who entered the courtroom from the public hallway was searched for weapons. None was found. There were only three men in uniform among the spectators.

Judge Wilson turned toward the jury. Had a verdict been reached? The foreman answered yes and handed a paper to the bailiff, who passed it up to the judge. Wilson read it quickly and looked up, puzzled. After a moment he said, "This verdict, gentlemen, cannot be received by the court."

The verdict acquitted Elmer Smith and Mike Sheehan. It held Loren Roberts to be guilty but insane. Britt Smith, O. C. Bland, James McInerney, Bert Bland, and Ray Becker were found guilty of second-degree murder and Eugene Barnett and John Lamb were guilty of "murder in the third degree."

There is no such thing as third-degree murder, the judge said. (The term "manslaughter" is used to de-

scribe slayings which are unintentional and unpremeditated, but the crime of murder is limited to two degrees — first, in which a killing is premeditated and deliberate, and second, in which a death is caused by deliberate action that was not planned in advance. The judge, however, did not explain these distinctions before he sent the jury back to deliberate further.)

At 8:40 the jury returned with a revised verdict. It was the same as the first except that Lamb and Barnett also were found guilty of second-degree murder. But attached to it was a message to the judge, which read, "We the undersigned jurors respectfully petition the court to extend the leniency (sic) to the defendants whose names appear on the attached verdict."

For a moment, after the amended verdict was read, there was silence as lawyers, defendants, and spectators pondered to make sure they understood it. It wasn't what anyone expected, so it took a while for its meaning to penetrate. Second-degree murder! How could that be? The most common reaction was perplexity. Two acquittals! And what about Roberts? Insane. What would be done with him?

Reporters were out of the room, telephoning, when the final verdict came in. The faulty first one had been explained to the attorneys by Wilson and then Abel wrote it out and gave it to the reporters, who rushed out to call in the news.

Vanderveer, irritated and crestfallen by the verdict, used the incident to vent his ire one last time on his foes across the table. "This is contempt of court — rotten contempt," he complained about the leaking. "If this court hasn't the courage to uphold its own dignity and self-respect, it certainly cannot expect to have other people respect it."

Abel, reconsidering what he had done, went to the press room on the first floor to ask that the first verdict not be transmitted on the three press association wires. Vanderveer followed and, in the presence of the reporters, said to Abel: "This is small-town stuff. You make an ass of yourself giving out a verdict told you in confidence, and then when you know it's too late to stop the story, you come down here and ask them to kill it."[8] Abel, embarrassed and angry, hurriedly left. He did not return to hear the final verdict.

Back in the courtroom Allen asked the sheriff to serve pre-prepared arrest warrants for the murder of McElfresh on all ten defendants, including the two who were acquitted. To his way of thinking a second-degree murder conviction was just not acceptable. There would have to be another trial, another chance to lay the basis for the most severe penalty short of death — life imprisonment.

The prisoners, their battle lost, walked back to their cells across the overhead bridge. When the warrants were served, Elmer Smith turned his face upward and began singing loudly one of the IWW's favorite songs — the words written by Ralph Chaplin, the IWW journalist who sat through the trial — "Solidarity Forever," to the tune of "John Brown's Body." The others joined him, press reports said, "and the defiant air rang through the prison."

23

Sentence and Appeal

The final act in the Montesano drama was the sentencing, answering the question everywhere being discussed — how would the judge treat the jury's plea for leniency? Would he take the unusual postscript to the verdict as it seemed intended — a notice to the judge that while the jury felt obligated to find the men guilty, as public opinion of the time demanded, it did not regard them as terribly guilty since, as was plainly revealed in the trial, their motive was defense of their union hall? Or would he disregard it as legally irrelevant since the degree to which a convicted person is punished is up the the court only, not the jury?

Judge Wilson, a strict man of the law, chose to ignore the plea. The statute provided that second-degree murder be punished by "imprisonment for not less than ten years." He construed that to mean that ten years was the minimum and there was no maximum. The eight Wobblies were sentenced to not less than twenty-five nor more than forty years. That included Loren Roberts. He was to serve the same length of time as the other prisoners but in a ward for the criminally insane.

The sentences were a severe shock to the men and their lawyer. They expected nothing so extreme. The IWW press had said the verdict was actually a victory for Vanderveer, considering the state of anti-IWW hysteria in Grays Harbor County, the obstinate refusal of the judge to permit evidence showing why the men defended their hall, and the jury being intimidated by bringing in army troops to defend the town against a danger that was nonexistent and only vaguely rumored. It was a victory also because the jury had recommended leniency — a request the judge could hardly ignore. Then, twenty-five years! The verdict itself was a blow to the men but the sentencing was as crushing as it was unexpected. Long years of prison lay ahead. At least ten years — maybe forty, the rest of their lives.

A verdict of innocence by the Labor Jury, rendered in Tacoma two days after the trial ended, was not much solace, but it did help ignite a blaze of indignation inside organized labor that never entirely died down. Not all AFL unions, however, approved the union jury verdict. In Seattle the painters' and the retail clerks' unions withdrew from the Central Labor Council because of it.

Britt Smith was the only defendant willing to talk to a reporter the day after the sentencing. "We are not worrying," he said. "The judge sure handed us a bunch. He put on every year he could and then some. We didn't look for anything else from a tool of the lumber barons. Say, but Vanderveer sure did roast the court and the lumber trust lawyers."[1]

No one expressed satisfaction with the court verdict. The great many who were unalterably convinced that the killing of four ex-soldiers could not be properly punished by anything less than life sentences or, better still, hanging expressed various degrees of disapproval. The verdict "is a travesty of justice," said Prosecutor Allen. "We will continue to prosecute these men until a proper conviction is procured. The McElfresh information and warrants are evidence of our intent."[2]

In his account of the case, prepared for the American Legion, Ben Hur Lampman wrote:

Grays Harbor County and the entire Pacific Northwest declared (the verdict) an impossible, monstrous miscarriage of justice. Both state and defense were in agreement for once, that but one of two verdicts could have logically been returned — guilty in the first degree or acquittal. And the local police declared that the unworthy fear of IWW reprisal, together with a desire also to placate public sentiment, led that incomprehensible jury toward a verdict its members considered a compromise.[3]

Newspaper editorials were generally critical. "The Montesano verdict violates both justice and common sense," said the *Oregonian.* "Here is a clear case of jury incompetence or of fear of personal consequences.... That there was a conspiracy to kill was plainly established in the mind of the jury, yet it acquitted the lawyer, Elmer Smith. If there was a conspiracy, here was the most culpable one of the lot...."[4]

The *Seattle Post-Intelligencer* deplored the verdict as well. Its editorial read, "Time has not abated one whit the horror and patriotic resentment aroused by the Centralia crime; the blood of our murdered servicemen calls no less loudly today than on the day of their death for the just reprisals that the law has the power to exact."[5]

State Senator Edwin Corman of Spokane joined those calling the verdict a "grievous miscarriage of justice." Then he made a prophecy: "Until these criminals either die or serve their sentences, it will become a political issue in this state to elect some governor who will either commute the sentences or grant a complete pardon. The seeds of another Mooney case are already sown in our midst."[6]

The verdict was indeed a compromise, as several jurors later conceded. The defendants were Wobblies. They couldn't be acquitted, not in the climate that prevailed in 1920. So it was decided to find them guilty, against the better judgment of at least some of the jurors, who were made to feel better about their decision by the plea for leniency.

Juror Inman, looking back upon the trial after a space of forty years, said he and others who were for acquittal were afraid of a hung jury. They feared that in a second trial the accused might be convicted of first-degree murder and hanged. Inman was resentful about the way the trial was conducted. Referring to the trial sessions, he said: "That was the damndest thing I ever listened to. Every time they had an argument they would shoo us upstairs. When we came back we could tell who won the argument. It was the prosecutors every time. The judge had his mind all made up."[7]

Vanderveer's first move after the sentencing was to move for a new trial. He based his request on newly discovered evidence that one of the jurors, Harry Sellars, was strongly prejudiced against the IWW and

before the trial began had been heard to say, "I am going to be one of the jurors and I will hang every goddamned one of them." Sellars denied saying that and swore that his accusers, four of whom signed affidavits, were IWW sympathizers, one even being a paid investigator for Vanderveer.

The judge chose to believe Sellars rather than those who swore to his prejudice. He rejected Vanderveer's motion for a new trial. The next move was to appeal the decision to the state supreme court. This called for producing a document detailing the reasons his clients were unfairly tried. Vanderveer could cite many reasons, collected every time Wilson sustained a prosecution objection. His appeal was lengthy and took two weeks to prepare.

Meanwhile Montesano gradually returned to normalcy. The hotels and rooming houses were emptied. The improvised dormitory and feeding station for the Legionnaires and prosecution witnesses in the fire station were closed. The troops from Camp Lewis gathered up their gear, folded their tents, and departed by train. They hadn't been needed. The soldiers had so much time for romantic pursuits in their off-duty hours in Montesano, reported the *Oregonian,* that "approximately 17 weddings are imminent and 18 engagements or near engagements have been announced. Fourteen romances will culminate in Hoquiam where the young people will make their homes."[8]

While the appeal was in process the prosecutors did nothing about a new trial. Elmer Smith and Mike Sheehan, though acquitted, remained in jail with the others. Not until May was Smith allowed to go free on bond furnished by an unexpected sympathizer — William Guderyan, an uncle of Arthur McElfresh.

During this period the costs of the Montesano trial were added up and they were so high local legislators were asked to get an appropriation through the next session to give the affected counties some relief. The big items on the expense list included $5,063 for jury fees, $5,000 for Cunningham's services, $5,000 for Abel, $1,899 for jurors' meals, $369 for prisoners' meals, $2,500 for Cunningham's services in helping prepare the state's response to the Supreme Court appeal, $1,119 for forty extra deputy sheriffs and jail guards, and $2,768 to pay the Luke May detective agency. The total was $51,809.38.

The costs were given considerable attention when the county commissioners discussed with the prosecutors the consequences of doing it all over again with a second trial.

Luke May remained in the lumber companies' employ even after the trial. His operatives continued to roam about picking up bits of information about the IWW. In one report "Operative No. 155" told of encountering two known Wobblies, Harry Drew and Joe Moore, who talked in Seattle about a mill fire in Chehalis. The Wobblies said the mill was owned by a "lumber baron" named Moore who, like Hubbard, sent paid Loyal Legion men to attend the trial in Montesano and was "firing all the Wobblies off the jobs in the camps and mill just as fast as the hired stool pigeons got wise to who they were." The operative said the two Wobblies predicted Hubbard would suffer a severe loss too before the summer was over. They also said "Brown and Hubbard were the cause of the Armistice Day shooting in Centralia and they were the two most active men against the Wobblies in Lewis County for the past several years . . . and they as well as others will suffer for this activity. . . ."[9]

Such reports reinforced the opinions of industrialists about the IWW. They were still dangerous.

Because the Centralia case was the last big ruckus involving the Wobblies to receive national attention, it came to be regarded as the dropping of a curtain on the IWW in the West, but in fact it was not so. The Centralia convictions were a severe setback, one from which the organization never fully recovered, but it was not the end. The employers knew this and did not let down their guard. For years afterward, if a fire broke out in a mill, or there was any other kind of trouble, Wobblies were thought of first as the likely culprits.

Vanderveer's appeal of the case to the Supreme Court had to be accompanied by a printed abstract of the trial transcript. It was a lengthy document, made long partly because Vanderveer cited so many ways the trial court, in his opinion, had erred. He was an experienced lawyer who had handled other appeals and knew the law so well he was convinced that the exclusion of pertinent evidence, the mistaken rulings of the judge, the bringing in of the troops, the evidence of public hostility toward the IWW in the county where the jurors were chosen and, in the end, affidavits swearing that one juror (Sellars) had his mind made up before the trial even began, were more than enough to convince the justices that a new trial should be granted. His opponent — in this instance Cunningham —

was just as sure that the trial he helped conduct, and win, was fair. So he gave equal attention to the preparation of his brief opposing a retrial. He was still looking forward, along with Allen, to trying the men on the new charge of murdering McElfresh and having a second chance to get a first-degree murder conviction. Having to try the men again for the murder of Grimm would interfere with that. Furthermore in a retrial there would be a different jury and a judge, who might not exclude as much defense evidence as Wilson did.

The crusading zeal of one who is sure he has righteousness on his side kept Vanderveer from realizing that the appeal was almost certainly foredoomed to rejection. For seven weeks he had argued over and over that it was not his clients who were in the wrong. They had to be considered in the right when, denied police protection, they took up arms to defend themselves. To do otherwise and submit meekly to another raid would have been unmanly if not cowardice. Now he was asking the supreme court to examine the evidence, not to find his clients innocent, but to find that they had been tried unfairly.

His appeal began with the argument that Wilson erred in granting a second change of venue, then reversing his decision.

In its decision the Supreme Court found that the judge merely expressed a preliminary opinion about the need for a second change of venue and so made only one ruling, which was final.

The second appeal claimed that the court erred in receiving a verdict of murder in the second degree. The prosecution tried to prove that the defendants conspired in advance to arm themselves for the purpose of killing men in the parade. A conspiracy must involve premeditation. But second-degree murder is defined as unpremeditated. How then, could the defendants be guilty of second-degree murder?

Cunningham in his brief denied that the prosecution specifically claimed a conspiracy. The word "conspiracy" did not appear anywhere in the information against the defendants.

Vanderveer argued that "the function of a verdict is to decide the issue. This verdict decides nothing. Did the defendants conspire or did they not? Yes, for otherwise they should have been acquitted. No, for otherwise they should have been convicted of murder in the first degree."[10]

The court was unimpressed with this logic. It did

note that Vanderveer requested the court to instruct the jury about murder in the second degree, indicating that the defense attorney had foreseen that such a verdict was possible.

Vanderveer contended that the court was wrong in excluding evidence of a conspiracy among business interests in Centralia to raid the IWW hall. But the court agreed with Judge Wilson that such evidence had nothing to do with the murder of Grimm. It noted that of 114 defense witnesses only 11 claimed Grimm was participating in a raid on the hall at the time he was shot. This, it said, did not outweigh the testimony of scores of prosecution witnesses who told of seeing Grimm standing at the corner of Tower and Second, far from the hall, when the shooting began.

Vanderveer argued that the trial court erred in refusing to let him attempt to show that Tom Morgan made his pretrial statements, which were never admitted as evidence, under duress and threats, and in sustaining objections to his questioning of witnesses about the kidnapping of Tom Lassiter and about prejudices they might have against the IWW.

The appeals court noted that Judge Wilson had instructed the jury on the latter point. It was not the IWW that was on trial, the jury was told, and any evidence of prejudice for or against that organization was to be disregarded.

When it came to the objection concerning Sellars, the court held that Sellars' prejudice, if any, could not have unduly influenced the outcome of the trial since he voted with the other jurors for a second-degree murder conviction.

Though Vanderveer couldn't realize it, the Centralia Wobblies had little more chance for a sympathetic hearing before the supreme court than before the Grays Harbor superior court, perhaps less. The appeal, of course, was denied.

Still George Vanderveer wouldn't yield. In one last desperate effort he petitioned the court for a rehearing "for the reason that manifest errors in both fact and law had been committed in deciding the case."[11] This was a seventeen-page document in which Vanderveer's exasperation with the rulings plainly showed. Again he described what went on in Montesano and Grays Harbor just before the trial — the vituperative editorials in the *Vidette* and the several circulars sent through the mail demanding punishment for the Centralia men. Any conclusion that these "poisoned pens" had no effect on those called for jury duty, argued Vanderveer, "is so manifestly at variance with the common judgment of sane men that it is entitled to no consideration whatsoever."[12] Later in the brief Vanderveer wrote: "This court may say if it will that there is no evidence to dispute the state's contention regarding the place and manner in which Warren Grimm was shot, or this court may, if it pleases, say that two plus two makes seventeen. But saying these things will not make either of them true. . . . "[13]

Such jibes did nothing for Vanderveer's case. He was denied a rehearing.

By this time it was mid-May. Seven months had gone by since Armistice Day, two months since the trial ended. The excitement had subsided and the passions aroused by the trial's outcome were cooling. Lewis County decided the cost of attempting to get more severe punishment for the Centralia Wobblies by trying them again was too high. After all, they were sentenced to at least twenty-five years in prison. Maybe that was enough. The McElfresh murder charges were quietly dropped.

Elmer Smith and Mike Sheehan now could go free. Their relief was great, but they were bitter about the fate of their eight companions, taken in handcuffs from the jail behind the courthouse in Montesano, where they had lived together for more than two months, and put aboard a train that would take them on the long journey across the state to the prison at Walla Walla. But it was not to be the end. Elmer Smith made that his firm resolve. Justice had to be done. He would never give up until those eight Wobblies were given their freedom, too.

24

The Struggle Goes On

Armistice Day, 1919, may be considered the climax of the Wobbly war in the West but it was not the end. The struggle continued, kept alive by the fierce determination of Elmer Smith and a few other crusaders to win release for the eight convicted men and by the equally firm opposition of those who didn't care if the men were ever let out of prison. Anti-Wobbly and antiprisoner sentiment remained at full heat while IWW leaders and their few allies went about shouting their outrage to the world and trying to tell what they were sure was the truth about the Centralia case.

Seeking a new weapon to use against the radicals, Sen. Miles Poindexter proposed federal antisyndicalism legislation fully as punitive as any of the state laws. Washington's statute was challenged in the state supreme court and it was not surprising that the same justices who approved all that went on in the trial at Montesano could find nothing wrong with a law that made it illegal even to belong to an organization advocating such radical reforms as those to be found in the credo of the IWW.

The courts continued to be cluttered with trials of men deemed deserving of prison for their beliefs and their loyalty to the organization that supported those beliefs. It was a time of suppression, of silencing radical dissent. The victory of the prosecutors at Montesano was taken as a signal to bear down on the cancerous labor situation before the Wobblies could recover from their defeat.

By the end of June 1920, two months after the trial, Elmer Smith was ready to begin a crusade aimed at carrying the Centralia story by word of mouth to every part of the state. He was an able speaker. He liked to speak. And people listened.

One of his first targets was Bellingham, in the northwest corner of Washington, where he scheduled an appearance on June 19. The Legion heard he was coming and protested immediately to the mayor. Don't let him speak, they demanded. The mayor complied, issuing orders to Police Chief Powell, who went to the hall rented for the occasion and found that Smith was appearing at what was billed as a Triple Alliance rally. The chief stayed. Smith mounted the platform and when almost immediately he shifted from politics to the Centralia case Powell jumped to his feet and called a halt. Don't talk about Centralia, he commanded. This was Smith's first confrontation with censorship and while he didn't accept it without a protest, he did not go the Wobbly way and become defiant to the point of being dragged off to jail. Jess Drain, the Legion adjutant in Bellingham, defined the Legion's stand: "We didn't want him speaking on any subject, even the weather, for any length of time, even a few minutes.... We do not wish to usurp any man's constitutional rights to free speech, but we are objecting to Elmer Smith speaking in Bellingham."[1]

The police chief, who was running for sheriff, was sure he knew the people's will. "By not allowing that man to talk on the Centralia affair," he said, "I think I was protecting the rights of the majority."[2]

He was saying that in his opinion free speech in Bellingham was not just what the majority wanted to be free to hear, but what the majority had the right to protect others from hearing, and if someone tried to say what the majority decided was not fit to be said, he must be silenced. As Elmer Smith learned in this first foray into the hostile hinterland, any discussion of the Centralia case from the IWW viewpoint was not something he could expect to be permitted without objection, if permitted at all, the guarantees of freedom of speech in the Constitution notwithstanding.

The Wobblies were not despised by all, however. The commonly accepted version of the "Centralia massacre" — that it was an unprovoked act of terrorism — came to be questioned in some sectors as details of the trial became more widely publicized. Some of those sectors were eminently respectable, such as the *Atlantic Monthly* which carried an article entitled "The Wild West" by Edwin Townsend Boothe in its December 1921 issue. Boothe went into some detail about the Centralia case and what he said was so offensive to Gov. Louis Hart that Hart sent a lengthy letter of protest and "correction" to Ellery Sedgwick, the editor of the magazine. Sedgwick replied to Hart, saying that his venerable magazine was certainly not sympathizing with radicals, but he did see some discrepancies in the Legion version of the Centralia affair. He could not believe, for example, that the IWW men set out deliberately to ambush veterans marching in a patriotic parade, as the Legion accounts charged, when such an ambuscade would lead to their own certain destruction.

Other widely read publications were troubled by aspects of the case usually glossed over, especially the lynching of Wesley Everest and the refusal of authorities to bring charges against the lynchers. J. W. Lockhart in *Current History* concluded an article on the case saying: "I hate and despise the doctrines promulgated by the IWW; their methods are those of reformers gone mad . . . but I can see no reason why the devil of mobbism should not be painted as black as the devil of IWWism."[3]

Centralia could claim it was no more anti-Wobbly than Seattle, Everett, Yakima, Spokane, or other cities that had done their utmost to suppress troublesome radicals. And its record of bloodshed in fighting the Wobblies was not as bad as Everett's, but Centralia suffered more unpleasant notoriety than any of the others because of the way the IWW propagandists were able to keep attention focused on the eight "class-war prisoners," as they came to be called, who were "buried alive" in the dank penal fortress at Walla Walla. Far more men died in the waterfront battle in Everett, but no one went to prison as a consequence. Unlike Centralia, it was no cause célèbre.

All through the 1920s Centralia was kept in the spotlight as demands for release of the prisoners mounted to a crescendo, and more and more persons, many of national prominence, became convinced by what the IWW, the ACLU, the AFL, and others who joined the fray were saying about Armistice Day and the trial in Montesano.

Centralia felt offended by all this — offended and angry. It did not feel apologetic about its militant anti-Wobbly stand. The lynching was regrettable but no cause for great shame. It was a spur-of-the-moment thing — anger prevailing over good judgment. Furthermore the one lynched by the townspeople was responsible for the deaths of two of the four slain young veterans. He had to die sooner or later. Didn't the city deserve some sympathy in this situation, some understanding?

There were enough who did not think so to make the years following 1919 uncomfortable ones for the railroad town in the valley of the Chehalis. Much of that discomfort could be attributed to the red-headed radical lawyer who, as Centralians knew, had a part in what took place on Armistice Day, came away unpunished, and now was back in town keeping the whole unpleasant thing alive.

Elmer Smith went back to Centralia in handcuffs, and in disgrace in the eyes of most of the townsfolk, but he was undaunted. He didn't leave. He stayed there among his enemies, possibly to taunt them, sure he had a chance for vindication. But as his daughter, Virginia Smith Waddell, observed in later years: "Nothing was ever to be the same again in Centralia for the Smith family. Father did not come through those terrible events unscathed. He came home from his imprisonment filled with a righteous anger and a determination to do everything in his power to correct what he felt to be a terrible miscarriage of justice."[4]

As a lawyer Smith knew that the fate of convicted persons rests with one body, the state parole board, and one person, the governor, who had the power to issue pardons, paroles, and commutations of sentences. He set himself the task of convincing one or both that the eight prisoners could not, by any standard of justice, be left in prison for as long as the twenty-five years Judge Wilson decreed in defiance of the jury's wishes, and should in fact be freed without further delay.

Smith did not embark on his crusade alone. The imprisonment of IWW members became so common after the war that the defense of those accused and

An early piece of defense committee literature sent out from Seattle in June 1920, shortly after the conviction of nine of those pictured. Faulkner and Smith were acquitted.

EUGENE BARNETT

BRITT SMITH

JAS. McINERNEY

WESLEY EVEREST

BERT BLAND

BERT FAULKNER

O. C. (COMMODORE) BLAND

MIKE SHEEHAN

JOHN HILL LAMB

ELMER SMITH

RAY BECKER

LOREN ROBERTS

Northwest District Defense Committee

GEO. WILLIAMS, Secretary-Treasurer

Box 1873, Seattle, Wash.

BRANCHES

BUTTE   SPOKANE   PORTLAND   SEATTLE

June 14, 1920.

Friend and Fellow Worker:

A few lines to let you know that we are going to hold an immense picnic near Seattle on the Fourth of July. The picnic will be held under the auspices of the Northwest District Defense Committee and the proceeds are to go towards the relief and defense of the class-war prisoners who are held by the hundreds in the penitentiaries and jails of the Northwest.

However apart from any benefits for those who are in jail the picnic is more important as a great-get-together rally for the workers in the Northwest—To lend support to the appeal in the Centralia case which comes up in September.

We want the Workers from all over the state to come to this picnic and help give an expression of SOLIDARITY that will be hitherto unequaled.

It will be well worth the trouble and expense to travel from any part of the State on this occasion. There will be games and sports with prizes for every one. Good accommodations are being installed so that families can find comfort and recreation. Also good music and dancing. Children under ten are admitted free. We are assured of the presence of W.D.(Big Bill) HAYWOOD at the picnic and also ELMER SMITH the Centralia attorney who was a defendant in the famous Centralia case.

As you probably realize it is necessary to have co-operation to make such large gatherings a success. We want your support to boost this picnic from an organization as well as a recreational standpoint. Will you help? Yes! Good. Here's what we want you to do:

If you can sell any tickets in your locality write in and let us know how many you can sell. The price is 50 cents. If there are some who cannot come urge them to buy a ticket anyway as the money derived from the sale of the tickets is badly needed to defend the hundreds of Fellow Workers in jail awaiting trial on Criminal Syndicalism charges, besides giving relief to their families who are in destitute circumstances because of the fact that their husbands and fathers are being held in Capitalist dungeons. You can also help in distributing dodgers announcing the picnic. You will be a great help in helping to advertise this picnic.

We would greatly appreciate a quick reply stating how many tickets you can handle; also some dodgers to advertise same.

Yours for Industrial Freedom.

Geo Williams

WITH DROPS OF BLOOD

THE HISTORY OF

THE INDUSTRIAL WORKERS OF THE WORLD HAS BEEN WRITTEN

Ever since the I. W. W. was organized in June, 1905, there has been an inquisitorial campaign against its life and growth, inaugurated by the Chambers of Commerce, Profiteers, large and small, and authorities of State and Nation in temporary power.

The Industrial Workers of the World is a Labor organization composed of sober, honest, industrious men and women. Its chief purposes are to abolish the system of wage slavery and to improve the conditions of those who toil.

This organization has been foully dealt with; drops of blood, bitter tears of anguish, frightful heart pains have marked its every step in its onward march of progress.

I. W. W. MEMBERS have been murdered.
I. W. W. MEMBERS have been imprisoned.
I. W. W. MEMBERS have been tarred and feathered.
I. W. W. MEMBERS have been deported
I. W. W. MEMBERS have been starved.
I. W. W. MEMBERS have been beaten.
I. W. W. MEMBERS have been denied the right of citizenship.
I. W. W. MEMBERS have been exiled.
I. W. W. MEMBERS have had their homes invaded.
I. W. W. MEMBERS have had their private property and papers seized.
I. W. W. MEMBERS have been denied the privilege of defense.
I. W. W. MEMBERS have been held in exorbitant bail.
I. W. W. MEMBERS have been subjected to involuntary servitude.
I. W. W. MEMBERS have been kidnapped.
I. W. W. MEMBERS have been subjected to cruel and unusual punishment.
I. W. W. MEMBERS have been framed and unjustly accused.
I. W. W. MEMBERS have been excessively fined.
I. W. W. MEMBERS have died in jail waiting for trial.
I. W. W. MEMBERS have been driven insane through persecution.
I. W. W. MEMBERS have been denied the use of the mails.
I. W. W. MEMBERS have been denied t he right to organize.
I. W. W. MEMBERS have been denied the right of free speech.
I. W. W. MEMBERS have been denied the right of free press.
I. W. W. MEMBERS have been denied the right of free assembly.
I. W. W. MEMBERS have been denied every privilege guaranteed by the Bill of Rights.
I. W. W. MEMBERS have been denied the inherent rights proclaimed by the Declaration of Independence—Life, Liberty, and the Pursuit of Happiness.
I. W. W. Halls, Offices, and Headquarters have been raided.
I. W. W. property, books, pamphlets, stamps, literature, and office fixtures have been unlawfully seized.

I. W. W. as an organization and its membership have been viciously maligned, vilified, and persecuted.

The charges set forth in this indictment would count for nothing unless evidence and proof were at hand to sustain them. A record of every charge can be found in the annals of the press, the court records of the land, the report of the Commission on Industrial Relations, and other reports of the Government of the United States.

Wobbly publicists listed twenty-six wrongs against the IWW in this red-ink-splattered appeal for public sympathy.

efforts to free those convicted became a major IWW activity. A General Defense Committee operated in Chicago, publishing tracts and sending out speakers. Several regional defense committees, including one in Seattle, supplemented the national effort. But Smith was not content to rely on the committees raising funds and championing causes all over the country. He was outside the Wobbly movement himself and his concern primarily was for the men who were tried along with him and who did not get off as had he and Mike Sheehan and Bert Faulkner.

There had to be a local organization and since the task ahead, as Smith saw it, was to engage in public education, he called it the Centralia Publicity Committee. Furthermore it might be easier to raise funds for one particular group of Wobblies, whose story made dramatic telling, than for the mass of men caught in the widespread antisyndicalism net. As the Centralia story became widely understood, Smith reasoned, public sympathy for the prisoners' plight would grow and pressure for parole or pardon would gradually build so much that the governor, who must be responsive to public opinion, could not ignore it, nor could the parole board, appointed by the governor.

Smith's fanatical loyalty to the Centralia men was interpreted by his chief courtroom foe, C. D. Cunningham, as evidence that he suffered pangs of conscience because it was on his advice that the Wobblies decided to defend the hall rather than submit to another smashup raid like the one in 1918. Without that advice, Cunningham believed, the ill-conceived plan to use gunmen stationed outside the hall might not have been attempted.

Whatever his reasons, Smith felt so strongly about his crusade that he was willing to give it all he had — his time, his money, his powers of persuasion as a speaker, and his services as a lawyer, although he did accept fees from the committee for some of his services. He never made a good living in the practice of law. His clients were mostly poor and could pay little if anything. Sometimes his family had barely enough for living expenses.[5] But he was able to sell the timber on his mining claim near Kopiah for twenty-five thousand dollars and most of this, over the years, was used to pay for printing, mailing, and the always-heavy travel expenses he and others incurred as they went from city to city repeating their story, appealing for sympathy, moral support, and, of course, funds. It was a difficult

time for his family.

Centralia did not extend the hand of forgiveness to the Smiths. The people of the town were not just cold toward them; they were hostile. Elmer belonged to the Woodmen of the World, a lodge. It cancelled his insurance. He felt obliged to resign. Their daughter Virginia grew into girlhood realizing that something was wrong. They didn't go to church like other families. She knew her father had enemies. She couldn't even go to school. Her mother taught her at home.

They were not completely ostracized. Old friends stood by them. But still Laura Smith and her daughter suffered severe feelings of embarrassment and shame, and it was particularly humiliating for Laura, the daughter of a judge who had not approved of her marriage to a poor Centralia lawyer-schoolteacher in the first place and who approved even less now that he was making a career of defending Wobblies.

Matters were made even worse when Elmer began to suffer from a severe stomach disorder — bleeding ulcers — which plagued him for the remaining years of his life. Laura would plead with him to get away from the stress of the prisoner crusade — the stress that surely caused the ulcers — but he would not listen.

She would plead with him also not to be so generous toward those needing help, especially in times when they had so little money. But his feeling of compassion for anyone in need was such that he would reach willingly into his pocket to help anyone he was sure needed money more than he. Often he brought home one of the downtrodden for dinner and sometimes to spend the night without consulting Laura. Usually she would submit to the intrusion meekly, but on one occasion her husband's generosity was more than she could take. The guest, a man who had nothing at all, was to have a meal and one overnight stay. She agreed providing it was for just one night. But he didn't leave. He had nowhere to go, explained Elmer. Day after day he was always on hand at dinner time. Her patience finally at an end, Laura left, saying she was going to stay with relatives and wouldn't be back until that man was gone.

Another time Elmer offered overnight accommodations to a Wobbly acquaintance who was accompanied by a daughter. Not until the next day when she found the bed sheets stained with blood did Laura learn that the daughter had just had an abortion.[6]

Smith could even be a soft touch for someone

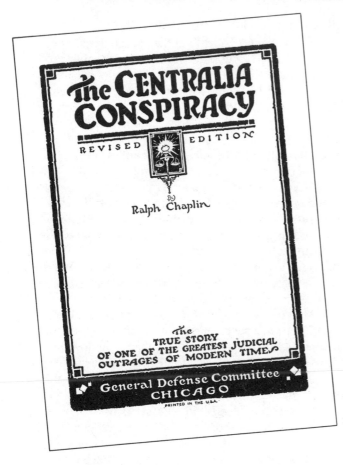

An account of the Centralia case entitled "The Centralia Conspiracy" was written by Ralph Chaplin shortly after the trial ended. It was published in several editions and was the most widely circulated of the many publications concerning the case.

merely posing as a needy person. One of Luke May's operatives, pretending to be a Wobbly, was working in Chehalis in June 1921, when several Wobblies were being tried on a syndicalism charge and Smith was defending them. May's agent was recruited by one of Elmer's brothers to be a defense witness. Fearing he might be exposed, he called May and asked him to send a telegram saying his mother was ill so he could have an excuse to get away. The telegram came and was shown to Elmer Smith, who arranged to have the man testify immediately so he wouldn't be delayed in getting home to his sick mother. He successfully impersonated a Wobbly on the stand and afterward Smith followed him out of the courtroom to ask if he had enough money to get back to Seattle. When the em-

ployer spy said no, Smith gave him some money, and arranged for a car to take him from Chehalis to Centralia, where the IWW had a makeshift hall by then. There he shaved and was given supper and put aboard the 4:30 train.[7]

Centralia's posttrial animosity was not confined to the Smith family. Dewey Lamb did not admit to being a Wobbly when he was arrested along with his father on Armistice Day, but he was considered to be one, and after John Lamb was convicted for his part in the defense — being present though unarmed in an upstairs room of the Arnold — the son was treated as if he should not have escaped punishment of some kind. He could not get a job in Centralia when he was recognized as John Lamb's son, and elsewhere, when he did find employment, he would be fired as soon as the employer found out who he was. He went to Aberdeen, hoping for different treatment. But he found himself blacklisted there too.[8]

Although Elmer Smith's standing in the community at large sank to new depths after the trial, he emerged as a man of courage and conviction among a sizable group of liberal thinkers who were trying to assert themselves through a third party — Farmer-Labor. He was nominated to run for attorney general on the party's ticket but declined so he could file for another office he thought he had some chance of winning — prosecuting attorney in Lewis County.

The *Farmer-Labor Call*, published in Centralia, reported that Smith was the worst-hated and the best-loved citizen in all Lewis County. It said,

> The hemp society gangsters of the lumber interests and the commercial interests of Centralia and Chehalis have centered their fire on him. . . . They used to fleece workingmen in Centralia out of their wages, to throw the injured or sick in the streets, to trick them in the courts and baffle them with the legal technicalities of unscrupulous attorneys. Then Smith came along. He defended workingmen in the courts. He kept them from going to jail for unjust reasons, saw that the state laws protecting them were enforced and was their friend on every occasion.[9]

Smith made defiant speeches, reported only in the Farmer-Labor press. On one occasion he said, "If I am elected prosecuting attorney the criminals in this town who were responsible for the Centralia tragedy — and I don't mean the little fellows — are going to Walla Walla."[10]

Smith challenged his chief opponent, Herman Allen, to debate on one of several subjects, one of which was that Allen had failed to prosecute the "rich and powerful" in Lewis County for the "crimes they have committed," referring to the Everest lynching and the raids on IWW halls.

If Allen had agreed to a debate it might have been difficult to find a place to hold it. According to the *Farmer-Labor* paper the "Republican machine in Centralia managed to keep every hall in the city closed to Farmer-Labor candidates including Bob Bridges, candidate for governor, and Homer T. Bone," who later beame a United States senator and a federal judge. "They had been scheduled to speak in the Rialto Theater but upon arriving found the doors locked. In a heavy downpour they led a procession to the Chatauqua grounds where they could speak outdoors."

As time went on Smith was much encouraged by the American Civil Liberties Union, led then by Roger Baldwin and Albert DeSilver who were completely in sympathy with the plight of the Wobblies. Their widely circulated pamphlet, *The Issues in the Centralia Murder Trial*, attracted wide interest. As early as February 9, 1920, while the trial was still going on, the ACLU sponsored a Centralia meeting in New York City. Among the speakers were Harry F. Ward, chairman of the ACLU and president of the Union Theological Seminary; Mrs. Carleton Parker, wife of the University of Washington professor who helped settle the wartime labor controversy in the Northwest; and J. T. (Red) Doran, a talented Wobbly speaker from Seattle. The next week Baldwin sent out a form letter to his mailing list of contributors across the country, appealing for funds to support a Centralia publicity and defense effort.

Baldwin also tried to stir up interest in Western Europe. He wrote to *Le Populaire* and *Humanities* in Paris and the *London Daily Herald*, describing the case and urging friendly editors to do what they could to arouse labor in their countries since "it looks as though only a demonstration on the part of foreign labor would save these men's lives."[11]

There was some response to these efforts in later years when several British unions passed resolutions adding their voices to the growing chorus in America demanding release of the Centralia prisoners.

In March 1921, a year after the trial ended, Elmer Smith judged the climate in Centralia to be such that he could come out in the open on home grounds with his free-the-prisoners effort. A mass meeting was held on Sunday, and it was a nasty day, according to the *Industrial Worker*, but hundreds attended. The crowd joined in a loud rendition of "Solidarity Forever" and then Smith spoke. He was the only speaker, but a good one. He had a voice that could be raised enough to be heard throughout a hall or auditorium, and spoke fluently and easily. He explained industrial unionism, reviewed the Armistice Day case, and gave a boost to the IWW, saying it had recently reopened halls in Portland and Seattle and soon would have one again in Centralia. He said Centralians were joining the IWW at the rate of at least one a day. At the end of the meeting a collection box was passed and fifty-four dollars taken in for the "class-war prisoners."

Two weeks later the IWW suffered its worst legal setback. The conviction of the union's national leaders, including Ralph Chaplin and William Haywood, the IWW president, under a federal wartime antisubversive statute, was upheld by the Supreme Court. The convicted Wobbly leaders, who had been set free on bail while the appeal was pending, had to go back to Leavenworth prison to serve sentences of from one to twenty years — all, that is, except Haywood. He jumped bail, went to Russia, and never returned. Regarded as a hero of labor by the Russians, he lived out his years in the Soviet Union and was buried inside the Kremlin walls.

Four days after the U.S. Supreme Court decision, the Washington State Supreme Court decision in the Centralia case appeal was announced. The *Industrial Worker* carried this banner headline:

CHICAGO AND CENTRALIA APPEALS DENIED;
Court Action Outlawed in Bosses' Courts,
Futility of Attempt at Court Action by
Wage Workers is Demonstrated;
ONLY COURSE LEFT IS ORGANIZATION TO
ABOLISH CAPITALISM.[12]

25

Old Foes and New Allies

The chief foe of the Wobblies in the Northwest was always the wood industry employers — those who stood to lose the most when the IWW organized workers, "sowed the seeds of discontent," called strikes, maybe drove spikes in logs and in other ways made life difficult for those who had their fortunes invested in an industry so full of economic risks and uncertainties that fomentors of labor trouble were intolerable.

The Wobblies understood this enemy. Employers were those who paid wages and it was an IWW objective to abolish the wage system. Another foe emerging with new strength after the war — one more difficult for the radical workers to oppose — were the patriots, those with a strong love of country, satisfaction with the status quo, and the feelings victors have about what they risk so much to defend. They opposed all who didn't like America the way it was and wanted to bring about change, and in particular the IWW and the Communists who were gaining prominence in the wake of the successful revolution in Russia.

The American Legion was founded by servicemen even before they left France as a kind of bastion of patriotism from which men still in a fighting mood could turn out on call to fight battles at home if need be. Servicemen returned to the Northwest, organized their Legion posts, and became aware at once that the region was still infested with a radical element that opposed and refused to support the war they fought, denounced it as part of a capitalist plot against the working class, and now were exhilarated by the overthrow of the government in Russia by the Bolsheviks. Antiradicalism became as firmly imbedded in the creed of the Legion as patriotism itself. The Centralia violence, bringing death to four of its members, was considered a call to arms.

Overnight, as the *American Legion Weekly* observed, "the name Centralia became as familiar to Americans as Chateau Thierry." The terror of Tower Avenue occurred at the very time the national executive committee of the Legion was in session and the young veteran leaders were shocked and alarmed by telegrams received from Centralia. The national commander immediately appointed F. R. Jeffery, commander of the Department of Washington, to head a committee to study the outbreak and report to the executive committee's spring meeting. Jeffery's committee, which included C. D. Cunningham, met in Spokane on May 7, 1920, and prepared a report that included recommendations for specific ways the Legion could wage war on Wobblies. If a member of the Legion's executive committee had not then been in trouble with the law as a consequence of some extremist Legion vigilante suppression in Ohio, the report,

By 1924 efforts to free the Centralia prisoners were in high gear. The IWW newspaper in Seattle, of course, added its voice to those of the national and regional defense committees and Elmer Smith's Publicity Committee in Centralia, all portraying the convicted men as class-war prisoners unjustly imprisoned. This illustration is one of the most elaborate used in the defense effort and appeared on page one of the Industrial Worker *on April 30, 1924. The poem at bottom reads:*

Mourn not the dead that in the cool earth lie
    Dust into dust —
The calm, swept earth that mothers all who die
    As all men must
Mourn not your captive comrades who must dwell
    Too strong to strive —
Within each steel-boned coffin of a cell,
    Buried alive;
But rather mourn the apathetic throng
    The cowed and the meek
Who are the world's great anguish and its wrong
    And dare not speak!

which carried Cunningham's signature, might have been adopted in its entirety.

The report identified both the Communist Party and the Industrial Workers of the World as unequivocally unlawful. Therefore, it said, the "National Americanism Committee of the American Legion should be empowered and directed to employ and send throughout the nation speakers charged with the duty of giving publicity to the vices and fallacies of the doctrines of such organizations. . . . "[1] The report recommended that the Legion engage in the printing and distribution of literature combating subversive doctrines; that Louis Post, assistant secretary of labor, be fired for failing to enforce the law requiring the deportation of aliens who advocated the overthrow of the government and the destruction of property; and that the Legion support a bill in Congress which would require aliens to become citizens and learn to read, write, and speak English within seven years or face deportation.

In a preface to a part of the report dealing with the Centralia case, Jeffery explained that

> loggers used to come to town and get drunk and probably have their pockets picked by the end of three days. They would then return to work wanting to do an honest day's work for the next two or three months. What is the condition today? The lumberjack comes in from the mills and the lumber camps and stays in Seattle and by paying his board for six months in advance he stays there. During that time he falls easy victim to headquarters that are provided by the IWW and other radical reds and he is thrown in their society and subjected to the doctrines and propaganda which is put out by these organizations.[2]

Jeffery related with a note of pride the part the Legion played in the Centralia case. He said the work of examining some six hundred veniremen called for the Montesano trial was undertaken by the intelligence committee of the Grant Hodge post. The Legionnaires questioned hundreds of possible jurors and furnished the prosecution with information about any Wobbly sympathy they might have. Jeffery held up a thick packet and said: "I hold here a list alphabetically arranged of the (IWW) members in Seattle which we have been able to capture in the raids upon their halls. It consists of over 6,000 names. The membership of the IWW today is in excess of 18,000 men. Now if you think

that doesn't present proportions that are worthy of the considerations of an organization which proclaims as one of its fundamental principles to defend the Constitution, then I miss my guess."[3]

Jeffery reviewed the evils of the IWW — preaching sabotage and singing terrible songs. He recited the often-quoted irreverent parody of "Onward Christian Soldiers." At this point a delegate from Wisconsin interrupted to suggest that Socialists also should be combatted by the Legion. From his experience in Wisconsin he concluded that "the Socialist is the arch-conspirator of the whole outrage."

The report prepared in Spokane made other specific recommendations: assist in the prosecution of those accused as radicals; report all radical activities to authorities; have Legionnaires attend all radical meetings; keep a card index in all Legion posts of suspected radicals in a city.

This course of action aroused some disapproval. Gilbert Bettman of Ohio spoke up in opposition: "I feel this whole thing is like opening a keg of dynamite. You are convicting men for their thoughts and not for their acts. . . . This is a subject that only the Supreme Court can decide. . . ."[4] He said the experience of hundreds of years would lead the court to say that you have got to have an act to make a crime.

Bettman had reason for caution. He was then one of the defendants in a suit filed against those who raided the Communist-Labor Party office in Cincinnati. Legionnaires heard about a large shipment of Communist literature arriving in town and decided to confiscate it. "I don't know that it will be entirely defended but we did it," he admitted. "We marched in a body up one of the main streets and scaled the outside of the Communist-Labor headquarters and got up on the second floor where they had this literature and made a bonfire of it." (At this point, the minutes note, Bettman was interrupted by applause.) "And that was the end of the Communist-Labor Party in Cincinnati. But we have been sued by the party and the trial is coming up May 20." He said they might all go to jail.

Bettman continued his words of caution:

> I do not think the American Legion in its infancy can safely go out and propagandize on great political and social questions of this kind. I mean it is dangerous. We cannot run the government of the United States. We can urge Congress to pass laws and as a result of the

Centralia trial the Americanism Committee can say we have investigated the trial and we believe that such and such a law is necessary. But that kind of thing has to come as a result of a mature reflection of our committee.[5]

Mature reflection tempered the official attitude of the Legion considerably but the Centralia case was never forgotten nor was the attitude of the Legion toward the IWW ever modified. All through the decade of the 1920s when Elmer Smith and others worked ceaselessly at stirring up sentiment favorable to what they termed progressive ideas and those who had such ideas, including, of course, Wobblies — and especially those unjustly imprisoned in Walla Walla — the Legion led in trying to make these efforts fail.

After the trial, anti-Wobbly feelings ran higher than ever because those held responsible for the Armistice Day killings got off with second-degree murder convictions. Demands were renewed for eradication of the IWW in Lewis County. The Wobblies were still around, shaken, perhaps, but not undone by the fate of Wesley Everest in the night of terror or of fellow workers tried in the shadow of the military in Montesano. Something, it was felt, had to be done about them — again.

When the supreme court of Washington upheld the antisyndicalism act, it gave sanction to "convicting men for their thoughts and not for their acts," as the cautious Gilbert Bettman put it. This was a signal for abandoning vigilantism and relying instead on the strong arm of the law. Prosecutors got busy.

Only a few weeks after the trial Herman Allen set out to do what he said in the fall of 1919 he could not do — deal with Wobblies by legal means. The antisyndicalism law was in effect in November 1919, and Allen could have sent the sheriff to arrest everyone in the IWW hall on the morning of November 11 if he had wanted to. Instead he stood on the sidewalk at Second and Tower when the parade went by to see what would happen. He would not enforce the law before the tragedy. Now he would.

The first arrest was made on June 3, 1920. Herman Nolan was picked up and charged with having been a member of the IWW on November 11, 1919. The next day the police chief raided what would ordinarily be called a hobo camp near the railroad tracks at the edge of town, calling it a gathering place for the IWW.

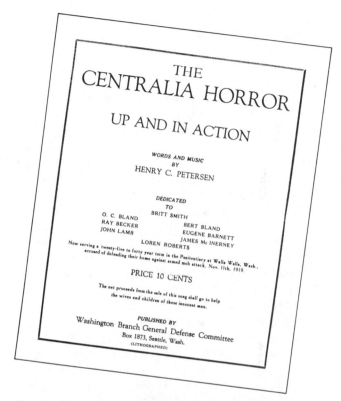

The sale of sheet music was one device used to raise defense funds. This one was dedicated to the eight convicted Wobblies still in prison. Its first verse: "Up ye toiler hard! A voice, a plea despair, a call, from men a sighing, and slowly dying, behind the slimy prison wall; help open the portal, fear no mortal, like a flood welling up, naught can stem your mass'd forces." Inside the cover was a chronology of the Centralia case from 1917 until 1927.

On the day that Mayor E. E. "Hi" Gill of Seattle came to town to make a speech warning that the Wobblies were making such gains that statewide membership increased 1,260 in one month, nine more men were arrested, one of them being Tom Lassiter, the partly blind news dealer who had been twice run out of town for persisting in selling the Seattle Union Record at his newsstand.

Elmer Smith, still free on a five-thousand-dollar bond on the McElfresh murder charge, and J. F. Emigh, an attorney with the firm of Vanderveer and Pierce, defended the man, calling Mary McAllister as one of the witnesses to relate what she knew of Wobblies from close observance. All but two of these brought to trial were convicted.

The Wobblies were not deterred by this new drive

against them. Centralia might be a town where businesses should be boycotted, in retaliation for the business community's hostile attitude and actions, but it was still considered a place where workers could and should be recruited into the ranks of the organization.

A rented house on the edge of Centralia served as a hall. A report sent to the *Industrial Worker* said: "We are well organized by this time. We are settled into a house with a complete corps of cooks, waiters and cooking equipment. We have two automobiles collecting food which is being contributed in good quantities by the farmers here about. Potatoes, chickens, eggs and other foodstuffs are coming in all the time."

Men were sent to sell IWW literature on the streets and when they did they were promptly arrested. Thomas Nash, one of the region's best organizers, was dispatched to Centralia to head a membership drive. "That was one hot spot, Centralia, let me tell you," he recalled when interviewed in 1961. "And I was arrested." And so were many others. One, picked up while distributing a Wobbly pamphlet house to house, told the police the "Wobs" were coming in such numbers that "we will fill your jails."

FBI agent Edwin Morse, doing IWW watch duty in Seattle at the time, reported the impending trouble. Luke May sent one of his operatives to pose as a Wobbly and report. This agent found an IWW member named Gust who was sure the trial beginning the following Monday would be "thrown out of court for lack of evidence." Elmer Smith, he said, "the fighting Centralia attorney," would get the boys off.

At this time Centralia stopped jailing Wobblies on antisyndicalism charges, possibly because, as the May agent observed, the jails were full and the Wobs liked it that way — liked being a burden on the establishment. Thus some were free to resume old activities, such as harassing the Salvation Army on street corners. The local IWW headquarters was found to be in a rented house at the eastern edge of town. May's man picked up the reassuring information that the IWW was not contemplating more violence but expected to make a convincing legal case.

More than the usual attention was given to the trial of Nash and four others. The *Industrial Worker* urged "all footloose" Wobblies around the state to go to Centralia, taking enough to "jungle up on," and pack the courtroom. These Wobblies were a defiant lot, wearing the largest IWW buttons available when they took seats in the courtroom, as if to dare anyone to arrest them too.

The defense consisted of attempts to convince the jury that there was so much good about the IWW that no one should be punished for being a member, no matter what the syndicalism law said. (This was the trial where one of the witnesses Elmer Smith called was a Luke May undercover agent who posed so successfully as a Wobbly that Smith afterward gave him train fare home to Seattle.) Smith tried to get charges against Nash and W. F. Moudy dismissed because both had been tried before in Seattle on the same charge and acquitted. It was double jeopardy, he claimed, but the judge, Ben Sheeks, would not listen.

The jury found Nash and Moudy guilty and acquitted the two others, G. I. Smith, one of Elmer's brothers, and Charles Beavers. This puzzled everyone concerned until Elmer Smith obtained an affidavit from G. Austin Goodell who swore he heard one of the jurors, Mrs. Walter Hill, say she did not believe the IWW was an unlawful organization and so none of the four were guilty, but the jury was divided, so it agreed to compromise — convict two and acquit two. They picked the two out-of-town men, Nash and Moudy, to be the ones who would have to go to prison while the local men went free. Moudy and Nash were sentenced to two to fifteen years in the state prison and went to Walla Walla, to join the Centralia prisoners and numerous others convicted under the syndicalism law.

It was easy enough in this period to prosecute Wobblies just for being Wobblies. The jails were crowded. But it was difficult to catch a Wobbly breaking any other law although they were often under suspicion. Shortly after the trial in Montesano the Coal Creek Lumber Company sawmill in the north end of Chehalis burned in a fire that began at three a.m. A night watchman said he discovered the blaze in a room that reeked with the fumes of gasoline. Barney Lee Clowers was arrested later on a charge of arson. He talked about an arson ring that was burning mills to get vengeance for the convictions of the Centralia men. A mill at Neuwakum in Lewis County was destroyed on March 1. Another at Lake Stevens in Snohomish County burned on May 31.

In Aberdeen on February 2, 1921, a man was discovered placing a charge of dynamite under the American Legion hall while seventy-five Legionnaires were meeting inside. The man escaped but a description of him was sent out with offers of rewards of five thousand dollars from the Aberdeen Chamber of Commerce, five hundred dollars from the state (authorized by Governor Hart), and one hundred dollars from the Legion for the dynamiter's capture. He was never found.

Luke May's operatives picked up alarming bits of information. Two known thieves told one of them in April that the southern part of the state was "in for a good bunch of trouble all summer." What kind of trouble? More fires. The same operative reported meeting Ben Swanson, a Wobbly, who told him the Chehalis fire was set by a fellow worker, but he didn't know who it was. Another mill fire in Kelso, he said, was set by a Wobbly.

Proof that Wobblies committed arson of course was lacking, just as it could not be proven that Wobblies drove spikes in logs or put sand in machinery. Sabotage is almost impossible to detect. But when they staged a boycott, which was entirely legal, all could see. Businesses that contributed to the Legion fund to pay for the prosecution of the men in the Armistice Day case were placed on boycott lists. A general absence of loggers in Centralia after the trial appeared to be the consequence of a common agreement that working men should not patronize business in that town. The Tower Cafe in Centralia closed, its owner blaming the Wobbly boycott. In Seattle the Our House Cafe, a well-known card room and lunch counter at Washington Street and Occidental, was accused of contributing to the Centralia fund and was boycotted with such effect that the cafe's owners sued the IWW for forty thousand dollars. Elmer Smith went to Seattle to defend the union, and did it successfully.

The lumbermen had other worries besides sabotage as the decade of the 1920s got underway. The lumber market went into one of its periodic declines. F. B. Hubbard was forced to give up. He resigned as president of the Eastern Railway and Lumber Company, selling his interest to the mill's manager, Jay Agnew, who had been associated with the company since it was formed in 1906. His son, Sam Agnew, succeeded him as manager.

An opportunity to track down one of the two missing fugitives in the Centralia case — Ole Hansen — seemed to have been passed up in this post-trial period. C. D. Cunningham received a letter from R. Y. Hutchings of Puyallup reporting that Hansen was seen near Bordeaux, not far from Centralia, wearing whiskers as disguise. That was in June 1921, and the following August Cunningham received another letter from Thomas N. Swale, a Seattle lawyer, saying that E. J. Kilman, an acquaintance just returned from the Orient, reported that Hansen was one of several men the U.S. consul in Manila put aboard the *City of Spokane* to be returned to the United States. Kilman, who knew Hansen, said that when Hansen realized he had been recognized, he jumped ship at Hong Kong.[8]

Hansen was never apprehended, nor was the mysterious John Doe Davis (Collins) who took a rifle to the Avalon and who, if he was alone there, was the one who killed Warren Grimm.

Troubles caused by or attributed to the Wobblies made Elmer Smith's task all the more difficult as he set out to win supporters for his free-the-prisoners crusade. The hostility he and others encountered in the early years showed that tolerance for pro-IWW speaking was no better than in past times. Some cities officially closed their doors when they heard Smith, James Rowan, or some other pro-IWW speaker was coming. On February 12, 1922, Smith was to speak in the Aberdeen Eagles Hall "on behalf of the class-war prisoners and especially the eight members of the Industrial Workers railroaded to the state penitentiary by the commercial interests of Centralia and the timber beasts. It was generally known that I was to tell in detail about the commercial conspiracy to raid the workers' hall on Armistice Day. . . ."[9]

Smith took the bus to Aberdeen where he found the police waiting for him. "On demanding to see a warrant," Smith said in his account of the affair, "the officer near me said: 'I have the only warrant I need right here on my belt.' " Mayor H. E. Bailey had issued a proclamation stating, "Whereas, a state of public feeling" exists in the city against Smith speaking publicly, it was necessary "to prevent acts of violence and to protect the lives of men, women and children, to prohibit him from speaking."

A crowd gathered at the Eagles Hall was told to disperse. The defiant throng then went to the Finnish hall where the police said Smith would be arrested if he tried to speak. Then, trailed by a loyal and persistent few, Smith walked to a nearby vacant lot where he started speaking, quoting first from the Declaration of Independence, "We hold these truths to be self evident . . . . " He had uttered only a few lines when a police officer took him by the arm, put him in a car, and drove him to the city jail where he was booked and charged with violating the mayor's proclamation. He was held until midnight, long enough to make sure the last of his curious and disappointed audience had gone home.

Smith had little reason to be encouraged by his free-the-prisoners efforts until May 1922, when he visited W. E. Inman, the Oakville rancher who served on the jury at Montesano. The former Texas Ranger had been carrying a gun ever since the trial but now, after two years, his fears were much diminished. He was not only willing to say that he felt the Centralia men were wrongfully convicted, he was willing to do so in a written affidavit. He thought L. E. Sweitzer, another juror, would also.

Smith was overjoyed, and the more so when he found that not just Sweitzer but E. E. Torpen also was willing to sign an affidavit. He interviewed all three the same day, wrote a brief of what they had to say, and had them sign it.

What the jurors did was unusual and might have been entirely unprecedented. They repudiated their own verdict, rendered while they were under oath. Inman and Sweitzer joined in signing the same statement. They confirmed that Harry Sellars said in the jury room what he was accused of saying before the trial began, "Every one of them is guilty and ought to be hung no matter what the evidence shows." They expressed the belief that all the defendants were innocent and said the reason they voted for conviction was fear that if there were a hung jury, another trial would be held and the men might be convicted of first-degree murder and hanged.

The statement closed with the assertion that "in the event of another trial and these affiants were to set as jurors in this case, and were permitted to receive in evidence what they now know, their verdict for each and all defendants would be 'not guilty. . . .' " [10]

Torpen swore that contrary to what others said, a trial ballot was taken as soon as the jury retired and that it was unanimously for acquittal. After some deliberations the second degree verdict was agreed to, he said, with the understanding that they would "recommend extreme lenience."[11]

When another juror, P. V. Johnson, then living in Oregon, heard what the others had done, he agreed also to recant. "If the jury," he said in his statement, "had been permitted to consider what I have since learned was a premeditated attack upon their hall, the jury would never have returned a verdict of guilty. It is my firm belief . . . that Warren Grimm was killed while advancing upon and engaged in an attack upon the IWW hall in Centralia."

Johnson said the determining element in securing conviction "was the bringing in of a large number of soldiers a few days before the conclusion of the trial. That these soldiers were brought in to protect the jury and as the jury was led to believe; that we were informed that a thousand or more IWW were hiding in the woods near the town. This tended to create a feeling in the minds of the jurors that the IWW was composed of outlaws and that therefore the organization was as much on trial as the individuals."[12]

Smith took the four affidavits to Aberdeen and showed them to Carl Hulten. He agreed with them readily and signed an affidavit saying that "the defendants did not have a fair and impartial trial and there is now in my mind no abiding conviction of their guilt of the murder of Warren Grimm. . . ." He said "the trial was conducted under extreme excitement and pressure which made it impossible to conduct a trial in a normal manner and leave the jury free and unhampered in their deliberations."[13]

These affidavits made sensational news — huge headlines in the labor papers and considerably smaller ones in the public press. Readers were thunderstruck. The jurors themselves saying the killers didn't get a fair trial? What made them say that? Were the affidavits genuine, and if so had they been obtained under some kind of duress?

Incredible though they seemed, the statements were genuine. A few months later Smith was able to get two more jurors — making seven in all — to join his crusade to right the wrong he was so sure had occurred in Montesano.

U. G. Robinson of Hoquiam, this time with George Vanderveer to witness his signature, stressed the intimidation resulting from bringing in the troops: "Nearly always when we were out for exercise between court sessions we would see those soldiers either marching around the streets or their camp. . . . There were three or four jurors as I now remember who so feared an assault (by the IWW) that they wanted guns for their own protection. It is my recollection that these same jurors were the ones who voted to find the defendants guilty of murder in the first degree."

Samuel Johnson repeated much of what the others said. He contended that most of the jurors wanted to acquit the men but agreed finally to a compromise verdict to avoid a hung jury.

Seven of the twelve jurors were now agreeing with what the Labor Jury found in its unofficial verdict. To what extent the affidavits and statements were made as a result of persuasion by Elmer Smith and how much was voluntary cannot be determined with certainty but later investigations, including an interview the author had with Inman, support a belief that the jurors recanted willingly and were even relieved at the chance to set straight a record that had been made wrong by their own doing.

The publicity committee made maximum use of the affidavits. Wobbly journalist Walker Smith was commissioned to provide a sequel to Ralph Chaplin's account, written just after the trial. He included, of course, the text of the juror affidavits.

Walker Smith interviewed Inman, who talked to him at length about the way the verdict was decided upon. Some jurors, he said, felt that if the men were acquitted they would be marked for lynching by the Legionnaires. He added,

Thinking wasn't very popular about that time. You thought what everybody else thought or you began to feel funny inside, as if you was a crook or something. When a man got an independent idea, chances was he dropped it quick and flopped over with the rest, like a fish. You found out about the strength of outside opinions in that jury room. I remember when we went to the window and got first sight of the soldiers from Camp Lewis, with their little tents hiked up everywhere, and the boys a promenadin' around. They was men in that courtroom you could-a knocked the eyes off with a pitchfork and never touched their noses. "My God," one of them said to me, "they're here to keep us from being shot."[15]

26

Tireless Efforts, Implacable Opposition

"It is the dominating tenet of tyranny to punish men for what they think — for what they believe. It is a cardinal rule under free institutions to punish men only and alone for what they do."[1]

Senator William E. Borah of Idaho made this memorable declaration in a New York speech in 1923. The wartime espionage act had been repealed, he said, but some fifty men convicted under it were still in prison. They were members of the IWW, "being punished for political offenses," and should be released.

Borah was not referring to the Centralia prisoners, yet they were considered by the IWW to be as deserving of release as those convicted under the criminal syndicalism acts. The Centralia men were identified in the defense literature and the labor press as "class-war prisoners" along with all the others locked up in the general but nonviolent prosecution of the war on Wobblies.

Others besides Borah and the IWW Defense Committees, with their shrill and unrelenting cries for release of martyred members, were applying pressure. The ACLU led this effort nationwide. It proved successful. President Harding was persuaded and Wobblies in prison under federal laws were set free.

This had no effect at all on Governor Louis Hart and other Western governors, who had similar powers to free men sentenced under state laws for what they said, thought, or believed. Hart was in office during the war when the Wobblies' reputation was blackened by their antiwar stance and their strikes and slowdowns in the lumber industry. He would yield to no one in Centralia or elsewhere in sustained, fierce hostility toward the IWW.

His attitude was not modified when the Farmer-Labor Party made the Centralia case a political issue. In the fall of 1923 the chairman of that bothersome third-party movement in Washington sent Hart a telegram saying "labor unions, farm organizations, progressive groups and the Farmer-Labor Party demand the unconditional release of the Centralia prisoners and all men convicted under criminal syndicalism law. . . ."[2] He received another resolution from a conference attended by fifteen hundred in Vancouver, B. C., and still another from a gathering of a thousand "citizens and workers" in Walla Walla. The Centralia case had indeed become a cause célèbre. Whenever any group with a liberal leaning met, it became virtually obligatory to pass a Centralia case resolution. Most were directed at the governor.

In 1923 the IWW felt it was time to apply pressure at the source of the original trouble. The Centralia branch of the union announced that a strike was called for September 4, in the woods and in the mills. "Now is the time for all men who believe in Freedom and Justice to lay down their tools for the release of the eight Centralia victims and all Class War prisoners," the posters declared. "Strike now! Strike hard! Establish your picket lines before leaving camps if possible." This gesture did little more than rekindle the anger Centralia generally felt toward the IWW.

The General Defense Committee in Chicago continued to apply pressure on Governor Hart, as did the ACLU. To the ACLU he replied, "You are entirely misinformed concerning Washington State prisoners." There were only five syndicalism law prisoners in Washington, he said, and "they could have had their freedom at any of the last three quarterly meetings of the parole board but refused to accept it until certain prisoners sentenced for murder were released, preferring the role of martyrs."[3]

Hart was referring to the stance taken by Tom Nash and others convicted under the syndicalism law who refused parole unless the Centralia men were permitted to leave prison with them. Their intent was to improve chances of release for their cell mates from Centralia, but there was not full agreement on this point. In a letter to "Fellow Workers Nash and Moudy" James McInerney explained:

> There has been some misunderstanding between the Centralia boys and the criminal syndicalism workers about the latter staying in here any longer. Some of the Centralia boys seem to think that you boys are a detriment to their case, while a few of us think different. So, yesterday, while in the big yard, we all came to the conclusion to settle this question in the mind of every fellow worker for once and forever. Dan Curtin is the fellow worker who brought this matter up; so we drew up a motion and everyone of us signed it but one. This action . . . has the sanction of Dan Curtin so now it is up to you boys to do your stuff. There was five of the Centralia bunch who think you are a detriment. . . . The other two believe it is high time for you to leave. My personal opinion is: Go out and root! You have waited for the workers long enough to prove themselves worthy of doing something for you, but they have not come across. We will have to do it ourselves. Go, thou, and stir them up.[4]

Enclosed with the letter was the following statement which had been signed by all of the eight except Ray Becker: "We, the Centralia defendants, are in favor of all criminal syndicalism boys going out next time the parole board sits."[5]

When the parole board next sat, they went.

The affidavits of the seven jurors did not have as much effect as the Publicity Committee hoped for. The statements lacked spontaneity. The jurors didn't come forward on their own to recant; they were persuaded — maybe pressured — by Elmer Smith and those working with him. And while the affidavits received top headline treatment in the IWW press and in defense pamphlets, the public generally did not see or hear much about them. Certainly the governor and the parole board were unmoved.

Still it was considered worthwhile to get even more affidavits, this time from witnesses, some of whom testified at the trial and many who didn't. These

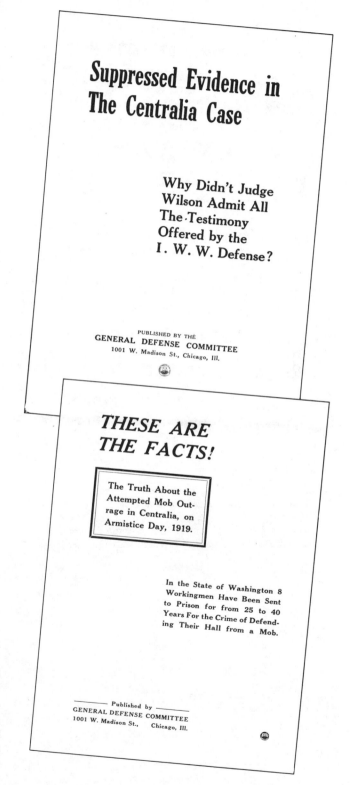

Suppressed Evidence in The Centralia Case

Why Didn't Judge Wilson Admit All The Testimony Offered by the I. W. W. Defense?

PUBLISHED BY THE
GENERAL DEFENSE COMMITTEE
1001 W. Madison St., Chicago, Ill.

THESE ARE THE FACTS!

The Truth About the Attempted Mob Outrage in Centralia, on Armistice Day, 1919.

In the State of Washington 8 Workingmen Have Been Sent to Prison for from 25 to 40 Years For the Crime of Defending Their Hall from a Mob.

Published by
GENERAL DEFENSE COMMITTEE
1001 W. Madison St., Chicago, Ill.

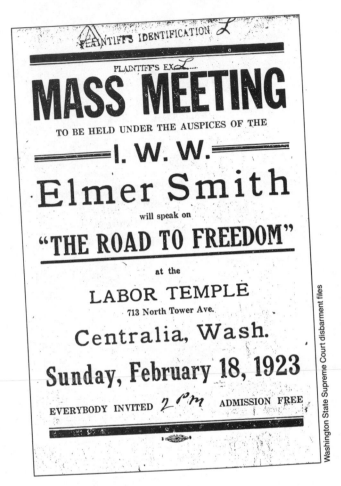

PLAINTIFF'S IDENTIFICATION L

PLAINTIFF'S EX L

MASS MEETING

TO BE HELD UNDER THE AUSPICES OF THE

I. W. W.

Elmer Smith

will speak on

"THE ROAD TO FREEDOM"

at the

LABOR TEMPLE

713 North Tower Ave.

Centralia, Wash.

Sunday, February 18, 1923

EVERYBODY INVITED 2 P M ADMISSION FREE

Washington State Supreme Court disbarment files

Elmer Smith went on the road through Washington to give impassioned speeches in defense of the Centralia prisoners. In February 1923 he dared to sponsor a mass meeting in the city where the trouble occurred. He was arrested. This poster, marked "Plaintiff's Exhibit L," was introduced as evidence at his subsequent trial.

were secured by Smith, Mark Litchman, and others through the first nine months of 1924.

They found D. E. Burrell, who was sent by the Lincoln Creek Lumber Company of Galvin to the October 1919 Elks Club meeting in Centralia, where plans for running the Wobblies out of town were discussed. He identified Warren Grimm as one who was appointed along with William Scales and F. B. Hubbard as a committee to carry out the sense of the meeting, which was to rid Centralia of the IWW. He said Grimm was the chairman. Burrell also stated that early in the afternoon of November 11 Arthur McElfresh told him "they have decided to raid the IWW hall after the parade," and that he expressed disapproval of the plan. Burrell then went to Elmer Smith's office and told him what McElfresh had said.[6]

Others signed affidavits at the behest of the defense committee. Cecil Draper, a member of Company M who served overseas with the Ninety-first Regiment, related a conversation on the evening of November 11 with Eldon Roberts, who told him that when the men in the parade stopped in front of the hall, McElfresh started for the hall with "a verbal message," and when he was halfway there someone shouted "Let's go!" Then the men broke ranks. Roberts told Draper that he reached the door about the same time as McElfresh. The two of them pushed against the door until it opened about three inches. "I looked through," Roberts related, "and saw a bunch of men lined up with guns inside. They started to shoot."[7]

Charles W. Green swore that a rifle found by a sign board near his home two weeks after Armistice Day, which the prosecution contended was left there by Eugene Barnett, could not have been placed there on Armistice Day because he (Green) was cutting firewood within six feet of the sign all day.

Mrs. Mary McAllister went into far more detail than she had a chance to do on the witness stand.

Thomas Duffy of Centralia told of seeing bloodstains on the sidewalk, leading from the door of the hall to Second Street, on the night of November 11 and again the next morning.

P. M. Crinion of Centralia said he knew Warren Grimm as a lawyer well by sight. From the southeast corner of Tower and Second he saw Grimm and a smaller man rush to the door of the hall and kick the lower part while hitting the top part with their elbows. Then the shooting began.

Cecil and Clyde DeWitte, high school students, told of seeing Grimm back out of the doorway of the hall after the shooting began, holding his hands over his abdomen.

William S. McKenzie repudiated the testimony he gave under oath as a trial witness. He and his brother-in-law, Clyde Tisdale, saw the start of violence from a car parked at the southwest corner of Second and Tower. At the trial he denied seeing the attack on the hall begin before he heard shots. He now said that was not true because it was literally "not safe to speak the truth at that time." Clyde Tisdale, who had been in the car with McKenzie, signed an affidavit saying more or less the same thing.

Elsie Hornbeck Sherlie at the trial identified Eugene Barnett as the man she saw leaning from a window of the Avalon Hotel while the shooting was taking place. When asked, "Will you say on your oath . . . that this is the man?" she answered, "Yes." But in her 1924 statement she said that answer was not intended to constitute positive identification, but rather that Barnett had the general appearance of the man she saw in the window, and "if it is a fact that my testimony was the principal factor in sending Eugene Barnett to prison, I feel it was a grave injustice. I would not want my own brother sent to prison on evidence no stronger than mine."[8]

S. J. Spears, P. M. Crinion, Allen Maynard, A. L. Bond, George E. Munk, A. O. Bond, Charles Carey, Percy Draper, and Joseph Church all made sworn statements saying much the same things — that the assault on the hall began first and that Grimm was not on the corner when shot.

These sworn statements favorable to the Wobbly cause, made four years after the event and for the purpose of helping get the men out of prison, cannot be given the same weight as direct testimony at the trial which could be subjected to cross-examination. And, it needs to be asked, why did they, like the seven jurors, agree to step forward and give such out-of-court testimony at a later time? Those who were not called, like Burrell, could have volunteered to be witnesses for the defense at the trial. They may have felt in 1920 that their testimony wasn't needed — that the defense would prevail. Clyde Tisdale was in the legislature when he recanted and expressed the hope that his admission of perjury would be kept quiet. His political reputation might be damaged. By 1924 he and others

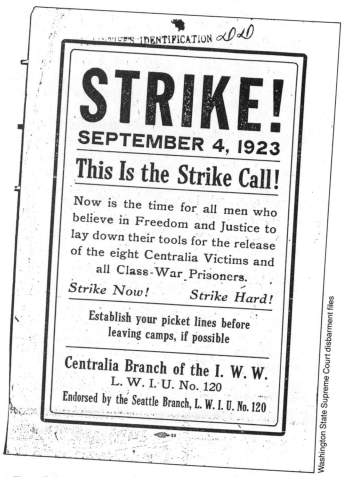

Washington State Supreme Court disbarment files

The strike weapon was used in attempts to intimidate employers and enlist their support in freeing the "Centralia Victims and all Class-War Prisoners." It was not successful.

were no longer fearful of telling the truth. Support for the convicted men was building. Seven jurors had recanted. In 1920, as some admitted, it wasn't safe to testify unless you had to, especially if what you saw wouldn't help convict the Wobblies. By 1924 those fears were largely gone and much of the truth that stayed hidden at the trial could come out.

Armed with the new batch of affidavits, the Centralia Publicity Committee made another attempt to make Governor Hart bend. He responded by repeating himself: The eight men had been given a fair and impartial trial. But how, the committee argued, could he say that in the face of all these affidavits? Hart refused to be drawn into an argument.

A new appeal was made to the parole board, buttressed by the new affidavits and resolutions from eleven labor unions. The appeal was given an emotional touch when the wives of six prisoners and the mother of Loren Roberts added a postscript saying:

> We are not asking for mercy. All we want is justice, that is, so far as it can be had at this late hour. We believe the people of the state of Washington now know the truth about this whole matter and we come before this parole board after years of anxious waiting and yearning in the hope that this board may find a sense of justice and a desire to right this great wrong so far as it can be righted. We want and need our husbands, fathers, and brothers and in you we place our last and only hope.[9]

This plaintive plea, like all others, was filed away and forgotten. The Centralia case was now a political issue and political concerns pushed the pursuit of justice into the background. The governor interpreted the public will as opposing any act of leniency toward the Centralia men. The parole board could only agree with him. Pleas from all quarters were ignored, including some even from far away. By 1924 the case had been given enough publicity in England to cause the Holderness Labor Party, the Beverley Labor Party of East Yorkshire, the National Union of Railwaymen of London, and the Hessle Labor Party of Hessle to dispatch resolutions to Governor Hart asking him to commute the sentences.[10]

The publicity committee distributed mimeographed resolutions to labor unions that needed only to be signed and sent. These poured into the gover-

nor's office and were ignored. The governor's secretary occasionally responded to a letter. In a typical response the official attitude was summarized: "Despite continued attempts at intimidations, threats and misrepresentations as well as widespread propaganda being carried through the nation, the good people of the state of Washington agree with Governor Hart that these men should not be released."[11]

This was a correct interpretation of the feelings of those who considered themselves the good people of Washington. The clamor in behalf of the Wobblies wasn't coming from them — the public at large. The resolutions poured in from labor circles as a consequence of the Centralia prisoners being elevated to martyrdom. Their foes were employers. Their cause was now labor's cause. Their release was therefore now intertwined with labor's struggles.

The liberal *New Republic* concluded that a nationwide protest was needed to bring the governor and the press of Washington to a "sense of responsibility." The protest was gathering momentum — enough to keep those engaged in the struggle encouraged — but it was not yet nationwide.

Elmer Smith kept on, little discouraged, as the passing months became passing years. Smith was like a traveling evangelist, always carrying the same message and heartened by the response of those who listened. At each speaking meeting a collection was taken and usually as much as fifty dollars in silver was dropped into the hats that were passed, enough to pay expenses. Other financial help came regularly from the ACLU and the General Defense Committee.

Opposition to these public appeals continued. The speaking procedure called for sending an advance man to a town to put up posters, engage a hall, and schedule a time. Montesano, Smith knew, was not a place where much sympathy could be expected, even four years after the trial, but still it was timber country where loggers were numerous, so a free-the-Centralia-prisoners meeting was scheduled there in May of 1924 with James Rowan as speaker.

Accompanied by F. W. Brown, Rowan drove to Montesano in the late afternoon and was flagged down on the outskirts by the town marshal. No speech, the marshal decreed. Montesano now had an ordinance against street speaking and the mayor had given instructions that no meeting in behalf of the Wobblies could be held.

National American Legion Library

Rowan, less courageous than Smith, yielded, turned his car west, and headed for Aberdeen. Others besides the mayor were prepared for Rowan's coming. Two miles out of town he and Brown saw that they were being overtaken by a caravan of cars. Aware like any Wobbly that he could be a victim of mob violence at any time, Rowan carried a gun, and while no sane Wobbly, after Centralia, would want to use a gun, this night he thought he might have to. Just before the pursuers caught up with him, Rowan turned his car into a farm yard and told Brown to run into the house

William Scales, left, and George Barner holding up the Grant Hodge post banner.

and tell the occupants what was going on. If there was going to be violence, he wanted witnesses. Rowan stayed in the car, his hand on the gun in his pocket.

The pursuers turned their cars into the farmyard and about twenty men jumped out and surrounded Rowan's car, an open black Ford sedan with no side curtains. "Where's that literature?" one of the men demanded. "We'll stop you ——— from spreading your damned lies around here, or you'll get the nicest coat of tar and feathers you ever heard of."[12]

One who appeared to be the leader, a gray-haired man in a business suit, seemed particularly aroused. "You're not spreading truth but a pack of damned lies," he shouted at Rowan, still seated behind the wheel of the car. "I sat in the courtroom and listened to the evidence and if I had my way those ——— would never have gone to jail at all; we would have taken 'em out and strung them up."[13]

A deputy sheriff came out of the crowd, pointed his revolver at Rowan, and ordered him out of the car. The gun in his pocket was taken away. At this point Brown emerged from the house with the farmer and his wife. They demanded to know what was taking place in their front yard. Wobblies, they were told.

Rowan's gun gave the deputy an excuse to arrest him on a charge of carrying a concealed weapon and lock him in the county jail for the night. Brown was allowed to drive on to Aberdeen, where he was able to engage a lawyer in time to get back to Montesano the next morning and convince the judge, when Rowan was brought into court, that any motorist has a right to carry a gun. Rowan was released. When Elmer Smith heard about all this he was predictably incensed. He notified the ACLU. He promptly scheduled another meeting for Montesano and dispatched a telegram to Governor Hart saying: "Elmer Smith will speak in Montesano May 22, 1924, and Elma, May 21, 1924. This is to inform you that mob violence will no longer be tolerated in Grays Harbor County and you will be held strictly responsible for any further mob violence to speakers in that county."[14]

Smith's assertiveness was sufficiently impressive to overcome further opposition. He was able to carry his message to Montesano and Elma.

The use of violence actually was rare in the Northwest in the 1920s but there was some elsewhere. Just a month after Rowan escaped a tar and feathering, a mob in San Pedro, California, identified as mostly sailors from the naval base, assaulted an IWW hall when a number of women and children were in the building. Some twenty of these were injured in the smashing and tearing up of the premises. Then some of the men were taken outside, smeared with hot tar, and showered with feathers.

The issue of the *Industrial Worker* reporting the San Pedro trouble carried a six-column-wide display on page one with two-inch-high letters: "BURIED ALIVE BY THE LUMBER TRUST." Under pictures of the eight Centralia prisoners was this: "They helped get you the eight-hour day. Let's bring them out!"

Some truth could be attributed to this claim. Any Wobblies during World War I who took part in strikes, slowdowns, sabotage, or any of the general mischief that accompanied the demand for the eight-hour day, all of which led the federal government to insist that the operators yield on that issue, could say they helped win the battle. The older of the Centralia men could legitimately make that claim.

Defense efforts in the mid-'20s were marred by suspicions that funds contributed to the cause were misused if not misappropriated. One who raised such a suspicion was Ray Becker, who began a crusade on his own from within the prison walls that was to endure for twenty years. Becker burned with resentment more than any of the others. He did not want parole. He demanded vindication. Nothing short of a pardon, accompanied by an apology for the wrongs which had been done to him, would satisfy Becker.

As the years went by and nothing encouraging happened, Becker concluded that those working in behalf of the Centralia men were not really doing much and were using the plight of the prisoners as an excuse to collect money for their own use. He said so in a letter to Samuel Gompers, AFL president, who sent it on to William Short, head of the AFL in Washington.

Short, whose regard for the IWW and its espousal of industrial unionism was low, wrote Becker agreeing that what he suspected was probably true. "I have seen many instances of this myself, especially in the Mooney case," he wrote, "where the Defense Committee operating out of Seattle collected . . . over $10,000 on behalf of Tom Mooney and had somewhere around $200 to be used for the purpose when the committee got through with their end of it. . . . I have seen much evidence to indicate that the IWWs have used the incarceration of yourself and associates to provide a meal ticket for themselves. . . ."[15]

Records confiscated in raids enabled the Seattle police "red squad" to obtain membership lists and information on the inside working of the IWW. A raid on the Finnish hall produced evidence that "the radicals were quarreling among themselves. Charges were made that some were pocketing funds collected for defense of prisoners. Former organizers said most of the money collected went to the radical officials and not to the prisoners."[16]

One who described himself as a "working liberal" wrote to the *Tacoma Times:* "I guess the Centralia defense committee will have to struggle along without my two bits and I don't mind saying why." He admitted to being sympathetic to the plight of the prisoners but said, "If I do any donating it will be sent to the fellows who are in prison and not to their 'friends' who are passing the hat outside. . . . "[17]

Funds collected were not carefully accounted for, but there is no record of serious accusations within the IWW except those of Becker, brooding over his fate in the Walla Walla prison. Smith and others traveling in behalf of the liberation cause used money collected for expenses. That is what it was intended for. The men in prison couldn't use money effectively to speak out or propagandize for themselves. If Smith kept any of the contributions for family expenses it was because he was spending more time working for the prisoners than for himself.

Another fund drive occasioned by the Centralia case was marred by some taint of scandal also. The funds were for a memorial to the four Legion men slain on Armistice Day.

Shortly after the trial William Scales recommended at a Chamber of Commerce luncheon that a memorial be erected to honor the four victims. He suggested a community building on the block facing the depot. This proposal was not pursued, but there was general agreement that some kind of memorial was in order. A committee headed by C. D. Cunningham decided on a statue — a work of art, something grand — providing recognition by the whole state of the sacrifice in blood these four men had made.

Statues were expensive, the committee soon learned. The kind of memorial they envisioned might cost a quarter of a million dollars. Such a sum certainly could not be raised in Lewis County alone, so a statewide fund-raising endeavor was launched. The Centralia Memorial Association Inc. was formed early in 1922 with Col. C. B. Blethen, publisher of the *Seattle Times,* as chairman and Lt. Gov. W. J. Coyle as vice-chairman. A professional fund-raiser, Frank Jackson, was retained at a salary of five hundred dollars a week plus expenses. Only half was to be paid during the drive with the rest becoming due when the goal of two hundred fifty thousand dollars was reached.

The drive ran into trouble immediately. The Wobbly side of the Centralia story was widely enough known by 1922 to raise many serious doubts about the truth of the contention that the four Legionnaires died as a result of IWW terrorism rather than a raid on a Wobbly hall. Refusals to contribute were common. Even some Legion posts in Eastern Washington would not give. A statement made by Edward Bassett, commander of the Butte, Montana, Legion post had wide circulation. He declared that "the IWW in Centralia who fired on the men that were attempting to raid the IWW headquarters were fully justified in their act. . . . The coroner's inquest showed that the attack was made before the firing began."

Only a little more than sixteen thousand dollars was collected or subscribed when the drive bogged down. The fund-raiser resigned, whereupon a suit was brought against the Memorial Association by A. D. Tasker, a creditor of Jackson who had been assigned the half of Jackson's salary to be paid when the goal was reached.

The committee, embarrassed by these troubles, modified its plans and its financial goal. It contracted with a Seattle sculptor, Victor Alonzo Lewis, to produce a modest-sized memorial to be placed in the city park. While Lewis worked the fund-raising went on. Much of Cunningham's time, meanwhile, was spent answering letters about the drive. One from Ellsworth French of the *Spokane Daily Chronicle* wanted to know about the charge that the sixteen thousand dollars originally collected had disappeared. In his reply Cunningham expressed exasperation that no sooner did he answer a letter such as this than another showed up. He decided to write an explanation about the whole matter and make copies to be sent out to inquirers. As for the sixteen thousand, he assured French, it was still intact — that is, what little was left after payment of expenses. Cunningham added: "I am more or less amused to have this question come from Spokane because it was there and in Yakima that we met the first united opposition to the erection of the memorial to the men who were murdered here."[18]

The kind of inscription to be put on the statue when it was finished presented a perplexing question. Four servicemen were being memorialized. Those who came to look at the statue would want to know what happened to them. They had been "murdered," as Cunningham put it, or at least murder had been proven against those held responsible for their slaying. Should the word "murder" be used in the inscription? If it were, the murderers would just about have to be identified. The committee deliberated about this for a long time. It was one thing to get a conviction for murder in court, but that conviction, they knew, would never be accepted by everyone, for by then a majority of the jury had recanted, witnesses were changing their testimony, the conduct of the trial was widely criticized, and Elmer Smith and the IWW and the ACLU were generating a hullabaloo in behalf of the imprisoned men that approached the hysterical. If the word "murder" appeared on the memorial's plaques, it would be an open invitation for a dynamiting.

So it was not used, nor were Wobblies identified as the killers. The memorial took the form of a soldier in uniform, heroic in size, standing on an eight-foot-high square pedestal on the sides of which were bas-relief likenesses of the four slain ex-servicemen — Grimm, Casagranda, Hubbard, and McElfresh. The inscription reads:

TO THE MEMORY OF
BEN CASAGRANDA
WARREN O. GRIMM
ERNEST DALE HUBBARD
ARTHUR McELFRESH
SLAIN ON THE STREETS OF
CENTRALIA, WASHINGTON,
ARMISTICE DAY, NOV. 11, 1919
WHILE ON PEACEFUL PARADE
WEARING THE UNIFORM OF
THE COUNTRY THEY LOYALLY
AND FAITHFULLY SERVED

The memorial was entitled "The Sentinel" and on its base was inscribed this somewhat confusing tribute:

IT WAS THEIR DESTINY—
RATHER IT WAS THEIR
DUTY — THE HIGHEST OF US
IS BUT A SENTRY
AT HIS POST

The others who served with Cunningham on the memorial committee were Lloyd Dysart, C. J. Oliver, C. W. Wells, A. J. Kresky, Louis Charneski, John E. Murray, and Dr. F. J. Bickford.

The memorial was ready for unveiling and dedication on Armistice Day, 1924. The arrangements committee decided that a parade would be appropriate and that it should follow the route used by the men being memorialized on the last day of their lives. Governor Hart was on hand. Three bands were assembled. The Legion scheduled its convention to coincide with the dedication so the city had an abundance of servicemen to march in the parade. The AFL carpenters' union sent a delegation. Boys from the state reform school in Chehalis were in the line of march. The Guard manned four tanks, women's patriotic groups and the Spanish War veterans filled out the ranks, and at the end of the procession was a car bearing an advertisement for D. W. Griffith's moving picture *America* then showing at the Liberty Theater.

The parade moved north on Tower Avenue, just as the parade had done five years previously. It passed Elmer Smith's office where one of the Wobblies' provocative placards, reading "BURIED ALIVE BY THE LUMBER TRUST," was displayed in a window; then it moved on past the site of the old hall in the Roderick Hotel, where everyone looked at the shabby building, remembering that this was the place where the men being memorialized were slain, and then up Tower past the new local headquarters of the IWW and office of the Centralia Publicity Committee in the new Labor Temple. Police Chief James Compton was seen sitting in his car on a side street, watching as the parade moved past the IWW headquarters. Then it made the turn at First Street and the return march, but with no pause or stop at the corner of Second and Tower.

Several thousand persons stood in the park around the statue and listened to speeches about patriotism and sacrifice, liberty and duty, justice and reverence for the Constitution. When his turn came, Cunningham said the four slain Legionnaires "sacrificed their lives in time of peace for the same principles and ideals that impelled us as a free people to enter the World War." Governor Hart, who followed him, said, "This memorial will be handed down from generation to generation as a shining emblem of the love of freedom, liberty and justice."

The principal speaker was Major General U. G. Alexander, who commanded the Thirty-eighth Infantry at the Marne. He deviated from the theme of the occasion to speak out against the League of Nations. "I don't want this published, if there are any reporters present," he said, "but if we keep out of European affairs we won't get into trouble." He also condemned

THE
SENTINEL·

IT·WAS·THEIR·DESTINY·
RATHER·IT·WAS·THEIR·
DUTY·THE·HIGHEST·OF·US
IS·BUT·A·SENTRY·
AT·HIS·POST·

TO·THE·MEMORY·OF

BEN·CASAGRANDA
WARREN·O·GRIMM
EARNEST·DALE·HUBBARD
ARTHUR·MC·ELFRESH

SLAIN·ON·THE·STREETS·OF
CENTRALIA·WASHINGTON·
ARMISTICE·DAY·NOV·11·1919·
WHILE·ON·PEACEFUL·PARADE·
WEARING·THE·UNIFORM·OF
THE·COUNTRY·THEY·LOYALLY
AND·FAITHFULLY·SERVED

A statue memorializing the four ex-servicemen slain on Armistice Day 1919 was erected in the park behind the Centralia Library. On one side are bas-relief portraits of Warren Grimm and Arthur McElfresh; on the other side, Dale Hubbard and Ben Casagranda.

disarmament, saying, "It is the strong man whose house is not attacked."

The committee asked for and received a telegram from the new president, Calvin Coolidge, who wired: "When on Armistice Day you unveil in memory of the four veterans of the World War who were murdered on Armistice Day, 1919, I wish to be among those who will join the expression of profound sorrow for the loss of those heroic lives and of gratitude that their memory is thus to be perpetuated."[19]

No mention was made of the IWW at the ceremony and certainly nothing was said about the men who were convicted of the slaying of one Legion martyr whose face, immortalized in bronze, was a part of the monument. Whatever the thoughts of Cunningham, Dysart, and others with vivid memories of the turbulent days of 1919, they were left unexpressed. The task at hand was to dedicate what was essential for Centralia, a lasting memorial, modest though it turned out to be in comparison with what had been originally envisioned, expressing the city's respect for the four who had fallen. The memorial could not say why they fell or even how it happened. They were slain — no question about that. They were wearing the uniform of their country, also unquestionable, and on the streets of Centralia. But that was all. The memorial was Centralia's expression: we acknowledge that it happened and it was sad. But we say no more.

The memorial endures to this day. It was never seriously defaced.[20]

27

The Turning of the Tide

In the spring of 1924, when only six months were left in the second term of Governor Louis F. Hart, John Nicholas Beffel, representing *The Nation,* went to Everett to interview the leading Republican candidate for governor, Roland H. Hartley. Hart rebuffed all appeals in behalf of the Centralia prisoners. Beffel hoped Hartley would say something to raise hopes that, if he were elected, the eight prisoners would have a better chance. He was disappointed.

When asked about his attitude on the Centralia case, Hartley bristled: "I don't know anything about the Centralia case. That hasn't anything to do with the political situation."[1] When Beffel said he thought it would be a major issue in the coming campaign, Hartley declared angrily: "Why should you come clear out here from New York to dig up this old issue that is dead? Why don't you let it stay buried? The people of this state don't want it dug up."[2]

Beffel explained that he had a personal interest in the case because he sat through the trial in Montesano and watched and listened while Judge Wilson barred all evidence showing there was a conspiracy to raid the IWW hall. "Do you doubt there was a raid on the IWW hall before the shooting?" Beffel asked. "Probably there was a raid."

Hartley responded, "There ought to have been a raid." Then Hartley called in an assistant, Harold King, who was district commander of the American Legion. King said yes, "they were raiding Wobbly halls all over the state at that time." Hartley added: "I believe in raids on Wobbly halls, if we can't get rid of the Wobblies in any other way. They are a menace to civilization."[3]

When Beffel persisted with his questioning, Hartley became angry. Red-faced, he demanded, "Why should you take it upon yourself to defend the IWW? Every decent man shuns them as he would a mad dog. They are a bunch of cutthroats and murderers. . . ."[4]

A month before the election the Centralia Publicity Committee asked each of the five candidates for governor to state his position on releasing the Centralia prisoners. Senator J. R. Oman, running on the Farmer-Labor ticket, answered immediately that he was for release. His party even had a plank in its platform pledging support for those working to free the prisoners. Emil Herman, candidate on the Socialist ticket, was so much for the prisoners that he challenged Hartley, the GOP nominee, to a debate at the corner of Hewett and Rockefeller Avenue in Everett on the subject. The challenge began, "Resolved, that the Republican party is responsible for the Centralia Armistice Day tragedy. . . ."[5] D. Burgess, the Socialist-Labor Party candidate, was sympathetic also. The Republican and Democratic candidates did not respond.

Washington was still a politically conservative Republican state in the 1920s and Hartley won the election easily. He was solidly a Tory who believed that too much was being spent on government and that taxes were excessive. It was just what the voters, most of them, wanted to hear. And he was against the IWW. They wanted to hear that too.

Hartley was fundamentally opposed to parole. "If the criminal doesn't beat us in the courts, he does after he gets in prison," he wrote in a message to the state legislature. "We have made it too hard for him to get in and too easy to get out. The alarming increase in crime and the practice of coddling prisoners go hand in hand. . . . When a man is committed to the penitentiary, he should be made to understand that the chances are he is going to stay there until the expiration of his sentence."[6] Hartley recommended legislation requiring fixed mandatory sentences and the abolition of the parole board.

In this same message Hartley said education was costing too much. The "staggering sum" of $33.4 mil-

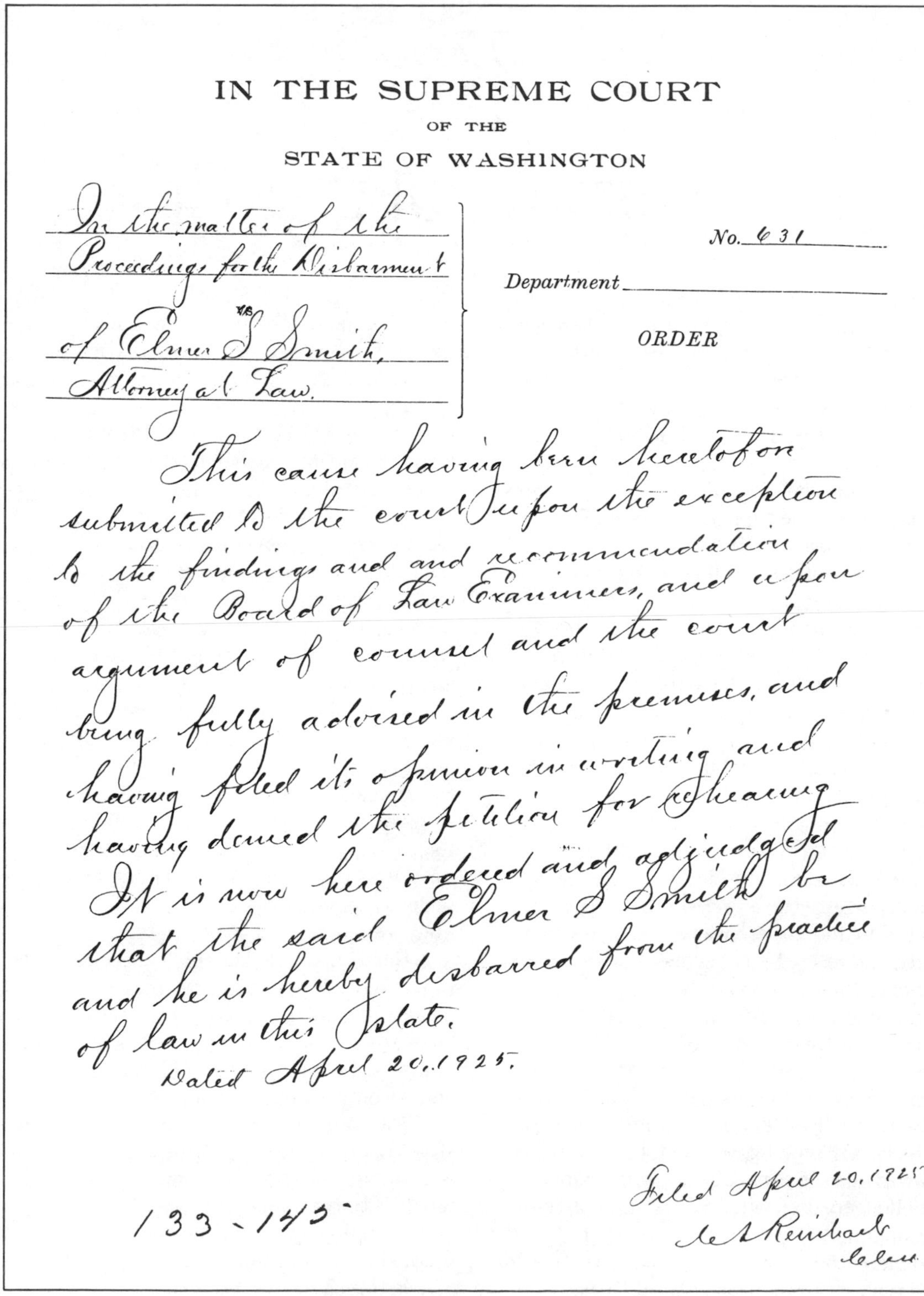

IN THE SUPREME COURT
OF THE
STATE OF WASHINGTON

In the matter of the
Proceedings for the Disbarment

vs.

of Elmer S Smith,
Attorney at Law.

No. 631

Department _____

ORDER

This cause having been heretofore submitted to the court upon the exception to the findings and and recommendation of the Board of Law Examiners, and upon argument of counsel and the court being fully advised in the premises, and having filed its opinion in writing and having denied the petition for rehearing

It is now here ordered and adjudged that the said Elmer S Smith be and he is hereby disbarred from the practice of law in this State.

Dated April 20, 1925.

133 - 145

Filed April 20, 1925
W A Reinhart
Clerk

The supreme court order disbarring Elmer Smith, April 20, 1925.

Washington State Supreme Court disbarment files

lion was spent on the schools of the state in 1924. He also deplored competition among the university and colleges for students and appropriations. He complained that the university's board of regents took its appropriation requests directly to the people, defying him, and recommended that the boards of regents of all five state schools of higher learning be abolished and replaced by a nonsalaried board of nine members. The university, he claimed, was so richly endowed that the rent money from the Metropolitan Tract in downtown Seattle would soon be enough to meet all the financial needs of the institution. Hartley said both the common schools and highway programs were too costly. He urged abolishment of the state library board and discontinuance of the traveling library.

Hartley's uncompromising attitude toward the IWW was not considered cause for abandoning or even lessening the defense efforts. The power of public opinion, Elmer Smith and his allies were convinced, eventually would wear down all opposition, even Hartley's. Their cause was just, they kept telling themselves and others; they would prevail.

The jurors who recanted were induced to take on the new governor. They were able to schedule a visit to tell him in person why they concluded the men were improperly convicted and should now be released. They also sent petitions and wrote individual letters. Hartley was unmoved.

When the parole board was scheduled to meet, Smith wrote to the governor, saying: "I thought you might forget to write the parole board calling up for consideration of the Centralia case and I am simply writing this as a reminder. I shall be in Walla Walla so as to be available in the event the board wishes any additional information about the case. It would certainly be splendid if you could find the time to be personally present during the consideration of this matter."[7] Hartley at least did not tear up the letter, if ever it was shown to him. It was preserved.

Cunningham, aware that the governor was being bombarded with defense literature and fearful that he might be influenced by the affidavits of the jurors and witnesses, wrote Hartley a long letter undertaking to disprove much of what was appearing in the defense committee pamphlets. The repentant jurors, he wrote, must have signed affidavits because they were Wobblies themselves or sympathizers. Cunningham said he was not trying to influence the governor in the matter of "extending or denying clemency to those convicted. That is a matter with which I feel I have no concern."[8] But he could not resist correcting what he considered to be misrepresentations in the published defense pamphlets.

The pamphlets, increasingly inflammatory, contained stinging accusations and lurid descriptions of events in pre-Armistice Day Centralia and in Montesano. The newly appointed health officer in Centralia was described as "the unspeakable Dr. Livingstone." Reference was made to his "alleged part in the lynching of Wesley Everest."[9] One pamphlet charged that the mayor of Centralia was trying to lure back loggers who were boycotting the town by offering the pleasures of a wide-open city.

The publicity committee, far from being discouraged by the attitude of the governor and the parole board, stepped up its activities. Elmer Smith and Rowan were on the road week after week, usually speaking out of doors, and doing so in spite of hostile Legionnaires, mayors, police chiefs, and others, such as a motorcycle rider who attempted to drown Smith out in one town by circling nearby with his noisy machine. In another place an airplane flew low over the assembled crowd several times to interrupt his speech. The street meetings always went on for more than an hour — sometimes two — depending on the weather and the temper of the crowd.

Occasionally Smith took his wife and two young children on speaking trips. They sat in the car and waited patiently while he told again the stories they had heard many times. Some meetings were enlivened by Henry Gehrig, a singer, who knew the labor songs and could make his loud baritone voice heard across several blocks while a crowd gathered. The crowd joined in when the meetings closed with a song.

Like many speakers called upon to repeat the same oration over and over, Smith developed an effective delivery and style. One writer, probably Nicholas Beffel, compared him to nationally known orators, saying: "I have heard Robert Ingersoll tune the chimes of his voice and entone his vision of a world without master or slave. I have heard James G. Blaine and Garfield. I have been part of assemblies where oratory has awakened enthusiasm, but never have I seen or imagined such an event as this Skidroad speech."[10] He was describing an oration Smith made to an estimated three thousand persons on a Seattle street on May 31, 1924.

By 1923 Elmer Smith felt that Centralia itself was ready to hear his story, but he was wrong. In February when posters announcing that he would give a public address were widely distributed, he was arrested. Just to announce that he had something to say publicly in behalf of the Centralia prisoners was sufficiently offensive to bring him into police court, where he reacted to the injustice of it all with such vigor that he was held in contempt of court for "unprofessional" conduct and penalized with a fine or three days in jail. He followed his customary practice of appealing to the supreme court and had no more success than usual. Rather than pay the fine, he served the jail sentence.

In August Smith traveled to the penitentiary at Walla Walla, where he was permitted to visit the "eight men buried alive." "It is hard indeed for me to express the feeling and emotions which swept over me as I visited the victims of the Lumber Trust," he wrote. "After five years of prison hell they stand erect, inimitable and unconquerable, their spirits untamed and still as much in the fight for a better world as the day they entered."[11] This was published on page one of the Wobbly paper, which had few issues in the middle '20s that did not carry some report about Centralia defense efforts and the need to sustain the work and support it with donations.

Others besides sympathizers sometimes listened when Smith and Rowan spoke. When Smith appeared in Yakima on July 23, 1923, Thomas E. Grady, a member of the State Board of Law Examiners, heard him describe Judge John Wilson as a "tool of the lumber trust" and as being "ever faithful to the lumber trust." Grady, himself a former judge, issued a statement to the press next day saying that such remarks, coming from a lawyer, were unprofessional and cause for disbarment. He took affidavits from three others who heard the same speech and commenced proceedings calling for disbarment. Besides disrespect for Judge Wilson, Smith was charged with speaking under the auspices of the IWW whose literature circulated by him "teaches both sabotage and criminal syndicalism as a means of enforcing industrial changes . . . and there is no reason why he should not be charged with all the responsibility that usually follows an abettor of a criminal act."[12]

Smith wrote to the ACLU saying the disbarment charges were based on his assisting and defending the IWW and advocating industrial unionism. He said he was to be tried for his social views and noted that the bar association committee preparing the charges included his old foes, C. D. Cunningham, Herman Allen, and Lloyd Dysart.

George Vanderveer was retained to represent Smith. He asked that the matter be heard by a jury. Both the bar association and the supreme court refused the request. Instead it was heard by the bar's Board of Law Examiners, sitting in Chehalis. The hearing went on for several days. Vanderveer wanted to subpoena Wilson, put him on the witness stand, and prove that he was indeed a "tool of the lumber trust," but he was denied that opportunity. At the conclusion the board voted for disbarment and the decision was promptly appealed to the supreme court.

Vanderveer in his brief before that court seemed to misunderstand the charges. He assumed that an attempt was being made to punish Smith for defending men under indictment, "thereby assessing punishment different from what would be meted out to other lawyers in the state who might likewise be charged with crime."[13] He said nothing in the brief about Wilson or the IWW literature. But the justice, K. Mackintosh, who wrote the majority opinion in the appeal, had much to say about the radicals that Smith defended. The literature passed out at Smith's speaking engagements with his knowledge, he wrote, was "vile. . . . It advocates many serious crimes. . . . Anyone who advocates such general principles is unworthy of the office of attorney at law."[14]

Mackintosh said Smith "has been pleased to denominate 'political prisoners' as persons punished because of their opinions and has in his public addresses advocated a general strike, a strike 'that will paralyze all the industries of the state,' as a means of coercing their liberation. On his admission to practice as an attorney the defendant took an oath to uphold the laws of the land, and, in our opinion, his conduct in this particular is a violation of that oath."[15]

Then Mackintosh quoted the "Onward Christian Soldiers" parody and a poem describing sabotage of a threshing machine. He also quoted a labor bulletin dated 1900, five years before the IWW was formed, describing the sabotage of machinery.[16]

In his summary Mackintosh said Smith had a right to advocate peaceful changes in government, but overstepped permissible bounds when he advocated change by "criminal and other unlawful means."[17]

The decision of the court was six to three against Smith. In a dissent Justice J. Parker said Smith was not a member of the IWW and he could find no evidence that he was advocating the views expressed in the quotations from the so-called IWW literature introduced in evidence, "nor can I agree that the record shows that Smith distributed or is responsible for the distribution of any of the literature. . . . "[18]

Smith actually was not, as the justice observed, a card-carrying member of the IWW, but he wished he could be, or a least said as much when he acted as chairman of a meeting attended by three thousand persons in the Seattle Hippodrome on April 6, 1924, called to hear James P. Thompson, IWW organizer and lecturer, who was appearing for the first time after being released from Leavenworth penitentiary. A report of that meeting said: "The chairman (Smith) expressed a wish to be an IWW but mentioned that he was ineligible due to his profession. He said, 'I am with the Wobblies because they would make a heaven out of this capitalistic hell.' "[19]

At that same April meeting, attorney George Vanderveer proclaimed his sympathies with IWW philosophy as well when he said: "The old idea that private property must be the cornerstone of all common effort is dying. A new order lies ahead. The cause of our enemies is decadent because it does not serve the common people, the honest people. I have faith in the future of freedom."[20]

So Elmer Smith was disbarred — prohibited from practicing law in the courts of the state. He could still engage in law work in his office, but in any filings or other actions involving a court, he would have to act through another attorney, and this he did. But the time when he could defend men accused under the syndicalism act was over.

The bar association thus succeeded in punishing the most vocal defender of the IWW. The Mackintosh opinion made it plain that the disbarment was approved less because of what Smith said or appeared to advocate than because the men he sought to set free were members of an organization that was still as much hated and feared as ever — and furthermore their literature was "vile."

Mackintosh was the justice who, two days after the Armistice Day violence, sent an often-quoted letter to George Dysart expressing appreciation for the "high character of citizenship displayed by the people of Centralia in their agonizing calamity. We are all shocked by the manifestation of barbarity on the part of the outlaws and are depressed by the loss of lives of brave men, but at the same time are proud of the calm control and loyalty to American ideals demonstrated by the returned soldiers and citizens."[21]

The disbarment was a blow to Smith and his family. It was one more humiliation. Disbarment is a rarely invoked penalty, usually associated with dishonesty, embezzlement, moral turpitude, and other irregularities and offenses that reflect shame on the person punished. In Smith's case it was quite plain why the legal profession wanted to read him out of its association as it tried to do with Vanderveer. Both were lawyers for and allies of those with whom society was still at war.

The disbarment was widely accepted as a battle victory in that war and was particularly welcomed by the Northwest Logging Operators Association, which decided in 1924 to accelerate efforts to rid the state of the IWW. It adopted a budget of fifty-five thousand dollars for the first year of a concentrated fight.

The continued concern of another employer group, the Federation of Washington Industries, could be seen in a paragraph from its annual report: "During the summer disbarment proceedings were brought against Elmer Smith, the IWW and radical lawyer of Centralia. . . . At the request of the attorney general's office the Federated Industries extended assistance in securing evidence for the prosecution."[22]

Elmer Smith could not accept the fierce opposition to his efforts with equanimity. The years of traveling and delivering long orations at the top of his voice for an hour or more at a time, the anguish over the continued imprisonment of the men he had sworn to get released, his inability to provide adequately for his family, and then the shock of being rejected by fellow lawyers, denounced by the supreme court, and banned from the bar, aggravated what developed soon after the Montesano trial — chronic stomach ulcers.

Smith's ulcers were bad. The pain was often severe, the bleeding frightening.

"I was aware that father was miserable," his daughter wrote,

but just how bad it was came home to me during one of our rare family outings. Father did love to fish and this particular Sunday we went down to the Toutle River for fishing and a picnic. Mother prepared lunch while Father slowly progressed along the bank of the river with his fishing rod followed by my brother Stuart, age two, and me. Father stopped to fish from a fallen log, hanging quite high over the water. We children were having great fun launching a driftwood flotilla when Stuart slipped and fell into the swirling stream. I screamed for help. After one startled glance Daddy jumped off the perch, a height of some ten or twelve feet, and waded to the rescue. Once we were safely back on dry land Father collapsed in agony and sent me to fetch Mother. Between us we managed to help him back to the car and into the driver's seat as mother didn't know how to drive. It was a nightmare journey home, with frequent stops. Two frightened children watched from the back seat as their father vomited blood into the dusty wayside bushes.[23]

No one in Centralia would rent office space to Smith so he built a small office building at 717 North Tower. Later half of Smith's building was rented by the IWW. The family moved into a large old house in the Logan district, on the east side of the railroad tracks.

"Our home remained a haven for many rootless men," his daughter remembered. "If a man came to Father with empty pockets, he never left that way, even though our cupboards were as bare as old Mother Hubbard's. Transients were never turned away from our door when they came asking to work for a bite to eat." Laura Smith endured it all but she was not happy. The quiet schoolteacher she married had turned into a firebrand defender of radicals with consequences that were increasingly unpleasant for the family.

The ulcers finally became so severe that Smith went to the well-known Coffee Clinic in Portland for surgery. The operation did not produce much relief and later he went to the clinic again seeking a surgical cure for the painful gnawing in his stomach. There was some relief but he was not healed.

The stress Smith lived with was sustained by the adamancy of Governor Hartley all through his first term in rebuffing every appeal in behalf of the prisoners, and then in 1928 Hartley was reelected. But then began a series of events that marked a turning point.

The year started badly enough. State Legion officers, who included Cunningham, met in Spokane and acted on a rumor that some of the prisoners were due for parole. They organized what they termed a "statewide protest" against any such act of lenience. Every

post in the state was asked to participate.

At the Legion's August convention in Centralia the Grant Hodge post was able to get approval of a resolution opposing any effort to obtain paroles for the Centralia prisoners. One post dared oppose the resolution, saying it was "railroaded" through without any discussion. This was the Royal Mines post in the mountain town of Leavenworth, which adopted a resolution of its own saying: "It is the belief of this Post that the four ex-servicemen killed on Armistice Day were slain in self-defense by the now deceased Wesley Everest," and that the eight "innocent prisoners soon to enter on their tenth year of incarceration should be immediately released." The Wobbly literature was being believed, at least in some circles.

Shortly after the Legion convention the Methodist Episcopal Church, holding its annual conference in Tacoma, injected a new note into the controversy — the concern of religious bodies — by resolving that the church undertake a search of records to look for evidence of injustice. This aroused a "storm of protest" in the Legion.[24] It was one thing for the Wobblies themselves, and their lawyer, to agitate in behalf of those the Legion had helped put in prison. That was to be expected. But here was a church daring to suggest that all may not have been right at Montesano. Cunningham couldn't imagine what would inspire a respectable church to take such an action.

He suspected that the Wobbly and ACLU propaganda was having an effect around the country because otherwise respectable persons were saying they were being convinced by what they read about the Centralia case. William Allen White, the "Sage of Emporia," was one.

In response to a request from the ACLU for an expression, White wrote to Governor Hartley saying he was a member of the Chamber of Commerce and a Republican and "I have no possible sympathy with the aims or methods of the IWW, but I think these men are entitled to fair play and to their constitutional rights. If this information set forth by the Civil Liberties Union is correct, they have neither. What the state of Washington seems to have done was done during the war hysteria and might have happened in any state. But it seems to me that we all are now in a cooler and more reasonable frame of mind, and I think you would be doing the cause of justice in America a service if you would release these men."[25]

When no building owner in Centralia would rent an office to Elmer Smith, he built this small building on North Tower and rented part of it to the IWW.

The parole board met on August 23, 1927, and again denied parole to the Centralia men.

Cunningham and the Legion leaders began to realize that the crusade they were battling now posed a danger greater than premature release of the eight prisoners; there was the awful possibility that a large segment of public opinion could be swung around to the belief that the raid on the hall did begin before shots were fired, and that there was injustice in Montesano when the judge consistently upheld the prosecution's objections to the introduction of evidence supporting the Wobblies' claim that they were defending their hall against a raid they knew had long been contemplated.

Cunningham was particularly displeased when even his fellow prosecutor, W. H. Abel, joined the growing chorus in behalf of the one prisoner whose guilt was most frequently questioned, Eugene Barnett. Abel wrote to the parole board: "Whether Barnett is innocent or guilty, I believe he has been sufficiently punished. Recently while on a visit to the penitentiary, I met Barnett and was very much impressed by his statement that he was entirely innocent of the charge of which he stands convicted. In any event I consider he has been fully punished even on the assumption that he is guilty. For these reasons I respectfully request that he be admitted to parole at this time."[26]

Ritchie M. Kinnear, a Seattle member of the parole board, did say publicly that he and other members of the board were "very much interested in Barnett" but Hartley, when asked about a rumor that Barnett was to be given a Christmas parole, said he didn't know anything about the matter and furthermore could not do anything unless a recommendation came from the parole board.

Then from an entirely unexpected source — the

The window of the new IWW hall the union dared open on North Tower Avenue in the early 1920s. It was never molested.

ranks of the American Legion itself — came an ally for the Centralia committee in mid-1928 so effective that he was enlisted by Elmer Smith to help carry on the arduous speaking campaign. He was Edward Patrick Coll, of Irish descent and a first cousin of Eamon De Valera, who came west in March 1928 to be an insurance agent in Grays Harbor County. Coll served as a captain in the army during the war and was an enthusiastic member of the American Legion. When he went into the mills to sell insurance policies, he asked those he identified as veterans to join the Legion. To his surprise they all shook their heads and gave him disapproving looks.

Workers explained to him later, he recalled, that "until the American Legion rectified what it did in Centralia in 1919, workers would not think of joining the Legion."[27] Coll read in the newspapers in 1919 about the Centralia events and knew that Wobblies fired on men marching in an Armistice Day parade and killed four veterans. Now, he wondered, was there something he didn't know? He was sufficiently curious to find out. He read newspaper files, the pamphlets put out by the Centralia committee, talked to a number of persons in Centralia, and read much of the court record at the courthouse in Montesano. He became convinced that the Legion was in the wrong. The eight men had been unjustly convicted.

He went to Robert Le Roux, Hoquiam weekly newspaper publisher and commander of the Legion post, to suggest that the post reexamine the case. Le Roux said it might be well, as Coll suggested, to have Sam Crawford, a reporter who covered the events, appear before the post and review the case. But before the meeting at which Crawford was scheduled to speak, Le Roux took Coll aside and told him that it had been decided not to have any discussion of the Centralia case because it contained enough "dynamite to wreck the post."[28] Le Roux said there would be discussion of the case at the forthcoming state convention, which turned out to be the one that had passed a resolution, written by Cunningham, opposing parole for the prisoners.

Coll then addressed a lengthy letter to members of the Hoquiam Legion post in which he denounced Le Roux for dictating the policies of the post and said the Legion's attitude on the Centralia case was a detriment to the post's growth and caused members to stay away from meetings. He went on to say that evidence in the case made plain that the men in the parade were the aggressors at Centralia, citing the affidavits of jurors and witnesses. Coll, well educated and a former candidate for the Catholic priesthood, had a flair for eloquence and concluded his letter saying:

As in the famous Dreyfus case in France, so in this state of Washington, a great wrong has been done and the innocent party has suffered. Yet the day is coming when the prison doors will also open to liberate the innocent Walla Walla prisoners. Yes, and as a Legionnaire I wish to prevent the "Shrine of the American Legion" from becoming the shame of the American Legion, for a day of justice will yet dawn when the memorial statue on the pedestal in that city park of Centralia will assume the appearance of the torn, battered and mutiliated Wesley Everest, and beneath that statue will be inscribed the terrible indictment — "Mobbed and lynched for upholding his constitutional rights."

The letter was mimeographed and widely circulated. When a copy reached the publicity committee, Elmer Smith and C. S. Smith, the secretary, were almost as incredulous as they were overjoyed. Here was a Legionnaire saying just what they were saying, only better perhaps.

They hurried to Hoquiam where they called at Coll's home on October 1. They stayed until midnight, excitedly discussing the case. Coll later wrote,

I wish you could have been in my home that evening when Elmer Smith and C. S. Smith visited my wife and me. For years these two men had been laboring for the release of the eight Walla Walla prisoners. . . . Only powerful public demand could force either the governor or his parole board to weigh the true facts of the case. Of late it seemed that even the friends of the prisoners were becoming a little faltering in their support. Some liberals had grown indifferent or given up hope. Then, by a mere accident of fate, I came along.[29]

The Smiths left Coll's home with authorization to use his letter to the Hoquiam Legion. They did not delay getting it into print for distribution.

A few weeks later Coll went to Centralia and visited Cunningham and Dysart in their offices. He told them of conversations he had with members of the Grant Hodge post who admitted they saw men from the parade rush the IWW hall. The two attorneys told him these men would never dare repeat such stories in public. Coll conceded that they would not, for fear of losing their jobs or being denounced as disloyal to the dead martyrs. Then he visited Elmer Smith who invited him to participate in a public forum in Seattle.

"I discussed the matter with my wife when I got home and it was decided to tell the story everywhere," he recalled. "I wrote Elmer Smith what we had decided and some weeks later he and I addressed an overflow house in the Eagles' big hall in Seattle."[30]

When Smith saw that Coll was as eloquent on his feet as with a pen he made him an offer: one hundred dollars a month to join the speaking tour on a part-time basis. About this time the lumber business slipped into what was to become a long and deep depression and Coll could sell no insurance in Grays Harbor where men were being laid off, so he was glad to accept the offer, supplementing this income by selling men's suits door to door.

After that he spoke frequently throughout the state, always identifying himself as an American Legion member — one who knew the truth and was not afraid to speak up about it.

What he learned in a conversation with William Scales, "really clinched the case for me," Coll said.[31]

When I asked Postmaster Scales at Centralia about the part he played that day, he told me: "I saw Warren Grimm coming from the direction of the hall, his arms over his stomach and he was bent over in pain. He rounded the corner and fell." Scales knew that Grimm had been at the head of the raiders on the hall and actually a bullet from the Colt automatic of Wesley Everest had been the cause of his death. He later appealed three times to Governor Hartley to have the prisoners freed, for Scales was anxious to atone for what had taken place. . . . [32]

Scales told Coll he "forgot" that he had seen Barnett in the lobby of the Roderick minutes after the shooting. He said nothing for the record because he was not called as a witness for the prosecution. There seems to be no explanation why Vanderveer did not subpoena him.

In a lengthy address on Easter Sunday in Centralia Coll said Scales also told him that when he and a group of other ex-servicemen went into the lobby of the Roderick Hotel in search of IWW members just after

the shooting, he saw a young man talking with the proprietor, McAllister. "As Scales and his companions edged along the wall (gun in hand), watching the door of the inner room, the young man cautioned the armed men that there was a woman in that other room," Coll said. "Then, Mrs. McAllister came to the door where she not only gave Scales to understand that the young man was Eugene Barnett but she also informed him that Barnett had been in the hotel lobby during the raid and shooting. . . . "[33]

Both Coll and Smith in their frequent speeches took the position that all four of the slain ex-soldiers had been killed by Wesley Everest, firing from inside the hall, a contention in direct conflict with the testimony of numerous witnesses, including Earl Watt, who was himself wounded along with Ben Casagranda around the corner from the hall.

C. E. Payne, a member of the IWW General Defense Committee staff, echoed the admiration the IWW developed for Coll in an article he wrote for The Nation entitled, "Captain Coll, Legionnaire." Payne extolled the courage of Coll in daring to stand up for the Centralia prisoners (he did not mention that they were Wobblies) and told of an incident in Hoquiam when Coll induced Cunningham to engage him in debate. He quoted Cunningham as saying, "Even if we admit that those within the hall had a right to shoot, that does not give those over on the hill any justification for shooting." To this Coll replied: "Listen Cunningham, in my neighbor's yard, not far from my home in Aberdeen, there is a big tree that commands a view of both entrances to that home. If I hear that you are coming with a mob to raid my home, I will get behind that tree with every gun I can lay my hands on, and when you do come I will shoot every damn one of you."[34]

As 1928 drew to a close the publicity committee received further encouragement. The Reverend Fred Shorter of the fashionable Pilgrim Congregational Church in downtown Seattle joined with 125 delegates from sixty-three unions and other groups at a meeting where Coll was the main speaker. The group voted to organize and named an executive committee that included Shorter and John C. Kennedy, director of the Seattle Labor College.

The Reverend Shorter had not conferred with his church board about his conversion to the Wobbly side in the Centralia case and he was soon after relieved of his pastorship. "Fortunately the Reverend Shorter had an understanding and well-to-do mother," Coll wrote, "and he actually started a little mission on the Seattle skid road. He smilingly called it a 'Shorter but better way to Heaven.' Yes, it took courage to take the unpopular side of the Centralia case in those days."[35]

Intensifying its efforts, the defense committee in March 1929 organized an automobile caravan to bring in people from within a hundred miles of Centralia to attend a mass rally. The many who did come heard one of Ed Coll's impassioned orations.

In April Elmer Smith told an open-air mass meeting of several hundred that the parole for the Centralia men would be sought again at the June meeting of the parole board. Another resolution was drafted, passed, and sent to the governor.

The committee members reminded the governor that seven jurors had repudiated their verdict and that a member of the supreme court, Chief Justice Kenneth Mackintosh, had revealed his prejudice when he wrote a letter to a friend in Centralia before the appeal came to the high court in which he commended the Legion men in Centralia for their attitude toward the IWW. Hartley did admit at this point that some of the men ought to be eligible for parole the next year.

But he was still irritated by the tactics being used. "You're on the wrong trail, men, in appealing from the class standpoint," Hartley told a visiting delegation, headed by Carl Brannin of the Federal Labor Union in Seattle. "There's too much propaganda coming to me for them. I get letters from the East. What does a preacher in New York know about this case?"[36]

Elizabeth Gurley Flynn was national chairman of International Labor Defense. She descended upon Seattle to speak her militant piece. "These men are not in jail because they committed a crime," she shouted, "but because they represent the organized labor interest of the country. If the tables had been turned and if it were the IWW who had invaded an American Legion hall, and the Legionnaires had shot the intruders, they would have been hailed as heroes."[37] She then denounced Hartley, the parole board and the American Legion for keeping the men imprisoned.

The parole board members, like Hartley, were getting irritated by the persistent, demanding attitude of those seeking the release of the prisoners, but they were also impressed by the prominence of some of those they heard from.

David Starr Jordan, who was the chancellor of Stanford University, wrote as early as July 1928, saying: "It is certain that the treatment of the Centralia affair has counted as a disgrace to the State of Washington, and was a piece of injustice to more or less ignorant people. I sincerely hope . . . unconditional pardon is given to these people."[38]

Stephen B. Penrose, president of Whitman College, wrote in 1930 that although he had never taken any active interest in the Centralia prisoners, "I feel that it would be wise public policy to parole these prisoners. . . . I think that the majority of the people of the state would approve. . . ."[39]

J. M. Phillips, superior court judge in Grays Harbor County where the trial was held, wrote that he had "always been of the opinion that they did not have a fair trial. At the time of the trial the public was still in the grip of war emotion and the defendants were tried in an atmosphere intensely hostile toward them, and which in my judgment blew steadily against them, and which swept the court and jury along with it. . . ."[40]

W. H. Abel renewed his plea, telling the parole board that Eugene Barnett deserved parole.

The Reverend Hubert N. Dukes, minister of the Pilgrim Congregational Church in Lewiston, Idaho, analyzed feelings toward the Centralia case a decade after the violence occurred and wrote: "There is still strong feeling against any leniency in the case for there are many blinded by old prejudices. . . . The parole board knows full well the pressure against any action on their part. But a rising tide of protest is destined yet to bring in belated justice."[41]

When the Washington State Federation of Labor met in Bellingham in July 1929, it adopted another resolution calling for the release of the Centralia prisoners. The same month the members of the Willard Straight post of the American Legion in Washington, D.C., impressed by the writings of Coll and others, voted to ask National Commander Paul V. McNutt to appoint an impartial committee to investigate fully the Centralia case, the members of the investigating committee to be "from without the State of Washington."

But by this time another outside investigation was under way — one that was to bring to a climax the long efforts to free the Centralia Wobblies.

28

Labor Martyrs
in a Cause Célèbre

By 1929 an almost continuous stream of letters, petitions, and resolutions, not just from the Northwest but from around the country, flowed into Olympia. The Centralia case became a national cause celebre and the eight imprisoned men were identified as authentic labor martyrs.

Roland Hartley seethed under the relentless pressure. These men were Wobblies, the scum of the earth in his opinion. They deserved no sympathy, yet here were all these people writing and arguing and saying he was not doing the right thing. It was getting so, it seemed, that no one was backing him up except C. D. Cunningham and the Legion. Cunningham undertook to help by drafting a suggested stock reply the governor could use in answering the scores of letters he received. Hartley wrote back to thank him for the "sample letter," saying "this will help me greatly in answering this voluminous trash that comes into this office on the subject."[1]

One of the first to receive the stock reply was Ed Coll, who had tried flattery in a letter to Hartley. He sent one of his printed pieces about the Hoquiam Legion and wrote across the top: "Excellency, you remind me so much of the late Theodore Roosevelt in your courageous handling of political situations. I am convinced that the moral courage needed to deal with the Centralia case will yet be your brightest jewel."[2]

The new stock letter of reply said:

> Appealing to class and group prejudices, spreading propaganda, getting petitions signed, and the like, has no bearing in such affairs.... Justice is neither bought nor sold in the office of the governor.... Tearing down the government under which (the prisoners) expect to live if released does not improve the situation. The man who cannot support the flag and institutions of the government under which he lives should move where he can. The quicker these men in Walla Walla cut loose from the agitators and propagandists, the brighter their future.[3]

Letters from outside the state were particularly irritating to the governor. The National Economic League of Boston wrote saying it intended to "study the administration of justice in your state" and informed him he had been nominated for membership. Among those listed as members of the league's executive committee were John Hayes Hammond; William Allen White; Charles Schwab, chairman of Bethlehem Steel; A. Lawrence Lowell, president of Harvard University; Roger Babson, economist; David Starr Jordan, chancellor emeritus of Stanford University; George Wickersham, former attorney general; and Nicholas Murray Butler, president of Columbia University. It was an impressive array of distinguished people but no fit company for Roland Hartley. He informed the league that David Starr Jordan the year before wrote him appealing for clemency for the Centralia prisoners. "This plainly shows he is meddling with a vital and important subject in the state of Washington of which he knows nothing," Hartley wrote. "I do not wish to be a member of any organization ... along with such men as David Starr Jordan."[4]

Francis Ralston Welsh, a Philadelphia bond broker, wrote Hartley to inform him that Jordan was a member of the national committee of the ACLU "on which he associates with Communists, anarchists, insurrectionists and pullers-down generally."[5]

Hartley thanked Welsh and remarked: "There seems to be a propaganda drive on regarding the eight

IWWs who are serving time in our penitentiary. The data comes to this office from all over the United States and carries the same lies and misrepresentations regarding that awful piece of business in Centralia. Have often wondered why it is that so many men engaged in educational work are so twisted in their viewpoint of affairs of this sort. Letter writing is a slow way to combat this outfit. Better to swat them right and left in the public press."[6]

The persistence and persuasiveness of Smith and his followers had some effect even in Centralia, where nearly one hundred persons in 1929 were willing to sign a petition urging release of the prisoners. In April a delegation of approximately one hundred persons from Lewis County, having announced they were coming, descended on the governor's office. Hartley confronted them and expressed his usual displeasure. "When the judiciary comes forward and says there has been a mistake," he said, "and the petitioning groups plead for clemency rather than demand it, I will take some action."[7]

Not all union groups joined in applying pressure. The Seattle Central Labor Council expressed disapproval of the methods being used by the Centralia committee — especially when it sponsored picketing in Olympia — and accused it of capitalizing on the plight of the prisoners for private ends. The Seattle Federal Employees Union also announced it was "voting against the IWW."

In October Hartley gave the first hint of relenting when he wrote to the head of the prison to ask if he had a "missing file" containing a "transcript of new evidence" presented by sympathizers three years ago. "There is much agitation here from the sympathizers for a pardon," he wrote. "Many of them claim the sentence was illegal; that the minimum for the crime . . . is fixed by law and that the judge arbitrarily raised it from ten to twenty-five years. I wish to inform myself more fully on the details of the trial so that I may know better how to talk with those appealing to me."[8]

The governor, almost against his will, was being forced finally to do what so many others undertook on their own — a thorough study of the case. He must have felt inadequately informed when confronted by someone such as Elizabeth Attridge, a woman with so strong a social conscience that when she began reading the defense material she felt compelled to become involved even though she lived in Wisconsin. She was

an employee of the secretary of state's office in Madison so the ACLU suggested she make contact with "some of the liberal thinkers" on the campus of the state university there. This she did and found that they were already among those contributing to the flood of letters Hartley and the parole board were receiving from outside Washington. She contributed some money and this brought her each new piece of literature as it came out. Her interest was so much aroused she decided to participate in the crusade.

At first she was content to help by sending out letters by the hundreds, echoing the appeals originating in Centralia. Then she took a leave of absence from her job and headed west to join the fray.

Miss Attridge began by gathering information on her own. She spent ten days in Centralia finding and interviewing witnesses, all of whom confirmed her belief in the justice of the Wobbly cause. "I have every reason to believe these people are truthful," she wrote to Hartley, for "I had nothing to offer them one way or another for the testimony they gave."[9]

She went to Walla Walla and was able to visit the prisoners. They filed into the visiting room, surprised to find a young woman — a stranger — who had come all the way from Wisconsin to see if there was something she could do to help them. "How glad they were for a caller," she wrote. And little wonder, for there weren't many callers, partly because Walla Walla was in a remote corner of the state, reachable only by a long journey by train or car, and partly because interest in their case was dwindling with the sheer passage of time. For ten years they had been locked up, their hopes frequently raised by the willingness of so many to work for their release, but as often disappointed by the failure of those efforts and the rock-hard wall of official opposition, as unyielding as the high walls of the old prison that held them.

A lengthy account of Elizabeth Attridge's independent investigation was published by the publicity committee and given the usual wide circulation.[10] Some dismissed her simply as a do-gooder from out of state meddling in local affairs. But her approach was like that of Ed Coll — someone coming into the case at a late date, knowing nothing about it, gathering information on her own, and coming to an independent conclusion. Her tract made persuasive reading.

One of the "liberal thinkers" to whom Miss Attridge wrote was Mrs. Kate Crane-Gartz of Altadena,

Courtesy of Virginia Smith Waddell

The Smith family in the 1920s: from left, Harry, Glen, Dorothy, Isobel (mother), Willard, Elmer, and James. The snapshot was taken by the children's father.

California, who wrote an appeal to Governor Hartley. This brought the standard form reply drafted for the governor by Cunningham. It asserted that the trial was fair, the law followed, and the men guilty of murder and being justly punished, and that anyone who thought otherwise was out of bounds.

Mrs. Crane-Gartz was not one to be put off. She wrote again, and again, and each time was rebuffed. Her indignation mounted until in May 1930, she fired off a last scathing volley:

> Is it possible that you enjoy the slings and arrows hurled at you for the last twelve years because of your adamantine front toward innocent men confined in the penitentiary? What more can the world do toward a man like you, who has the power of life and death over human beings, and remains adamant, despite beseeching appeals from softer hearted people for innocent men? . . . What can we do to or with our public servants to make them human beings first? They are the ones who believe in force and violence and so the just words of just people fall on deaf ears. They are waiting for a big noise to jolt them off their pedestals. . . .[11]

What more could the world do toward a man like Hartley? No one knew. If there had been no IWW issue involved, and it was merely a question of whether the trial was fair, Hartley might have reacted differently. But in a state with a law that made it illegal even to belong to the IWW — and these eight men were admittedly Wobblies — he could muster no sympathy for them at all. As he said in his stock letter of reply, "Tearing down the government under which they expect to live, if released, does not improve the situation." He was saying that the men should continue to be kept locked up not because of what happened in Centralia but because they were Wobblies. If the men had renounced allegiance to the IWW and claimed they were reformed and now believed in capitalism and the flag and all they stood for, it is likely that Hartley would have approved parole, perhaps even granted pardons with a gesture of triumph like an evangelist welcoming converts down front at the close of a preaching engagement. But they defied him. They wouldn't recant. And so they stayed locked up.

Elmer Smith of course was discouraged. He had worked for ten years and nothing happened. But he

208

wouldn't admit failure. He kept looking for new ways to dent the opposition. He wrote Herman Allen, by then living in San Diego, pleading with him to do as W. H. Abel had done. "Will you join with us at this late hour and try to right the wrong that has been committed against these men so far as this can now be done?" he wrote.[12] If Allen replied at all it was to reject the request. Abel was the only one of the prosecutors who could bring himself to recommend any leniency.

Smith tried appealing to sympathy. Eugene Barnett wrote Smith to say he was shattered because his wife served him with divorce papers, and asked Smith to tell the governor that if he could be put on the list for consideration at the next parole board meeting, his wife might reconsider. Smith sent Hartley a copy of the letter, adding, "No comment is necessary other than to say it will surely give you some idea of the tragedy of keeping innocent men in prison."

One letter Hartley was glad to receive came from Warren Grimm's widow, who took the position of librarian of the American Legion when the national library was established in Indianapolis. Verna Grimm said she had

carefully followed the strong demand that is constantly being made by various elements upon you and the parole board to free the men who were guilty of Warren's death. I have noted your splendid attitude in the matter and want you to know I deeply appreciate it.

I am not vindictive nor do I want other wives and children to suffer, but to free these men ... would seem to justify their act and reflect upon the sacrifice made by Warren and the others who died.... The continuous agitation and unscrupulous methods have distressed me greatly but I am comforted by the thought that the responsible officials of my state have a true sense of right and have held to it."[13]

Sometimes the defense speakers, in their zeal to get a reaction from the crowd at hand, would say something detrimental to their cause. An example was a speech Ed Coll made on Easter in 1929 before a large gathering in Centralia. He said the innocent minds of children were being given a perverted version of true history when they were shown the wording on the statue erected to the memory of the four servicemen "slain on the streets of Centralia," which made no mention of the fifth ex-servicemen who also was slain that day. Coll then said he intended to found a Wesley Everest Memorial Hall in Chehalis and urged the formation of a "Committee to Clear Wesley Everest."[14]

Coll's suggestions were not followed. Thirty years were to pass before the IWW even got around to putting a small marker on Everest's grave. The suggestion that Everest, too, deserved a memorial in Centralia was not one that could be expected to alleviate Hartley's chronic and incurable case of the "Wobbly horrors."

29

Enter the Church

It was the church, of all things, that came at last with an effective rescue effort for the Centralia prisoners. Church interest came unexpectedly to the fore in 1929 but it was not of spontaneous origin, unlike that of the many who, when finally informed, felt a crusading urge to help straighten out a great social injustice. It began as early as 1919 when some segments of organized religion in the Northwest showed at least a little interest in the plight of loggers. But the religious community was just as stunned by the events in Centralia as the populace generally and little sympathy was expressed for Wobblies from pulpits or in church literature for the next ten years.

The early miserable conditions common to logging and sawmilling caused a few men of the cloth to dare say that such earthly matters should be the concern of those charged with carrying Christ's teachings into the twentieth century. One of these was Rev. Worth M. Tippy, a Methodist with a strong sense of missionary zeal who came to the Northwest in the winter of 1919 amid the hysteria occasioned by Centralia. He picked up enough information about working conditions to produce a detailed report on logging camps, together with recommendations for making improvements.[1]

The Reverend Tippy observed what to him seemed to be strange customs. Men worked eight hours for forty to ninety cents an hour, but, he wrote, "at meals the men eat in silence and it is a part of the etiquette that no one shall talk. In one of the camps I found a sign posted to this effect. They ate so rapidly that I was not more than half through when the men got up almost en masse and went out."[2]

For most people, dining together is a social matter, providing a time for pleasant conversational exchanges, but not so in logging camps. The Reverend Tippy may have heard that the custom of silence

originated from a desire to forestall complaints about the food, the wage scale, or the stinks and discomforts of bunkhouse living, but whatever it was, the Reverend Tippy didn't consider it normal. He also noticed the almost complete lack of reading matter in camp except the inflammatory journals of discontent smuggled in by the IWW. He noted that the camp superintendents were "uncompromisingly against the IWW" and discharged all IWW organizers.

The Reverend Tippy suggested to his church that a system of industrial chaplains be established. These chaplains could reside in central places and visit surrounding camps, showing movies, giving classes in English and Americanization, and holding discussions of religious and social questions, thereby "relieving the loneliness of the forest and the long evenings." He said the present suppression of free discussion in the camps was ineffective. "At the same time it is forcing one-sided and fanatical social propaganda," he wrote. "The men would be brought to see that there are various methods of social reconstruction."[3]

In the years following 1919 a few hardy ministers did undertake to work in the logging camps. The new Long-Bell logging town of Ryderwood in Cowlitz County had a company-paid minister and a church building from its beginning in 1924. Another Methodist pioneer was Robert C. Hartley whose work among loggers and lumbermen was commended by Dr. (later Bishop) G. Bromley Oxnam.

"Sky pilots," the preachers who worked the logging camps were called, but there were nine hundred camps in the region and only a handful of ministers to do the missionary work. Occasionally a Wobbly organizer would get admission to a camp by posing as a "sky pilot," taking advantage of the superintendents' willingness to extend a welcome — anything to get the men's minds off IWWism and discontent.

Robert Hartley preached in McCleary, a company town owned by Henry McCleary, for seven months on Sunday nights. He found the men "respectful and responsive." The nearby Simpson Logging Company made major improvements in its camps — steam heat, hot water in the bunkhouses, and free towels and soap. As a consequence its turnover was small and it had no Wobbly trouble.

The Episcopal church also saw opportunities to tell loggers there was a gospel better than that preached by the IWW. In 1920 it considered establishing the equivalent of YWCA hostel houses in the logging country. Blanch Wenner, who served the YWCA overseas, told a church gathering that "with a cup of coffee and a piece of pie backed up by the influence of a couple of good women we were able to stand off the onslaught of beer halls, wine dives, and the scarlet women in our little upstairs room in Germany." The establishment of similar huts in logging camps, she was sure, would convince loggers that the church did not represent the capitalism they abhorred.[4]

The Episcopalians were so intrigued with what looked like an opportunity to do something in a peaceful way to combat the IWW that it appropriated twenty-five thousand dollars to carry on the work.

The Methodist organization included a Social Service Commission which concerned itself with labor matters, sending its representatives to union conventions, influencing union voting on the "wet-dry" issue, and appealing for settlement of labor-management disputes "on the basis of human welfare and the pronouncements of Jesus Christ."[5] The commission members leaned toward the side of labor and proved their sympathy by saying, "We believe that the first charge upon any industry is an adequate living wage approximating the American standard for the toilers in that industry." Then, "in the name of justice," it called upon President Harding to review the cases of all prisoners held for violation of the wartime espionage act.[6] Finally, the commission baldly recommended what the Wobblies were crying out for, to the consternation of the American Legion — repeal of Washington's antisyndicalism law "so as to make impossible the imprisonment of men who have not so much as given expression to opposition to government much less have committed an overt act."[7]

Through the 1920s the churches continued to do some missionary work among the loggers but saw the need for it diminishing as working conditions improved and better roads made it possible for men to get out of the woods more often, and for more reading material other than IWW literature to get in. The isolation of the woods also was lessened by an innovation of the time — radio.

Those men of the church who worked with loggers, reading and hearing much about the Centralia case and the plight of the prisoners, gradually became convinced that there were sufficient overtones of injustice about the case to justify the organized church getting involved. They so informed their respective denominational superiors.

When the Methodists gathered in annual convention in 1927 their Social Service Commission was ready to recommend action. It presented a resolution calling for a committee "to make a thorough and impartial investigation of the alleged crime of these men and their convictions in order that we have a complete, reliable and unbiased information on all matters relating thereto . . . ."[8] And it shouldn't be a Methodist committee only. The help of the Federal Council of Churches "and any other organization that may help us come to wise conclusions" should be sought.

In debate on the resolution one minister expressed the fear that such an investigation would stir up trouble, perhaps even "dynamitings and explosions." But a majority did not share his timidity and the resolution was passed.

The Grant Hodge Legion post was disturbed by this unexpected show of interest. This was the first time any respectable state organization had said publicly that there was anything about the Centralia case that should be investigated. The Legion post that rounded up those responsible for the deaths of four of its members and helped try and convict them could not understand why anyone except radicals and their friends would raise questions now, ten years later.

A statement running to nearly a thousand words was addressed to the Puget Sound conference of the Methodist Episcopal church and printed for widespread distribution. In it the Legion expressed disbelief that the church was suggesting that the convicted men might not be criminals. "It must be the purpose of this investigation," it said, "to determine the honesty, integrity and fairness of the judge . . . and of the members of the supreme court who affirmed the judgment."[9] A second purpose could be to determine whether errors of law had been committed.

The statement was signed by J. C. Hampe, commander, and G. D. Rowe, adjutant, but the language, with its legalese, was unmistakably Cunningham's.

It was assumed, the statement went on to say, that the committee would only do what the clergymen authorized — that is, investigate only the record and the judgment made on such findings, and not examine statements or affidavits or other information gathered after the trial that had not been subjected to the scrutiny of cross-examination. This was the lawyer speaking — Cunningham — who, like Judge Wilson, insisted throughout his life that a trial is a trial and that the result of it cannot be evaluated on the basis of anything not presented in the courtroom. The Legion statement undertook to instruct the church committee and to caution it against being misled by pseudo-evidence and testimony put together by others after the trial and supreme court review.

The expectation that an independent committee would be governed by the Legion's demands — and they were indeed expressed as demands — was an unrealistic one.

The churchmen were more likely to be sympathetic with the views of the Reverend Aaron Allen Heist, pastor of the Grace Community Church in Denver, who wrote to the parole board in late 1928 to say that he had been pastor of the First Methodist Church in Aberdeen in 1919 and had an

> unusual opportunity to study the case. . . . There was never any doubt in my mind that the conviction and sentence of the eight men was a flagrant miscarriage of justice. . . . You and I know full well that the attitude of "He is a Wobbly and so deserves anything you can give him" has been all too prevalent in the state of Washington. It seems to me that the supreme evidence of the unfair attitude of the public is to be found in the fact that there never has been a demand for the punishment of the brutal mutilation and lynching of Welsey Everest.[10]

The Social Service Commission could not have been surprised when the Centralia Methodist Church formally expressed sharp dissent with the proposal of the Puget Sound conference to investigate the case. That church had too many relatives and friends of the victims in its congregation to allow it to approve anything that might question the black guilt of the men who fired the fatal shots on Tower Avenue.

The boldness of the Methodists in daring to raise an issue about the case impressed other denominations. The Congregationalists, when they met in the spring of 1929, approved the appointment of a five-member committee to work with the Methodist committee and together they petitioned the Federal Council of Churches in New York, which responded enthusiastically and invited the Central Conference of American Rabbis to join in, making the endeavor an ecumenical one.

The Baptists were more cautious. Their convention, held in Everett in May, was "thrown into an uproar," the press reported, when the Reverend Marion E. Bollen, pastor of the University Baptist Church in Seattle, introduced a resolution asking for a Centralia investigating committee. The motion to pass was tabled. But three days later the uproar died down enough to get it approved.

The Legion's alarm mounted. The national office proposed a counteroffensive consisting of a nationwide education effort to instruct Legionnaires on the right answers to give when asked why church groups were investigating the case.

Ed Coll was delighted with the developments. A devout Catholic himself, he used his church connections to encourage Catholic participation. When Coll studied for the priesthood in the North American College in Rome, a fellow student was Robert McGowan. Coll left the college to join the military when the war began and never returned, but McGowan did and became a priest. By 1929 he was assistant director of the Social Action Group of the Catholic Welfare Conference. Later he became a bishop.

Coll sent a thick bundle of material about the Centralia case to Father McGowan who passed it on to Father John A. Ryan, director of the Department of Social Action. In May Coll wrote to Father Ryan to say that the Reverend Worth Tippy, now with the Federal Council of Churches, called to discuss the Centralia case and said he was endeavoring to get the Catholic Welfare Conference to participate in the planned investigation. Coll tried to see Bishop S. J. O'Dea in the fall of 1928 in Seattle but could not get past Monsignor Theodore Ryan, chancellor of the diocese. Ryan told Coll the bishop couldn't get involved but would not oppose any action taken by the Catholic Welfare Conference. It was a hopeless cause anyway, Ryan said, and he doubted if the Federal Council of Churches would really make an investigation.[11]

In June Coll made a final attempt to influence Bishop O'Dea. He wrote to Monsignor Ryan,

It has taken months of arduous work to bring about the present favorable attitude of these great national groups, the Federal Council and the Council of Rabbis and our own National Catholic Welfare Group — and I know you would not checkmate our efforts by withholding Father Ryan's entry into the coming investigation. It is not my wish to inconvenience Bishop O'Dea, so I am going to ask you, Monsignor, to advise me whether his Lordship would be willing to grant me a personal interview with you some day to review this case. . . .[12]

Bishop O'Dea was not interested in hearing from anyone on the IWW side of the issue. He knew quite enough already about the Wobblies. But he was moved to seek the advice of some prominent Catholic laymen about the propriety of the Northwest church joining an investigation of the Centralia case. Among these was W. W. Conner, a Seattle insurance broker and a close friend of Governor Hartley.

Conner informed the bishop it was all a political matter, with the American Legion on one side and the IWW on the other. Even if pardons were recommended by the churches, he said, the governor would not grant them. Conner claimed he had been offered several thousand dollars, because of his closeness to the governor, to help obtain pardons. "I do not believe the state should interfere with religious matters," Conner wrote. "I do not believe the church should inject itself into state matters. I believe it is our duty to accept the verdict of the jury as approved by the trial court and the supreme court."[13]

That was enough for Bishop O'Dea. He instructed Monsignor Ryan to write to Father John Ryan saying that "because of the general sentiment prevailing here regarding the notorious Centralia case, the bishop believes that it is inadvisable for the National Catholic Welfare Conference to become involved in this affair. However, should the conference deem otherwise, the bishop will have no objections."[14]

Father John Ryan read Conner's letter and was dismayed. Any doubts he had before about the Centralia case, he said, were "considerably strengthened" by the letter. Ryan had worked for two years in behalf of

men sentenced to from one to twenty years under the federal espionage act. "By any fair test none of these men should have received a longer sentence than ninety days," he wrote.

Nevertheless it was for a long time impossible to get prominent persons interested in their plight, mainly because they listened to arguments such as those set forth by Mr. Conner, namely, that the prisoners belong to a detested society and therefore are presumably guilty of whatever crimes are charged against them; that on general principle they ought to be in jail anyhow; that they must have had a fair trial since they had a trial; and finally, that the persons most interested in seeking pardon are members of unrespectable associations and therefore presumably actuated by unworthy motives. Of course none of these contentions touches the main question — which is whether these men had a fair trial.[15]

Father John Ryan then wrote to Archbishop Hanna of San Francisco, chairman of the National Catholic Welfare Conference, and urged that the conference join in the investigation despite the opposition of Bishop O'Dea. Hanna agreed.

So finally the interchurch alliance was completed. And it was an impressive one, and rare — Protestants, Catholics, and Jews — all agreeing that after ten years the "notorious Centralia case," with eight men still locked in prison on account of it, was so tinged with implications of injustice that it deserved the undivided attention of the country's combined religious community.

A plan was agreed upon. An investigator would be sent to the Northwest to get the facts. He would then prepare a report that would be issued in the name of all three church bodies. It would be studied and edited, then published. That would be all. No campaign would be carried on in behalf of the imprisoned men if the investigation favored their cause.

The man chosen to study the case was considered ideally qualified because he was both a graduate of Union Theological Seminary and a lawyer. He was DeWitte Wyckoff, forty-two, legal counsel for the American Bankers Association in New York. The association gave him a leave of absence to undertake the unusual assignment. As a lawyer he was expected to have an understanding of the workings of the law in the case, and as a theologian he would not overlook the humanitarian aspects of it.

Wyckoff met with representatives of the three sponsoring bodies to get his instructions in October 1929, and on November 4, almost ten years to the day after Armistice Day 1919, he and his wife and two young sons set out for the West to learn the truth, once and for all, about the celebrated Centralia case.

A cooperating committee had been appointed by the several church groups in the Northwest to help with the investigation. The chairman was the Right Reverend S. Arthur Huston, bishop of the Episcopal diocese of Olympia. Others on the committee included Dr. J. Ralph Magee, district superintendent of the Methodist church; Rabbi Samuel Koch of the Temple de Hirsch; and the Reverend E. Raymond Attebury, who acted as secretary.

"This committee has been earnest, active and efficient in its cooperation," Wyckoff wrote at the conclusion of his six-month stay in the Northwest.

Certain of its members participated in conducting interviews. An extensive study has been made, with the aid of legal counsel, covering the entire court record, newspaper files, and much other documentary material. Many personal interviews were had, with the governor, the trial judge, the present chief justice of the state supreme court, who wrote the opinion of the court in the case, members of the staff of the prosecution, ministers, American Legion members, members of the Industrial Workers of the World and their sympathizers, nine of the jurors, and all of the prisoners."[16]

Wyckoff devoted every day of his stay to the investigation. Most of his time was spent in Olympia, Centralia, and Seattle, with shorter stays in Montesano, Hoquiam, Aberdeen, Walla Walla, and Portland. The person who worked most closely with him was the Reverend Frank E. Carlson, pastor of the United Congregational Church in Olympia. The clergy in Centralia carefully avoided him except one, the Reverend Fred Lucas, who was the pastor of the Emmanuel English Lutheran Church.[17]

At the end of each day Wyckoff dictated a report on his findings to Mrs. Wyckoff. She transcribed it and sent it to the Council of Churches offices in New York. Thus the sponsoring committee of Jews, Catholics, and Protestants had the benefit of the vast amount of material concerning the case that resulted from

DeWitte Wyckoff, sent to investigate the Centralia case by three national church bodies in 1929.

Courtesy C. Campbell Wyckoff

Wyckoff's painstaking day-by-day investigation. The report subsequently published was written originally by Wyckoff upon his return to New York, but those who worked with him in drafting it and editing it were men who by then knew as much about the case as Wyckoff himself. The report was not the judgment of the investigator alone.

When Wyckoff was satisfied that he had talked to everyone connected with the case whom he could reach and had read the court record, studied newspaper accounts, and conferred at length with persons who were as much convinced that the Centralia prisoners had been fairly tried as others were that they had not, he packed the great volume of notes he had accumulated and returned to New York. There he devoted several weeks to the task of condensing the information into a report that was submitted to the committee of the three sponsoring church groups. The committee members were Father McGowan, Rabbi Edmund Israel, and Dr. Ernest Johnson. The New York committee wanted the sponsoring committee in the Northwest to review the report while it was still in the editing process. Episcopal Bishop Arthur Huston, chairman of the Northwest committee, made a last attempt to get Bishop O'Dea involved. He wrote inviting O'Dea to appoint someone to join in reviewing the report. The records do not show that he did.

The first draft of the report was reviewed not only by the church committee but by Cunningham, who was given a copy by the Reverend Attebury and told he had a week in which to submit written comments. Cunningham sent his comments directly to Wyckoff in a lengthy eighteen-page letter, in which he was critical in the extreme since Wyckoff had done just what the Legion demanded originally not be done — give consideration to what was not in the court record. He said that if the report were going to contain details about anti-Wobbly activities in Centralia prior to Armistice Day, it ought also to tell about the things that produced anti-Wobbly feelings — "sabotage, destruction of crops and farm machinery, dynamiting of buildings and other acts of violence including the hijacking and robbing of workmen who refused to join the IWW; their unpatriotic actions and conduct during the war, and by their advocacy of the overthrow of all orderly government."[18] Cunningham wrote that "there is nothing stated in the report, or that has come to this writer's attention in the years that have gone by since the trial that has ever caused a change of that opinion."

Cunningham did concede, "Looking back now after a lapse of years, and taking a judicial view of the whole affair, it must be admitted that mistakes were made, both by the prosecution and by the defense. That is to be expected."[19]

Cunningham also was consulted about details in the report. A member of the federal council staff wrote asking about the accusation that funds raised by the Legion to use in prosecuting the IWW were not opened for inspection. Cunningham disclaimed any knowledge of such fund-raising, except for some money that was raised by individual Legion posts to send observers to the Montesano trial.[20]

The passing around of the manuscript and the editing of it through several drafts took months. It was gone over meticulously for, as the committee well knew, it was being awaited by many eager to find flaws that would justify criticism if the report did not favor their side of the story. Wyckoff did not approve of all the editing, feeling that several items he considered to be of vital importance were omitted in the finished draft.[21] On the whole, however, he was satisfied with the report after it was edited down to a remarkably tight fifteen thousand words and published in a forty-eight-page pamphlet.

The report related the background of the case, telling of the reputation of the IWW, the early instances of violence involving the IWW in the Northwest, and the organization of the Citizens Protective Association in Centralia in the spring of 1919 to cope with the local Wobbly problem. It told of the efforts of Mrs. McAllister to get police protection and quoted from the printed appeal of the Centralia Wobblies that was distributed a few days before the parade. The events of Armistice Day were described in detail.

The report stated that the main question in dispute was which side was the aggressor. "While a prior rush toward the hall is not conclusively shown," it reads, "it appears more probable that this occurred than that the shooting took place first."[22]

Other conclusions of the church report included the following:

1. The mass of evidence "casts serious doubt on the charge that Barnett was present in the Avalon and participated in the defense of the hall." The jury's original finding that he was guilty of "third-degree murder" indicated it did not believe he was the one

who fired the shot that killed Warren Grimm.

2. The weight of testimony at the trial indicated that Lieutenant Grimm did not participate in an attack. The positive assertions of those working for the release of the prisoners that he actually led an attack on the hall was based chiefly on affidavits made after the trial, and must be considered much less reliable than courtroom testimony.

3. The story of the mutilation of Everest could not be verified.

4. The American Legion made a "quiet, determined resolve" to insist on further prosecution, in order that the crime should not go "inadequately punished." These declared intentions, however, were not carried out. Vanderveer moved for a new trial. This afforded an opportunity for the prosecution to secure what it would consider a "proper conviction," under the rule in the state of Washington that a prior conviction for a lower degree of crime does not preclude a conviction of higher degree on a new trial. But the motion for a new trial was strenuously resisted by the prosecution and was denied by the court.

5. The halting of the Centralia contingent in front of the IWW hall was probably by design, since some of the Legionnaires immediately interpreted it as a signal for hostilities and offered to rush the hall. Some one of the waiting Wobblies either inside or outside the hall could have precipitated the affair by firing sooner than his comrades in the hall expected or intended. At the distance of Seminary Hill it would be easy to confuse a bunching of men in the street with an actual attack on the building.

6. It is probable that Grimm was shot from the Avalon Hotel, and while he was standing in the street at the head of his contingent.

7. It is probable that Barnett was not in the Avalon but the Roderick, and therefore did not shoot Grimm.

8. As to the question of whether the rush on the hall or the shooting occurred first, no exact answer is possible. The most that can be said with assurance is that the movement of the paraders in front of the hall made it appear to the waiting IWWs that an attack was commencing, or, at least, was imminent.

9. Waiving legal technicalities, it is difficult to see how the exclusion of evidence concerning the raid on the IWW hall, which had occurred during the year previous, could be other than prejudicial. The same can be said of the exclusion of evidence concerning the

activities of the Citizens' Protective League and the employers' meeting of October 20. By judicial ruling matters of the utmost significance in interpreting the acts of the defendants were excluded from the trial.

10. The presence of federal troops at Montesano created an atmosphere that was not conducive to the rendering of impartial justice.

11. The theory underlying the verdict seems to have been that the prisoners had not conspired to kill wantonly but had intended to defend their hall from attack, but that, on the other hand, they were acting illegally in placing armed men outside the hall. Thus the verdict appears to have dealt what the jurors, in their own minds, considered to be rough justice.

12. It is impossible to exclude from consideration the many acts of violence against the IWW for which no one was prosecuted. The earlier raid on the IWW hall, the destruction of that organization's property on this occasion, the deliberate lynching of one of their number, the violence committed during the manhunt, as well as earlier acts of violence, have gone without investigation or punishment.

13. The lynching of Everest before the death of the man he shot was a particularly revolting affair. The reason assigned by the prosecuting attorney for not prosecuting those responsible is that the perpetrators are not known. There is evidence, however, that the names of some who took part could be ascertained. The severe treatment accorded this little group of radicals considered alongside the immunity given to those who committed the crimes against them makes a deadly parallel.

14. The action taken by the members of the Citizens' Protective League at their meeting prior to Armistice Day was unjustifiable and lawless. The mood of revolt which had come over these Wobblies was fortified by a deep sense of social injustice and economic disadvantage and the plan to deal with them by violence only deepened their resentment and goaded them to violent resistence.

15. Failure of the police to give protection to the hall was neglect of duty, inasmuch as the police had been informed a raid was possible.

16. Legion leaders who took part in the planning of violent measures against the IWW must have known that they were allowing the patriotic impulses of the Legion to be exploited by the interests of lumber operators in a way that concerned many of the Legion

members not at all. This attack was no noble patriotic demonstration. Economic interest and class solidarity were powerful and obvious influences in the tide of feelings which broke into hysteria and fury on that Armistice Day. The fact that the desired result could not be arrived at by legal measures should have been an effective deterrent to men of patriotic spirit.

17. The course the IWW took in deciding to defend the hall with arms, rather than removing their effects and absenting themselves until after the parade, was clearly wrong since it involved almost certain loss of life on both sides. As it was they lost everything and completely frustrated their own purposes.

18. The verdict was manifestly a compromise. The jury was apparently seeking the closest possible approximation to justice. The effort, however, was thwarted by the court in the imposition of long sentences. It is at this point that the disinterested student of the trial gains the strongest impression of injustice, which is sharply accentuated by the fact that shameful crimes against the IWW have gone unpunished.

The church report concluded with the following observations:

Throughout this whole tragedy passion reigned. Businessmen, raiders and IWWs alike were in a state of mind which does not lend itself to reason. The fury of the lynching, the hunting down of the IWW, the killing of a posse member and the plea that such killing was accidental and even justifiable because the man was mistaken for an IWW, the policing of the city by Legionnaires, and the conduct of the trial, are indications, after the event, of the state of mind which led to the tragedy. The outstanding feature of this whole series of events was the passion of the community, which made sound moral judgments impossible. Both sides used social dynamite and neither seems to have realized the magnitude of its offense.

The Centralia story is a vivid warning of his duty to the man who feels the pull of a current of mass excitement and the quickening of the pulse that heralds the surrender of reason to mob passion. Those who feel the rising tide of passion, who lend themselves to its increase, or make no effort to lessen its force, are far from guiltless of the consequences. The six IWWs in Walla Walla penitentiary are paying the penalty for their part in a tragedy the guilt for which is by no means theirs alone. They alone were indicted: they alone have been punished.[23]

30

End of the Long Road

The joint church report was issued simultaneously in New York and Seattle on October 13, 1930. It made headlines but not very large ones except in the IWW press. Summaries of it were difficult for news writers because the report did not come right out and say that all was wrong on one side and all was right on the other. It found faults on both sides, but it was not another compromise verdict. It said the Wobblies did have reason to believe their hall would be raided and so had valid motives for defending it, although the way they chose to do it was foolish.

The conclusion that the men in prison were paying the penalty for a guilt that was not theirs alone suggested that it was time to set them free, and Episcopal Bishop Arthur Huston announced immediately that the report would be used as the basis for renewed efforts to achieve that long-sought objective. The report was not similarly interpreted, however, by the many, probably still a majority, whose IWW prejudices were too deeply ingrained ever to allow them to concede that anyone involved in the gunfire of the "Centralia Massacre" should be shown any leniency.

The IWW hierarchy in Chicago was not pleased with the report either because it did not endorse the official IWW position — that the Legionnaires who raided the hall should have been punished, not the courageous men who defended it. The sardonic headline in *Industrial Solidarity* read:

CENTRALIA CASE REPORT
MADE BY CHURCH BODIES INDICATES BIAS
OF ALL SUCH FOLK IN CLASS WAR.

To the IWW not even priests, pastors, or rabbis could be unbiased when it came to social justice. "All such folk" were always biased. The Centralia defendants, said *Industrial Solidarity*, were neither legally nor morally guilty.

The *Seattle Times*, as unyielding as ever on the Wobbly issue, called the report "shameful." The Federal Council of Churches, it said, should have enough to occupy its attention without running "off into matters that cannot be construed as any of their business." But "once again the agents of the Federal Council are adventuring in a matter that they have no qualifications to discuss. . . . The men who signed the report blaming everybody but the IWW for what happened at Centralia ought to be ashamed of themselves."[1]

Elmer Smith and the Centralia Publicity Committee did not share Chicago's views. They were pleased enough with the report's conclusions to publish them in full immediately and to commend the "splendid and sincere efforts of many honest and upright men back of this investigation by the churches." They could not, however, refrain from criticizing portions of the report for giving what they said was undue weight to evidence submitted by the prosecution at the trial — evidence they termed "schooled perjury."

The joint committee and DeWitte Wyckoff made no comments about reactions to their report. They were not, after all, purporting to speak as one voice for all of Catholicism, Protestantism, and Jewry. They were only the social action arms of three religious bodies which were assigned to make an investigation and that was done. Their task was finished. If there was to be any follow-up, any action taken, it would be up to others.

Ministers and church boards in the Northwest and elsewhere read summaries of the report, and some read the report itself, and wondered what if anything they should say or do about it. Social action was not something churches felt they needed to give much attention to in 1930. It was the year the Great Depression began, leading to drastic reforms in thinking about governmental obligations to accept responsibility for reforms in social areas, but the reforms had to wait until the political upheaval of 1932 and so also did most of the Centralia prisoners.

A few church publications had the courage to discuss the report. One of the more influential and widely read, the *Christian Advocate,* published the conclusions of the investigation just as the Centralia committee had done. This prompted a reader to inquire why such a respected journal would devote so much space to the sordid Centralia case. The *Advocate's* editorial board responded in its next issue with four reasons why Christians should concern themselves with the case:

1. Though the Centralia killings occurred in a remote corner of the Union, they might have happened in any state. The feelings which clashed there did not originate in local grievances, but in a generally prevalent state of mind. The warning which the investigators uttered in the closing paragraphs is as valuable in New York as in Skykomish.

2. There is a widespread belief that at the time of the Centralia killings, the Mooney affair in San Francisco and other outbreaks of violence, the feverish state of mind in America made it difficult for the courts to administer justice with an even hand. Ten years have passed and presumably have calmed the troubled seas. It is a propitious time to appeal from Philip drunk to Philip sober. Hence a justification of the opening of the case.

3. Justice is a quality of religion. If injustice has been done at Centralia or elsewhere it is the business of Christian men who are aware of the facts to bring them to light and see that justice is done, however tardily. The Master did not draw any line between secularity and spirituality. All life was to be lived well and in the spirit of a God of love. Could the Christian ministers of the Pacific Northwest stand in their pulpits on Sunday and preach love and mercy and justice while their fellow men were rotting in jail under what many believed to be an unjust sentence?

4. The Centralia case had been lifted out of its local setting into national prominence and significance. It had become in a sense a test of the churches, whether they retained enough of the spirit of Christ to undertake an unpopular investigation and carry it through. That it was done, impartially and thoroughly, is, in our opinion, greatly to the credit of the Federal Council's Research Commission.

Finally, why should the *Advocate* print it? Simply because most of the dailies would not. . . .

Furthermore, Armistice Day is at hand. It is a day when we feel in duty bound to exert ourselves not only to prevent the recurrence of war, but to prevent the recrudescence of the spirit which grows out of war, and out of which wars grow. Centralia was a private war, a war in miniature, with passion and a bloodthirst that make war hateful.[2]

The *Advocate* identified the conflict properly. It was a war, but hardly a private one. The forces that told Bishop O'Dea to keep Northwest Catholics on the sidelines while other Catholics joined in getting at the truth — the forces which caused successive Washington governors to reject all appeals — were stronger in the Northwest than the editors realized.

A former national vice-commander of the Legion, John J. Sullivan, came forward with an idea he hoped might counter the church report. He suggested that Governor Hartley appoint an impartial commission to hear evidence from both sides on what actually did occur in the trial and make a recommendation concerning the release of the prisoners. As usual Hartley saw no reason to do anything. He agreed with Cunningham. The courses of the law were followed. Judge Wilson, called upon for a comment, took that position also. W. H. Abel, by then a superior court judge, said those making an investigation ten years after the event could not get as good a grasp of the circumstances as the judge and jury were able to during the trial.

A minister who claimed he was threatened with lynching in San Jose, California, the night of November 11, 1919, when he said something construed to be defensive of the Wobblies, made an evaluation of the report that was published in *Christian Century.* It read, "The point of primary emphasis . . . is that there was a commission of this character, and such a report. Nothing of this kind has been so much as attempted before in all the history of the labor movement. . . . Nothing of the kind has been so much as proposed in our own day by any body of professional men of anything like equal intellectual and social standing. . . ."[3]

This evaluation was probably correct. However else it may be described, the Centralia case, in legal terms, was a criminal matter. Catholics, Protestants, and Jews neither before nor since have been confronted with any other criminal case that was so badly handled or influenced so much by unreasoning bias that they felt justified in joining to give their combined weight to an investigation of the facts.

Because of the report the Centralia Publicity

Committee could change its worn and familiar tune. No longer was it merely a few zealots, including one who was himself briefly one of the Centralia prisoners, saying there was good reason for releasing the prisoners. It wasn't just Elmer Smith and Ed Coll and others shouting at crowds on street corners. Here was a report made by those whose sense of morals could not be questioned — men of the church, no less — and their findings amounted to a recommendation that freedom be granted.

As it turned out, it was not pardon or parole that first brought freedom to a Wobbly prisoner; it was death. On August 13, 1930, two months before the release of the church report, James McInerney died in the prison hospital. The forty-six-year-old Irishman contracted tuberculosis in prison. While suffering from this disease he became infected also with spinal meningitis, the ultimate cause of death.

Elmer Smith knew McInerney had no relatives outside Ireland and when news of his death came the publicity committee asked for the right to take care of his remains. It would have been simple enough, and cheaper, to allow the body to be buried in the prison cemetery in Walla Walla, but the Centralia committee concluded that the cause would be helped by a large funeral in the city where all the trouble started. What's more, McInerney was a martyr. He deserved a special kind of funeral.

The one he was given was just that. The date was set well in advance, August 20, which by coincidence or otherwise was the same day the national commander of the Legion was scheduled to stop in Centralia on his way to the state convention in Aberdeen. The Legion event was announced on August 14, the day after McInerney died.

The funeral was to be no quiet gathering of friends. Handbills announcing it were printed and scattered about Centralia and other towns, urging union men to attend, as if it were another rally, which, in truth, it was.

Centralia was disturbed. All those radicals coming to town? There could be trouble again. The *Chronicle*, the only local daily surviving in 1930, printed nothing at all in advance about the funeral.

Around noon on the 20th caravans of cars began arriving from Seattle, Tacoma, and other places where delegations were recruited to make a good showing of those who wanted not just to pay their respects to a departed fellow worker, but to demonstrate to Centralia how much a great many cared about the imprisoned martyrs. Nor were they all Wobblies. The attention given to the event by the AFL papers indicated to what extent the Centralia cause by then was embraced by organized labor generally. Extra police, sheriff's deputies, and state patrolmen were brought out to assure order. The Fissell & Reynolds funeral home, next door to the new Elks temple and across the street from the monument in the park, was the beginning point of a funeral procession that stretched for more than a mile and moved slowly through the city to the Mountain View cemetery at the northwest corner of town. There the casket containing the body of the militant Wobbly who survived the violence at both Everett and Centralia was set beside an open grave while Ed Coll and Elmer Smith spoke their pieces.

Coll was assigned the role usually performed by a priest or minister. He gave the eulogy, ending, "Greater love hath no man than this, that he lay down his life for his friends. Brave man, brave men, my friends, death has finally liberated James McInerney."[4]

Elmer Smith could not resist giving his usual speech, reviewing the whole Centralia story. "Don't mourn the dead," he concluded. "Go ahead with the fight for the freedom of the workers."[5]

The *Chronicle* had some difficulty deciding how much news attention to give to the funeral of a Wobbly. The paper might have ignored the event entirely. But a funeral attended by two thousand! That was impressive. City editor Vance Noel decided to send a teenage reporter, David James, to cover the event, advising him "not to get carried away." James, in his first newspaper job, was impressed by the crowd's "thunderous" rendition of "Solidarity" at the cemetery and the fiery talk by the red-headed lawyer, Elmer Smith.[6] He returned to the office "bursting with ideas" and wrote enough copy to fill two columns. Noel cut it to five paragraphs and ran it on page ten the next day. The report of the Legion commander who placed a wreath on the sentinel monument later the same day received more prominent news play on page one.

The first Centralia prisoner actually to gain freedom turned out to be Loren Roberts, and it did not come about through executive clemency or parole. Roberts, judged insane at the Montesano trial, was committed originally to the state hospital for the criminally insane near Spokane but was shortly afterward transferred to the prison. His insanity, if there was any, was of short duration. The verdict for Roberts had been "guilty but insane." This was taken to mean he was guilty, sane or insane, and so had to serve as much time as the others. But the chance that it could mean otherwise led to a concerted effort in 1929 to obtain his release on a legal technicality. He was granted a hearing before a jury. It took place in Montesano, in the same courtroom where he was sentenced ten years previously, and the prosecutor this time was W. H. Grimm, brother of the slain Warren Grimm. Grimm began by saying he would not try to prove that Roberts was insane but that he had always been sane and had faked insanity in the hope of getting off. Superior Court Judge W. R. Campbell ruled, however, that the jury must accept the finding of the jury in 1919 that Roberts was insane at the time.

Roberts's attorney told the jury he spent his years at Walla Walla working in the automobile license plate mill and in the cannery kitchen. His record was good and he planned to return to his mother's home near Grand Mound. The jury required only fifteen minutes to find that Roberts was sane and should be released.

This verdict was unacceptable to Grimm, who announced that an appeal would be made to the supreme court. Roberts was required to return to prison while the appeal was processed. Then Grimm, for lack of supporting evidence or otherwise, decided not to pursue the appeal and Roberts was allowed to leave prison on August 20, 1930, after serving nearly eleven years of the minimum twenty-five-year term specified by Judge Wilson.

By the fall of 1930 Elmer Smith knew there was little chance public opinion would build enough to move Governor Hartley to action. He began working on a legal approach, basing it on the contention that the statute set ten years as the minimum penalty for second-degree murder, and that the men had served longer than ten years already and therefore should be paroled. Furthermore the original verdict had been "third-degree murder," the equivalent of manslaughter, which is unintentional killing, and that should be taken into consideration. Smith engaged a pair of Walla Walla attorneys to work for release on these premises, offering them $1,900 if they could accomplish the release of all the prisoners by October 1 when the parole board next met — or $285 for each one who was released.[7]

This offer was possible, Smith explained, "because of some money which has come in to the committee which we are at liberty to use as we see fit." The Walla Walla attorneys made the effort but it was unsuccessful.

After the church report new pressure for releases came from churches and unions. The men weren't mere Wobblies anymore. They were victims of injustice in the eyes of churchmen, and workingmen martyrs in the view of organized labor. J. W. Taylor, president of the Washington Federation of Labor, took a personal interest in the case, making his own appeals to the parole board.

The governor as usual continued to be displeased by anything done in behalf of the imprisoned Wobblies. He still hated them. But he was a politician and in 1932 his second term would be up. He was thinking of running again.

At the parole board meeting in April 1931, it was evident that support for release was mounting. Taylor was on hand to say that the combined forces of organized labor — the mighty AFL — were there to demand belated justice for the men. The governor himself was in attendance for the first time. A sizable delegation of churchmen was there, including Raymond Attebury of the Grace Methodist Church, Seattle; Theodore R. Vogler, First Congregational Church, Walla Walla; and Dr. Lucius O. Baird, state superintendent of Congregational churches. Both Attebury and Vogler were members of the Legion.

The board listened and the governor listened. They had heard it all before, over and over, and now they heard it again. But it was all to no avail. It was still not the time, the board ruled, to issue any paroles.

There was, however, one breakthrough. A special appeal was made in behalf of Eugene Barnett, whose wife, not having divorced him, now was ill with cancer and needed him to help care for her. Hartley was sufficiently moved by this to announce after the hearing that Barnett would be given a "six-month reprieve" so he could be with his sick wife. "We are glad to show this element of mercy and six months from now Barnett will return to prison to serve his sentence," Hartley announced.

So on May 27, 1931, Eugene Barnett became the second of the Centralia men to leave prison. A man of varied talents, including some writing ability, Barnett wrote the words to a song, "Wallowa Love, a ballad dedicated to Mrs. Eugene Barnett," with music by Harry Chandler. After a joyful return to his wife's home in Idaho he went door to door, selling the sheet music of the song for thirty-five cents a copy to raise money needed to take his wife to a cancer clinic in Missouri.

Barnett, ever the militant, could not resist using page two of the song sheet to make a statement under the heading "Historical Note." Referring to the Wallowa Valley in the northeast corner of Oregon, last home of the widely admired Nez Percé Chief Joseph, Barnett wrote: "The whites who live there today would fight as bravely and desperately to maintain their homes against invaders as did Chief Joseph and his little band of three hundred braves whose courage and prowess won the admiration of their opponents. . . ."[8]

The trip this song helped pay for ended tragically. Mrs. Barnett, her case diagnosed as hopeless, died on the train returning home from Missouri. Barnett, however, was not required to go back to prison at the end of his reprieve. By then, the end of 1931, the shattered state of the economy in Washington overshadowed all other public concerns and, while parole for the prisoners was not a forgotten issue, it was submerged in the general unrest created by widespread unemployment, wage cuts, bank closures, and other manifestations of chaotic economic developments. Hartley, hoping to win a third term in the fall of 1932, decided to yield a little to union demands and included Barnett and O. C. Bland among a number of prisoners to be given "Christmas paroles." These took effect, not before Christmas, but the day after.

So Commodore Bland went out. Barnett stayed out. That left four — John Lamb, Ray Becker, Bert Bland, and Britt Smith.

Elmer Smith welcomed Commodore Bland home and sent his congratulations to Barnett, but he was troubled by it all. No one of the men was more deserving of release than another. Yet four remained locked up after eleven years. For all of those years he lived with an obsession — a duty, self-imposed, to prove to the world at large that the Centralia convictions were unjust. He had not been able to do that and, as the years lengthened into a decade, the inner hurt he felt did not lessen, nor did the physical pain persisting in his stomach. He went to Dr. Coffee in Portland a third time, but again there was no relief.

In the summer of 1930, five years after his disbarment, Elmer Smith concluded that it was time to ask for reinstatement. By then few were still seriously afflicted with the "Wobbly horrors." The IWW's radical appeal to the working man had faded. Old animosities had subsided so much that many of the once-hostile lawyers in Lewis County were willing to write letters supporting Smith's eight-page petition for a rehearing in which he admitted that his radical feelings were now much modified.

Among those who sent letters of support for Smith's reinstatement were three superior court judges — J. M. Phillips, H. W. B. Hewen, and George Abel. W. H. Cameron, a lawyer in Centralia since 1907, wrote that

> within the hearts of a large percentage of the city of Centralia, who number forty thousand, there lodges great respect for the honesty and sincerity of purpose of Elmer Smith. . . . (I) sincerely trust that the honorable court will . . . admit him into the practice of his profession, feeling assured that the blight upon his past career will be smothered up and forgotten by a future life spent in loyalty to the flag, patriotic to his country's institutions, unflinching integrity in his attitude toward court and client, and a wholesome factor in the community in which he lives.[9]

The bar association submitted a set of questions to Smith to determine whether, since 1925, he had changed his views sufficiently to deserve being ranked again as a respectable attorney at law. He was asked first if he still supported the philosophy expressed in the preamble of the IWW creed. His reply:

> Insofar as the Preamble . . . can be construed as advocating the organization of labor to accomplish more of the good things of life, shorter hours, better working conditions and general improvement of the status of workers, I approve of the same; otherwise, I do not approve of the ideas and the principles therein set forth, nor do I believe that such ideas are a desirable goal for society in this country. I do not wish this answer to be construed that I do not believe in the right of public ownership by the people when accomplished through due process of law. I do believe in such public ownership.[10]

Smith denied emphatically that he favored attempts to change the government by use of force.

Asked if he approved of IWW literature, he conceded that "in some of their literature there are principles and ideas set forth that I deem vicious and of which I do not approve." These he said included sabotage, syndicalism, and any violation of the law in an attempt to achieve social reform or changes. "I believe," he wrote, "that all worthy objects, to achieve which labor has the right to organize, can be accomplished by law through unions organized in harmony with our laws and institutions and by the ballot."[11]

The Bar Association read his replies with approval and was able to agree that five years of punishment for a member who expressed radical views was sufficient. It joined those telling the court that he should be reinstated, and he was, effective November 17, 1930.

Near the end of winter in 1932 Smith was convinced by someone — his family never knew who — that a doctor operating a clinic in Puyallup had good success treating stomach ulcers. Desperate by then and willing to try almost anything, Smith went to him. He may have had cancer, although he never mentioned that possibility. His family later wondered. Perhaps Coffee had told him and he kept it from his family. Cancer was still considered something so horrible that few would even discuss it. Smith went to the clinic in Puyallup and agreed to submit again to surgery. He bled to death on the operating table. The date was March 20, 1932. He was forty-four years old.

Smith's death occured just as a judicial subcommittee of the U.S. Senate commenced an investigation of his disbarment in connection with the nomination of Kenneth Mackintosh to a federal judgeship. Because it was Mackintosh who wrote the scathing opinion upholding the disbarment of the Centralia attorney in 1925, the nomination was vigorously opposed by labor leaders — so much so that Mackintosh was denied the judgeship. Wobbly leaders, some now good members of the AFL, were elated. They had gotten even.

The extent to which Centralia's attitude toward Elmer Smith had modified by 1932 could be seen in the respect shown him on his funeral day. While the city did not turn out en masse by any means, attendance at the services on March 22 was large. Judge J. M. Phillips of the superior court in Grays Harbor County where, twelve years before, Elmer Smith had been tried for murder, came over from Aberdeen to deliver the funeral oration. Members of the Lewis County Bar Association — some of whom were among those who refused as a body to defend any of the accused in 1919 — were willing now to attend in a body the funeral of one who was again considered a respected colleague. Burial was in Mountain View Park.

Elmer Smith left his family virtually nothing. All his resources had gone into the crusade. Laura, fortunately, was able to get a teaching appointment for the next school year in Mendota, a small community in eastern Lewis County, where Elmer's brother and his secretary, Nora Beard, were on the school board. One of the few wandering Wobblies Smith brought home who ever met with Laura's approval was a bowlegged logger-journalist with courtly manners, Archie Sinclair, and he was adopted by the family. He was of great help to the family in this period of adversity, moving the Smiths' possessions to Mendota where they made a home in a small cabin near the James Smith house. Seeing an immediate need, Sinclair quickly built a two-hole privy near the cabin.

They remained in Mendota through 1933, Laura much saddened by widowhood but relieved at being freed from the tensions of the Wobbly struggle which preoccupied her husband almost from the beginning of their marriage. She did not miss anything about Centralia, especially the rough characters she was frequently called upon to feed and house at home — so much "riffraff," she called them.

With Elmer Smith gone, the defense effort faltered. At the spring meeting of the parole board John Lamb counted on being released. His wife and daughter went to Walla Walla expecting to take him home, but they were disappointed. Again his application for parole was rejected.

The publicity committee, now having to rely on C. S. Smith, its secretary, for leadership, issued a bulletin suggesting that the action on Lamb indicated Hartley was taking advantage of Elmer Smith's passing, "thinking the fight is over. . . . We want to assure Hartley that it is not. This committee considers it a duty not only to Elmer Smith but all of the Centralia victims to fight this case through regardless of what stands in the way and we are confident that our many friends will stand by us."[12]

The committee then made an urgent appeal for funds, stating, "Governor Hartley has announced himself a candidate for reelection and if we are to accomplish anything we will have to work hard. The secretary is cutting expenses to the bone. He is also cutting his wages from $14 to $12 per week starting May 1. He is the only one being paid by the CPC."[13]

The Democratic nominee for governor in 1932 was Clarence D. Martin, a wealthy grain-elevator owner in Cheney, near Spokane. He was an employer and had little more regard for Wobblies than either Hart or Hartley had, but was aware of the political change taking place.

Washington generally was as Republican as it was unfriendly to organized labor through all of the first three decades of the the twentieth century, but confidence in the traditional political leadership was shattered as lumber orders fell off and mills went on short work weeks, banks closed, wages were cut, and across the land a word seldom heard before became common — depression. The conservative Republicans had been in office so long, however, that a swing to the left was not certain, so Clarence Martin went looking for support wherever he could find it. The unions, weak as they were outside Seattle, were eager to replace Hartley, so Martin listened when they spelled out their wants. One of them was freedom for the "class-war prisoners" — including the Centralia men. Martin put his ambitions ahead of his prejudices and agreed to grant the long-denied paroles if he were elected.

He was elected, as were Democrats throughout the country in that year of discontent. Martin took office in January 1933, but it was April before he got around to his campaign promise about the Centralia prisoners. John Lamb came first. He went out on parole April 13. Britt Smith was next, on June 24; then Bert Bland, on July 1.

With those three gone, McInerney dead, Commodore Bland already paroled, Eugene Barnett released on a reprieve, and Loren Roberts freed by a jury, the only one of the eight left in prison was Ray Becker. He would not accept parole when it was offered. His sense of outrage at the injustice of the whole affair by this time had led him into a crusade of his own — the pursuit of vindication. Freedom alone was not enough. Ray Becker wanted the forces that put him in prison to admit they were wrong. His obsession kept the Centralia case from ending in 1932.

The paroles granted by Martin did not create much of a stir. There were no strong protests from Legion men or others. This could not be construed as a sign of general agreement that thirteen years of the minimum twenty-five-year sentences were considered enough punishment. It was just that everyone was relieved to get the clamor stopped. People were weary of hearing about the Centralia prisoners, just as they grew tired of the incessant protests about Tom Mooney's continued imprisonment. Now there would be no more speeches about Wobbly martyrs, no more demonstrations for them in Olympia, no more resolutions, no more appeals. No one wanted to prolong the decade of public agonizing over the Centralia men, whether they were guilty or not.

31

The Last Man

Anyone inclined toward superstition could look at the number assigned Ray Becker in prison — 9413 — and say he was fated to have the ill luck that followed him all the years of his adult life. Others might say the bad luck was not so much the result of fate as of his perverse and rebellious nature. He came west from his home in Chicago at the time of World War I, leaving behind a father and two brothers, who, judging from their lack of interest in his plight later, did not sorrow over his departure. His father was a minister who hoped that Ray would follow him in that career, but the son would not finish school. In Washington he learned the hard trade of the logger.

He was recruited by the IWW, whose radical doctrines suited his temperament so well that when the time came to register for the draft he refused. As the Wobblies insisted, it was a capitalist war. He said he would rather die than join the army. His choice, however, was to register or go to jail and he chose the latter, but fled at the first opportunity and became a fugitive, living under an assumed name, Ralph Bergdorff. He was picked up by the police in Spokane and sent back to Bellingham to serve out his jail term.[1]

Released, he took to the road and it led him by unfortunate chance to Centralia the day before Armistice Day, 1919, where he walked into an explosive situation he had no part in creating. Yet he was a Wobbly and well enough aware of the widespread animosity toward all "fellow workers" to understand what was up when he went to the local hall and was told that a raid was expected next day. He was there when guns were gathered and armed men stationed across Tower Avenue. It was an exciting day and he hung around. He saw the shooting. He ran with the others to seek refuge from the attackers in a cold-storage locker. And he was caught, tried, convicted of murder, and sentenced with the others to a minimum term of twenty-five years in prison.

His sense of being outrageously wronged by all this left him at the outset not speechless but silent. He alone among the accused ten did not tell his story. He made no statement prior to the trial and did not go on the witness stand. Either Vanderveer was afraid to use him or he refused to testify.

His silence was soon broken, however, after the doors at Walla Walla closed and he began to ponder the string of events and circumstances that put him in such a serious predicament. He came then to a firm and resolute conclusion: He had been railroaded. He had committed no crime. He did not shoot anyone. Yet here he was convicted of murder. It became his unshakable resolve not merely to get out of prison but to obtain redress, to get the wrong righted, to force an admission from those who wronged him that they committed grave errors.

The other Centralia prisoners were content to be labor martyrs, attributing their convictions to the fact that they were Wobblies who dared resist those who hated them and all their kind. But Becker's allegiance to the IWW was not strong. He was in prison, he was sure, because evil men conspired against him and if the IWW had any part in the conspiracy, the IWW was blameworthy too.

Becker became an articulate champion for himself and over the years carried on a voluminous correspondence with a number of persons with such effective pleading that he won not only their liking and respect but in a few instances their deep affection.

He began his campaign for vindication by trying to enlist the support of labor newspapers and was disappointed when they did not consider his battle one that should be fought in every issue they published. He would send requests for publicity to editors by registered mail, but had to admit in a message published by the *Farmer-Labor Call* in Centralia, "All my requests have been treated by silence."[2]

Becker believed the widely circulated rumor that a Pathe news cameraman took pictures of the November 11 violence and that his camera and film were destroyed by a mob. He said that the information had been suppressed.

"Widespread and persistent publicity being our only hope, is it to be wondered that I am beginning to consider that we are less the victims of the mob than victims of the indifference of our fellow workers?" he asked.[3] The *Call* not only carried his appeal but promised to publish any information that might turn up about the mysterious newsreel. None ever did.

Becker had one communication from his father just before Christmas in 1922. He replied, thanking him for the "package and the money" but chided his father for expressing the hope that he would have a Christmas replete with "bountiful blessings." "I guess you forgot where and what I am," he wrote.[4] The father, the Reverend Angus Becker, said he was going to South America and was urged by his son to go before labor bodies of whatever cities or towns he happened to visit, and "acquaint them with the great game of 'frame up' played in the U.S. against members of the working class." He added, "You will do this, won't you?" He signed the letter, "Yours with filial love."[5]

Becker's ignorance of the law during his early years in prison caused him to become furious when he heard that an appeal to the supreme court was being planned. "It means the stool pigeon and yellow element is in control of the IWW," he wrote to William Moran at the IWW office in Seattle. "It means a Judas kiss is about to be bestowed upon us and the other survivors of the Centralia mob."[6] He was afraid a supreme court action would delay other efforts to obtain release for possibly two years.

By 1923 the other prisoners as well as Becker were getting impatient with those they counted on to get them released. They were sending money to Elmer Smith, although acknowledging that it was enough to pay only some of his expenses. Becker learned the craft of bead working and offered to send Smith his output to sell so he could pay a stenographer to take down his speeches and send them to newspapers. He told Smith he was speaking for the two Bland brothers, Gene Barnett, James McInerney, and Loren Roberts when he said, "We are utterly disgusted with the

dilatory tactics of the defense committees."[7] He authorized Smith to organize an independent publicity committee to take over the task or privilege of collecting money for the Centralia prisoners.

Soon Becker became disenchanted with Elmer Smith also even though he was giving the defense effort his all — time, money, legal service — and sometimes risking bodily injury in fulfilling speaking engagements in hostile towns. In the spring of 1924 Becker wrote a scathing letter severing relations with the prisoners' own chief champion. He accused Smith of using the imprisoned men to further his political ambitions and charged that funds collected were being mishandled or misappropriated and that as a consequence the IWW soon would be disgraced.

The break with Smith was completed three months later when Becker forbade Smith to use his name or picture in soliciting any more funds to add to those he had "most shamefully used." "Something for which you have won my contempt is your begging for a trial or pardon for us," he wrote. "The decent thing to do is to demand the immediate and unconditional release of the men railroaded to prison cells to cover up the dirty work of the lynchers of Wesley Everest and shield them from punishment and to clamor for the trial of the perpetrators of the outrages which have made Centralia and Montesano towns of darkest memories."[8] Smith, although he was dismayed by Becker's ingratitude and hostility, was not deterred in his resolve to struggle on for the others who did not share Becker's view that vindication was more to be desired than freedom.

Becker's early suspicions about misuse of defense funds turned out to be sufficiently justified to cause most of the other prisoners to renounce a group in Seattle calling itself the "Centralia Liberation Committee" and to urge "support for defense committees which we have already recognized as sincerely working in our behalf."[9]

Having broken with Smith and other defenders, Becker decided, as prisoners with time on their hands often do, to study law and acquire enough skills to write his own appeals. He learned about writs of habeas corpus and how they could be used to get a hearing. His general knowledge broadened also as he read books sent him by a wealthy New Yorker who learned of his idealistic stand from the ACLU. This was Robertson Trowbridge, an elderly wealthy bachelor and a member of the exlusive Union League Club who displayed one chink in an otherwise solid armor of conservatism — he admired the way Wobblies went to jail rather than renounce their ideals and beliefs. He was a heavy contributor to ACLU funds raised to defend Wobblies and others accused and often convicted under the federal espionage act. Trowbridge admired one young Wobbly, Pierce Wetter, so much that when Wetter was released from prison he was invited to bring his family and live at the Trowbridge house in Washington Square. This they did and the arrangement was so amicable that Trowbridge adopted Wetter as his son.

At this time Becker met and became enchanted with a beautiful young woman, Julia Godman of Springfield, Oregon, who accompanied her radical father to Walla Walla for a visit with the prisoners. This began an association bordering on the romantic that was to endure and brighten his life over the next sixteen years.

Letters exchanged among Becker, Trowbridge, and Godman were frequent, strange relationship though it was among a wealthy old man with a high sense of social consciousness on the East Coast who had never seen Walla Walla, an idealistic occupant of the state prison, and a compassionate young liberal woman living in Portland, all working toward a common goal. Trowbridge became well enough acquainted with Becker through letters to understand his nature and the difficulties he caused those who tried to help him. In one letter to Julia he sympathized with her because Becker was so hard to deal with. He hinted at this conclusion about her loyalty to the prisoner when he wrote, "You have probably suspected that I am in love with Ray myself. . . . "[10] He ended his letter, "Your brother in love." Trowbridge offered to take Becker in if he were released, and was so sure this would happen that he sent word he had a room waiting. It remained vacant and his adopted family referred to it as the "Ray Becker room." Wetter, Trowbridge wrote, would find a job for Becker when he came to New York.

Becker tried to be his own attorney in 1929, bringing an action in habeas corpus before the federal district court in Spokane. It was quickly dismissed as being without merit. It was four years before his next legal move which took the form of a hand-printed, 141-page brief written in support of a plea to the state supreme court for a writ of habeas corpus. This plea

Ray Becker at the time of his arrest. He and Wesley Everest were the only Wobblies who fired at servicemen through the door of the hall.

227

also was denied.

But Becker did not have to fight his battle alone after the Centralia men were released. The IWW lost interest in him, but the AFL did not. The woodworkers, the largest union in the state, at their convention in 1936, besides endorsing Franklin Roosevelt for president and denouncing their own international president, William Hutchinson, for supporting Alfred M. Landon, devoted a full page in their resolutions report to the Ray Becker case. It condemned Senator Wesley Jones for expressing approval of the lynching of Wesley Everest, quoted the jurors' affidavits, criticized Governor Martin for not releasing Becker, and ended by demanding a congressional investigation "of the vicious frame-up of Ray Becker and of the whole Centralia case."[11]

Becker never belonged to an AFL union but by 1936 he qualified as a genuine labor martyr and the newly militant unions, given new power and respectability by the Wagner Act, needed something to agitate about since the economy was still so depressed there were few economic objectives that could be fought for successfully.

Baldwin and his associates in the ACLU did not sympathize at all with Becker's stubborn refusal to accept parole. They argued with him. Becker paid no heed and bided his time, encouraged by the increased interest organized labor was showing — and then there was Julia.

Julia Godman was a kind of latter-day Anna Louise Strong in that she was acutely aware of flaws in an American society that kept those labeled as "workers" in a state of subjugation. It distressed her immensely. She was brought up on radicalism. Her family lived for a time in a country setting where her father, in the manner of Elmer Smith, welcomed those seeking refuge or comfort or just a few regular meals. She heard the Centralia case discussed time and again and it wasn't all history for then, after 1933, there was still a final chapter to be written — one man still in prison, one man holding out for his principles, one man willing to suffer more misery for the sake of an ideal.

She was fascinated by Ray Becker's stand, and furthermore he was a nice man, she thought, a good deal older than she, but friendly and desperately in need of friends. She became his good friend.

In 1936, after an acrimonious internal conflict, a substantial number of sawmill workers and loggers broke away from the conservative carpenters' union and formed the International Woodworkers of America, structured along lines the IWW stood for — one big union for all those engaged in one industry. Many Wobblies eagerly joined this new confederation, and so it was not surprising that one of the IWA's first acts was the setting up of a Free Ray Becker committee with headquarters in Portland. Julia Godman became the committee secretary.

This committee, like the ACLU, considered Becker's efforts to climb out of prison on his own through some kind of legal loophole a futile endeavor, and decided to help by providing good legal assistance. One of the attorneys the Free Ray Becker committee was able to interest in the case was Irvin Goodman of Portland, a lawyer with considerable experience in labor cases. He reviewed the situation and decided that if new evidence favorable to the convicted men could be dug up in Lewis County — evidence that was suppressed or otherwise kept out of the trial — some chance of obtaining the exoneration Becker sought might emerge. Julia said she would try to get that evidence.

She went to Elmer Smith's old law office in Centralia looking for records of the Centralia Publicity Committee. They were there, in the back room, and when the lawyers still using the office went out to lunch, she appropriated them all and took them with her. These papers and some instructions from Becker provided her with leads she undertook to follow.[12] She went to the courthouse, looking for a record of an inquest that might have been held in the Everest lynching. There was none. But she found other material. She went to Montesano and read much of the lengthy transcript of the trial. Her great hope was to find someone who might know some dark secret that now, after all this time, could be revealed safely. She put up at a cheap hotel and stuck a note on the door saying when she would be there. "It was surprising how many persons came to see me or left an unsigned note under my hotel room door," she wrote. She spent mornings in the room, then

the rest of the day I would go out, trying to verify reports, interviewing people, checking, rechecking, and cross-checking stories told me. The Eagles and the Lamb family and many others became friends. . . . I shall always remember my surprise at the impact time had upon the personalities of people; how the part individuals had played when they were younger — cruel, brave, criminal, or merely weak — had colored their lives, their family relationships, and the pity I felt for several who had once played very discreditable roles. It was interesting to learn what had become of the members of the lynch party and others who had helped break in the jail and had participated in the overall conspiracy to raid the hall and cover up the responsibility for the tragedy. . . . One man asked me again and again to understand why he could not sign an affidavit, admitting what he himself had done and what he knew because of the suffering and shame it would bring to a family he had not had at that time and who knew nothing of his connection with the events of Armistice Day, 1919. Even more moving, of course, was the courage and dignity revealed in some of the stories told me as those who had been participants in another way in the tragedy, who had been beaten, lost jobs or been jailed, related their accounts of those happenings.[13]

Julia Godman interviewed the Montesano jurors and obtained new affidavits repeating what they had sworn to in 1924 but with new emphasis on the injustice of the verdict.

She was particularly impressed with one juror, Carl Hulten. He came from his home near Lake Quinault to meet her in Aberdeen and insisted on taking her to lunch in the dining room of the best hotel.

He was very simply dressed but he had immense dignity, and I shall never remember anything as moving as his saying to me: "Saying he is afraid is not what a man can say — it would take a long time to say it to yourself. If you were a man you would know this." Then he looked at me, while I sat at the table with its dazzling white cloth and fine silver, hardly breathing, and at last he said, "I have said it to myself, and now it can go in your paper." It must have come to Mr. Hulten slowly over the years: the fear that he had felt — the gradual perception of what actually happened in Montesano.[14]

Julia felt she was responsible for causing one juror, P. V. Johnson, to leave self-imposed isolation in an Oregon forest and return to Portland. "He suffered more from guilt than anyone I have ever known," she wrote. It had caused him to leave Grays Harbor County and go to Portland, but even there "he sometimes fancies people might know he was the one who sent them all to prison. He retreated into an almost inaccessible spot in the forest, far from any road, between Scapoose and Vernonia. There he set up a crude home in a clearing where everything he needed he could not make had to be carried in by backpack."

Johnson, she found, had held out for acquittal longer than any others, but finally gave in. "He had tried in vain to think of 'what he had done' in hanging the jury for such a long time as a noble action, and still had moments of insisting to himself, or so he once told me, that 'this was what saved them from first-degree.' To me he was a Hamlet in a plaid shirt."[15]

The Free Ray Becker committee, financed with funds raised mainly among IWA members, used information gathered by Julia to plead for Becker just as the CPC pled for most of the previous ten years for all eight of the prisoners. But the Democratic governor in Olympia was no more sympathetic than the Republican governors before him. Clarence Martin didn't understand a man who would refuse parole when it was offered to him. A man like that ought not be let out. He must be up to something.

Becker, impatient as usual, soon was as critical of the Portland committee that bore his name as he had been ten years earlier with Elmer Smith's efforts. He broke with the committee and it was disbanded. Attorney Goodman tried on his own to carry on, but soon Becker turned on him with one of his characteristically vitriolic letters. Goodman patiently replied, answering each charge Becker made, and then explained that the only interest he had in Becker was his status as a "political prisoner."

"The day we first met," Goodman wrote, "you told me that one of the differences between Mooney's case and your case was that your case had been forgotten. I believe the primary reason is, and herein lies one of the tragedies of your case, that you have neither faith nor hope in the working class. Ray, I emphasize with all the power at my command that in the working class you must establish your faith and your hope."[16]

Becker turned against all who tried to help him except Robertson Trowbridge and Julia Godman. He called Walker Smith, the Centralia pamphleteer, "a capitalist agent."[17] He called the ACLU the "snivel liberties bureau." He said the joint church report was inspired by the American Legion.[18]

While he had no faith in attorneys, he clung to his hope for legal redress of some kind and in 1937, on his own, again filed a petition for a writ of habeas corpus, this time in the federal court in Tacoma. It was, like the others, denied, whereupon he used his newfound knowledge of the law and filed an affidavit of prejudice against Judge J. Stanley Webster. It was ignored. He filed for a writ again in 1938. It was the fourth attempt and again he struck out.

Baldwin realized he could not do much for Becker by correspondence from New York. He needed allies on the scene. He found one in Mary Farquharson of Seattle, a member of the ACLU and a state senator. She suggested that Baldwin get Benjamin Kizer, a prominent Spokane attorney who also was a member of the ACLU, to take an interest in Becker's case. Kizer was well acquainted with Clarence Martin and was appointed by him as chairman of the newly formed Washington State Planning Council, the state's first attempt to provide some guidance for legislators and others making decisions that affected the future.

It was Kizer who came up with a new idea for solving the Becker problem. He could be released by simply having his sentence commuted to the time already served. In this way Becker's prison term would be brought to an end. He could no longer remain in prison because his sentence would be finished. Like it or not, he would have to get out.

Baldwin knew Becker would not like this at all, so he was not told about it. By this time the parole board had a new chairman, Louis F. Bunge, and while he agreed that commutation of sentence would be effective since it could be imposed on the prisoner without his consent, he was concerned about what would happen to such a celebrated prisoner, especially one of his temperament, once he was released. Governor Martin was concerned too. He was afraid Becker might be more of a troublemaker outside prison than in.

Martin indicated he might commute the sentence if he could be given assurance that Becker would be turned loose somewhere outside Washington state. Baldwin then asked Arthur Garfield Hays to write Martin offering to provide Becker with a job and money for transportation to New York, but expressed concern about who would handle the delicate job of meeting Becker upon his release from prison and getting him on his way. Because of Becker's hostility toward the ACLU, Baldwin did not want to offer the help of that organization directly.[19]

Weeks went by and when nothing happened

Baldwin wrote Martin directly asking him, "Hasn't the time come when he (Becker) should no longer be penalized for misguided obstinance?"[20] Senator Farquharson suggested that Reverend Shorter, then operating the "Church of the People" on Seattle's skid road, and himself a member of the ACLU, accompany her to Walla Walla to serve as a two-person release committee to take Becker by the arm when he emerged from the prison and escort him to Portland, where the IWA wanted to give him a fitting welcome.

This was agreeable to Martin, but he waited until after the legislature adjourned before finally signing the commutation on September 20, 1939, reducing Becker's sentence to the time served — eighteen years, three months. Baldwin sent expense money to pay for Farquharson's and Shorter's trip to pick up the last of the Centralia class-war prisoners.

By this time Bunge had been succeeded as parole board chairman by William J. Wilkins. He wrote to the warden instructing him to get Becker ready to be released and to use his own judgment on whether to wait until Senator Farquharson and Reverend Shorter arrived before telling Becker he had to go. Wilkins was afraid that Becker, denied the pardon he held out for all those years, would be infuriated and try to resist the order that evicted him from his prison home. The fear proved unfounded. Becker received the news calmly. It wasn't parole. Instead he would be completely free. And the governor was restoring all his civil rights. He could go out, if not victorious, at least with his head up. The arrangement was acceptable.

But before he left he must send a telegram to his benefactor, Trowbridge, assuming, incorrectly, that he did not know what was taking place. That done, he walked away from the place where he had spent more than eighteen years. Then the three — a female state senator, a rarity then; a Protestant minister who lost his church because of his radical views; and a man, young at twenty-six when he went to prison, and now forty-five — headed for the railroad station and a train that took them west to Oregon and on to Portland.

Becker's friend Julia was married by this time. Her name was Bertram, but she was there at Union Station in Portland to greet him — she and a delegation of union men so numerous that Becker, when he saw the crowd, became confused and frightened and started to run. He was quickly overtaken and assured that the crowd was not a mob come to harm him.

His release was widely compared to that of Tom Mooney, whose sentence of twenty-five to forty years in California for a parade bombing was commuted on September 22, just two days after Becker was released. Both were hailed as labor heroes and a great fuss made over them at union meetings. When he visited union halls Becker was always greeted with prolonged applause and sometimes cheered. He was taken on the rounds, from meeting to meeting, making short speeches exhorting all his listeners to be loyal to labor's cause. Irvin Goodman had accused him of lacking true allegiance to the working class, but any such lack didn't show up on his visit to Portland.

The industrial union that rose to challenge the old AFL was the Congress of Industrial Organizations of which the IWA was a part, and jurisdictional friction between it and the AFL unions was severe in 1939, but, said the labor press, all differences were forgotten in the triumphant welcome for Ray Becker. He stood for labor's cause — the common cause.

The welcome culminated in a banquet, the preparations for which ran into difficulties when the restaurant where it was scheduled informed the committee that no blacks could be allowed and there were some blacks in the unions who planned to attend. Racial prejudice was not something that could be successfully opposed in that time so another restaurant had to be found. It turned out to be one owned by the parents of Richard Neuberger, later a U.S. senator from Oregon. At the banquet the drama of the occasion was accentuated when an unsigned message from one of the Montesano jurors was read. It said:

> I held out until the very end for release of the defendants. But finally on the last evening, because I could sense the temper of the community and two of the jurors had threatened me that I would never leave there alive, and I could smell the fate that would await me when I left the room, in fear of my life, I gave in and voted with the others for conviction, after they had agreed to send a recommendation for leniency to the judge. There were other jurors who felt as I did. . . . Perhaps more than anyone else I have reason to be thankful and rejoice that Ray Becker is free."[21]

In a few weeks the period of adulation was over, Becker had new clothes, and the time had come, Julia told him, to go on to New York where his friend Trowbridge was waiting. Becker seemed uneasy, Julia noticed, and it was not only because it still seemed strange to be away from prison restrictions, having to make decisions on his own, and not knowing what lay ahead day to day. She theorized about his state of mind. In prison his dogged pursuit of vindication became a career, extending over eighteen years. Suddenly and unexpectedly it was all over. Now he didn't have anything to do. He was out. He hadn't planned beyond that.

Money was at hand for the trip to New York and so he went, taking the long, slow way, by ship from Portland down the coast and through the Panama Canal and up to New York, there to be greeted by a man who said he loved him but had never met him. But Becker was not like Wetter who was only twenty-five when Trowbridge took him in as an adopted son. Becker was middle-aged and felt uncomfortable in the opulent environment of a Washington Square mansion. He appreciated the hospitality and the friendships, which he recognized as genuine, but he couldn't stay. Another war was raging in Europe. It was on the first anniversary of the end of the last war that his freedom was taken away. Now those same powers that fought the war he refused to join in 1917 were at it again. It upset him and he wanted to return to the Northwest, where he had friends also. After only a short stay in New York he left.

32

Centralia in the Aftermath

The Centralia case settled uneasily into twentieth-century history. When the long drama ended with the eviction from prison of Ray Becker, Centralia, disturbed at having developed an image as a city of violence, turned away from the past, hoping the storm of controversy that swirled about it for two decades finally would die out. It did subside, but never quite died. By 1939 the war on Wobblies was long over in Centralia but the old battles were not forgotten, nor would they ever be.

Twenty years is the time span of a generation. After two decades the young generation in Centralia had no memories at all of the tumultuous events of 1919 and 1920. They never saw the headlines denouncing the IWW as ruthless murderers, although many did remember reading about Elmer Smith and Ed Coll, the church report, the affidavits of jurors and witnesses, and the insistent hammering at successive governors demanding leniency for the imprisoned Wobblies. The soldier martyrs — the four men memorialized on the statue in the park — were not forgotten. There were always editorials and speeches about them on Armistice Day. And it was hard to forget the men who went to prison when the clamor in their behalf kept up year in and year out. Their story was told so often that it took on an aura of plausibility even among those who would never concede that the shooting was in any degree excusable.

The older generation in Centralia of course could not forget. They could only try to draw a curtain and wait for memories to fade, curiosity to diminish, and notoriety to end while their once-placid city returned to normal, peaceful ways. As if by common consent, the case was seldom discussed in Centralia. A new minister could come to town, live there for six years next door to Warren Grimm's brother, see him every week at Kiwanis, and never once hear him or anyone else even mention the case.[1]

The public library for thirty-five years was not allowed to keep any clippings, books, or other printed material pertaining to the case.[2] The Tacoma library, aware of the ban in Centralia, tried to make up for it by collecting all the material it could find.

For the principals in the case there was certainly no forgetting. They were haunted and disturbed by it for the rest of their lives. Eugene Barnett visited Centralia several years after his release and called on William Scales, the one man who could have verified the alibi that he was in the lobby of the Roderick Hotel at the time of the violence and so could not have shot Warren Grimm from a window of the Avalon. Scales, he was sure, had seen him there a few minutes after the shooting began, but he would not appear as a witness at the trial.

Barnett knocked on Scales' door. When it was opened, he stepped inside, closed it, and stood facing the man he held responsible for his eleven years of imprisonment. Scales had a patch over his right eye and peered with surprise at his visitor. Barnett described what was said:

"Do you remember me?"
"I don't believe I do."
"I'm Eugene Barnett, the man you wouldn't come and identify."
He became very excited at this, and told me, "I want you to know I went to the governor three times trying to help you."
I said, "Yes, after it was too late. You wouldn't come to the trial when it would have done some good."
I heard he was dying of cancer. I just wanted to see if it was true. I guess there are worse things than being innocent in prison. As I left and walked away I felt sorry for him. After all, he was only a weakling afraid to oppose the industrial tyrants.[3]

Barnett remained a militant rebel and served for a time as a CIO organizer. He also operated a fox farm in Idaho, worked in the mines again, and operated a ride in a carnival in the summers. He wrote a short instructional manual about a skill he learned in prison — making articles of horse hair, which was published.[4] He died in 1973 at the age of 83.

Loren Roberts went back to logging and became an honored member of the International Woodworkers of America, the industrial union that proved to be a haven for Wobblies when they realized in the 1920s that the IWW's time was past. In 1960 he was living with his wife in Bucoda and had taken up landscape painting. Interviewed about the Centralia case, he expressed apprehension that publicity might result in his losing his gun collection. He took the interviewer to see Britt Smith, then seventy-three and living alone in a small house in Bucoda. Smith talked readily about the case. He said the hall really wasn't worth defending but the men felt the time had come to take a stand. He said he had never set foot in Centralia again since then and never would.

Commodore Bland returned to his family in Centralia where he died about 1938. His younger brother Bert moved into the Midwest where he died a few years later. Even in 1986, nearly seven decades later, older members of the Bland family declined to comment on the Centralia affair. Roberts died in 1976 and is buried in the pioneer cemetery in Grand Mound. Smith died in Bucoda in the 1960s.

Ray Becker, when he returned from New York to Portland, supported himself until his death in 1950 by plying handicraft skills he learned in prison, selling his wares in a small shop in Vancouver.

John Lamb returned to Centralia after earning a diploma from a school that trained masseurs, and spent the rest of his life successfully operating a massage shop with the help of his son, Dewey. The son recalled when Dr. David Livingstone, well advanced in age, was in the hospital, terminally ill. Mrs. Lamb was a nurse in the hospital and Dr. Livingstone, knowing who she was, said he would like to talk to Dewey. He went to the hospital but just as he reached the door of the doctor's room, Livingstone suffered a seizure and became greatly agitated, flailed his arms about, and cried: "Get those IWWs off of me. Get those IWWs off me!" Death came minutes later before he could tell Lamb whatever was on his mind.[5] Livingstone was well aware of the role which the IWW repeatedly declared him guilty of in the Everest lynching, and it literally haunted him to his dying day.

John Lamb died on Christmas Eve, 1949, of smoke inhalation after rescuing his children, grandchildren, and wife from their burning home.

C. D. Cunningham settled back into his law practice after the Montesano trial but remained the most articulate defender of the Legion position in the case throughout his life, which ended in 1963. He was Centralia's authority on the case and responded to inquiries about it, never deviating from the position that the trial in which he was a prosecutor was fair and that the eight men were justly convicted and sentenced. He did not like to discuss the case but he gave full cooperation to those doing research. With a fine sense of historic worth, he kept his files and a copy of the trial transcript, consigning them before his death to the Legion National Library in Indianapolis. He was an understanding and affectionate father who wrote long letters to his sons at regular intervals while they were in service in World War II and lent needed early support to his third son, Mercier, as he was getting established as an innovative classical dancer, a career he pursued with such success that he was named to Washington state's centennial hall of honor in 1983. Another son, Dorwin, served as a superior court judge in Lewis County for sixteen years. The family's youngest son, John Marshall, remained in Centralia as a practicing attorney.

George Vanderveer lived a turbulent life in the two decades after his last big IWW trial. In 1922 he finally agreed to a divorce and then lived openly with Kitty Beck. Though regarded still in Seattle legal circles as a renegade, his abilities were respected and his skills were much in demand in criminal cases. He prospered in the 1920s and built a spacious home in Lake Burien where he and Kitty attempted to gain new friends by frequent entertaining. But his background was too well remembered and the acceptance he yearned for was not forthcoming. Then he immersed himself in work and alcohol. Living with the George Vanderveer of that period of proved too much for Kitty, and in 1924 she took poison and died.

Vanderveer invested in real estate and became moderately wealthy. In 1927 he married Ethel Hoover of Tacoma. He bought the Seattle baseball club, which proved a financial disaster, but he was rescued when an influential client, Dave Beck, head of the Teamsters Union, persuaded Emil Sick, owner of the Rainier Brewing Company, to take over.

When President Herbert Hoover nominated Justice Kenneth Mackintosh of the state supreme court to be a federal circuit court judge, Vanderveer, still bitter about the opinions Mackintosh wrote in the Centralia appeals and in the disbarment of Elmer Smith, openly demanded that organized labor oppose the appointment. Considerable pressure was applied by the legal fraternity, which supported Mackintosh, but Vanderveer, stubborn as ever, was unyielding, and the anti-IWW judge didn't get the appointment.

In 1942, driving while drunk, Vanderveer suffered a punctured lung in a car accident. He died as surgeons worked unsuccessfully to keep him alive.

A career as unusual and eventful as his deserved to be recorded, and it was, in a 1953 biography entitled *Counsel for the Damned*, by Lowell S. Hawley and Ralph Bushnell Potts.

Centralia's general attitude concerning the case, bordering on paranoia, came in for a behind-the-scenes discussion in 1954 when a history of the city was produced as a part of a community development study sponsored by the University of Washington. The director of the study, Frank Anderson, had been in town only a short time when he learned that the Armistice Day affair was something one didn't talk about. Nevertheless it was a significant event in the city's history. How could it be ignored? Anderson consulted a friend, James Stevens, a prominent Northwest author, who recommended that Centralia not appear to be trying to hide an unpleasant chapter in its history, but rather to deal with it forthrightly without undue emphasis and trust that the city would be judged by its good qualities and accomplishments rather than by "one sordid affair."

"The historical committee," Stevens wrote, "should first place the IWW affair in its true historical perspective and proportion. In that light, despite the bloodshed and the succeeding trial, it was simply an incident in the course of regular human events. . . . And that is how it should be presented, in low key, in bald terms. It was simply a violent, glaring spot in a workaday American town and in a workaday American industrial environment."[6]

The history committee, emboldened by Stevens's advice, set out to gather information and was immedi-

ately rebuffed. The schools, the committee members were told, certainly should have no part in writing anything about the awful business involving the IWW. As a consequence, the entire matter was covered in a brief paragraph:

> It was not surprising that Centralia, in the heart of the lumber producing sections of the Pacific Coast, should have a share in the history of this class warfare. Here, as in other localities in this region, feelings ran high between industrial leaders and patriotic groups on one hand and the leaders of change and revolution on the other. In such a conflict, violence is very likely, and the Centralia Armistice Day tragedy of 1919 in which four Legionnaires were killed and three more wounded, and one IWW hanged, was the direct result of this long and violent struggle which occurred in many parts of our country during this period.[7]

Thus the one event which brought fame to Centralia, however unwelcome it was, received but bare mention in its local history, and the emphasis in that mention was not on what occurred but on attempting to convince readers that since such things were commonplace at the time Centralia's industrial troubles were not to be singled out as being any worse than those of other Western cities.

In a 1977 interview a Centralia resident told a researcher that "vigilante-type control imposed on the town after the massacre was deeply resented by many laborers in the community" and that the "unfriendly atmosphere around Centralia" caused many loggers, miners, and railroad men to avoid the town.[8]

The city's image was damaged most by the persistent story that Wesley Everest was emasculated before he was hanged and that the prominent men in the community who were responsible never were brought to account. The same researcher wrote,

> The claim that fair evidence to prove the IWW version of the raid was destroyed by the Legionnaires gave a bad public image of the Legionnaires and businessmen in Centralia. It was at this time that an unofficial boycott was put into effect by many workers around Centralia. Those suspected of killing Everest, allowing the vigilante groups to control Centralia . . . were avoided. A local doctor was shunned because of his suspected guilt in castrating Everest; a hardware-store owner received few customers as he was ac-

cused of selling shells for the rifles used by men that raided homes in Centralia and Mendota; the employment agency in Centralia saw many jobs available with the Hubbard-owned mill but received few if any takers for many months."[9]

The curtain Centralia drew down on its most unpleasant period was never raised. Those who tried to pull it aside to get at hidden facts were usually discouraged or rebuffed. Mrs. Jackie Morgan of Chehalis was employed as a federal CETA trainee to do work for the Lewis County Historical Society in 1981. On her own she went on a quest for new information about the "massacre." The board of the historical society, informed of what she was doing, called her in and suggested that she stop making inquiries about the case because it might be harmful to "the museum" located in the abandoned Chehalis railroad depot. She persisted, however, but gave up after the board twice more told her that it was not proper for a person representing the local society to dig into a part of the past the local people wanted to forget.[10]

But 1919 could not be forgotten in 1983 any more than in previous years when it was the frequent subject of articles pertaining to labor history and especially in publications of the IWW, for however much the union was weakened and depleted in ranks, it survived. The case remained such a cause of chagrin that in 1963 the *Centralia Chronicle,* under new ownership by then, decided to end local silence on the subject. An editorial on page one headed "Let's Refute the 1919 Armistice Day Dishonor" was considered sufficiently unusual to be reported on the Associated Press news wires.

What bothered the *Chronicle,* undertaking to speak for the community it served, was that after forty-four years there was still a flow of material concerning the "massacre," some of which

pictured Centralia as the scene of an unfinished American tragedy, dwindling in size and existing in humility and without self-respect. . . . It is time Centralia and Centralians start insisting the record of 44 years ago is history, and admittedly one no community could be proud of. Yes, the city was not the only one in those years to have bloodshed on the same issues. It was here that reactionary forces of the time collided in a manner and moment that brought unforgettable attention from the whole nation. Centralia today is no shattered community. Its population is almost twice that of 1919. . . . No one asks that what happened be forgotten. What Centralia asks and deserves today is that the record remain, but without the dishonor contemporary historians insist is there. It is time to command accuracy and respect. The community that fails to do that permits the continuing conviction that its name and character are worthless.[11]

Three years later the *Chronicle* broke the code of silence concerning details of the case by publishing the first comprehensive account ever to appear in print locally. It was doing so, the editor explained, to dispel confusion created by contemporary writers who, without supporting facts, sought to put new light on what happened.

This account mentioned the 1918 raid in which the IWW hall was destroyed and the Wobblies driven from town. In 1919, it said, the IWW came back and opened a hall. "Businessmen and civic leaders gathered to discuss the situation. At this point the turmoil in the Northwest had as its concern the Red menace rather than unionism. Responsible public opinion had been led there by the war, propaganda, sabotage and violence." The account conceded that "there were some threats that the Wobblies' hall would be attacked again." It did not make a judgment on who was the aggressor when the parade halted in front of the hall. It merely described the two contentions — "one, that the Legionnaires broke from the parade line and charged the IWW hall. . . . The other contention, and just as solidly argued, is that shots whipped into the columns of veterans as they marked time. They could have come from Seminary Hill or from several nearby buildings whose second-floor windows faced the street. The Legionnaires, some battlefield veterans whose instinctive reaction was to get cover, raced for protection."[12]

The *Chronicle* admitted that the Wobblies had a right to protect themselves if attacked, but asked, "But were they? Did one of them strike first, and in one moment of kaleidoscopic terror did the others mistake men fleeing for cover as attackers?"[13]

The account had little to report about the lynching of Wesley Everest but did concede that he "was mutilated" and hanged from the Mellen Street bridge and that none of the lynchers was ever prosecuted. It said nothing about the Montesano trial except that it resulted in convictions.

This first account of the case, published in Centralia forty-seven years after the events, was so well accepted by the townspeople that it was republished in its entirety three years later on November 11, 1969, for the "enlightenment of younger generations." This was the fiftieth anniversary of the tragedy.

In the 1950s the country generally turned on domestic Communists and those suspected of being Communist sympathizers with a ferocity that could be compared with the "Wobbly horrors" of an earlier time. It gave the Legion an opportunity to boast that it was fighting the Reds long before anyone else. The editor of the *American Legion Magazine* in 1959, Robert Pitkin, reminded Legionnaires that "early Reds incited many vicious local crimes by giving organized leadership to deluded or ignorant men with potentially criminal mentalities." One of these crimes occurred at Centralia, he wrote, at the very time the Legion was holding its first national convention.

> Fourteen armed members of a radical, communist labor group, the International (sic) Workers of the World (IWW) ambushed Centralia's first Armistice Day parade as it marched down Tower Avenue....At a signal the concealed Reds opened fire on the parade from upstairs rooms of three buildings and a nearby hilltop. . . . The assassins later came to trial and escaped the death penalty on their lawyers' plea that they had been incited to their crime by radical intellectuals who were too smart to take part themselves. Which was true.[14]

This commentary on the Centralia case, though flagrantly inaccurate, so pleased C. D. Cunningham that he wrote a letter to the Legion magazine editor, telling with pride of the part he played as a prosecutor in the case. Then he complained,

> From the date of the arrest of the defendants, and for a period of 30 years thereafter, and even since then, there has been a steady barrage of literature of all kinds propagated by the communists and their sympathizers condemning the courts and all those who had to do with the prosecution, charging that the accused were denied a fair and impartial trial and, among other things, proclaiming the existence of a conspiracy by the "Lumber Barons" against "Labor" and that the American Legion was a tool in their hands to carry out the conspiracy....[15]

The Legion fought those who followed the Communist and Nazi line in broadcasting lies about the

Centralia case, Cunningham wrote, and "sometimes it seems that it stood alone."[16] He did not question the accuracy of Pitkin's description of what occurred on Armistice Day and what motivated the violence.

No action was ever taken on suggestions that something be done to memorialize Wesley Everest in Centralia. No labor school was named for him, as Ed Coll proposed, no statue. The very size of the marker placed on Everest's grave by the IWW, and the terse inscription on it, suggested that none was left among the Wobblies in the after years who, like Ray Becker, burned with a desire for vindication or some kind of admission of guilt on the part of Centralia.

One citizen came close to such an admission in a letter to the editor of the *Chronicle* in 1979. "You know the black cancer that has slowly, over the years, crept into our town," he wrote. "We have something (the statue) in our park...that was produced out of fear and hate and something that reeks of wrongdoing and death. It is something that has no right standing in the sun. This thing should be buried along with thoughts of hate and fear."[17]

Though much was written about Everest, he was not accorded a degree of martyrdom comparable to that of some others such as Joe Hill. There was never a "Friends of Wesley Everest" organization like the "Friends of Joe Hill" who picketed the offices of the *New Republic* in New York in 1948 to protest an article by Wallace Stegner which seemed to convict Hill anew of a murder which, after thirty-two years, many believed him innocent. Ralph Chaplin responded to the Stegner article with a five-page letter of denunciation to the *Industrial Worker*.[18]

Chaplin, author of the original comprehensive Wobbly account of the Centralia case, went to San Francisco in the late 1930s as editor of a labor newspaper at the height of jurisdictional struggles between the old federation and the new industrial union offshoot, the Committee for Industrial Organization. The Communists were using unions to further their ends at that time and pressure from them forced Chaplin to give up his job after only three months. He was identified as an enemy of the Communists and his life was threatened.[19] Chaplin then took a job in which he exposed the CIO's connections with Moscow. This took him to Long Beach where he lived with an armed guard posted at his door.

"Imagine," his wife wrote to a friend, "Ralph, who

had spent the best years of his life fighting for the underdog, to be placed in a position where he needed armed force to protect him from a so-called labor union! That lasted only two months. Then Dave Beck, head of the Teamsters Union in the Northwest, asked him to go to Seattle to edit a publicity organ to combat the CIO influence there."[20]

He was forced out of that job, his wife contended, when local Communists, deeply involved in local and state politics, as was Beck, agreed to support Beck's slate of candidates in an election if he would get rid of the anti-Communist publicity bureau and Chaplin.

Chaplin lived out his years in Tacoma as editor of a labor paper there. Then, turning to history, he worked for several years as a volunteer consultant to the Washington State Historical Society.

A rare instance of official admission of injustice in the war on Wobblies occurred in May of 1987. The Nevada State Board of Pardons voted six to one to grant posthumous pardons — the first in the state's history — to Morrie Preston and Joe Smith, convicted of a Goldfield killing in 1907. Both men were considered to be IWW radicals. Smith, an organizer, had called for the boycott of a restaurant owned by a John Silva, who had docked the pay of a waitress who left without notice. Preston was picketing the restaurant when Silva, pistol in hand, went out in the street to drive him and other pickets away. Preston drew a gun and shot Silva, killing him. Smith was at home with his family at the time, but was arrested on a charge of

conspiracy in the killing and the two were quickly convicted of murder in a trial atmosphere strongly redolent of anti-Wobblyism.

Recent research uncovered a 1914 letter in which the prosecutor admitted that two key prosecution witnesses, one a member of Butch Cassidy's outlaw gang, had lied on the witness stand. A hearing was held in Carson City and the convictions of the two Wobblies, long dead, were declared to have resulted more from prejudice than from the facts of the case.

Wesley Everest's place of burial remained unmarked and its location known only to the few who were present when the grave was dug until the late 1930s when a modest granite headstone was purchased from a Centralia monument maker and placed on the grave in the southwest corner of the Sticklin Greenwood Memorial Park near the northwest outskirts of Centralia. In one corner of the marker is the IWW emblem. The inscription reads:

In memory of
Wesley Everest
Killed Nov. 11, 1919
Age 32

In the early 1980s flowers began appearing on the grave, raising a much-discussed question: Who, after all these years, would be putting them there? The mystery was solved when Jackie Morgan, whose interest in the case was only heightened by the efforts to get

her to stop digging into it, "staked out" the grave, as she put it, and found that an elderly woman, Goldie Horst, was walking from her home in Centralia to decorate the grave of Centralia's one lynch victim.

Her explanation was simple. She had been a close friend in Aberdeen years before of an Oliver Smith who was a friend of Everest in the service. Smith asked her to let him know if she ever found the location of his old friend's grave. Smith was dead by the time she located the grave, so she was simply doing what she knew her friend Smith would be doing if he were there. Smith told her that Everest was a "devil-may-care" sort of person, full of fun and "with lots of guts."[21]

On the sixtieth anniversary of the Centralia violence the Pacific Northwest Labor History Association sponsored a commemorative visit to Montesano and Centralia. An estimated 150 persons went first to the courtroom where the trial was held and heard Prof. Albert Gunns of the California State College at Long Beach present an account of the case. On the way to Centralia a stop was made at the site of "Hangman's Bridge" where the lynching took place. Then, after a visit to North Tower Avenue, the group gathered for dinner, a slide show, and more talks at Centralia Community College. Julia Ruuttila was there, still feisty enough to rise and dress down Professor Gunns for not telling the story the way she believes it should be told — with all the blame for the trouble going to the Centralia business community and full vindication being accorded the Wobblies.

Sixty years after Armistice Day, 1919, Centralia no longer suffered from the consequences. Few were left who remembered. It was all history now, remaining to be told right. So much time had gone by that even those familiar with the case could drive past on the freeway, see the "Centralia" signs, and not reflexively associate the name with the dramatic events of long ago.

33

Conclusions

Accounts of conflict in the West usually follow a pattern. Good men oppose bad. In this familiar pattern it is usually made plain who are good and who are bad.

In Centralia on Armistice Day, 1919, the bad men were easy enough to identify in terms of that day's standards. The Wobblies were considered so bad that a substantial portion of the good citizens wanted them run out of town, as they had been run out before, and that is just what was attempted. Towns existed as islands. Each sought to rid itself of any undesirable element, in this case the Wobblies, just as Seattle and Tacoma tried to cleanse themselves of Orientals in the late nineteenth century. Expulsion — forced deportation — was the solution, it being of no concern to the people of one town that their expelled undesirables would have nowhere to go except the next town.

The IWW was considered to be the prime evil element in the Northwest in the first quarter of this century, and evil will thrive, as the saying goes, if good men do nothing about it. It could not have occurred to the men in Centralia who wanted to do something about the evil presence of the IWW in their midst that they were motivated by anything other than a desire to do a good thing. So they were both surprised and dismayed as time went on to find that what they did or wanted to do was not considered by all reasonable persons to be good.

The men identified in Centralia as bad were not all bad, it turned out, nor the good men all good. This resulted in confusing evaluations which were accentuated by the attention focused on something unique in such conflict situations — opposing martyrs. This clouded issues that otherwise might have been seen more clearly after everyone's tempers simmered down. Here were four men returned from risking their lives in defense of their country, shot down on the streets of their hometown while engaged in a patriotic exercise. Everyone was stunned. The inconceivable had happened. The shock was a long time wearing down. Centralia grieved, buried its martyrs, and erected a monument to them.

The eight men who were arrested, tried, and convicted, plus Wesley Everest, came to be identified as martyrs also — martyrs to the cause of labor — as Elmer Smith and others went about the task of proving that a great wrong had been done.

The Centralia case, like the one involving Tom Mooney, had enough emotional appeal to make it a rallying point for union leaders needing something dramatic to talk about in their organizing efforts. And as the years went by the continued imprisonment of the Centralia men, and the unceasing clamor in their behalf, made the case a political as well as a labor issue. Lines of contention between employers and unions tightened around it. To employers and others who never heard or read anything good about the IWW, it was unthinkable that any leniency should be shown to IWW members found guilty of murder. Thus employer opposition came to be identified as the chief obstacle in the efforts to gain the men's freedom. And if it were an employer objective to keep them in prison, it must then be a labor objective to get them out. This made the Centralia men not just Wobbly martyrs but class-war martyrs as well. Much of the defense literature does not even mention the IWW.

Employers in 1919 were understandably afraid of the IWW. Not only was it a labor union of sorts, which made it automatically threatening to those who never intended to give collective bargaining serious consideration, but it was also a radical band bent on destroying the American economic system. Furthermore the Wobblies did unpopular things. They engaged in strikes. When they worked they "dogged it." They published radical tracts and sang songs that mocked respectable institutions. They were blasphemous and irreverent. Worst of all they engaged in sabotage. They denied it, but their literature preached it. They denied it, but reports of it by responsible men were too numerous to be doubted.

Hostility toward the IWW was accentuated by the brief but frightening display of union power in the Seattle general strike earlier in the year. Also everyone remembered the Everett violence and the refusal of Wobblies to support the war effort in any way.

So tempers in Centralia flared in the fall of 1919 when brash Wobblies dared open another hall, this time right on Tower Avenue, and with a big sign in the window. Eighteen months previously they had been run out. Now they were back. Something had to be done. Since no one was punished or even criticized, outside the labor press, for Centralia's raid on the hall in 1918, there was no reason to conclude that similar action in 1919 would not be entirely in order. So a raid was planned, or at least talked about, in an open meeting in October. Other towns were taking action, the secretary of the employers' association told Centralia employers. It was time they did something also.

No firm evidence supports the contention that a raid was planned by those who marched in the parade, but it is indisputable that the marchers knew of Centralia's mood and that some of the marchers, at least, expressed a willingness to take part in a raid moments before it occurred.

The Centralia Wobblies knew it was coming. They appealed for protection under the law and were rebuffed. They appealed to public opinion through a widely distributed circular and received no sympathetic response at all. Their alternatives were to give in — to step aside and let the hall be raided — or to put up a defense, something that was almost never done. Wobbly hall raids were common but resistance to them was not. This was partly because such raids came unexpectedly. Vigilantes customarily didn't issue warnings. But in Centralia what amounted to a notice of intention to raid was given at a meeting in the Elks hall three weeks before Armistice Day. The men who gathered in the IWW hall had a long time to consider their plight. They asked Elmer Smith if they had a right to defend the hall and he said that they did. He was essentially right, but he was wrong in not counseling them that a defense should not include the stationing of snipers at posts outside the hall to catch raiders in a cross fire.

A central question always has been: Who was the aggressor? Which came first, a rush by men in the parade who halted directly in front of the hall, or shots from the defenders? The testimony of many witnesses is so conflicting on this point that it has always been possible to argue the question. But it has never been reasonable to contend that all the men in the parade were standing in the street, fifteen feet or more from the hall's door, when the first shots were fired, nor that those who admittedly broke into the hall were seeking shelter. Bullets came out through the door from Wesley Everest's gun but not before soldier feet and shoulders broke it open.

A raid on the hall was intended. It was willed by the mood of the city if not planned by those bold enough to take action. And it occurred, whether at a time planned or as a result of a sudden decision when the opportunity made it seem easy. A raid with enough men would not need to take more than a few minutes. The patriotic program still remaining would not even be interrupted. And so it happened.

The raid came as no surprise to the Wobblies. The surprise was on the other side. They didn't expect resistance of any kind, much less gunfire. Elmer Smith knew about the guns and he might have prevented the slaughter if, after leaving the hall, he had issued a warning. But whom could he warn? The police? The police had all but admitted an unwillingness to act in the face of a townwide resolve to take vigilante action. Still the police might have intervened if Smith had warned that the Wobblies were armed.

Whether Warren Grimm was shot from a window of the Avalon while he stood at the corner of Second and Tower or when he hit the door of the hall like a football player smashing a line was made a point of great magnitude at the trial because the judge, agreeing with the prosecution, was determined not to allow any testimony that would tend to show any need for defense of the hall. This made little difference in the final outcome. The anti-Wobbly mood was just as prevalent in Montesano as in Centralia and so, with federal troops camped in the shadow of the courthouse to protect good people from the danger of further bloodshed at the hands of some other lawless Wobbly band, the accused men — all but three of them — stood no chance at all of acquittal, no matter what the evidence, even at the hands of a jury that was reluctant to convict and whose members, most of them, later publicly recanted and acknowledged that their verdict was wrong. These men were marked for punishment as surely as was Everest, the one Wobbly who was a killer beyond doubt because he shot young Dale Hubbard right before the eyes of C. D. Cunningham and the other pursuers on the banks of the swollen Skookumchuck. The urge to retaliate was too strong to suppress in the early dark of Armistice Day. Infuriated vigilantes dragged Everest out of jail, then hanged him, and pumped bullets into the limp body that almost certainly also had been maimed.

Judge Wilson was as much infected with the anti-Wobbly spirit of the day as the justices of the supreme court, but he was not given the chance to give voice to it as did Justice Mackintosh when he wrote the stinging decision affirming the Montesano conviction. Wilson's prejudice showed in the repeated rulings that kept from the jury evidence supporting the contention that the armed defense of the hall was brought on by the expectation of the raid. Wilson's disappointment at the verdict — second-degree murder — was on a level with that of the prosecutors and he undertook to overrule it and demonstrate that no leniency toward Wobblies would come out of his court when he ignored the jury's plea for light sentences and imposed the harshest penalties the statute books would allow.

The Centralia case came to be called the "Centralia massacre." It was a bloody mess, all agreed, and very unfortunate, except that it proved something about the Wobblies and perhaps set them back so much they would never recover. That hope came to be realized in the decade that followed, although it is not reasonable to conclude that the Centralia affair alone brought on the IWW's decline. The setback dampened Wobbly ardor and made the IWW more cautious in its random pursuit of goals not as easily defined as the eight-hour day and elimination of bedrolls — objectives attained long before 1919.

The IWW couldn't sign contracts, unlike any other union. There was no one to sign, no one who could speak for the IWW unless it was to repeat the Wobbly creed proclaiming total disinvolvement with capitalism, the wage system, and the right of one class to subject another to the humiliation of subservience.

Two old Wobblies engaged in a philosophic exchange of views in 1960. One was Richard Brazier, a writer in his young years of firebrand verse that went into the Little Red Song Book, and later a speaker, organizer, and "defense worker." The other was T. J. Bogard, another early-day Wobbly with the intellectual capacity to look back and seek an understanding of what he had devoted his life to.

After telling Bogard that he would rather be remembered for his songs than for going to jail for a principle — because jail was merely a part of the way of life for a fellow worker — Brazier wrote: "You ask what was wrong with the IWW and why did we fail? My answer is that in one sense we did not fail because, you see, Tom, we never were much more than a propaganda organization. We never had any large amount of job control. . . . We never had control long enough to solidify gains. In a way we were just missionaries going around spreading the gospel of industrial unionism and the necessity of working class solidarity."[1]

Bogard said the IWW "sowed the seeds of industrial unionism." This could be its only claim to lasting achievement beyond the gains that were forced upon timber industry employers by the government during the war to buy peace in the woods and mills and stop the strikes and slowdowns that impeded war production. It took another decade and more for the industrial union concept to gain decisive support in a labor movement as devoted to craft unionism as employers were to freedom from organized-labor involvement of any kind. It took form in the first faltering steps of a labor offshoot calling itself the Committee for Industrial Organization, headed by John L. Lewis. Then it had to shake off the clawing hands of domestic Communists, whose objectives were enough like those of the IWW to cause the two often to be lumped together as equally objectionable, and became the powerful Congress of Industrial Organizations which later merged with the AFL. Into the CIO went many of the Wobblies, taking with them their unshakable belief in "one big union" and gaining for the CIO the recognition and acceptance the IWW was groping for but lost forever with setbacks such as Centralia.

Because the IWW began losing ground instead of emerging as a dominant force after World War I, it might be concluded that the repressive ways used against it were successful and so could be used again. But the raids and the head knockings and the tar and featherings came to an end. Not even the hated Communists after World War II were dealt with as harshly

241

as were the Wobblies after World War I.

Might it be concluded, then, that the Centralia case had a sobering effect on the nation? Did citizens generally, seeing what could happen in an atmosphere as intolerant as the one that developed in Centralia, resolve that such a thing would never happen again? No, for the citizens, most of them, never learned what actually happened at Centralia. The full story wasn't told. What motivated the IWW in firing their guns was little known and even less understood. Public opinion was formed on the basis of early newspaper accounts which only reported that armed Wobblies killed four Legionnaires. It was affirmation in blood of the worst that was believed about the Wobblies. Any claim that the hall was attacked could be easily dismissed as an attempt to alibi out of a predicament.

The Wobblies suffered also because of their utter disregard for public opinion as they set out in their own erratic ways to achieve objectives intended for the betterment of the "working class." So when trouble came, and the troublemakers were arrayed against as respectable a group as the American Legion, it was obvious who would have the public's sympathy.

Judgments about the case, however, were being made more than sixty years after the event. In a renewal of the perennial controversy over capital punishment in 1985, the ACLU sponsored a research project that compiled a list of innocent persons who have been convicted of murder or sentenced to death since the turn of the century. The total number, according to the study, was 343, among them "seven members of the IWW convicted of murder in Montesano in 1920."

When a cause, long pursued, eventually prevails, whether it be political, revolutionary, or other, whatever occurred on the road to success tends to become sanctified. After the downfall of the IWW in the late 1920s, the cause of labor came to prevail in a resounding way, but under different names, and there could be seen, in recent years, a tendency to paint the Wobblies with quite different colors than those used in earlier times. Plays and novels were written about the Centralia case, and about the Wobblies, placing emphasis on their romantic characteristics — free spirits defying tradition and authority, clinging loyally to unpopular beliefs, adhering to a code of ethics with curious aspects, such as rejection of what might be "dehorn," and along the way singing, always singing, loud, off-key songs of defiance.

The Wobblies became latter-day heroes to some of the young in the later part of the century. Some of the young admirers even made attempts at revival.

But new and revived attitudes toward the Wobblies of old contribute nothing to a long-delayed understanding of the episode known as the Centralia case, nor do they help dispel the wrongness of so much that has been published by those trying desperately to prove a case — their side of the case — with good and evil plainly identified in black and white.

Neither side in the war on the Wobblies deserves to be called all good or all bad. Each should be judged by what actually was done, and what motivated the deeds, at a point in American history when attitudes about labor were as unlike those of today as attitudes about race are from those of recent yesteryear.

NOTES

FOREWORD

1. John Dos Passos, *1919* (New York: Harcourt, Brace, 1932), pp. 456-61 (vol. 3 of *U. S. A.*, New York: Harcourt, Brace, 1930-1936). Dos Passos followed the pro-IWW account of Chaplin (see note 2, below).

2. Until *Wobbly War* the leading works on the Centralia episode were: Ralph Chaplin, *The Centralia Conspiracy,* pamphlet (Seattle: n. p., 1920), the IWW version; Ben Hur Lampman, *Centralia: Tragedy and Trial,* pamphlet (Centralia: American Legion, c. 1920), an anti-IWW account; Federal Council of Churches *et al., The Centralia Case,* pamphlet (New York: Federal Council of Churches, 1930), an unbiased, objective study; and Robert L.Tyler, *Rebels of the Woods: The I.W.W. in the Pacific Northwest* (Eugene: University of Oregon Books, 1976), chapter 6 of which, although only one chapter in a larger study, is an able, balanced essay on the Centralia episode. All of these accounts, whether slanted or objective, are inadequate in comparison to the thorough research and full treatment represented by *Wobbly War.*

3. For further reading, see Thomas R. Cox, *Mills and Markets: History of the Pacific Coast Lumber Industry* (Seattle: University of Washington Press, 1974), and Ellis Lucia, *The Big Woods: Logging and Lumbering — from Bull Teams to Helicopters — in the Pacific Northwest* (Garden City, N.Y.: Doubleday, 1975).

4. The leading study of the IWW is Melvin Dubofsky, *We Shall Be All: A History of the Industrial Workers of the World* (Chicago: Quadrangle, 1969). Other recent general works on the IWW are Joseph R. Conlin, *Bread and Roses Too: Studies of the Wobblies* (Westport, Conn.: Greenwood, 1969), and Patrick Renshaw, *The Wobblies: The Story of of Syndicalism in the U.S.* (Garden City, N. Y.: Doubleday, 1967). Encyclopedic but slanted is Philip S. Foner, *History of the Labor Movement in the United States: Volume IV: The Industrial Workers of the World, 1905-1917* (New York: International Publishers, c. 1965). Fred Thompson and Patrick Murfin, *The I.W.W.: Its First Seventy Years* (Chicago: Industrial Workers of the World, 1976), is the official history of the IWW. The most complete bibliography of the IWW is Joseph R. Conlin, ed., *At the Point of Production: The Local History of the I.W.W.* (Westport, Conn.: Greenwood, 1981), pp. 237-318.

5. For further reading, see Joseph R. Conlin, *Big Bill Haywood and the Radical Labor Movement* (Syracuse: Syracuse University Press, 1969), and Peter Carlson, *Roughneck: The Life and Times of Big Bill Haywood* (New York: W.W. Norton, c. 1983).

6. Conlin, *Bread and Roses.*

7. Joyce L. Kornbluh, ed., *Rebel Voices: An I.W.W. Anthology* (Ann Arbor: University of Michigan Press, 1969). See, also, Donald E. Winters, Jr., *The Soul of the Wobblies: The I.W.W.*

Religion, and American Culture in the Progressive Era, 1905-1917 (Westport, Conn.: Greenwood, 1985), chapters 3 and 5.

8. Tyler, *Rebels of the Woods.*

9. Ibid., chapters 2-3. See also Norman H. Clark, *Mill Town: A Social History of Everett, Washington, from Its Earliest Beginnings on the Shores of Puget Sound to the Tragic and Infamous Event Known as the Everett Massacre* (Seattle: University of Washington Press, 1970). The best overall treatment of violent industrial relations in American history is Philip Taft and Philip Ross, "American Labor Violence: Its Causes, Character, and Outcome," in Hugh Davis Graham and Ted Robert Gurr, eds., *Violence in America: Historical and Comparative Perspectives: A Report to the National Commission on the Causes and Prevention of Violence* (2 vols.; Washington, D. C.: U.S. Government Printing Office, 1969), pp. 221-301.

10. Andrew Mason Prouty, *More Deadly than War! Pacific Coast Logging, 1827-1981* (New York: Garland, 1985).

11. See Vernon H. Jensen, *Lumber and Labor* (New York: Farrar & Rinehart, 1945); Harold Hyman, *Soldiers and Spruce: Origins of the Loyal Legion of Loggers and and Lumbermen* (Los Angeles: University of California Press, 1963); and Robert E. Ficken, "The Wobbly Horrors: Pacific Northwest Lumbermen and the Industrial Workers of the World, 1917-1918," *Labor History*, 24 (Summer, 1983): pp. 325-340.

12. Carlos A. Schwantes, *Radical Heritage: Labor, Socialism, and Reform in Washington and British Columbia, 1885-1917* (Seattle: University of Washington Press, 1979).

13. Robert W. Smith, *The Coeur d'Alene Mining War of 1892: A Case Study of an Industrial Dispute* (Corvallis: Oregon State University Press, 1961).

14. Arnon Gutfeld, *Montana's Agony: Years of War and Hysteria, 1917-1921* (Gainesville: University Presses of Florida, 1979), chapter 3.

15. James W. Byrkit, *Forging the Copper Collar: Arizona's Labor-Management War* (Tucson: University of Arizona Press, c. 1982); A. Yvette Huginnie, "Copper-coated Dreams: Labor Organization and Community in the Southwest and Northern Mexico" (unpublished paper, annual meeting of the Western History Association, Billings, Montana, October 16, 1986).

16. Robert L. Friedheim, *The Seattle General Strike* (Seattle: University of Washington Press, 1964).

17. See William Preston, *Aliens and Dissenters: Federal Suppression of Radicals, 1903-1933* (Cambridge: Harvard University Press, 1963), chapters 4-8; David M. Kennedy, *Over Here: The First World War and American Society* (New York: Oxford University Press, 1980), chapter 1; H. C. Peterson and Gilbert C.

Fite, *Opponents of War, 1917-1918* (Madison: University of Wisconsin Press, 1957); and Joan M. Jensen, *The Price of Vigilance* (Chicago: Rand McNally, c. 1968).

18. Robert K. Murray, *Red Scare: A Study in National Hysteria, 1919-1920* (New York: McGraw-Hill, 1955).

19. Richard Seelye Jones, *A History of the American* (Indianapolis: Bobbs-Merrill, c. 1966), pp. 25-26.

20. Michael Kammen, ed., *The Past Before Us: Contemporary Historical Writing in the United States* (Ithaca: Cornell University Press, 1980), chapter 11.

21. Clark, *Mill Town*. An even more recent example of the local-history approach to the IWW is Conlin, ed., *At the Point of Production*. See also Kammen, ed., *Past Before Us*, chapter 10.

22. Richard Maxwell Brown, *Strain of Violence: Historical Studies of American Violence and Vigilantism* (New York: Oxford University Press, 1975), chapters 4-6.

23. Carlos A. Schwantes, "The Concept of the Wageworkers' Frontier: A Framework for Future Research," *Western Historical Quarterly*, 17 (January, 1987): pp. 39-55.

CHAPTER 1

1. Early in its history the Industrial Workers of the World acquired a nickname — Wobblies — that came to be considered a proper name, used interchangeably with the initials IWW. Several theories on the origin of the name Wobbly have been advanced, but the one most frequently heard, and most likely true, concerns a Chinese man. Stewart Holbrook, writing in the *American Mercury* of January 1926 on the subject "Wobbly Talk," explained that an enterprising Chinese laundryman, following the Canadian Northern railroad construction crews through Saskatchewan in 1914, realized it was good business to make friends with the men who either were "packing red cards" or at least had leanings toward the IWW. "But the heathen tongue was not equal to the letter W," wrote Holbrook. " 'Me likee I Wobbly Wobbly' was the best it could do. It proved enough. Wobbly spread from man to man and, by mysterious, unseen jungle news channels, from camp to camp, until now it is used by all Western headline writers."

2. Mrs. Will Marion Oliver, interview, Lewis County Historical Society records, page 11/T131.

3. *Coast Magazine*, March 1909.

CHAPTER 2

1. Clyde Lowe, letter to author, 17 April 1961.

2. *Los Angeles Times*, 26 December 1913.

3. Quoted in Nathan Douthit, *The Coos Bay Region, 1890-1944*, 1981, p. 120.

4. Ibid., p. 121.

5. Ibid., p. 121.

6. Leigh H. Irvin, *Un-American Ambitions* (Employers Assn. of Wash., n.d.); Northwest Collection, University of Washington Libraries.

7. Hawley and Potts, *Counsel for the Damned* (N.Y.: Lippincott & Co., 1953), p. 174.

8. *Everett Labor Journal*, 15 September 1916.

9. Hawley and Potts, *Counsel*, p. 180.

10. A black cat was one of the Wobblies' sinister symbols used to intimidate employers.

11. Walker C. Smith, *The Everett Massacre* (Chicago: IWW Publishing Bureau, n.d.), p. 85.

12. Norman Clark, *Mill Town*, p. 201.

13. William J. Williams, "Bloody Sunday Revisited" in *Pacific Northwest Quarterly*, Vol. 71, No. 2, p. 50.

14. Hawley and Potts, *Counsel*, p. 17.

CHAPTER 3

1. Herbert Hunt and Floyd C. Kaylor, *Washington West of the Cascades* (Chicago: S. J. Clarke, 1917), p. 285.

2. This episode is described in detail in Hunt and Kaylor, *Washington West of the Cascades*, and also in Clinton A. Snowden, *History of Washington* (New York: Century History Company, 1909), vol. IV, p. 277.

3. Richard Maxwell Brown, "The American Vigilante Tradition," in Hugh Davis Graham and Ted Robert Gurr, eds., *Violence in America: Historical and Comparative Perspectives: A Report to the National Commission on the Causes and Prevention of Violence* (2 vols.; Washington, D.C.: U.S. Government Printing Office, 1969), p. 123.

4. Kina Bower, *In the Service, the Great World War: Honor Roll*, (Centralia: n.p., n.d.).

5. Ibid., p. 25.

6. *Industrial Worker*, 29 April 1916.

7. *Industrial Worker*, 13 May 1917.

CHAPTER 4

1. Tom Copeland, "The Story of Elmer 'Red' Smith, '10," *Macalester Alumni Magazine*, September 1972.

2. Hunt and Kaylor, *Washington West of the Cascades*, p. 315.

3. Louis Adamic, *Dynamite* (New York: Viking Press, 1931), p. 395.

CHAPTER 5

1. Proceedings, National Lumber Manufacturers Association (Chicago, 1912), p. 23.

2. *Syndicat* is a French word meaning a grouping together. "Syndicalism" was used to describe the process of grouping, in the case of unions for conspiratorial purposes. The new anti-syndicalism laws were aimed at gatherings of those who advocated revolution and resistance to the national objective — winning a war.

3. Memorandum for the attorney general, including "an extract from a letter written by an Olympia lawyer 'of high repute'" who lived near the governor's apartment; Department of Justice file 186701, National Archives.

4. Report of the President's Mediation Commission to the President of the U.S., *Unrest in the Lumber Industry*, p. 14; cited in J. S. Gambs, "Decline of the IWW," in *Studies in History, Economics and Public Law*, No. 361 (New York: Columbia University Press, 1932), p. 37.

5. Ibid.

CHAPTER 6

1. *Centralia Chronicle*, 16 August 1917.

2. *Industrial Worker*, 10 March 1917, p. 2.

3. *Chehalis Bee-Nugget,* 10 May 1918, p. 2.

4. Ibid.

5. *Bee-Nugget,* 21 June 1918.

6. Ibid.

7. *Chronicle,* 15 May 1917.

8. Lucien Birdseye was the father of Story Birdseye, for many years a Superior Court judge in King County. Story Birdseye as a boy witnessed the raid and destruction of the Centralia IWW hall in 1918. He recalled being shocked at seeing a typewriter and furniture thrown out of a second-story window.

9. *Centralia Hub,* 2 February 1918.

10. *Chronicle,* 6 May 1918, p. 1.

11. W. A. Blackwood to Wesley Jones, 30 January 1918; Department of Justice file 186701-49, National Archives.

12. Quoted in letter from attorney general to Clarence Reames, 3 October 1918; Department Justice file 186701, National Archives.

13. Lister papers, Box 2, Washington State Archives.

14. Thomas Elliott to Lister, 20 March 1918; Lister papers, State Archives.

15. Elliott to Lister, 21 March 1918; Lister papers, State Archives.

16. Fourth message of Gov. Ernest Lister to the state legislature, 16th session, Olympia, 1919.

17. *Congressional Record,* Vol. 56, Part 4, 65th Congress, 21 March 1918, p. 3821.

18. Robert W. Bruere, *Following the Trail of the IWW* (reprinted from the *New York Post,* 1918), p. 22.

19. Reames to attorney general; Department of Justice file 186701-49-75, National Archives.

CHAPTER 7

1. *State vs. Lowery,* 104, Wash. 521.

2. Session Laws, 1919, Chapter 174.

3. Session Laws, 1919, Chapter 173.

4. Washington's sabotage law remains on the statute books, an enduring Wobbly legacy. The antisyndicalism law was left standing, little noticed, until 1937 when it was repealed.

5. *Oregonian,* 4 July 1919, p. 1.

6. Thompson and Murfin, *The IWW,* p. 55.

7. *Chronicle,* 27 June 1919.

CHAPTER 8

1. Cunningham to Karl C. Peterson, Stanford, California, 1947; Cunningham papers, Legion Library.

2. *Chronicle,* 17 March 1917, p. 1.

3. *Chronicle,* 20 March 1917, p. 1.

4. Eugene Barnett, interview, n.d.; Labadie collection, University of Michigan Library.

5. Copies of many raid warrants from various parts of the country are in the Reuther Library, Wayne State University, Detroit.

6. *Industrial Worker,* 12 January 1918, p. 1.

7. *Chronicle,* 28 April 1917, p. 8.

CHAPTER 9

1. *Chronicle,* 3 November 1919.

2. *Oregonian,* 10 October 1919, report from Marshfield, Oregon.

3. L. H. May to attorney general, 17 March 1919; attorney general file 186701-49, National Archives.

4. Hart papers, Washingon State Archives.

5. *Montesano Vidette,* 17 October 1919.

6. Ibid.

7. *Oregonian,* 9 November 1919, p. 1.

8. *Seattle Union Record,* 18 September 1919, p. 1.

9. Ibid.

CHAPTER 10

1. Robert W. Berry, son of John Berry, letter to author, 25 August 1968.

2. *Chronicle,* 2 October 1919.

3. *Chronicle,* 8 October 1919.

4. D. E. Burrell, affidavit; IWW papers, Archives of Labor History and Urban Affairs, Wayne State University.

5. Ibid.

6. *Seattle Union Record,* 24 October 1919, p. l.

7. *Chronicle,* 21 October 1919.

8. *Tacoma News-Tribune,* 21 Oct. 1919, p. 9.

9. Ralph Chaplin, *Wobbly* (Chicago: University of Chicago Press, 1948), p. 58.

10. *State vs. Smith,* transcript of trial in Montesano, January-March, 1920, p. 2,394. C. D. Cunningham's copy of this transcript is in the National American Legion Library, Indianapolis, and a microfilm copy is in the manuscript division, University of Washington Libraries.

11. Ibid.

12. *To the Citizens of Centralia We Must Appeal,* undated one-page leaflet. Text reprinted in *Eight Men Buried Alive* (Chicago: General Defense Committee, IWW, 1924).

13. Ibid.

14. J. G. Parkin, Westlake Fuel Co., Seattle, *To Whom It May Concern,* n.d.; Ruuttila papers, Oregon Historical Society.

15. Carl Dickey, Centralia, letter to author, April 1965.

16. Charles Everest, brother of Wesley, interview with author, 5 March 1982.

17. Ibid.

18. Dorwin Cunningham, son of C. D. Cunningham, interview with author, 28 February 1983.

19. Loren Roberts, supplementary statement made to C. D. Cunningham and other prosecutors in presence of his mother, Mrs. Edna Roberts, 24 November 1919; Cunningham papers, Legion Library.

20. Chaplin, *Wobbly,* p. 317.

CHAPTER 11

1. Hollis B. Fultz, *Elkdom in Olympia* (Olympia: BPOE, 1966).

2. Loren Roberts, statement at sheriff's office, November 12, 1919; Cunningham papers, Legion Library.

3. Ibid.

4. Dewey Lamb, statement at sheriff's office, November 12, 1919; Cunningham papers.

5. Tom Morgan, statement at sheriff's office, November 24, 1919;

Cunningham papers.

6. Roberts statement, Cunningham papers.

7. Ibid.

8. Britt Smith, statement at sheriff's office, November 18, 1919; Cunningham papers.

9. John Lamb, statement at sheriff's office, November 15, 1919; Cunningham papers.

10. Florence Casagranda Mahar, affidavit, October 17, 1924; IWW papers, Centralia Public Library.

11. Ibid.

CHAPTER 12

1. Dr. Herbert Y. Bell, testimony at coroner's inquest, 13 November 1919; transcript in courthouse, Chehalis.

2. Adrian Cormier, testimony at coroner's inquest.

3. Dr. Frank Bickford, testimony at coroner's inquest.

4. Centralia Defense Committee affidavit, signed by Percy Draper, 14 November 1924; Ruuttila papers, Oregon Historical Society.

5. Eyewitness accounts of the capture of Everest are in letters from C. D. Cunningham to Karl J. Peterson, Stanford, California, 8 November 1947, and to Stewart Holbrook, Portland, 9 November 1937; Cunningham papers, Legion Library.

6. State vs. Smith, transcript of trial, p. 924.

7. Chronicle, 6 November, 1981, p. 7.

8. Ibid.

9. Report of Luke May operative, quoting Forest Nealey, bartender in the Olympic Club pool hall who marched with the Elks band; Luke May papers, University of Washington Libraries manuscript collections.

10. Oregonian, 12 November 1919, p. 1.

11. Helen and Marjorie Ort, interview with author, San Francisco, 27 April 1982.

12. State vs. Smith, transcript, p. 828.

13. Ibid., p. 829.

CHAPTER 13

1. Hollis Fultz, interview with author, Olympia, 5 November 1974.

2. Oregonian, 12 November 1919, p. 1.

3. Tacoma News-Tribune, 12 November 1919, p. 20.

4. May papers, A-1.1-1, University of Washington Libraries manuscript collections.

5. Lloyd Dysart, interview with Sue Toy, Lewis County Historical Society, 10 January 1975; IWW collection, Centralia Public Library.

6. Ibid.

7. Windsor to attorney general, 24 November 1919; attorney general files, State Archives.

8. Lew Selvidge, interview with author, Olympia, 12 January 1962.

9. Eugene Barnett, letter to author, 27 September 1961.

10. Chaplin, The Centralia Conspiracy, p. 75.

11. Julia Ruuttila, notation on lynch suspect list; Ruuttila papers, Oregon Historical Society.

CHAPTER 14

1. This account of Barnett's capture is based on an interview with Dysart in Centralia, and on later correspondence between the author and Barnett.

2. Aberdeen World, 12 November 1919.

3. Ibid.

4. Washington Standard, 12 November 1919, p.1.

5. Chronicle, 19 November 1919.

6. Ibid.

7. Chronicle, 20 November 1919.

8. Ibid.

9. Transcript of inquest, 13 November 1919; Clerk's Files, courthouse, Chehalis.

10. Bert McDonald, letter to Frank Bayley, Sr., Seattle, 1 December 1959; files of Christopher T. Bayley, Seattle.

CHAPTER 15

1. Oregonian, 13 November 1919, p. 6.

2. Saunders to attorney general, 13 November 1919; Department of Justice file 186701-74, National Archives.

3. L. L. Thompson to attorney general, 19 November 1919; Department of Justice files, National Archives.

4. Chronicle, 13 November 1919.

5. Ibid.

6. Aberdeen World, 15 November 1919, p. 4.

7. See Anna Louise Strong, I Change Worlds (New York: H. Holt, 1937).

8. Seattle Post-Intelligencer, 14 November 1919, p. 2.

9. Short to Palmer, 15 November 1919; Department of Justice files, National Archives.

10. Chronicle, 14 November 1919, p. 1.

11. Post-Intelligencer, 18 November 1919.

12. William Short to attorney general, 18 November 1919; Department of Justice file 1806701-74, National Archives.

13. Post-Intelligencer, 21 November 1919.

14. Ibid.

15. George Ryan to Joseph Tumulty, 18 November 1919; Department of Justice file 186701-74-47, National Archives.

16. Saunders to attorney general, 8 March 1920; attorney general files, National Archives.

CHAPTER 16

1. These statements are in the Cunningham papers, Legion Library.

2. Washington Standard, 28 November 1919.

3. Published statement, City of Centralia, 24 November 1919.

4. Chronicle, 18 November 1919.

5. Cunningham papers, Legion Library.

CHAPTER 17

1. Montesano Vidette, 5 December 1919.

2. Northwest District Defense Committee, Workers, Judge for Yourselves About Centralia (Butte, Mont.: IWW, n.d.).

3. Americans, Judge for Yourselves About Centralia, pamphlet (n.p., n.d.); exhibit B, State vs. Smith.

4. *Truth Vs. Lies!,* pamphlet (n.p., n.d.); exhibit C, *State vs. Smith.*

5. *Will IWW Threat Affect the Jury's Verdict?,* pamphlet (n.p., n.d.) exhibit E, *State vs. Smith.*

6. *State vs. Smith,* transcript on appeal to Washington Supreme Court, 36A.

7. Ralph Chaplin, *Wobbly,* p. 86.

CHAPTER 18

1. *The Issues in the Centralia Murder Trial,* pamphlet (New York: American Civil Liberties Union, 1930).

2. *Raids, Raids, Raids,* pamphlet (IWW: n.p., n.d.).

3. F. R. Jeffrey, Kennewick, Washington, to Lemuel Bolles, national adjutant, American Legion, 27 February 1920; Cunningham papers, Legion Library.

4. The five were H. H. Martin Lumber Company, Eastern Railway and Timber Company, Chehalis Mill Company, Lincoln Creek Lumber Company, and Coal Creek Lumber Company; May papers, University of Washington Libraries manuscript collections.

5. May papers.

6. *Vidette,* 23 January 1920.

7. F. Kaffre in the *Farmer-Labor Call,* quoted in *Industrial Worker,* 5 March 1921.

CHAPTER 19

1. *Vidette,* 30 January 1920, p. 4.

2. *Industrial Worker,* 21 February 1920.

3. Ibid.

CHAPTER 20

1. *State vs. Smith,* transcript of testimony, p. 594.

2. Ibid., p. 595.

3. Ibid., p. 598.

4. Ibid., p. 1029.

5. Ibid., p. 689.

6. Ruuttila papers, Oregon Historical Society.

7. *State vs. Smith,* p. 935.

8. Ibid., p. 936.

9. Ibid., p. 570.

10. Ibid., p. 1089.

11. Ibid., p. 1095.

12. Ibid., p. 923.

13. Ibid.

14. Ibid., p. 2352.

15. *Oregonian,* 15 February 1920.

16. *State vs. Smith,* p. 1158.

17. *Oregonian,* 19 February 1920.

CHAPTER 21

1. Dewey Lamb, interview with author, Centralia, 12 September 1984.

2. *State vs. Smith,* transcript of trial, p. 1430.

3. Ibid., p. 1431.

4. Ibid., p. 1607.

5. Ibid., p. 1619.

6. Vanderveer, letter to Roger Baldwin, 23 February 1920; ACLU papers, University of Washington Libraries manuscript collections.

7. *State vs. Smith,* p. 1936.

8. Ibid., p. 1969.

9. *Chronicle,* 1 March 1920.

10. *State vs. Smith,* p. 2964.

11. Ibid., p. 2979.

12. *Vidette,* 12 March 1920, p. 5.

13. *State vs. Smith,* p. 1520.

14. Ibid., p. 1535.

15. Ibid., p. 1380.

16. Ibid., p. 1383.

17. Ibid., p. 1638.

18. Ibid., p. 1650.

19. Ibid., p. 1339.

20. Ibid., p. 1351.

21. Ibid., p. 2021.

22. Ibid., p. 2027.

23. Ibid., p. 1759.

24. Ibid., p. 1788.

25. Ibid., p. 1740.

26. Ibid., p. 1742.

27. Ibid., p. 1744.

28. Ibid., p. 1748.

29. Ibid., p. 2003.

30. Ibid., p. 2009.

31. Ibid., p. 2013.

32. Ibid., p. 1588.

33. *Hub,* 20 October 1919, p. 1.

34. *State vs. Smith,* p. 2367.

35. Ibid., p. 2383.

36. Ibid., p. 2388.

37. Ibid., p. 2904.

38. Ibid., p. 1912.

39. Ibid., p. 2950.

40. Ibid., p. 2918.

CHAPTER 22

1. *Vidette,* 14 March 1920.

2. The text of Judge Wilson's instructions to the jury is in unnumbered pages at the conclusion of the trial transcript.

3. *Industrial Worker,* 9 March 1920.

4. Ibid.

5. William Inman, interview with author, Oakville, 13 February 1960.

6. Ibid.

7. Ibid.

8. *Industrial Worker,* 2 April 1920.

CHAPTER 23

1. *Vidette,* 16 March 1920.

2. *Post-Intelligencer,* 14 March 1920.
3. Ben Hur Lampman, *Centralia: Tragedy and Trial,* p. 29.
4. *Oregonian,* 15 March 1920, p. 9.
5. *Post-Intelligencer,* 16 March 1920, p. 8.
6. Ibid., 15 March 1920, p. 1.
7. William Inman, interview with author, Oakville, 13 February 1960.
8. *Oregonian,* 22 March 1920, p. 1.
9. Report of operative 155, 30 March 1920; May papers, University of Washington Libraries manuscript collections.
10. *State vs. Smith,* 115 Wash. 405, 115.
11. *State vs. Smith* et al, No. 16354.
12. *State vs. Smith,* petition for rehearing, p. 2.
13. Ibid., p. 12.

CHAPTER 24

1. *Chronicle,* 29 June 1920.
2. Ibid.
3. *Current History,* 20 August 1922.
4. Virgina Smith Waddell, unpublished autobiographical sketch in her possession.
5. Ibid.
6. Ibid.
7. Report of operative 26, 15 June 1921; May papers, University of Washington Libraries manuscript collections.
8. Dewey Lamb, interview with author, Centralia, 12 September 1984.
9. *Farmer-Labor Call,* 22 October 1920, p. 4.
10. Ibid.
11. Microfilm reel 1, p. 167, ACLU papers, University of Washington Libraries.
12. *Industrial Worker,* 15 April 1921.

CHAPTER 25

1. Minute book, American Legion National Executive Committee, 18 May 1920, p. 7; Legion Library.
2. Ibid.
3. Ibid., p. 274.
4. Ibid.
5. Ibid., p. 306.
6. *Industrial Worker,* 6 November 1921.
7. Thomas Nash, interview, *Post-Intelligencer,* 28 August 1961.
8. Cunningham papers, Legion Library.
9. *Farmer-Labor Call,* 16 February 1922.
10. Affidavit, 15 May 1922. These and other affidavits by jurors were widely published in newspapers and IWW literature. Copies in Ruuttila papers, Oregon Historical Society, and Cunningham papers, Legion Library.
11. E. E. Torpen, affidavit before O. M. Nelson, notary, 17 May 1922.
12. P. V. Johnson, affidavit before B. A. Green, notary, 29 May 1922.
13. Carl O. Hulten, affidavit before J. M. Phillips, 1 June 1922.
14. Walker Smith, *Was It Murder?,* pamphlet (Centralia: Centralia Publicity Committee, n.d.).

CHAPTER 26

1. Senator William E. Borah, speech, New York, 11 March 1923; political prisoners file, Box 136, Wayne State University Library.
2. Hart papers, State Archives.
3. Ibid.
4. McInerney, letter to Moudy and Nash, 14 November 1926; parole board files, State Archives.
5. Ibid.
6. D. E. Burrell, affidavit, 13 February 1923; Archives of Labor History and Urban Affairs, Wayne State University.
7. Cecil Draper, affidavit, 14 November 1924; Ruuttila papers, Oregon Historical Society.
8. Elsie Hornbeck Sherlie, affidavit, 5 November 1924; Archives of Labor History, Wayne State University.
9. Archives of Labor History, Wayne State University.
10. Hart papers, State Archives.
11. Hart, letter to W. W. Whalen, Buffalo, Oklahoma, 17 September 1924; Hart papers, State Archives.
12. *Industrial Worker,* 14 May 1924.
13. Ibid.
14. Ibid.
15. Short, letter to Becker, n.d.; Ruuttila papers, Oregon Historical Society.
16. *Seattle Times,* 14 August 1925, p. 6.
17. "D.K.M." in *Tacoma Times,* n.d.; papers of DeWitte Wyckoff in author's files.
18. Cunningham, letter to Ellsworth French, 4 June 1924; correspondence file, Cunningham papers, Legion library.
19. *Industrial Worker,* 19 November 1924.
20. The bayonet on the soldier's rifle was broken off once.

CHAPTER 27

1. *Industrial Worker,* 12 November 1924, p. 2.
2. Ibid.
3. Ibid.
4. Ibid.
5. *Industrial Worker,* 18 October 1924.
6. Proceedings of Extraordinary Session, Washington legislature, 9 November 1925, p. 36.
7. Smith, letter to Hartley, 23 November 1926; Hartley papers, State Archives.
8. Cunningham, letter to Hartley, 18 February 1927; Hartley papers, State Archives.
9. *Think or Surrender,* pamphlet (Centralia: Centralia Publicity Committee, n.d.).
10. IWW collection, Archives of Labor History, Wayne State University.
11. Ibid.
12. *In re Smith en banc,* before supreme court, 24 February 1925, p. 146.
13. Brief on behalf of defendant Elmer Smith, *State Bar Association vs. Elmer Smith,* before supreme court, n.d.; Archives of Labor History, Wayne State University.
14. *In re Smith,* p. 145.

15. Ibid., p. 147.

16. The court was provided with an abundance of IWW literature to peruse while weighing the merits of the bar association's finding that the Wobblies' lawyer was unfit to practice. The books and pamphlets, used as exhibits in the case, included the report of George Williams, the IWW delegate to the First Congress of Red Trade Union International at Moscow in 1921 (which reported that the Communist Party was already in control of the revolution and that the party scorned the IWW as small and ineffective); *The IWW in Theory and Practice,* by Justus Ebert; *The New Unionism,* by Andre Tridon; *The IWW,* by Vincent St. John; *The Revolutionary IWW,* by Grover H. Perry; *Sabotage,* by Elizabeth Gurley Flynn; *The Red Dawn,* by Harrison George; *The Advancing Proletariat,* by Abner F. Woodruff; *Sabotage, its History, Philosophy and Function,* by Walker C. Smith; *The Onward Sweep of the Machine Process* (The IWW); *Industrial Communism,* by Harold Lord Varney; *The Evolution of Industrial Democracy,* by Abner Woodruff; the opening statement by George Vanderveer in the case of *USA vs. William. D. Haywood, et al;* and numerous copies of the *One Big Union Monthly.*

17. *In re Smith,* p. 153.

18. Ibid., p. 154.

19. *Industrial Worker,* 12 April 1924, p. 1.

20. Ibid.

21. *Industrial Worker,* 12 April 1924, p. 10.

22. Ibid.

23. Virginia Waddell, unpublished biographical papers.

24. *Post-Intelligencer,* 21 September 1928.

25. William Allen White, letter to Hartley, 12 May 1927; Hartley papers, State Archives.

26. W. H. Abel, letter to parole board, 29 October 1928; parole board files, State Archives.

27. Edward Coll, letter to author, 26 January 1960.

28. Ibid.

29. Coll, letter to author, 25 September 1972.

30. Coll, letter to author, 26 January 1960.

31. Ibid.

32. Ibid.

33. *Speeches by Elmer Smith and Capt. Edward P. Coll, On the Centralia Case,* 21 March 1929 (Centralia Publicity Committee).

34. *The Nation,* 10 July 1929, p. 38.

35. Coll, letter to author, 22 February 1960.

36. *Post-Intelligencer,* 17 April 1929, p. 3.

37. *Post-Intelligencer,* 18 March 1929, p. 2.

38. David Starr Jordan to H. B. Clausen, chairman, parole board, 10 July 1928; parole board files, State Archives.

39. Stephen B. Penrose, letter to H. B. Clausen, 15 June 1929; parole board files, State Archives.

40. J. M. Phillips, letter to H. B. Clausen, 15 June 1929; parole board files, State Archives.

41. "The Centralia Case — Ten Years Afterward," article in *The World Tomorrow,* June 1929.

CHAPTER 28

1. Hartley, letter to Cunningham, 30 April 1929; Hartley papers, State Archives.

2. Ed Coll, letter to Hartley, 20 April 1929; Hartley papers.

3. Hartley, letter to Coll, 29 April 1929; Hartley papers.

4. Hartley, letter to National Economic League, 4 October 1929; Hartley papers.

5. Francis Ralston Welsh, letter to Hartley, 2 April 1929; Hartley papers.

6. Hartley, letter to Welsh, 8 April 1929; Hartley papers.

7. *Post-Intelligencer,* 17 April 1929, p. 3.

8. Hartley, letter to C. E. Long, 30 October 1929; Hartley papers.

9. Elizabeth Attridge, letter to Hartley, 9 September 1929; Hartley papers.

10. Elizabeth Attridge, *My Findings in the Centralia Case,* pamphlet (Centralia: Centralia Publicity Committee, n.d.).

11. Kate Crane-Gartz, letter to Hartley, 15 May 1930; Hartley papers.

12. Elmer Smith, letter to Herman Allen, 16 April 1929; Ruuttila papers, Oregon Historical Society.

13. Verna B. Grimm, letter to Hartley, 18 May 1929; Hartley papers.

14. *Industrial Worker,* 20 November 1962, p. 1.

CHAPTER 29

1. Worth M. Tippy, *Report on the Logging Camps of the Pacific Northwest with Recommendations* (New York: Joint Committee on War Production Communities, Commission on Church and Social Service, 1919).

2. Ibid.

3. Ibid.

4. *Chronicle,* 5 February 1920, p. 3.

5. Report of Social Welfare Commission, Puget Sound Conference, Methodist Episcopal Church, 1922; Methodist archives, University of Puget Sound.

6. Ibid.

7. Ibid.

8. Report of forty-fifth annual meeting, Puget Sound Conference, Methodist Episcopal Church, 1927: Methodist archives.

9. Statement of Grant Hodge post, American Legion, n.d., signed by J. C. Hampe, commander, and G. D. Rowe, adjutant; Legion Library.

10. A. A. Heist, letter to R. M. Kinnear; parole board files, State Archives.

11. Ed Coll, letter to Father John A. Ryan, 27 May 1929; Catholic archives, Seattle.

12. Coll, letter to Theodore Ryan, 5 June 1929; Catholic archives.

13. W. W. Conner, letter to Father Theodore Ryan, 20 May 1929; Catholic archives.

14. Father Theodore Ryan, letter to Father John Ryan, 21 May 1929; Catholic archives.

15. Father John Ryan, letter to Father Theodore Ryan, 31 May 1929; Catholic archives.

16. *The Centralia Case: A Joint Report on the Armistice Day Tragedy at Centralia, Washington, November 11, 1919,* issued by the Department of Research and Education of the Federal Council of the Churches of Christ in America; the Social Action Department of the National Catholic Welfare Conference; and the Social Justice Commission of the Central Conference of American Rabbis, October 1930, p. 5.

17. D. Campbell Wyckoff, son of DeWitte Wyckoff, interview with author, Princeton, New Jersey, 20 May 1960.
18. Cunningham, letter to DeWitt Wyckoff, 4 September 1930; Cunningham papers, Legion Library.
19. Ibid.
20. Cunningham, letter to Benson Landis, 25 February 1930; Cunningham papers.
21. Mrs. DeWitte Wyckoff, letter to author, 17 November 1960.
22. *The Centralia Case*, p. 15.
23. Ibid., p. 48.

CHAPTER 30

1. *Seattle Times*, 14 October 1930, p. 10.
2. *Christian Advocate*, 30 October 1930.
3. Robert Whitaker, "Centralia and the Churches," *Christian Century*, 3 December 1930.
4. *Tacoma Labor Advocate*, 5 September 1930.
5. *Chronicle*, 21 August 1930.
6. David James, letter to author, 20 January 1983.
7. Smith, letter to Earl Benson, 19 July 1930; Ruuttila papers, Oregon Historical Society.
8. Eugene Barnett, *"Wallowa Love,"* song sheet, 1931.
9. W. H. Cameron to supreme court, 22 May 1930, petition for rehearing No. 631; supreme court clerk's office, Olympia.
10. Elmer Smith to Dix H. Rowland, Tacoma, 2 July 1930, petition for rehearing in Matter of Proceeding for disbarment of Elmer S. Smith; court records, Olympia.
11. Ibid.
12. Centralia Publicity Committee Bulletin, 2 June 1932.
13. Ibid.

CHAPTER 31

1. Spokane police to Luke May, 26 December 1919; May papers, University of Washington Libraries manuscript collections.
2. *Farmer-Labor Call*, 16 February 1922.
3. Ibid.
4. Becker, letter to the Reverend Angus Becker, 13 January 1922; parole board files, State Archives.
5. Ibid.
6. Becker, letter to William Moran, 13 January 1922; parole board files.
7. Becker, letter to Smith, 26 April 1933; parole board files.
8. Becker, letter to Smith, 17 July 1924; parole board files.
9. *Seattle Times*, 20 June 1927, p. 13.
10. Robertson Trowbridge, letter to Julia Bertram (nee Godman), 31 July 1936; Ruuttila papers, Oregon Historical Society.
11. Resolutions passed at 1936 convention of Sawmill & Timber Workers' Union, Oregon Shingle Weavers Association, Plywood, Veneer & Ship Workers Union, Boommen and Rafters Council — all affiliates of the International Brotherhood of Carpenters and Joiners; Ruuttila papers, Box 2, Folder 1, Oregon Historical Society.
12. "Some remarks on how the affadavits and information were secured"; Ruuttila Papers. Oregon Historical Society.
13. Ibid.

14. Ibid.
15. Ibid.
16. Irvin Goodman, letter to Becker, 22 April 1936; Ruuttila papers.
17. Becker, letter to Bertram, 17 December 1935; parole board files.
18. Becker, letter to Bertram, 2 January 1936; parole board files.
19. Farquharson papers, Box 3-1; University of Washington Libraries.
20. Ibid.
21. Unidentified labor press clipping, n.d.; Ruuttila papers.

CHAPTER 32

1. Reverend Erle Howell, interview with author, Seattle, 2 March 1983.
2. Mrs. Barbara Bruhns, Centralia librarian, letter to Mary W. Jeffries, librarian, Longview Public Library, 3 February 1961; Longview library files.
3. Barnett, letter to author, 14 February 1961.
4. Eugene Barnett, *The Art of Hitching Horsehair* (Longview: Longview Publishing Co., 1965).
5. Dewey Lamb, interview with author, Centralia, 12 September 1984.
6. James Stevens, letter to Frank Anderson, 29 October 1954; manuscript collection, Centralia Public Library.
7. *History of Centralia*, Centralia Community Study Group, Proceedings, Part VI, 1954-1955.
8. William M. Haag, *Riot and Reaction: The Short-Term Consequences of the Shootings at Centralia, Washington, on November 11, 1919 Upon the First World War Economic Recovery of the Community, 1919-1924*, unpublished dissertation (Western Washington University, 1977).
9. Ibid.
10. Mrs. Jackie Morgan, interview with author, Chehalis, 21 February 1983.
11. *Chronicle*, 11 November 1963.
12. *Chronicle*, 11 November 1966.
13. Ibid.
14. Robert B. Pitkin, "The Legion's 40 Years Against Communism," *American Legion Magazine*, December 1959, p. 23.
15. C. D. Cunningham, letter to editor, *American Legion Magazine*, March 1960.
16. Ibid.
17. John L. Lawrence, letter to editor, *Centralia Chronicle*, 9 November 1979, p. 6.
18. *Industrial Worker*, October 1979, p. 2.
19. Edith Chaplin, letter to Agnes Inglis, 12 May 1941; Chaplin papers, Special Collections, University of Michigan library.
20. Ibid.
21. Goldie Horst, interview with author, Centralia, 3 October 1981.

CHAPTER 33

1. Richard Brazier, letter to T. J. Bogard, n.d. (probably 1960); Bogard papers, Washington State Historical Society.

INDEX